1/18

SILENCED IN THE LIBRARY

SILENCED IN THE LIBRARY

Banned Books in America

Zeke Jarvis

GREENWOOD™

An Imprint of ABC-CLIO, LLC
Santa Barbara, California • Denver, Colorado

Library of Congress Cataloging-in-Publication Data

Names: Jarvis, Zeke, author.
Title: Silenced in the library : banned books in America / Zeke Jarvis.
Description: Santa Barbara, California : Greenwood, an imprint of ABC-CLIO, LLC,
    [2017] | Includes bibliographical references and index.
Identifiers: LCCN 2017004973 (print) | LCCN 2017032642 (ebook) | ISBN
    9781440843952 (ebook) | ISBN 9781440843945 (hardcover : acid-free paper)
Subjects: LCSH: Challenged books—United States—Bibliography. | Prohibited
    books—United States—Bibliography. | Libraries—Censorship—United States—
    History. | Censorship—United States—History. | American literature—History and
    criticism. | Literature and society—United States—History.
Classification: LCC Z1019 (ebook) | LCC Z1019 .J37 2017 (print) |
    DDC 098/.10973—dc23
LC record available at https://lccn.loc.gov/2017004973

ISBN: 978–1–4408–4394–5
EISBN: 978–1–4408–4395–2

21 20 19 18 17   1 2 3 4 5

This book is also available as an eBook.

Greenwood
An Imprint of ABC-CLIO, LLC

ABC-CLIO, LLC
130 Cremona Drive, P.O. Box 1911
Santa Barbara, California 93116-1911
www.abc-clio.com

This book is printed on acid-free paper ∞

Manufactured in the United States of America

CONTENTS

ALPHABETICAL LIST OF TITLES

1984, George Orwell
The Absolutely True Diary of a Part-Time Indian, Sherman Alexie
The Adventures of Huckleberry Finn, Mark Twain
The Adventures of Tom Sawyer, Mark Twain
All the King's Men, Robert Penn Warren
American Psycho, Bret Easton Ellis
An American Tragedy, Theodore Dreiser
The Anarchist Cookbook, William Powell
And Tango Makes Three, Peter Parnell and Justin Richardson
Angus, Thongs, and Full-Frontal Snogging, Louise Rennison
Annie on My Mind, Nancy Garden
Are You There, God? It's Me, Margaret, Judy Blume
Arizona Kid, Ronald Koertge
As I Lay Dying, William Faulkner
Asking about Sex and Growing Up, Joanna Cole
Athletic Shorts, Chris Crutcher
The Autobiography of Malcolm X, Malcolm X and Alex Haley
Batman: The Killing Joke, Alan Moore
Beloved, Toni Morrison
Black Boy, Richard Wright
Blankets, Craig Thompson
Bless Me, Ultima, Rudolfo Anaya
Blood and Chocolate, Annette Curtis Klause
Blubber, Judy Blume

ALPHABETICAL LIST OF AUTHORS

Alexie, Sherman
Allard, Harry
Anaya, Rudolfo
Angelou, Maya
Atwood, Margaret
Auel, Jean M.
Bannerman, Helen
Bechdel, Alison
Blatty, William Peter
Blume, Judy
Bradbury, Ray
Brittain, Bill
Brown, Dee
Burgess, Anthony
Burroughs, William S.
Capote, Truman
Chbosky, Stephen
Cleaver, Eldridge
Cole, Brock
Cole, Joanna
Collier, Christopher
Collins, Suzanne
Conly, Jane Leslie
Conrad, Joseph

Cooney, Caroline B.
Cormier, Robert
Courtenay, Bryce
Crutcher, Chris
Dahl, Roald
Dreiser, Theodore
Dugard, Jaycee Lee
Duncan, Lois
Ellis, Bret Easton
Ellison, Ralph
Ewing, Lynn
Faulkner, William
Fitzgerald, F. Scott
Fitzhugh, Louise
Frank, Anne
Friday, Nancy
Gaiman, Neil
Garden, Nancy
George, Jean Craighead
Ginsberg, Allen
Golding, William
Greene, Bette
Haley, Alex
Handford, Martin

TOPICAL GUIDE TO TITLES

RACE

The Autobiography of Malcolm X
The Adventures of Huckleberry Finn
Beloved
Black Boy
The Bluest Eye
Bury My Heart at Wounded Knee
The Color Purple
Gone with the Wind
Heart of Darkness
I Know Why the Caged Bird Sings
Invisible Man
Song of Solomon
Soul on Ice
The Story of Little Black Sambo
Their Eyes Were Watching God
To Kill a Mockingbird

RELIGION

All the King's Men
An American Tragedy
Are You There, God? It's Me, Margaret
As I Lay Dying

Bless Me, Ultima
The Boy Who Lost His Face
The Bridge to Teribithia
Bumps in the Night
The Call of the Wild
Cat's Cradle
The Chocolate War
Cross Your Fingers, Spit in Your Hat
The Dead Zone
The Exorcist
Final Exit
The Giver
Goosebumps (Series)
The Grapes of Wrath
The Handmaid's Tale
Harry Potter (Series)
The Jungle
Moby Dick
Of Mice and Men
The Power of One
The Satanic Verses
Scary Stories to Tell in the Dark (Series)
Slaughterhouse V

Fear and Loathing on the Campaign
   Trail
Go Ask Alice
The Great Gatsby
Naked Lunch
The Outsiders

Junie B. Jones (Series)
A Light in the Attic
My Brother Sam Is Dead
One Flew over the Cuckoo's Nest
Staying Fat for Sarah Burns
The Stupids (Series)

BAD BEHAVIOR

The Adventures of Tom Sawyer
The Anarchist Cookbook
Captain Underpants (Series)
Catcher in the Rye
Catch-22
A Clockwork Orange
Crazy Lady
Cut
Fahrenheit 451
Family Secrets
The Great Gilly Hopkins
Harriet the Spy
How to Eat Fried Worms
James and the Giant Peach

GRAPHIC NOVELS

Batman: The Killing Joke
Blankets
The Color of Earth
The Dark Knight Returns
Fun Home
The Graveyard Book
The League of Extraordinary
   Gentlemen
Maus
Palomar (Series)
Pride of Baghdad
Saga (Series)
SideScrollers
Watchmen

PREFACE

This book represents a careful examination of censorship in its many forms when it comes to literature in America. While it does extend to works and challenges outside of America, it generally focuses on the challenges within America in order to focus on the notion of freedom and the limits of freedom. The new productions of texts and new technologies will push censorship and discussions of what is appropriate for young readers. This means that the set of challenged or banned texts will continue to evolve, but this book will help to give context and reflection to help readers navigate concerns of what texts are appropriate and necessary in years to come.

Although there is much discussion of books being banned, it is important to recognize that challenges to books can have a significant impact upon their sales and reputation. A banning can be an outright removal from a classroom curriculum or a library. In more extreme cases, banning books meant that it was illegal to sell them even to adults, as was the case with James Joyce's *Ulysses*, D. H. Lawrence's *Lady Chatterley's Lover*, Vladimir Nabokov's *Lolita*, and William S. Burroughs's *Naked Lunch*, though all of these controversial novels were eventually made legal again. Challenges come when there are attempts to ban a book, but the attempts do not result in a full-on removal. However, this lack of banning does not mean that the books and authors do not face any consequences. In some cases, the books may be put into restricted sections of libraries, making it more difficult for young readers to access them. Challenges can also have the effect of making teachers wary of discussing or recommending these books, meaning that while there is not an official ban, the fear of parental complaints can lead to what is effectively a removal from class discussion. Of course, not all authors view these challenges as hurtful. Some, like Sherman Alexie, take the perspective that challenged books are a kind of "forbidden fruit" and that such challenges increase the publicity for and desirability of the books. For authors like Alexie, challenges are welcome. Still, the informal challenges can be overlooked if discussions and records focus solely upon outright bans. As stated previously, challenges can create practical barriers to making a book available for students, making the need for careful attention to challenges all the more important.

In terms of the organization of the book, entries have been categorized according to topic. The chapters cover topics of race, religion, graphic portrayals of sex, sexual orientation, graphic violence, drugs and alcohol, and bad behavior. Additionally, there is a chapter on graphic novels. The separation of the final chapter comes largely because the emergence of graphic novels as a legitimate genre is a relatively recent phenomenon, so the challenges that these works face are often different from the novels and nonfiction books included in the other chapters. Of course, some of the books face challenges on multiple grounds (the Harry Potter series, for instance, has faced challenges for its portrayal of witchcraft as well as its seeming lionization of children who break rules). In these cases, the books have been placed in the section that recognizes the most frequent or most significant reason for the challenge. This requires some analysis based upon critical reaction, but the critical consensus is generally clear enough to make this determination. Of course, critical reaction and interpretation is always a complex topic, so the entries have been designed to recognize the multifaceted nature of these struggles rather than oversimplify them. To this end, each entry provides a brief description of the book under discussion, situates the work within the original publication's historical context, and reviews the challenges the book faced and outcome for the struggles. From this full discussion, the significance of both the book and its challenges will become clear.

INTRODUCTION

One of the reasons that scholars study literature is that it represents the culture that produced it. If literature does represent a culture, then the study of literature might well include not only what gets published and shared but also what is forced into hiding, what people go out of their way to not talk about. Every culture has some sense of what is open for comment and portrayal and what is unspeakable, and these sorts of topics can change significantly over time. While one generation or geographic location might find that the subject of marital infidelity is so troubling and immoral that it should not be discussed at all, a subsequent generation might find this topic particularly interesting, resulting in its being covered in a number of texts in various genres and media.

What this means is that it is very important to view what a culture or society tries to keep unspoken, because it tells us a good deal about that culture's values and ideas. Of course, in the same way that some texts might represent niche or fringe elements of a culture, the move to censor certain works or topics does not always represent a general sentiment from a culture. Sometimes, the vocal few can overpower the reasonable (or even apathetic or unaware) majority. Many readers will be surprised to see some of the works that have been challenged. (Where's Waldo? series tends to surprise many people, for instance.) While this book series does not ask the reader to judge or to take sides in any debate over censorship, it will often use hindsight to illuminate the nature of the conflict between the two sides of the censorship issue, recognizing the difference between how issues of race or sex were viewed differently during the times of the text's creation and how they have been viewed in later years.

The question of censorship changes from generation to generation, and it is well worth examining whether each generation has learned from the problems of the previous one. If we follow Mark's Twain's definition that "censorship is telling a man he can't have a steak just because a baby can't chew it," we might assume that all censorship is bad. But do we want a world where every child has quick and immediate access to any text of any topic or delivery? It is hard to accept the argument that, if something is published, then it needs to be accessible to every reader of every level. In addition, Twain's quote, while incisive, does oversimplify the argument. In particular, the comparison of literature to steak implies that all banned books are of good quality. However, some literature might be hard to defend on the grounds of quality. When shock rap group 2 Live Crew's album *As Nasty As They Wanna Be* received a legal triumph, being acquitted of the obscenity charges that originally landed some of the members in jail in 1990, comedian Dennis Miller acknowledged the importance of free speech but quickly followed that acknowledgment with the observation: "But it really was a bad album." Of course, Miller is not the first figure to make such an observation. Voltaire coined the phrase, "I disapprove of what you say, but I will defend to the death your right to say it" in the early 1700s, and the sentiment has been around for even longer than the phrase. To return to Twain's quote, then, even if a man can eat a good steak, and even if men should be free to eat steaks of varying quality, it doesn't automatically follow that everyone will work to defend every steak, and it also does not automatically follow that men being able to eat steak should imply that we should try to feed it to babies.

However, as stated before, this book will not concern itself with taking sides, but the recognition of the difference between the *quality* of a text and the *importance* of a text is crucial to the examinations contained within this book. In fact, some scholars have argued that the attempts to ban a book can actually serve to increase its importance and prominence. Literature can help a culture to identify which barriers or issues not only exist for it but also which are ready to be broken. Often, the controversial texts are the ones that identify changes in our morals or standards. From Barbara Park's series, Junie B. Jones (originally published in 1992), which focused on a child character who behaved more disrespectfully than well-behaved children of previous generations, to *Slaughterhouse V* (Kurt Vonnegut's book originally published in 1969), which discussed sex and death in frank ways that would not have been acceptable even a decade before its publication, books can be the battlegrounds for shifts in perspective and values.

THE GOVERNMENT, THE DISTRIBUTORS, AND THE PUBLISHING INDUSTRY

Not all censorship comes from the government. In fact, many artistic industries self-regulate, using policies or boards like the Comics Code or the rating board in the film industry. In order to have the Comics Code symbol on the cover, publishers would have to agree to avoid certain topics like rape and certain portrayals like overly sexualized characters. These self-regulatory mechanisms are specifically designed to prevent controversial texts from reaching the public, where they might come under fire and draw scrutiny to the entire industry. However, there are often loopholes within these sorts of structures. DC Comics, for instance, publishes the Vertigo Comics imprint, which is labeled for mature readers, thus gaining a greater level of freedom than other publications remaining solely under the Comics Code. At the same time, some retailers (including major chains like Wal-Mart) refuse to carry or support some texts and records, leading publishers and record companies to release censored versions so that they can be sold in Wal-Mart. What all this means is that there are multiple ways that a text can be banned or censored outside of governmental regulation.

Of course, the government does often take part in these debates and struggles. One way that this has often come into play is through the mailing of controversial or obscene texts. Novels like Vladimir Nabokov's *Lolita* and William S. Burroughs's *Naked Lunch* faced significant challenges. *Lolita* was banned and seized in London after its publication in 1955. *Naked Lunch* was published in 1959 but was illegal to ship because of U.S. obscenity laws relating to pornography. In both cases, the ensuing legal action brought a tremendous amount of publicity to the text. In the case of *Lolita*, by the time it was available in the United States, it had developed such a reputation in Europe that it gained a significant critical and commercial following, selling enough to go into a third printing shortly after its initial release. In the case of *Naked Lunch*, major literary figures like Norman Mailer and Allen Ginsberg testified at the trial, defending the literary merit of the work.

The government also takes a role in the debates in less direct ways, particularly when it comes to public school libraries and classroom assignments. Because of the unique nature of public schools (partially governmental office but also partially public space), decisions about the appropriateness of works are often particularly interesting. Some subtle differences, such as the distinction between purchasing books and keeping them on the shelves once they have been purchased, have played key roles in struggles over challenged books.

"THINK OF THE CHILDREN"

Perhaps no genre of writing has seen more challenges than children and young adult literature. Part of the cause for this is simply that the genre of young adult literature is a relatively new one, so the boundaries and expectations are still evolving, but some of the struggle is also rooted in the unclear nature of who has the authority to make decisions about what children read. While teachers, administrators, and librarians obviously all have a clear voice in what schools teach or keep in the library, how students, parents, and publishers involve themselves in these discussions is still evolving, and there have been a number of cases (*Annie on My Mind*, *And Tango Makes Three*, and Captain Underpants, just to name a few) where fans, lawyers, or the American Civil Liberties Union have gotten involved in the dispute over what books are available to children. In the case of *Annie on My Mind* and *And Tango Makes Three*, there was concern over the portrayal of homosexuality, and in Captain Underpants, the concern was over bad behavior and material relating to bodily functions.

Interestingly, some of the struggles involve content that young readers might not even recognize as being controversial, so the move to censor the book has actually resulted in calling more attention to the book's potentially problematic content. Book series like Dav Pilkey's Captain Underpants and Barbara Park's Junie B. Jones clearly involve either crass humor or children who are openly disrespectful to adults, but many of the texts, like the aforementioned *And Tango Makes Three*, that subtly or obliquely examine sexual orientation or gender roles receive a good deal of resistance, whether there is any evidence that the young readers directly recognize the significance of the material or not. Of course, another issue is whether a text uses the questionable material as part of an organic, meaningful study of cultural transitions or whether the potentially offensive material is used simply to shock or gain attention. This can be surprisingly difficult to tell. Again, the example of Junie B. Jones can be seen as simply using a "bratty child" for simple and quick humor, but it can also be viewed as a recognition of how children try to navigate the world as they work to achieve a sense of independence. Likewise, although some conservative parents and commentators challenged the Harry Potter series for including magic in a way that did not fit their narrow conception of proper views of religion, the book series actually included a number of allusions to Christian iconography and concepts like forgiveness and sacrifice. These sorts of debates and misunderstandings show that the challenges toward books often take on a life of their own, sometimes moving beyond the books themselves.

Still, many of the books that are challenged by one generation become some of the favorites of the next. D. H. Lawrence, for instance, faced ban for nearly every book that he wrote during his lifetime, but he went on to become a major literary figure for generations after his death. One of the impacts of a once-banned writer's mainstream acceptance is that readers of a subsequent generation can fail to recognize what boundaries were once needed to be tested or broken. Although D. H. Lawrence was not writing young adult literature, the transition from edgy to accepted has happened for writers like Judy Blume, who has transitioned from receiving harsh criticism for her discussion of sexuality to being remembered as beloved and influential by many readers who grew up with her work.

CHANGES IN PUBLISHING

In addition to the points discussed earlier, there have been significant shifts in how technology and printing have impacted reading habits and senses of propriety. While there have been books with illustrations or etchings for centuries, advances in printing technology make it easier and more affordable to publish graphic novels. In addition, the ease of both online publishing and self-publishing has changed the overall landscape of the publishing industry, allowing for both more voices and a wider variety of voices. While this diversity has had some positive effects, it also can lead to greater splintering and niche publishing and marketing, creating greater barriers and sometimes hostilities between groups. This shift in the way that books (and other writings from articles to blogs) are published, marketed, and distributed has also had an impact on the way that texts are challenged or defended.

In addition to changes in publishing, the changes in how social and literary movements form and communicate have impacted the nature of debates over books. Online petitions, Facebook posts, and other digital discussions can make movements to either challenge or defend a book move more quickly than in previous eras. In 2015, for instance, New Jersey saw both a call for censorship and an online petition to fight censorship of Bernard MacLaverty's book *Cal* after it was included in some school curricula. These developments can make the discussions even more virulent (though sometimes more temporary) than debates from previous eras. While there were people leading challenges against books for reasons of publicity or political posturing in the pre-Internet era, that phenomenon has seemingly become even more common in the Internet era, where public figures are often looking to use public debates to help establish their prominence or build their base of support. Still, while there may have been some debates that have been largely for show, the new media have helped to expand the debate about what is and is not appropriate for readers of various ages.

1

RACE AND CENSORSHIP IN AMERICA

Even before America was officially a nation, racial tension has played a part in its history. As literary scholars look for narratives representing the Native American experience, they run into two different problems. The first is that many narratives have been lost or deliberately destroyed. The second is that many were translated by European explorers who either were hostile toward Native Americans or had particular political or social agendas that impacted the translations. As the settling process continued, there was some cooperation between European explorers and Native American tribes, but there was also a great deal of tension and conflict. As the old adage "History is written by the winners" indicates, Americans of European descent were able to focus the historical narrative on America's rebellion against Britain rather than on the harmful interactions with Native Americans. This led to many Americans being ignorant of both the nature and the extent of the oppression that Native Americans faced. After a few generations of focusing on America as the land of freedom, movements to recontextualize our nation's history often face significant criticism from figures outside of academia. Howard Zinn's texts uncovering not only some of the treatment of Native Americans but also the systemic issues that lead to their continued suffering faced not only criticism but also outright challenges when then Indiana governor Mitch Daniels made public statements condemning Zinn's work as un-American in 2010. The criticism from Daniels was seen as more political than academic or intellectual, but it was a very public controversy nonetheless. While Native American literature is now thriving in academic and literary circles, books dealing with Native American struggles still face challenges, like Sherman Alexie's *The Absolutely True Diary of a Part-Time Indian*, published in 2007. Although many of the challenges lodged against the book focus on its sexual content, it is another example of Native American voices facing harsh criticism.

Of course, Native Americans are not the only group to face significant challenges. African American writers have also faced a variety of challenges as they have gradually made their way into the literary canon. As with some Native American authors, the struggles faced by these writers have not always been confined solely to their discussions of race. While both Richard Wright's novels *Black Boy* and *Native Son* made many readers uncomfortable for their content dealing with race, his comments on religion and politics were also part of the motivations of people objecting to his books. Likewise, Toni Morrison's book, *Beloved*, clearly troubled many readers for its frank and disturbing portrayal of the conditions faced by African American slaves. However, there were also complaints about its portrayal of a mother murdering her child and acts of bestiality.

One likely reason for the incorporation of challenging content into African American literature is the very brutality of African American history itself. While many parents still feel that only a basic and general discussion of the history is appropriate for students, there are a number of scholars who see a clear need for direct discussions of the individual sufferings during events or periods like the Trail of Tears, the era of slavery, and the Holocaust. This has led to parties disagreeing not just on the texts themselves but also upon the basic grounds of how what should be banned is argued. For free-speech advocates, if young readers perceive slavery as something simply bad rather than truly horrific, then they might never truly understand the lasting impact of the slave system—the lingering aftereffects of slave owners breaking up families and forbidding slaves to learn to read or otherwise gain any sort of tool or power that might help them.

This argument about the necessity for realistic or authentic portrayals of the suffering of oppressed people is not the only ground that advocates for books like Wright's *Native Son* and Morrison's *The Bluest Eye* have sought out. While it can be understandable for a reader or critic to react negatively to disturbing portrayals of violence or sexual content, it is very difficult to isolate one portion of the book, either arguing that the "inappropriate" sections of the book outweigh its cultural and historical significance or that the primary challengers of the books were objecting only to those portions and not to the way that the books portray issues of race as well. In the end, as with Native American literature, African American literature has been accepted into the literary canon, but there are still attacks upon individual works.

Although there are many areas of commonality among different racial and cultural groups representing their experiences, it is important not to assume that all controversies involving race are the same. Some controversies surrounding portrayals of race do not arise until generations after the text's original publication. One clear example is Mark Twain's *Huckleberry Finn*. For some eras, *Huckleberry Finn* represented a positive discussion of race, skewering the racist assumptions of the dominant culture and presenting an interracial friendship that made the book a seemingly progressive text. However, as more documents were uncovered discussing Twain's past and some of his views, and more attention was paid to the end of the book (where the interracial friendship largely unravels), more readers found the book to be offensive in how it used its characters. Of course, like *The Bluest Eye* or *Native Son*, the treatment of the characters was hardly the only reason why the book was challenged and banned. The frequent use of the word "nigger," the use of curse words, the questioning of religion, and the general "bad behavior" of the characters have made it a very controversial text.

While *Huckleberry Finn* might be the most prominent book to get banned for reasons related to race, the history of controversies related to race in American literature is long and complicated. Often, the controversies related to books are influenced by outside factors. For instance, during the Civil Rights Movement, the support for or attack upon a book was often a political stance as much as it was a moral one. In the age of the Internet, reality television, and cinema blockbusters, it can be difficult to appreciate just how major a controversy over a book could be.

TIMELINE

1768—Phillis Wheatley writes "To the King's Most Excellent Majesty," making her one of the first African American poets to publish

1795—Treaty of Greenville signed between U.S. government and Native American Western Confederacy, establishing a series of treaties that would often be neglected by the U.S. government. This pattern established a pattern of distrust and animosity between Native Americans and the federal government

1845—*Narrative of the Life of Frederick Douglass, an American Slave*, Frederick Douglass, published

1852—*Uncle Tom's Cabin*, Harriet Beecher Stowe, published, bringing issues of slavery into the national conversation

1863—Emancipation Proclamation ordered by Abraham Lincoln

1885—*The Adventures of Huckleberry Finn*, Mark Twain, published

1889—*The Story of Little Black Sambo*, Helen Bannerman, published

1890—Jim Crow laws officially enacted segregation

1902—*Heart of Darkness*, Joseph Conrad, published

1909—National Association for the Advancement of Colored People founded

1931—Toni Morrison born

1936—*Gone with the Wind*, Margaret Mitchell, published

1937—*Their Eyes Were Watching God*, Zoran Neale Hurston, published

1939—*Gone with the Wind* adapted into a film

1940—*Native Son*, Richard Wright, published; Hattie McDaniel becomes first African American to win an Oscar

1942–1946—Asian Americans held in Japanese internment camps during World War II

1945—*Black Boy*, Richard Wright, published

1948—U.S. military desegregated by Harry S. Truman

1952—*Invisible Man*, Ralph Ellison, published

1954—Desegregation ended by *Brown v. Board of Education* U.S. Supreme Court decision

1955—Montgomery Bus Boycott begins the Civil Rights Movement

1965—*The Autobiography of Malcolm X*, Malcolm X and Alex Haley, published; Malcolm X assassinated; Voting Rights Act passed, prohibiting discrimination based upon race

1966—Black Panther Party formed; Sherman Alexie born

1968—American Indian Movement formed; *Soul on Ice*, Eldridge Cleaver, published; Martin Luther King Jr. assassinated

1969—*The Way to Rainy Mountain*, N. Scott Momaday, published, becoming one of the first major works of Native American literature in the modern era; *I Know Why the Caged Bird Sings*, Maya Angelou, published

1970—*Bury My Heart at Wounded Knee*, Dee Brown, published; *The Bluest Eye*, Toni Morrison, published, marking the beginning of Toni Morrison's publishing career

1976—"Negro History Week" expanded to "Black History Month" in America

1977—*Ceremony*, Leslie Marmon Silko, published, marking Leslie Marmon Silko's entry into Native American literature

1982—Challenges to books dealt a major blow by the *Island Trees School District v. Pico* U.S. Supreme Court decision; *The Color Purple*, Alice Walker, published

1984—*House on Mango Street*, Sandra Cisneros, published, marking Sandra Cisneros's entry into both Hispanic and young adult literature

1985—*The Color Purple* adapted into a film

1988—"Hispanic Heritage Week" expanded to "Hispanic Heritage Month"

1989—*Joy Luck Club*, Amy Tan, published, adding a major voice to Asian American literature

1990s—A number of challenges lodged against *Malcolm X*, *Adventures of Huckleberry Finn*, and a number of other books

1990—Oscar Hijuelos awarded the Pulitzer Prize for literature for this book, *The Mambo Kings Play Songs of Love*, making him the first Hispanic author to earn the award; "Asian-American Heritage Week" expanded to "Asian-American Heritage Month"; "Native American Heritage Month" proclaimed

1992—*Malcolm X* adapted into a major motion picture

2008—Barack Obama elected as first African American president of the United States of America

2011—Sherman Alexie's response to challenges against *The Absolutely True Diary of a Part-Time Indian* published in *Wall Street Journal*

2016—#OscarsSoWhite movement formed to protest lack of diversity within the Academy Awards

The Autobiography of Malcolm X, Malcolm X and Alex Haley
(Grove Press, 1965)

The Autobiography of Malcolm X is a book largely narrated by Malcolm X and transcribed and edited by Alex Haley, who also wrote the book *Roots*, which inspired the widely acclaimed television miniseries. *The Autobiography of Malcolm X* examines the path of Malcolm X from impoverished child to criminal to prominent member of the Nation of Islam in America. The book begins with background on the family of Malcolm X (born Malcolm Little). He discusses growing up poor in Michigan. After his father died and his mother began a descent into mental illness, Malcolm had to fend for himself. This led to hard work and, eventually, criminal behavior. In addition to discussing these issues of social struggle, Malcolm also makes observations about more mundane cultural issues, like straightening his hair and working to afford fashionable clothes, though even these topics are often related to issues of race and class in America. After becoming involved in crime, Malcolm was caught and sent to jail, where he began a program of self-education. He describes reading the dictionary and recopying the words in order to enhance his vocabulary and get used to writing properly. In prison, he also gets exposed to Islam, an experience that would shape the rest of his life. After being released early from prison, Malcolm X began his work for the Nation of Islam, quickly ascending to prominence because of his passion and his public speaking skills. He also made a pilgrimage to Mecca, where his commitment to the religion deepened, and where he got to see another nation's systems and structures. Although Malcolm X was a popular and respected figure within the Nation, his fiery speeches and penchant for individualism also led to tension within the movement. Before the book could be entirely finished, Malcolm X was assassinated. The killer was never successfully found, and some theorize that the Nation of Islam orchestrated the assassination because Malcolm X's comments (in particular, some about the Kennedy assassination) had led him to fall out of favor with the core membership of the Nation. Of course, his outspoken nature and his commitment to civil rights made him a target for any number of groups. Haley does discuss the assassination in the book. He also, in an epilogue, reflects upon the interviews that he conducted with Malcolm X to generate the material for the book, giving discussion of Malcolm X as a person.

The book was a sensation, going into over forty editions and selling well over a million copies. While the book originally was commissioned by Doubleday, they backed out after the assassination over fear of controversy. Grove Press quickly stepped in and had a major commercial and critical success. In addition to the strong sales, the book has earned high praise for both its construction and its social significance. It has also been translated into a number of languages from Arabic to German to Indonesian. In addition, there have been multiple attempts to adapt the book into a screenplay. For years, novelist James Baldwin had been asked to work on a script. Eventually, parts of the script were published in book form, but it was never produced. Two decades later, in 1992, Director Spike Lee used Baldwin's work to create a screenplay that he successfully adapted into a film. The film met with widespread and significant acclaim, with Denzel Washington (who played Malcolm X) earning a nomination for Best Actor for the Academy Awards.

Although it was popular and well received, the book also had met challenges almost immediately from its publication. While the true reasons for some books' challenges can be difficult to determine, most of the early challenges to the book directly commented on the radical nature of the book's content. Beyond the challenges from concerned parents, the book, like its core figure, remains controversial for a number of parties. Not all Muslims have agreed with Malcolm X's characterization of the Nation of Islam, and many cultural commentators have objected to his characterization of race relations as well, though these challenges have been more informal rather than direct challenges made to library or school boards. In the 1990s, there were formal challenges to the book in a number of places in Florida and in New York, with parents arguing that the book promoted violence between races. A number of challenges did result in the book being placed on a list of books that could only be checked out with parental permission, but it was also taught in classrooms across America, and it holds a significant place in both American literature and American history.

FURTHER READING

Miller, D. Quentin. "Lost . . . and Found? James Baldwin's Script and Spike Lee's Malcolm X." *African American Review*, Winter 2013, Vol. 46, Issue 4, pp. 671–685.

Nikpour, Golnar. "Revolutionary Journals, Revolutionary Practice: The Hajj Writings of Jalal Al-E Ahmad and Malcolm X." *Comparative Studies of South Asia, Africa and the Middle East*, 2014, Vol. 34, Issue 1, pp. 67–85.

Norrell, Robert J. *Alex Haley and the Books That Changed a Nation*. New York, NY: St. Martin's, 2015, pp. xi, 251.

Worden, Daniel. "Neoliberal Style: Alex Haley, Hunter S. Thompson and Countercultures." *American Literature: A Journal of Literary History, Criticism, and Bibliography*, December 2015, Vol. 87, Issue 4, pp. 799–823.

The Adventures of Huckleberry Finn, Mark Twain
(Charles L. Webster and Company, 1884)

The Adventures of Huckleberry Finn follows two characters, Huck Finn and Jim, as they travel up the Mississippi River in an effort to escape from their surroundings. For Huck Finn, this means escaping both his alcoholic, troubled father and the "civilizing" efforts of his adoptive caretaker, the Widow Douglas. For Jim, the escape means literal freedom as he leaves the slave states for the North. Prior to setting off for the North, Huck fakes his own death to evade following. While the two enjoy each other's company, they also run up against a wide variety of characters and situations that make escaping a challenge. From the search parties sent to recapture Jim to the Duke and the King, grifters who take advantage of Huck and Jim—all of them creating a number of problems that make the trip to freedom slower and more difficult. After some of these difficulties, Jim and Huck get separated. When Huck discovers Jim's current location, he strikes out to find Jim. When he arrives, he is mistaken for his good friend Tom Sawyer. Huck uses this mistake to help gain information about Jim's whereabouts. Ironically, Tom Sawyer shows up. Sawyer knows that Jim's former owner has died and that Jim has been freed, but, rather than helping Huck to free Jim, Sawyer decides to construct an elaborate plan to free Jim only after enjoying an adventure. After Tom Sawyer has had his fun, he lets everyone know that Jim is free and that Huck's father has died, helping Huck to strike out on his own. At the end of the novel, Huck is glad to have helped free Jim (despite the fact that, at one point, he assumes that freeing Jim would be equivalent to stealing, meaning that he would go to hell for helping Jim), and he decides to set out on his own into "Indian Territory."

The Adventures of Huckleberry Finn is not only one of Mark Twain's most famous works but also a very controversial one. Interestingly, the book was originally published in the United Kingdom and Canada rather than in America due to the success of Twain's previous works and his travels in Europe. The book picks up from Twain's previous work, *The Adventures of Tom Sawyer*. While *Huckleberry Finn* included many of the same characters, it had some differences in tone and style. In particular, *Huckleberry Finn*'s narrator (the title character) used a more colloquial style, including slang and unintentional (and intentional) vulgarity. Upon its release, the book almost immediately received negative reactions. While many readers enjoyed the humor of the work, multiple libraries refused to house it, citing the "coarse language" as a primary reason. Like many later writers, Twain's reaction to the refusal to include his book was hardly negative.

He is reported to have told his publisher that the refusal would only lead to greater sales.

Interestingly, later generations also objected to Twain's work, but for largely different reasons. Many readers have harshly criticized Twain's work for both its use of the word "nigger" and also for its treatment of African American characters. While readers of some generations had seen Twain's treatment of African American characters as progressive for his era, many readers and critics from eras after Twain (among them, noteworthy figures such as Ernest Hemingway) have seen the treatment of Jim in the concluding chapters as racist and deeply offensive because Tom Sawyer sees Jim as a toy that he can use for his own amusement. In fact, in the 1990s and 2000s, the book was once again challenged, being deemed unfit for reading in the classroom by some teachers and administrators.

Part of the difficulty in determining Twain's position on race and its representation in his text is the satiric nature of Twain's work. Unlike other writers and works that give a clearer and more earnest presentation of an issue, Twain's work in general, and *Huckleberry Finn* in particular, takes on a number of issues, including race, religion, and social class, often critiquing behavior without suggesting any kind of safe or correct position. In particular, the characters often employ clearly faulty logic, from the feuding families who hear a sermon in church about forgiveness, but who refuse to apply the message to their interactions, to Huck's absurd logic that his caring for Jim will lead him to hell. Twain's narration is playful and his presentation is satiric, making it hard to definitively state what Twain's position is.

Interestingly, there have been a number of editions of the book that have omitted the word "nigger." These editions have met with varied reactions. While some teachers have expressed appreciation for the less controversial versions of the book, many critics feel the omission of the racial slur actually sanitizes both the history of race relations in America and Twain's views on race. This sort of move has been perceived by some as sidestepping the core problems and debates of the text. Beyond the teachers appreciating less charged language, some critics and readers point out that the word "nigger" is used much differently in contemporary times than it would have been by Twain. This can lead to debates in more recent times that are fundamentally different from those that would have occurred in Twain's time.

Regardless of the challenges that the book has faced, it has been consistently read and referenced in American culture. The book has been adapted for both film and television from 1920 through the present day. There have also been many playful references to the storyline or characters, ranging from *The Simpsons* to the work of German composer Kurt Weill. This widespread and lasting impact makes it clear that *The Adventures of Huckleberry Finn* will retain a sense of cultural prominence that will likely outlast any challenge it faces.

See Also: *The Adventures of Tom Sawyer.*

FURTHER READING

Ernsberger, Richard, Jr. "Have We Misread Huckleberry Finn?" *American History*, April 2015, Vol. 50, Issue 1, pp. 26–28.

Kraus, Daniel. "Race in Mark Twain's Huckleberry Finn." *Booklist*, March 15, 2010, Vol. 106, Issue 14, p. 41.

Rule, Henry B. "A Brief History of the Censorship of *The Adventures of Huckleberry Finn*." *Lamar Journal of the Humanities*, Spring 1986, Vol. 12, Issue 1, pp. 9–18.

Beloved, Toni Morrison
(Alfred A. Knopf, 1987)

Beloved is one of Toni Morrison's most noted works. Published in 1987, the book was a finalist for the National Book Award and won the Pulitzer Prize in 1988. Like many of Morrison's books, the novel looked at issues of race and gender, but its direct portrayal of slavery is part of what made the book both so striking and so controversial. The book traces slaves as they try to escape from the Southern states, making their way to the free states in the North. Many of the brutal realities of slavery are portrayed, including horrible whippings that leave scars, the separation of families by slave owners, and the use of sex as a form of trade. When one of the main characters, Sethe, fears that she and her children will be taken back to their master after she thought they had escaped, Sethe kills one of her children rather than letting them be taken back. This child eventually comes back in the form of a ghost, Beloved, who haunts Sethe and the people around her. In particular, when Sethe tries to start a family with a new man, Paul D, the story of Sethe killing her child surfaces, and Paul D must come to terms with the disturbing history of Sethe and the South in general.

Interestingly, *Beloved* is not the only novel where Morrison portrays a mother killing her child. In *Sula*, a mother kills her son when she discovers that he has become addicted to heroin. As she realizes what has happened to her son, the character decides that she has given too much to raise and protect her child to give him over to drugs, and she sets him on fire while he is stuck in a drug haze. Not surprisingly, both of these books have been met with resistance from some readers, though for slightly different reasons. Starting in the mid-1990s, the book began receiving challenges from parents for being too violent and having portrayals of race and racism that made some parents uncomfortable. There were also concerns raised about the frank portrayals of sex in the book, particularly the passages that dealt with bestiality and rape. Most of these challenges were short-lived and unsuccessful. Still, the number of challenges that came from around the country made the book noteworthy, not just for its literary impact but for its controversy as well.

Even though the book has faced multiple challenges, it continues to be taught in schools, carried by libraries, and hailed by critics. In fact, the novel was even adapted into a film in 1998, largely thanks to the efforts of Oprah Winfrey. Although the film adaptation was not nearly as well received as the original novel, the film did help to bring an even larger readership to the book.

See Also: *The Bluest Eye* and *Song of Solomon*.

FURTHER READING

Colbert, Soyica Diggs. "Assessing 'What Was African American Literature?'; or, The State of the Field in the New Millennium: On Tradition." *African American Review*, Winter 2011, Vol. 44, Issue 4, pp. 575–578.

Magras, Lydia. "Popular Reception of Toni Morrison's *Beloved*: Reading the Text through Time." *Reception: Texts, Readers, Audiences, History*, 2015, Vol. 7, Issue 1, pp. 29–44.

Reames, Kelly Lynch. *Women and Race in Contemporary US Writing: From Faulkner to Morrison*. Basingstoke, England: Palgrave Macmillan, 2007, p. 200.

Black Boy, Richard Wright
(Harper & Brothers, 1945)

Black Boy is a memoir largely examining Richard Wright's experiences living as an African American man first in the South and then in the North. Wright is honest yet playful in his discussion of his early years, showing himself to be a mischievous boy but one whose rebellion is partially impacted by what he perceives as a breakdown in his culture's strict expectations for behavior of women and more permissive attitude toward male behavior. The tension continues to build as Wright becomes more and more aware of the impact that the systemic racism found in the South during the 1920s has upon his family. Things worsen as Wright's father leaves his family. Wright bounces from household to household until he and one of his aunts travel north to Chicago. There, Wright finds a relatively high level of tolerance, but he still does not find either real opportunity (most of his early life is spent working menial jobs during the day, building his education on his own at night) or a place to fit in (although he attends meetings for the Communist Party, he finds them to be exclusionary and paranoid). In the end, then, the book does not present a positive opportunity for a free-thinking African American in either the North or the South.

The two-part nature of Wright's life led him to split the book into two sections: one, "Part One: Southern Night" discussing his time in the South, and the other, "Part Two: The Horror and the Glory" focusing on his time in Chicago.

Originally, the book was published through the Book of the Month Club but only included the first section. Wright meanwhile serializes small excerpts of the second section in a variety of magazines. Eventually, Harper & Brothers published the book in its entirety, and it sold very well.

Although some of the challenges toward *Black Boy* have cited obscene language and sexually explicit material as reasons for their objection, it is clear that the majority of the issues revolve around Wright's social commentary. Wright directly discusses his atheism, which, particularly at the time of the book's publication, made many readers quite uncomfortable. In addition, the book is a blistering critique of social structures in both the North and the South, demonstrating the difficulties faced by African Americans in any geographic region. Finally, Wright's political discussions, both his critiques of the southern, traditional culture and of the Communist Party, alienated segments of both the mainstream culture and the counterculture. Not surprisingly, the book received some of the harshest critiques of any book from conservative commentators. From testimony before Congress to the *Board v. Pico* case that was heard by the Supreme Court, *Black Boy*, along with its frequently challenged partners like *Slaughterhouse V* and *The Naked Ape*, has been part of landmark battles and decisions. The case focused on the presence of these books in either school curriculum or libraries. While the objections ranged in nature, *Black Boy* was mainly being criticized for its perceived anti-American nature. In the end, the Supreme Court found that students had the right to have access to these books, and *Board v. Pico* established the precedent that a school could not ban a book simply because of disagreements with the content. This was a major precedent in censorship in the United States.

In addition to the legal importance of *Black Boy*, it also helped to establish a new and vibrant set of texts from African American authors. The boldness and frankness of *Black Boy* helped to pave the way for later texts such as Ralph Ellison's *Invisible Man*. It also was noteworthy for being an early African American text to be commercially successful. This further helped to open many doors for African American authors looking to challenge the literary establishment and dominant culture. While *Black Boy* might seem relatively tame to readers now more than a half century after its original publication, its boldness and importance make it one of the more memorable books in American history.

See Also: *The Invisible Man*.

FURTHER READING

Butler, Robert. "Seeking Salvation in a Naturalistic Universe: Richard Wright's Use of His Southern Religious Background in *Black Boy* (American Hunger)." *Southern Quarterly*, Winter 2009, Vol. 46, Issue 2, pp. 46–60, 15p.

Hobbes, Dwight. "A Forgotten Pioneer: Richard Wright's *Black Boy.*" *Colors: Minnesota's Journal of Opinion by Writers of Color,* November–December 1995, Vol. 4, Issue 6, pp. 37–39.

Thaddeus, Janice. "The Metamorphosis of Richard Wright's *Black Boy.*" *American Literature,* May 1985, Vol. 57, Issue 2, p. 199, 16p.

The Bluest Eye, Toni Morrison
(Holt, Rinehart and Winston, 1970)

The Bluest Eye follows two sisters, ages nine and ten, as their family takes two people into their home: one, a tenant that the family takes in to help ends meet, and the other, a foster child coming from a difficult background. The foster child, who is African American, wishes that she were white and with blue eyes, particularly when she hears others refer to her as ugly. The child, Pecola, is eventually twice raped by her stepfather, and she becomes pregnant as a result of the rape. In a particular disturbing twist, some of the characters in the book perceive the rape as the only way that the father could possibly show Pecola love, with even Pecola taking it as a sad form of affirmation. This sort of perverse logic is a key part of the book's theme, looking at how the African American community can be hostile toward its own members and also looking at how deeply people can internalize messages about their appearance and worth. The child Pecola carries after being raped eventually is born prematurely, and it dies. At the book's end, Pecola seems to have gone insane, believing that she has actually had her wish granted and that she now has blue eyes, making her beautiful by the standards of the dominant culture.

Not surprisingly, the book's material had a very polarizing effect. While some readers appreciated the careful study of the complexities of race, gender, and class, many readers and politicians attacked the book for its material. In Alabama, in particular, the book met a good deal of resistance. While the book was challenged in over 130 school districts across the country, the harshest criticism came from Alabama state senator Bill Holtzclaw, who claimed that the book was inappropriate for both content and language. Although Holtzclaw did not initially object to the book, when he felt pressure from some of his Republican colleagues for not being vocal enough about problems with Common Core readings, Holtzclaw began calling the book entirely inappropriate and demanding that it not be included in classroom discussions. In the end, the book was not removed, though Holtzclaw remained critical. Although the challenge in Alabama might be one of the most public that the book has faced, it has literally had challenges from coast to coast, as far West as Bakersfield, California, and as far East as Brookfield, Connecticut, and many places in between. Still, the book helped to catapult Morrison to public prominence.

See Also: *Beloved* and *Song of Solomon*.

FURTHER READING

Pal, Payel, and Gurumurthy Neelakantan. "Morrison's Prostitutes in *The Bluest Eye*." *Notes on Contemporary Literature*, March 2014, Vol. 44, Issue 2, pp. 4–7.

Peoples, Tim. "Meditation and Artistry in *The Bluest Eye* by Toni Morrison and *Their Eyes Were Watching God* by Zora Neale Hurston." *Midwest Quarterly*, Winter 2012, Vol. 53, Issue 2, pp. 177–192.

Saunders, James Robert. "Why Losing a Tooth Matters: Shirley Jackson's *The Tooth* and Toni Morrison's *The Bluest Eye*." *Midwest Quarterly*, Winter 2012, Vol. 53, Issue 2, pp. 193–204.

Bury My Heart at Wounded Knee, Dee Brown
(Holt, Rinehart and Winston, 1970)

Bury My Heart at Wounded Knee is a nonfiction book looking at the history of Native Americans. The author, Dee Brown, opens the book with a general overview of the first contact with Columbus and other Europeans to the era shortly before the Civil War. The core point of this section of the book is to discuss the generally peaceful nature of the Native Americans in regard to the first settlers. Brown concludes that Native Americans only truly became hostile after losing a good deal of land to the Europeans. This claim worked against much of what was accepted as common knowledge about Native Americans at the time. Prior generations had generally portrayed Native Americans as either savage or primitive. After this initial correction of general American history of the time, Brown begins to focus on individual tribes and their histories, focusing on the Navajo, the Sioux, the Apache, and a half dozen other tribes. In the study of these tribes, Brown discusses a history of America failing to uphold the treaties made with the Native Americans and of a number of acts of hostility from both European settlers and the American government. In addition to the unfair treatment by the government, Brown looks at particular cruelties, like forcing tribes off of their land and onto reservations and the impact that disease brought by European settlers had upon Native Americans. By the end of the book, Brown had effectively rewritten a major piece of American history.

The book was a major success, both critically and commercially. It remained on the bestseller list for over a year, and it received positive reviews from mainstream publications like *TIME* magazine as well as from Native American authors and scholars, such as N. Scott Momaday. Many readers were surprised to find out that Brown was white rather than Native American, given the viewpoint of the book and the access to historical records that Brown was able to obtain. Part of the book's success was rooted in the emerging interest in Native American culture and history coming from developments like the counterculture movement of the 1960s and 1970s and the formation of the American Indian Movement, an activist group that occupied Alcatraz and Wounded Knee in protest of the American government's policies toward and treatment of Native Americans. Brown's book very naturally fed into these trends, but the book has also had significant staying power, consistently staying in print and being translated into a number of languages. In 2007, HBO aired a film that was adapted from the later parts of the book. It also was well received, earning a number of award nominations.

Despite its generally positive reception, the book did receive some criticism and a clear challenge. The criticism was that the book had a clear sense of bias, and even Brown admitted that he wanted the book to do the work of retelling the settling of America from the perspective of its Native people. The challenge to the book came in Wisconsin, where the book was banned by a school district in Wild Rose in 1974. The reason for the book's banning was simply that it was "controversial." Despite this lack of precise objection, the ban was successful for some time. Wisconsin has often had a high level of interracial tension between Native Americans and whites, with protests about spearfishing rights and other issues, and this certainly helps explain the success of the challenge. Subsequent bans and challenges have typically had similar, vague criticisms that many see as trying to hide the racist undertones of the objections. Still, the overall reputation of the book is very positive, and it is seen as one of a set of books (including Howard Zinn's *A People's History of the United States*, for instance) that have helped to add a level of depth and complexity to the teaching of history that had been absent for decades.

FURTHER READING

Fixico, Donald L. "*Bury My Heart and Wounded Knee* and the Indian Voice in Native Studies." *Journal of the West*, January 2000, Vol. 39, Issue 1, pp. 7–15.

Heffernan, Virginia. "There's an Allegory in Those Hills." *New York Times*, May 2007, Vol. 156, Issue 53955, pp. E1–E4, 2p.

Moses, Sarah. "*Bury My Heart at Wounded Knee* Debut." *Indian Life*, July/August 2007, Vol. 28, Issue 1, pp. 1–5.

The Color Purple, Alice Walker
(Harcourt Brace Jovanovich, 1982)

The Color Purple is a novel written by prominent African American author Alice Walker. The book centers around Celie, a poor, teenaged girl living in the South in awful conditions. Specifically, Celie is beaten and raped by Alphonso, the man whom she believes to be her father. As a result of the rapes, Celie has two children, both of whom are taken from her by Alphonso. To add to Celie's misery, her mother curses Celie as she dies. After the death of their mother, Celie and her sister, Nettie, find out that Nettie has a suitor. Rather than allowing Nettie to marry, Alphonso forces the suitor (whom Celie knows only as "Mister" at the time) to marry Celie. Celie finds herself in a rundown home taking care of Mister's children, who are extremely difficult. Mister also treats Celie poorly, though she is able to get some semblance of control in the house. Just as this begins to happen, Nettie escapes from Alphonso by moving into Celie and Mister's house. While Nettie is living in the home, Mister propositions her, sexually. Celie tells Nettie that she might be able to escape by taking refuge with a well-to-do African American woman who had adopted one of Celie's children from Alphonso. Although Nettie promises to keep in touch with Celie, Celie does not hear from her again. As the book progresses, Celie assumes that Nettie is dead. Celie focuses on raising Mister's children, who come of age and begin to strike out on their own, though one of them, Harpo, a son, impregnates and marries a young woman. Harpo's wife is not nearly as submissive to Harpo as Celie has been to the men in her life, and Celie advises Harpo to beat his wife in order for him to feel more in control. When Harpo attempts to take this advice, he ends up being injured himself. Celie apologizes to Harpo's wife, Sofia, for advising Harpo to beat her. Sofia discusses resisting with Celie, and Celie begins to seriously consider the possibility of standing up to Mister. However, Mister moves his ailing mistress into the home. At first, Celie is actually pleased, because she is fascinated by the mistress, who is a lounge singer. The mistress, Shug, is initially rude to Celie, but as Celie helps nurse Shug back to health, the two become friends, with Celie coming to develop strong feelings for Shug. Still, Mister feels pressure from the rest of his family because he and Shug have had three illegitimate children together, and their presence sometimes raises questions. When Shug returns to health, she begins working as a singer in a bar run by Sofia, who has left Harpo as a result of his attempts to exert control over her. Shug stays with Celie and Mister, partially to keep Mister from beating Celie. While things temporarily look promising, Sofia is put in jail after an altercation with the town's mayor's wife. Harpo's new girlfriend, Squeak, takes care of his and Sofia's children, and Sofia strikes up a friendship with Squeak. When Sofia is released from prison, she works as the mayor's wife's maid, which leaves her bitter and humiliated. Meanwhile, Celie and Shug develop a sexual relationship, and Shug helps Celie to find out more about her sister, Nettie. Celie discovers that Mister has been hiding the letters that Nettie had been sending Celie. Celie discovers a good deal from the letters, from the fact that Alphonso is not her biological father (her father had been lynched by cruel and bigoted white men) to the details of her mother's mental collapse (and Alphonso's subsequent manipulation of her). Celie also discovers that the woman that Nettie has befriended had also adopted both of Celie's children, though Nettie did not immediately recognize this. All this time, Nettie had been doing missionary work in Africa, though, partway through her letters, it is clear that Nettie had grown disenchanted with the work. All of these revelations lead Celie to leave behind her previous, submissive ways. After confronting Alphonso, who confirms the information from Nettie's letters, she decides to leave Mister, cursing him as she moves out. Along with Squeak and Shug, Celie strike out. Celie settles in Tennessee, where she works as a tailor. Mister tries to reconnect to her, even proposing to her, but Celie refuses to allow any real connection, and Mister's success declines, as though Celie's curse had come to pass. Alphonso also suffers, dying unexpectedly. This means that Celie inherits the land she grew up on. After moving back, Celie finds out that Shug has fallen in love with one of the members of her band. While Celie is disappointed, she vows to maintain her love for Shug. After the female missionary she traveled with dies, Nettie marries the male missionary. They return, with Celie's children in tow. Shug also returns, having ended things with the member of her band. At the end of the book, Shug, Celie, and Nettie are all together, finally getting to be together rather than just hearing of each other.

The Color Purple truly was a landmark book, opening up new discussions of gender, race, and acceptance. The stark portrayals of male dominance and the impact of racism upon the main characters of the book helped to shine a light on the systemic oppression found in America. It also gained a good deal of support from readers who felt that their experiences had not been represented in American literature up to that point. From gays and lesbians to the working class to African American women, many groups who typically found themselves represented only as side characters in literature and mainstream culture now had a significant literary text that put them in the main role. In fact, the book's treatment of sexuality and sexual preference was particularly complex and nuanced for its era, not labeling Shug or Celie as purely lesbians or heterosexual but instead presenting sexuality as fluid, with the potential for characters to change over time. Even more, the book presented the importance of sisterhood and female collaboration. The support that Shug and Celie give each other or the friendships that Squeak and Sofia strike up show the power of female friendship, and, conversely, the initial animosity Shug feels toward Celie and that the female missionary displays toward Nettie show the damage that anger between women can do.

In addition to its importance as cultural analysis, the book was very well received for its writing. In 1983, *The Color Purple* won the Pulitzer Prize for fiction. Although it earned critical accolades, the book was challenged in 1984. In Oakland, California, the book was challenged, with critics claiming that it had inappropriate material for high school readers, citing both portrayals of sex and "disturbing" portrayals of race and racial tension. Although the discussion of the book's appropriateness lasted for some time, it was eventually validated by the Oakland Board of Education, making it eligible for inclusion on high school reading lists.

In 1985, the book was adapted as a film, which was directed by Steven Spielberg, who was, up to that point, known for more commercial work like *ET* and *Indiana Jones*. While the film was critically well received, there were some controversies that came out of it. The film had received 11 Oscar nominations, but it did not win any, which led many to suggest that the film was snubbed because of its portrayal of racial tensions, preventing what many considered to be the best film of the year from winning the award for Best Picture. On the other side of the coin, some critics complained that Spielberg's treatment tried to pass over the issue of lesbianism too much, not valuing the relationship between Shug and Celie to the extent that it should have. In addition, there was some criticism that the portrayal of black men in the film was overly harsh. In 2005, Oprah Winfrey (who had appeared in the film adaptation) coproduced a musical adaptation of the book, with the musical earning nomination for a number of awards and winning the Tony Award for Best Lead Actress.

FURTHER READING

Jones, Liz. "Purple Reign." *O, The Oprah Magazine*, December 2015, pp. 150–157.

Singh, Sonal, and Sushma Gupta. "Celie's Emancipation in the Novel *The Color Purple*." *International Transactions in Humanities & Social Sciences*, July 2010, Vol. 2, Issue 2, pp. 218–221, 5p.

Williams, Kam. "Alice Walker: *The Color Purple* 30th Anniversary." *Journal of Pan African Studies*, December 2015, Vol. 8, Issue 9, pp. 156–160, 5p.

Gone with the Wind, Margaret Mitchell
(Macmillan Publishers, 1936)

Gone with the Wind is a major American novel that was also made into a major motion picture. The book is set in the South, Georgia in particular, during the Civil War and the period immediately following it. The book follows the O'Hara family, with Gerald and Ellen being well-to-do plantation owners. The pair have a teenaged daughter, Scarlett, who is well liked and able to live up to the expectations of the Southern aristocracy, interacting with people with charm and grace. Mitchell uses the development of the family's farm to give a sense of the development of the South and the system supported by slavery and the plantation system. Tensions are mounting as some of the men are called away to the war. Meanwhile, Scarlett continues to think about marriage, weighing the possibilities of her suitors. She is distressed when she hears that one of them, Ashley Wilkes, will be marrying his cousin rather than pursuing Scarlett. Scarlett tells Wilkes that she loves him, hoping that he will change his mind and propose to her. He tells her that he has feelings for her as well, but he does not think that they would go well together.

After this, Rhett Butler, who was eavesdropping on the exchange, tells Scarlett that he admires her unladylike approach to courting Ashley. Scarlett becomes angry with him and storms off. Scarlett ends up marrying Charles Hamilton, and she even becomes pregnant with his child, but Hamilton dies of disease, leaving Scarlett to raise a child on her own. She also must wear black and avoid interactions with young men because of the expectations of the Southern gentry. Scarlett feels frustrated and isolated. Scarlett perks back up when she goes to stay with her aunt in Atlanta. She becomes part of the community, volunteering and helping others. While she is taking part in a benefit dance for the Confederacy, she sees Rhett Butler again, and he bids an inordinate amount of money to get a dance with her. She discovers that Rhett does not believe in the South's efforts in the war, thinking that they will lose. Instead of supporting the South, he has been making money illegally. Rhett's interest in Scarlett (a young widow) causes a scandal among the attendees.

Soon, the Civil War begins to intrude upon Atlanta, with the Union starting to bring troops through the South. Melanie, Ashley Wilkes's wife, who was also living with Scarlett and his aunt, gives birth with only Scarlett to help her. As the city is besieged, Scarlett, Melanie, and the newborn boy have to go into hiding. Scarlett forces a slave girl to find Rhett for her. When Rhett goes to Scarlett, she begs him to save her and her family. Rhett initially laughs off her request, but he does find them a horse and carriage, and the group heads out of Atlanta. Partway to Scarlett's family's plantation, Rhett decides to have the others travel on by themselves so that he can enlist in the Confederate Army, joining the war effort despite the difficult position of the South's army. Scarlett reaches her family home to find things in disarray. Her mother has died, and her father is too overwhelmed by grief to function. All the slaves have left her family's plantation, and the Union army had burned their fields.

Scarlett gives a now-famous speech about protecting her family and making sure that they never go hungry again. Scarlett does, indeed, protect her family and begin to grow food again, giving some to returning soldiers and keeping

Union soldiers off of her land, even killing one. Two Confederate soldiers, one of them Ashley Wilkes, stays on, though one of them is unable to give much help. Just when things are beginning to improve for Scarlett and her family, new taxes threaten to close down the plantation. Scarlett seeks out Rhett, hoping that he will have the money to keep the plantation open. When she is in Atlanta, Scarlett discovers that Rhett is in jail. She finds Frank Kennedy, who is engaged to Scarlett's sister. In hopes of keeping the plantation open, Scarlett charms Kennedy and convinces him to marry her instead. The two then go back to the plantation, and Kennedy gives Scarlett the money to keep the land. When Kennedy falls ill, Scarlett takes control of the books of the store that he owns. After she finds out that many people owe him money, she begins to change the store's practices, leading to tension between Scarlett and Kennedy's regular customers. She also borrows money from Rhett Butler to buy a sawmill, which she also runs in a savvy, almost ruthless way. This connection to Rhett leads to further gossip among the community. Scarlett has to relent when she learns that she is pregnant. She calls upon Ashley Wilkes to take over the running of the sawmill, and Ashley and his wife, Melanie, move to Atlanta, where Melanie becomes a prominent member of the community.

After Scarlett is attacked in an attempted robbery, Kennedy and members of the Ku Klux Klan go into a poor section of town, trying to get vengeance. Kennedy, though, is shot dead, leaving Scarlett a widow for the second time. To make matters worse, the other men involved in the attempted revenge are questioned by Union forces. Rhett comes to the rescue, claiming that the men were with him drinking and with women at a brothel. The men are grateful, but the wives are unhappy, because they have to depend upon the brothel owner to confirm the stories, putting them in the debt of someone who violates the politeness codes of the Southern aristocracy. Waiting for Kennedy's funeral, Scarlett drinks and feels devastated. Rhett finds her in this vulnerable position, and he asks her to marry him. At first, she tells him that she does not love him, but, as he continues to pursue the topic, kissing her, she relents.

Within a year, the two are married. They have an extravagant honeymoon in New Orleans, but, almost as soon as they return, the two begin bickering. Things worsen until Scarlett tells Rhett that she is pregnant with his child, and she will have the child, but she does not really want it. When the child, Bonnie, a daughter, is born, Scarlett talks to Ashley, finding that she still has feelings for him. Meanwhile, Rhett focuses his affection on Bonnie, spoiling his daughter. Ashley's wife hosts a birthday party for him, but, before the party begins, Ashley and Scarlett talk alone. When she begins to cry, Ashley comforts her, but when Ashley's sister sees the two embracing, she suspects that her brother is having an affair, and the rumors begin to fly. That night, Rhett comes home drunk, and he brings Scarlett to the bedroom after a confrontation, and the two sleep together.

Rhett leaves the house with Bonnie the next morning, and Scarlett wonders if they can be happy together. Not long after, she discovers that she is pregnant again. When Rhett returns, Scarlett tells him that she is pregnant, and Rhett asks her if the child is actually Ashley's. The two have a confrontation, and Scarlett falls down the stairs, ending up miscarrying her child. She takes her two children from previous marriages back to her family home, looking to recover after her fall. When she recovers and returns, she and Rhett have a relatively flat but inoffensive marriage. Rhett continues to spoil Bonnie. One day, Bonnie is riding her horse, and she asks Rhett to help her set up a dangerous jump. Her horse does not make it, and, when it falls, Bonnie breaks her neck and dies. Rhett takes to drinking again, and he and Scarlett start to drift apart, though Scarlett indicates that she believes that they can reconcile.

The book was a tremendous commercial success, topping the bestseller list, and it continues to be one of the bestselling books in American history. The initial critical reaction, however, was mixed. While some prominent critics spoke highly of the book, noting its emotionally engaging story and boldness of vision, others felt that the book was a bit sprawling, asking too much of its readers. An even greater source of criticism was its portrayal of African Americans. The book made unflattering comparisons between slaves and animals, and it treated the slave owners in the South sympathetically rather than painting them as people who had profited off of the labor and suffering of slaves. Still, the book won a number of awards, including the Pulitzer Prize and the National Book Award.

Despite its popularity and significant reputation, the book has been challenged a number of times for its racial slurs and portrayal of African Americans. In addition, the book has been challenged for its profanity and its discussion of sexuality. The book was challenged in a number of places, though it generally was kept in libraries if not on reading lists for courses. From the time that it was published, the book received some criticism for its language (in particular, its use of the word "damn"), but it took some time before formal challenges came. In 1984, the book was challenged in a school in Waukegan, Illinois, for its use of racially charged language. *Gone with the Wind* was not, in the end, removed, though this may have been because it was included with other books such as *Uncle Tom's Cabin*. Although this challenge was not successful, the book was successfully banned for a time in 1978 in Anaheim, California. The book also has been met with more informal challenges and controversies. One such controversy was the retelling of the book from the perspective of the African American characters, *The Wind Done Gone* by Alice Randall. The holders of the original book's copyright tried to sue Randall, stopping the publication. However, the courts found in favor of Randall. Poet and performance artist Vanessa Place also tweeted the book in its entirety, receiving a significant backlash for her continuing of the use of racial slurs. Place tried to argue that she was trying to raise awareness of racial tensions, but many readers and members of the publishing industry found it offensive and self-indulgent. Despite these many and varied challenges, the book continues to sell well and to be the focus of much critical discussion, keeping it as a major work of American literature.

FURTHER READING

Barkley, Danielle. "No Happy Loves: Desire, Nostalgia, and Failure in Margaret Mitchell's *Gone with the Wind*." *Southern Literary Journal*, Fall 2014, Vol. 47, Issue 1, pp. 54–67, 14p.

Clukey, Amy. "Plantation Modernity: *Gone with the Wind* and Irish-Southern Culture." *American Literature*, September 2013, Vol. 85, Issue 3, pp. 505–530, 26p.

Leff, Leonard J. "*Gone with the Wind* and Hollywood's Racial Politics." *Atlantic*, December 1999, Vol. 284, Issue 6, p. 106.

Heart of Darkness, Joseph Conrad
(William Blackwood, 1902)

Heart of Darkness was originally published serially in *Blackwood's Magazine*. It is a novel partially based upon the experiences of the author, Joseph Conrad. The book follows Charles Marlow, the captain of a river steamboat. The book opens with Marlow telling his fellow sailors about his time off the coast of Africa. In particular, he remembers what he sees as being chaotic, with a lack of productive use of machinery as well as explosions that do not seem to be tied to any purpose. Even beyond this level of disorganization, Marlow sees brutality and exploitation among both the natives and the colonists. In particular, he sees native Africans being enslaved and worked to death. What strikes him as particularly disturbing is that these enslaved Africans are often overseen by other Africans, though the natives running the system are clothed in uniforms that mark them as being part of the colonial system that exploits the others. When Marlow goes ashore, he begins to hear about Mr. Kurtz, an agent who is particularly successful at supplying the corporations with ivory. When Marlow makes his way to the ship that he was meant to captain, he finds that it has been destroyed after someone tried to take it out in order to find Mr. Kurtz, who had apparently fallen ill. At this point, Marlow characterizes the people around the river as being greedy and lazy. While waiting for his boat to be repaired, Marlow continues to inquire about Mr. Kurtz, and he finds that, beyond his ability to bring in ivory, Mr. Kurtz is actually a very problematic figure, with many people disliking him and feeling that he got to his position only through unfair advantages from friends. Once Marlow begins heading up the river, he finds more and more ominous signals about his trip. His crew is made up partially of what he refers to as cannibals, and on the trip, he finds a note indicating that he should proceed quickly and carefully as he goes up the river. Eventually, the trip becomes difficult because of fog, and, shortly thereafter, they are attacked, with arrows being shot at them. The crew fires out with their rifles, but they still suffer losses, with Marlow having to take the wheel and with the crewman who had been steering impaled in Marlow's plain view. When the crew reaches Kurtz's station, they are hailed ashore by a figure in garish, multicolored clothes. This figure turns out to be a Russian wanderer who has met Kurtz. The wanderer tells Marlow that Kurtz is a remarkable man and that the natives worship him. He also tells Marlow that Kurtz has given him new views of the world and life. Marlow listens to the wanderer, but, after listening, he suspects that Kurtz is insane. This feeling is only confirmed when Marlow uses a telescope to get a better view of the station. He sees that the station has the severed heads of natives hanging from it. At this point, Kurtz is brought to the crew by a group of natives. Kurtz is brought on a stretcher, and he looks gaunt and emaciated. Marlow becomes nervous, because he sees the crowd of natives that look ready to fight them. Fortunately for Marlow, Kurtz stops them from initiating any violence. Kurtz comes aboard the ship to talk to the manager. While Marlow watches a native woman walk along the shore, he overhears Kurtz and the manager arguing. He hears Kurtz insisting that his work at the station has not been completed and that he must not be interrupted. After Kurtz and the manager finish arguing, the manager takes Marlow aside and tells him that Kurtz's methods are endangering the company's reputation and future. The Russian wanderer then talks to Marlow, telling him that Kurtz had originally planned on having the natives attack and kill the crew, believing that they had been sent to remove him and possibly kill him. Marlow confirms to the wanderer that there was discussion of hanging Kurtz in order to get rid of him. At this point, the wanderer advises Marlow to leave on a canoe while he still can. That night, Marlow wakes up at midnight and finds that Kurtz has left the boat. Marlow leaves as well, eventually tracking Kurtz down. He finds that Kurtz is so ill that he can only crawl away. Marlow warns him that if he calls the natives, he will kill Kurtz. Kurtz begins to confess that he wishes that he could have done more in the area. Marlow tells Kurtz that he is still held in very high esteem in Europe, and that he will be in an excellent position if he returns. Kurtz agrees, and Marlow carries Kurtz back to the boat. The next day, the crew are preparing to leave with Kurtz. The natives, including the woman that Marlow had watched while Kurtz and the manager had argued, are all watching. They begin to shout, and, fearing an attack, Marlow sounds the boat's horn until the natives scatter, though the woman holds her ground, keeping her arms stretched out. As the boat pulls away, the crew fire their rifles at the natives. While they are returning, Kurtz becomes even weaker than he was when the crew found him, and Marlow begins to fall ill as well. As Kurtz becomes very weak, he gives Marlow a report that he had been commissioned to write along with a photograph. The next day, Marlow speaks to Kurtz, and Kurtz passes away, uttering the famous words, "The horror! The horror!" Marlow does not tell anyone that he saw Kurtz die. Later that night, one of the native crew members announces that Kurtz has died, and the next day, Marlow sees the native crew members burying something. As the trip progresses, Marlow becomes even more ill. In the end, Marlow does pull through and survive the trip back to Europe, where a number of figures seek out Kurtz's report. Marlow eventually offers Kurtz's report to one of the company's men, though Marlow has taken off a closing piece that recommended that the company kill "all the brutes." The company employee rejects this offer, confirming Marlow's suspicion that the company's only interest is finding the remaining ivory that Kurtz claimed to have had. Not knowing what else to do, Marlow decides to turn the report over to a journalist. He also gives some of Kurtz's personal effects to someone claiming to be his cousin. The book closes with Marlow visiting a woman who was supposed to be Kurtz's fiancée. He talks to her at length, and the woman asks Marlow what Kurtz's last words were. Rather than tell her the truth (that Kurtz ended his life with the words "The horror! The horror!"), Marlow tells her that the last thing that Kurtz said was her name.

Heart of Darkness has been a tremendously influential book that has received both lasting attention and significant criticism. Interestingly, during Conrad's life, the book received little attention, but since his death, it has received a great deal of study and analysis, with prominent literary critic Harold Bloom making the claim that it has been studied more than any other book. While not every scholar would agree with this, the novel has been very influential in the establishing and development of postcolonial studies, the field of literary analysis that examines the impact of outside cultures on indigenous people and cultures. In 1975, Nigerian novelist Chinua Achebe delivered a lecture in which he denounced *Heart of Darkness*, discussing the deep and consistent racism found in the book. Many other scholars in the field sided with Achebe, recognizing that Conrad tended to employ existing stereotypes even while he tried to denounce the influence of the British Empire upon developing countries. That said, there are some writers and scholars who not only study but also continue to celebrate the book. Prominent author Joyce Carol Oates has called the book "great, if troubling," demonstrating its ambiguous nature as an important but problematic book.

In addition to its influence upon literary studies (postcolonial criticism in particular), *Heart of Darkness* has had lasting and widespread influence over a number of media. In 1938, Orson Welles adapted the book as a radio play for CBS radio, and, the year after, he tried to adapt it to film, though the project fell through for a number of reasons. There were other adaptations that had varying degrees of success, but the most celebrated adaptation was likely Francis Ford Coppola's

1979 film, *Apocalypse Now*. The film used many aspects of the original text (the chaos, the brutality, and the dark influence of the Western portion of the world) to examine the Vietnam War. The film received significant critical acclaim, receiving two Oscars, and it helped to popularize portrayals of the Vietnam War in film.

Although *Heart of Darkness* has clearly had a significant and lasting impact upon literary and popular culture, it has met with challenges from readers as well. The book frequently uses the *N*-word, and this has been a major part of the challenge. While there still are some scholars who argue that the use of the term is ambiguous (generally, they take the position that Conrad is trying to illustrate the problematic views held by the colonists and that he is a product of his time, not meaning to assert problematic views but simply being part of his historical context), the majority of scholars and critics agree with Achebe, feeling that Conrad cannot separate his views from the problematic views of his audience, even if he tries to demonstrate that the views are troubling or outdated. Although there have been challenges (and the book actually has been banned in a number of U.S. schools) based upon his use of offensive racial epithets, the book continues to be used and taught in schools across the nation, though often more in colleges rather than high schools. Like Mark Twain's *The Adventures of Huckleberry Finn*, the book has such a prominent place as both a piece of literature and an influence upon subsequent generations of writers, it is difficult to remove *Heart of Darkness* from study in general or the literary canon in particular. Whatever its place in literature, *Heart of Darkness* is likely to remain an object of study for generations to come.

FURTHER READING

Achebe, Chinua. "An Image of Africa: Racism in Conrad's *Heart of Darkness*." *Massachusetts Review*, Spring 2016, Vol. 57, Issue 1, pp. 14–27, 14p.

Dilworth, Thomas, and Joseph Labine. "Two Black Hens in Conrad's *Heart of Darkness*." *Explicator*, 2013, Vol. 71, Issue 1, pp. 44–48, 5p.

Gramm, Christie. "Figure and Ground in *Heart of Darkness*." *Conradian: Journal of the Joseph Conrad Society*, Autumn 2014, Vol. 39, Issue 2, pp. 61–79.

I Know Why the Caged Bird Sings, Maya Angelou
(Random House, 1969)

I Know Why the Caged Bird Sings is an autobiographical novel written by prominent poet Maya Angelou. The book follows the main character "My" (short for "Maya") as she struggles with a number of negative forces (racism and sexism, for instance) in the American South. After My and her brother are abandoned by their parents, the pair of siblings go to live with their father's mother and their disabled uncle. While living in Arkansas with their grandmother and uncle, the pair suffer under the repressive, dehumanizing forces of their bigoted white neighbors. My's family is stuck in a difficult position, being well-to-do in some ways (My's grandmother owns a general store, giving her a source of income) but are also subject to the ridicule of even the lower-class white members of the community, as exhibited in an incident in which a lower-class white woman shows her pubic hair to My's grandmother (called "Momma" by My and her brother). Even worse, My sees her grandmother having to hide her disabled uncle when members of the Ku Klux Klan come by the house, looking to lynch adult, African American men. There are also other examples of degradation that My suffers, like having her name changed to "Mary" by her employer, who makes no effort to take into account My's preferences or interests, instead dismissing My's desires and level of self-worth out of a simple but troubling sense of bigotry. Even in school, My feels that her race is put down when a speaker at her eighth-grade graduation ceremony explains to My and her classmates that their race gives them limited potential and opportunity. Other examples of My feeling oppressed because of her race include a white dentist refusing to treat her, even though My's grandmother had lent the dentist money during the Great Depression. That said, there are moments when My is able to feel pride for African Americans, like when Joe Louis wins a championship boxing match. She feels a part of something, and she recognizes the significance of this sense of community. Although My has positive relationships with her grandparents, her father eventually comes back to town. He takes My and her brother, only to end up leaving them with their mother in St. Louis. After My's father disappears from her life again, she begins being sexually abused by her mother's boyfriend, Mr. Freeman. My eventually tells her mother, and Mr. Freeman is made to stand trial. After being convicted, Mr. Freeman flees, only to turn up dead. My believes that her uncles killed Mr. Freeman rather than letting him get away. All of this leads to My becoming isolated and withdrawn. Eventually, she leaves the care of her mother to return to her grandparents, though she remains generally withdrawn and quiet upon her return. Fortunately for My, Mrs. Bertha Flowers takes an interest in her, encouraging My to express herself. While My does start to express herself again, she and her brother feel the pressures and dangers of the South, and her grandmother decides to send the siblings back to their mother, though their mother now lives in San Francisco rather than St. Louis. In San Francisco, My begins to thrive, studying acting and dance and becoming the first African American streetcar conductor. Unfortunately, not all of My's experiences in California are positive ones. When she visits her father, she has to drive him home after he is too intoxicated to handle the wheel. In fact, the drive is her first time operating a car. Even worse, after an argument with her father's girlfriend, My is temporarily left homeless. My also finds herself dealing with anxieties and insecurities, most notably that she suspects that she might be a lesbian. In an attempt to disprove this possibility to herself, My initiates a sexual relationship with a boy, and she ends up pregnant. The book ends with My both graduating from high school and becoming a mother.

I Know Why the Caged Bird Sings is one of seven of Maya Angelou's autobiographical works, but it is the most widely and consistently acclaimed. Almost immediately after publication, the book became a bestseller, and it was hailed by critics as a significant work of American literature. The book was seen as both an important continuation of African American literary traditions (having affinities with texts like *Incidents in the Life of a Slave Girl* by Harriet Jacobs) and also opening up a new line of discussion for women of color. The book has also been noted as an influence for many different cultural figures, from director, actor, and activist Julian Mayfield to Oprah Winfrey. The book also catapulted Maya Angelou to a place of cultural prominence that she has held since, serving as a major figure in both literature and cultural struggles. Since her rise to noteworthy status, Maya Angelou has been included in a wide variety of cultural and political events. She read a poem at President Bill Clinton's first inauguration, she has appeared on the children's show *Sesame Street*, and she has won a Grammy for her reading of her work. Given her breakthrough and her staying power, it is hard to overstate the importance of Angelou as an African American writer or simply as a poet and writer in general.

Despite these significant accomplishments and recognitions, the book has received both criticism and challenges. Author Francine Prose has critiqued the book harshly, claiming that Angelou overdramatizes her life in order to get cheap or easy sympathy from the reader. In addition, a number of readers and groups have felt that the material covered in the book is inappropriate for many readers. Because of its discussion of the rape of a child and its open discussion of sex and sexual desire, the book has been challenged in fifteen states. Although the book remains in libraries and as part of class curriculum, some schools have requested that teachers provide alternatives for students and parents who find the book's themes and content too objectionable. Although the book has a wealth of defenders, it was third on the American Library Association's (ALA) list of one hundred "Most Challenged Books" of 1990–2000.

Despite these challenges, Maya Angelou's work has been taught, studied, and read for decades now, and it will likely continue to be regarded as a major literary work. When Maya Angelou died in 2014, many readers celebrated her life by returning to *I Know Why the Caged Bird Sings*, affirming Angelou's prowess as a writer and cultural critic.

FURTHER READING

Barnwell, Cherron A. "Singin' de Blues: Writing Black Female Survival in *I Know Why the Caged Bird Sings.*" *Langston Hughes Review*, Spring 2005, Vol. 19, Issue 1, pp. 48–60.

Bejan, Remus. "Nigrescene: Mapping the Journey in Maya Angelou's *I Know Why the Caged Bird Sings.*" *Romanian Journal of English Studies*, 2007, Vol. 4, Issue 3, pp. 200–207.

Walker, Pierre A. "Racial Protest, Identity, Words, and Form in Maya Angelou's *I Know Why the Caged Bird Sings.*" *College Literature*, October 1995, Vol. 22, Issue 3, pp. 91–108, 18p.

Invisible Man, Ralph Ellison
(Random House, 1952)

Invisible Man is a major American novel examining the role of African Americans in the mid-20th century. The book opens with the narrator explaining the book's central metaphor. Although he is not literally invisible, the narrator points out that people do not really see him when they look at him. Instead, they see the assumptions and stereotypes that they carry with them rather than his true self. Rather than bemoaning this invisibility, the narrator claims that it has allowed him to do things that he otherwise could not. In particular, he claims that his invisibility has given him the ability to "live underground," by which he means that he has been able to live on the margins of society, observing how it works and preparing himself to write the book that the reader is reading.

After giving these prefatory remarks, the narrator begins to describe his life. He grew up in the South, and he was a gifted speaker. Because of his natural talents, the narrator is invited to speak to a group of whites. The white men congratulate him on his speech, but instead of rewarding him for it, they force him to compete in a large, blindfolded boxing match with other young African American men. As part of the humiliation and torture of the young African American men, the white men (all of whom are well-to-do) force the African American men to crawl over each other on an electrified blanket in order to get what they believe to be gold coins but are actually fakes. After this incident, the narrator has a nightmare that what he believed to be a scholarship was hoax and that the paper he was given calls him a "Nigger Boy."

Despite these misgivings, the narrator does attend college, thanks to the scholarship. After a few successful years at college, the narrator is given the task of driving a wealthy trustee around the campus. Although the trustee dominates the conversation, things go fairly well until the trustee begins asking about a poor, African American man who committed incest, impregnating his daughter.

After hearing the unsettling story, the trustee decides that he wants to take his mind off of it with a drink, and the narrator takes the trustee to a bar that also serves as a brothel, primarily catering to African American men. Not surprisingly, trouble starts. After a fight breaks out in the bar, the trustee faints. He is tended to be an African American veteran who has experience as a medic. Although the veteran treats the trustee, he also belittles both the trustee and the narrator, telling them that they are both ignorant of the true nature of race relations in America.

The narrator then takes the trustee back to the college. The narrator listens to a speech about the college's founder, extolling the founder's virtue. Afterward, the narrator is called in by the college president, who tells the narrator that he heard what happened with the trustee. The narrator is expelled, and the president tells the narrator that he should have shown the trustee events and areas that make African American life seem simple and happy. Still, the president does give him some letters of recommendation and some leads for jobs in New York City. When the narrator arrives in Harlem, he finds that the letters of recommendation do him little good, and he struggles to find work. After the search for work becomes overly frustrating, the narrator seeks out the person to whom the letters are addressed (another trustee of the college). Although the narrator does not find the trustee, he does find the trustee's son, who tells the narrator that the letters are actually quite derogatory and are likely preventing him from finding a good job. Feeling betrayed, the narrator is dejected, but the trustee's son at least helps to find the narrator an entry-level job at a paint company. Ironically, the company's most popular color is called "Optic White." This job proves to be an unhappy one as the person that the narrator assists accuses him of working for the union. During a fight between the two men, an unattended tank explodes, knocking out the narrator.

The narrator wakes up to find that he has lost his ability to remember things and to speak. Rather than treat him with conventional means, the white doctors at the paint factory hospital decide to use electroshock therapy. The narrator does, eventually, recover his memory, but the shock treatments have left him in a bad state. After collapsing on the street one day, the narrator is taken to the home of an African American woman named Mary. Mary treats the narrator with kindness, letting him live at her home free of charge and directing him to value his African American culture. After experiencing this support and direction, the narrator begins to speak out, defending an elderly African American couple when he sees them being evicted. The narrator's speech in their defense energizes a crowd on the street, watching things unfold. One of the crowd members, Brother Jack, offers the narrator a job working for the Brotherhood, a social and political organization fighting for civil rights. The narrator begrudgingly accepts the offer, not having a genuine interest in the group but wanting to help Mary with some money.

Although the group is primarily focused on pushing forward African American rights, it is a white member of the group that trains the narrator in how to speak and how to represent the Brotherhood. As part of this initiation and training, the narrator is forced to take on a new name. When the narrator is sent to the post determined by the Brotherhood, he meets very different models for African American activists. On one end of the spectrum is Tod Clifton, a black youth leader, and on the other is Ras the Exhorter, who advocates for a domination by African Americans that would essentially replace white Americans in a position of power. After being seen talking to both of these activists, the narrator receives a note warning him that he must remain loyal to the Brotherhood. Shortly thereafter, he is publicly accused of seeking only to further his own interests. The narrator is put under investigation by the Brotherhood. During the investigation, the narrator is moved to a different area and asked to advocate for women's rights rather than the rights of African Americans. After speaking at a gathering, the narrator has sex with a white woman. After this, the narrator is sent back to Harlem, where he discovers that Tod Clifton has disappeared and many people are dissatisfied with the work being done by the Brotherhood. When the narrator does eventually find Clifton, he is selling dolls that are caricatures of African Americans. While Clifton tries to sell his dolls, he is accosted by white police officers who find that he does not have a license to sell them on the street. The confrontation ends horrifically, with Clifton being shot and killed by the officers.

Disturbed, the narrator holds a funeral for Clifton, extolling his virtues. Despite the positive response that the narrator gets from some of the attendees, the Brotherhood tells the narrator that he was wrong to hold the service for Clifton. The narrator argues with the members of the Brotherhood who are chastising him, including Brother Jack. After the narrator argues that Brother Jack is insulated from true battle and true sacrifice, Brother Jack takes out one of his eyes, showing the narrator that he has a glass eye from earlier fights. This silences the narrator, making him docile. The narrator is then sent back to the white member of the Brotherhood who originally had trained him. As the narrator talks to this member, he learns about new operations that the Brotherhood has set up in Harlem. Although the narrator is doing the work of the Brotherhood, he still resents Brother Jack, and he finds himself looking for ways to undercut Brother Jack's status.

While working in Harlem, the narrator finds that racial tensions are rising. In this combustible atmosphere, the narrator runs into Ras the Exhorter, who puts the narrator down and criticizes the Brotherhood for lack of action and pressure. In fact, Ras begins to send people to find and attack the narrator, so the narrator disguises himself, playing on the books "invisible" motif. The narrator goes to the apartment of the white member of the Brotherhood who trained him. The brother tells the narrator that the Brotherhood is shifting its focus away from racial matters, leaving the narrator bitter. Instead of outright attacking the Brotherhood, though, the narrator decides to take it down from the inside, and he pursues a woman close to one of the high ranking members of the Brotherhood, trying to seduce her. While the woman does give the narrator the opportunity to have sex (though it is clear that she sees him just as a black man, not as an individual), she apparently knows very little about the Brotherhood's operations. During a conversation with this woman at the narrator's apartment, the narrator receives an urgent phone call asking him to return to Harlem. The narrator does so, finding that a riot has started. In the midst of the riot, the narrator takes part in arson, setting fire to an apartment building. The narrator also finds Ras, who initiated the riot, and Ras tries to have his followers attack the narrator. As the narrator tries to escape, he falls down a manhole, and his pursuers ridicule him, covering the manhole. It is at this point that the reader comes to understand that the narrator is literally underground and that the opening lines worked on both a literal and figurative level.

The novel was been hailed by critics from its first publication. Many critics and scholars have recognized its significance both as a work of African American literature, drawing on a number of themes and conflicts that continue to permeate race relations in America, and as an experimental novel, playing with both form and sentence structure, reportedly influenced by Ellison's experience as a musician. It also had a number of subtle references, satirizing American culture of the day. The book continues to be studied largely because of its complex rendering of American racial conflict, finding issues with many positions in these conflicts. Large organizations like the Brotherhood are portrayed as inefficient and overly political, not achieving the change that they seem to advocate for. In addition, some African American activists, most notably Ras the Exhorter, are portrayed as dangerous extremists. The narrator does not find a viable alternative to either of these problems. This kind of grim vision of race relations makes the book an interesting and captivating study for many teachers and scholars.

Of course, *Invisible Man* has received a good deal of criticism as well. Its use of racial slurs and its portrayal of both sex and violence have led it to be the subject of attack by parents. While these portrayals have often been the stated reasons for the challenges to the book, many readers and social commentators have indicated a belief that the real reason for the book receiving attacks is that it puts forward "dangerous" views on race. In 1975, the book received two challenges, first having excerpts banned in a school in Butler, Pennsylvania, and then being removed from the reading list for a class in St. Francis, Wisconsin. In 1994, the book was challenged in Yakima, Washington, but it ultimately stayed in schools. In 2013, the book was challenged in North Carolina. Interestingly, some of the books challengers said that not only did the book have problematic portions, but it also lacked literary merit while others (groups in Pennsylvania, Washington, and Wisconsin) claimed that the book was too intellectual for younger readers. Proponents of the book were shocked by the former complaint, given the long history of positive reviews and criticisms that the book received. Despite this support, the book was banned in all three states. Still, the book's reputation has, overall, remained positive among literary circles and is often included on supplemental reading lists in history and literature courses.

FURTHER READING

Diller, Christopher G. "Signifying on Stowe: Ralph Ellison and the Sentimental Rhetoric of *Invisible Man.*" *Modern Language Quarterly*, December 2014, Vol. 75, Issue 4, pp. 487–509, 23p.

Sheokand, Anu. "Survival of Blacks: A Study of Ralph Ellison's *Invisible Man.*" *Language in India*, November 2012, Vol. 12, Issue 11, pp. 149–165, 17p.

Tucker Abramson, Myka. "Blueprints: *Invisible Man* and the Housing Act of 1949." *American Studies*, 2015, Vol. 54, Issue 3, pp. 9–21, 13p.

Song of Solomon, **Toni Morrison**
(Alfred A. Knopf, 1977)

Song of Solomon is one of Toni Morrison's early novels. The book follows Macon "Milkman" Dead III, so named because he was breastfed well past the typical age. When the neighborhood discovers that he is still being breastfed even though he has progressed out of diapers, he becomes the object of ridicule for being a "mama's boy." Macon comes from a troubled family with two sisters and a father who is ridiculed by Macon's mother for not living up to the standard of her father, who is the town's only black doctor. Macon's mother has an unhealthy connection to her father, with Macon's father claiming that when her father died, she laid in bed with the body, sucking its fingers, though his mother claims that she was only kissing the fingers. The tensions between Macon's parents increase, as Macon's father accuses his mother of committing incest with her father. When Macon's father strikes his mother, Macon becomes violent with his father in retaliation. Macon's parents are not the only unusual members of his family. One of his aunts, Pilate, was born without a belly button, and she seems to adhere to an "Earth Mother" mentality. She has both a child and grandchild, who she cares for with great nurturing. The granddaughter, Hagar, first falls in love with Macon, but, after he fails to reciprocate, she tries to kill him. Macon also is threatened by his friend, Guitar, after Guitar suspects that Macon has tried to cheat him out of gold that they are seeking. Ironically, the gold was meant to help fund revenge killings against people who had killed blacks. Despite these hostilities, Macon and Guitar help each other to search for gold around the farm that Macon's family used to work at in Pennsylvania. There, he meets Circe, a former slave who still lives, though the likelihood of someone her age living to the age that she is in the book is low. Circe tells Macon his family's history, though the tale seems like it could be partially a myth, because his great grandfather supposedly escaped slavery by flying all the way from the farm to Africa. She also claims that he left behind a large number of children, a fact that contributed to Macon's great grandmother insane (echoing the dissolution of Macon's own family). Macon decides to leave without finding the gold, and when he returns, he finds out that Hagar, the cousin who loved him but also tried to kill him, has died of a broken heart. Macon feels bad for his aunt, Pilate, and he brings her to the place where he found the farm his family formerly worked on. When they arrive, Guitar ends up killing Pilate, though he meant to kill Macon. Macon jumps at Guitar, though the end result of the jump is left ambiguous.

Like other novels of Morrison's, *Song of Solomon* incorporates a mixture of African American history, magical realism, and biblical allusions. Also like many of Morrison's other books, the novel was well received by a wide variety of readers. It received positive commentary from a number of literary critics and writers. It has also been listed as a favorite by President Barack Obama, and it was the inspiration for the Pennsylvania-based punk band The Dead Milkmen, showing the wide range of readership that the book has had.

Still, the violence, language, and sexual overtones of the book have led to it receiving a number of challenges as well. In 1993, the book received its first official challenge in Columbus, Ohio. The book was, in the end, retained, but it did have successful challenges in other areas. In Richmond County, Georgia, for instance, the book was removed from the "required reading" section of a library, though it was not banned outright. In Maryland, the book was also removed from the school library. The complaints were often vague, simply referring to the book as "filthy" or "trash." However, some complaints claimed that the book was degrading to African Americans. Still, the book continues to receive study and a consistent readership as part of Toni Morrison's larger body of works.

See Also: *Beloved* and *The Bluest Eye*.

FURTHER READING

Dubek, Laura. " 'Pass It On!': Legacy and the Freedom Struggle in Toni Morrison's *Song of Solomon*." *The Southern Quarterly*, Winter 2015, Vol. 52, Issue 2, pp. 90–109.

Pocock, Judy. " 'Through a Glass Darkly': Typology in Toni Morrison's *Song of Solomon*." *Canadian Review of American Studies*, 2005, Vol. 35, Issue 3, pp. 281–298, 18p.

Terry, Jennifer. "Buried Perspectives: Narratives of Landscape in Toni Morrison's *Song of Solomon*." *Narrative Inquiry*, 2007, Vol. 17, Issue 1, pp. 93–118, 26p.

Soul on Ice, **Eldridge Cleaver**
(Rampart Press Inc., 1968)

Soul on Ice is a memoir examining racial politics in America. The book was written by Eldridge Cleaver while he was in prison. Cleaver discusses growing up in Arkansas in the 1930s before his family moved to California in 1946. There, Cleaver began to join in groups of youths committing petty crimes, and he started his history of going in and out of jail. His first major arrests were for possession of marijuana, an offense that led to a two-year prison sentence, and for sexual assault with intent to murder, which led him to be housed in San Quentin and Folsom prisons, both known for their tough reputations. During his stay in prison, Cleaver earned his high school degree and began to focus on reading and writing. It was also during this period that he gave some of his writings to his lawyer, who brought them to *Ramparts* magazine, where they were published as individual articles and essays. The popularity of these publications led *Ramparts* magazine to offer Cleaver regular work when he was released from prison in 1966. Two years later, they published a collection of his essays as the book *Soul on Ice*. Cleaver showed an interest in history and literature, mixing his references of contemporary figures like Muhammad Ali and Malcolm X with references to Voltaire, Thomas Paine, and W. E. B. Du Bois. He also was very candid about his own crimes, admitting to raping young black women with the idea that this would help him to prepare for raping white women. In addition, Cleaver wrote regularly about the difficulties of being black in a society that was largely run by the white, wealthy elite.

The book was polarizing from the moment that it was published. Significant cultural and literary figures like Norman Mailer praised Cleaver for his ability to bring attention to issues that had largely been ignored in mainstream culture. In addition, many critics saw Cleaver as making astute observations about the systemic problems in America that led to racial strife, class inequality, and civic unrest. Other readers found Cleaver's claims disturbing, and they were even more horrified to see his success and validation by critics and writers. Still others appreciated Cleaver's comments about race and the corruption of systems in America but were disturbed by his views on gender and homophobic comments made throughout the book. Cleaver's involvement with the Black Panther movement tended to intensify the position taken by both sides. Despite (or perhaps because of) this controversy, the book has been read and referenced wisely, with a number of hip-hop artists titling either albums or individual songs "Soul on Ice" as an homage to Cleaver.

Cleaver's book has been kept in school libraries and even taught or put on recommended reading lists in some schools. Not surprisingly, it has faced a number of challenges. In particular, it was one of the books put on the list for the *Island Trees Union Free School District v. Pico* trial, which was heard by the U.S. Supreme Court (see the discussion in the entry on *Black Boy* for greater detail). The Supreme Court found that these books were generally challenged on the basis of their conceptual content rather than their level of obscenity, meaning that banning them from school libraries would interfere with the authors' rights to free speech. Despite this ruling, multiple dissenting opinions were issued by some of the justices who felt that the school board should have local authority to ban or allow books or that the school is an educating agent, not a governing agent, and so the banning of books from school libraries is fundamentally different from banning them in stores. Its involvement in the landmark case is certainly part of what made *Soul on Ice* one of the most important books in recent history. But even beyond this, the book is significant for its opening of discussion about race relations, the prison system, and a host of other topics that continue to be examined and debated in American political discourse.

FURTHER READING

Doherty, Brian. "Hugo Chavez, Black Panthers and Pig Power." *Reason*, June 2013, Vol. 44, Issue 2, p. 16.

Felgar, Robert. "*Soul on Ice* and *Native Son*." *Negro American Literature Forum*, 1974, Vol. 8, Issue 3, p. 235.

Lavelle, Ashley. "From *Soul on Ice* to *Soul on Fire*: The Religious Conversion of Eldridge Cleaver." *Politics, Religion & Ideology*, March 2013, Vol. 14, Issue 1, pp. 75–93, 19p.

The Story of Little Black Sambo,
Helen Bannerman
(Grant Richards, 1899)

The Story of Little Black Sambo is a highly controversial children's book. In it, the title character is out for a walk when he is approached by four tigers. Rather than panicking, Sambo gives the tigers each a piece of his clothing, and then he hides while the tigers begin to fight among themselves over which one has the best clothing. Eventually, the tigers chase each other for so long and so quickly that they turn into butter. When this happens, Sambo takes his clothes back, dresses himself, and returns to his mother and father (named Black Jumbo and Black Mumbo).

The book had several editions, and different editions were met with different reactions. The original was illustrated by Bannerman herself, and it was generally seen as simplistic in a way that was not uncommon for children's books. Subsequent editions, though, had images of Sambo, Mumbo, and Jumbo that seemed closer in appearance to stereotypical portrayals of Africans and African Americans or even like characters appearing in the exaggerations of blackface. More recent versions have, in some ways, reclaimed the story, using more realistic images and focusing on the intelligence of Sambo rather than portraying him in a stereotypical way, and these editions have met with a positive response from a number of critics.

Some of the responses to the book also came from the wide variety of adaptations and references to the book. A number of these adaptations, such as a board game in the 1920s and a cartoon in the 1930s, also incorporated the offensive images of some of the book's editions. Other references, like Ishmael Reed's book, *Mumbo Jumbo*, were more playful and critical in their use of terms and figures from the book. Still, references to the book were generally seen as problematic, and they met with significant backlash. One example is a restaurant chain that was named Sambo's and had images from the book's inside. People were so outraged (in addition to community groups, the NAACP got involved) that, even after most of the restaurants changed their names, many still had to close. This example was, of course, outside of the editions of the books themselves.

The book itself received a number of challenges. Most clearly, it has received clear challenges from sources that stemmed from its portrayal of race. For the first few decades of its publication, the book received relatively few challenges. However, in the 1970s, with the rise of the Civil Rights Movement, the images in the book began to come under fire. The first major challenges came from librarians in Chicago. There had been complaints prior to that, but the Chicago challenges gave a deeper level of detail in the reason for these challenges. In particular, there were complaints that the images looked like performers from offensive minstrel shows in which white performers would put on makeup to appear like exaggerated versions of African Americans and would behave in ridiculous ways, denigrating the African American race. They also pointed to existing African terms and names that may have influenced the names within the book and had problematic references, like "Zambo," which was a derogatory term for a person of mixed race. The book has faced challenges over the last century, but with the new, more realistic or sensitive versions of the story, the story itself is still widely circulated; the older, more offensive versions have generally fallen out of favor, though they can still be found by collectors.

FURTHER READING

Sircar, Sanja. "Little Black Sambo: Perplexities and Patterns." *Journal of Children's Literature Studies*, March 2006, Vol. 3, Issue 1, pp. 40–71.

Van Der Horn-Gibson, Jodi. "Dismantling Americana: Sambo, Shirley Graham, and African Nationalism." *Americana: The Journal of American Popular Culture* (1900–present), Spring 2008, Vol. 7, Issue 1.

Yuill, Phyllis. "Little Black Sambo: The Continuing Controversy." *School Library Journal*, March 1976, Vol. 22, Issue 7, pp. 71–75, 5p.

Their Eyes Were Watching God, Zora Neale Hurston
(J.B. Lippincott, 1937)

Their Eyes Were Watching God is perhaps the best known of Zora Neale Hurston's novels. The book is told by Pheoby Watson, though its protagonist is Janie Crawford, an African American woman. Janie's family has a troubling past, with her mother being the product of a relationship between Janie's enslaved grandmother and her master. Janie's mother, Leafy, became pregnant with Janie when she was raped by her teacher. Unable to deal with the pressures of motherhood, Leafy disappeared, leaving Janie to be raised by her grandmother. After the troubles with Leafy, Janie's grandmother is very cautious not to let Janie go astray. In attempt to control her, Janie's grandmother arranges for her to marry Logan Killicks, someone significantly older than Janie. Janie is not interested in Killicks, seeing him as someone who would be more akin to a business partner than a spouse whom she could love. This leads to friction between Janie and her grandmother. Not long after this fighting, Janie's grandmother dies, and she runs off with Jody Starks, trying to find someone whom she believes she can love. The two move to a small town where Jody and Janie run a general store. Eventually, Jody becomes mayor of the town, and, around this time, Janie begins to feel objectified, seeing Jody use her to show his power and position in town. Their marriage deteriorates as Jody becomes more controlling, expecting Janie to run the general store and publicly ridiculing her. Eventually, Janie ridicules him back, and Jody hits her. This leads to the two splitting up, and Jody falls ill shortly thereafter. Janie visits him on his deathbed, telling him that his controlling ways prevented him from recognizing who Jody was as a person. Although Jody and Janie had parted ways, they were still legally married, so when Jody dies, Janie inherits a substantial estate, and a number of men become her suitor. Janie chooses a younger man who goes by the name of Tea Cake. Janie sells the store, and they move to the Everglades, where they run a bean farm. The pair do fight at times (with Tea Cake abusing her to demonstrate his control, echoing the actions and attitude of Jody). Still, Janie feels that this is the best of her three relationships. During a hurricane, Tea Cake is bitten by a rabid dog in his attempt to keep it from attacking Janie. Though he survives, the disease takes hold of him, and he deteriorates, eventually coming at Janie with a gun. Janie shoots Tea Cake before he can shoot her, and she is charged with murder. Tea Cake's friends testify against Janie at the trial, but with the support of some white women in the area, Janie is found innocent by an all-white jury. Having lost Tea Cake, Janie gives him a respectable funeral and then returns to the town where she lived in with Jody, recognizing that she is the focus of gossip among the townspeople, but also having the confidence to not be influenced by them.

The book received a wide variety of reactions upon its publication. While Hurston did receive some acclaim, she was also attacked by both white and African American writers and critics. Hurston wrote out of the South, and many of the prominent African American writers of the day lived in the North, taking part in the Harlem Renaissance. Some of these writers criticized the novel as being too melodramatic. Many white critics were positive in their reviews. The book even received a positive review from the *New York Times*. Still, the book was not immediately a major commercial success. In the 1970s and 1980s, the book found new audiences, largely on college campuses where it became a regular part of African American literature curricula. It also was recognized as a significant work of feminist literature, showing the harmful effects of male-dominated relationships. New African American women writers like Audre Lorde and Alice Walker became champions of Hurston and her work. In the late 1970s, a major biography of Hurston came out, continuing to reignite interest in her career, and, by 1981, a Zora Neale Hurston Society was founded, giving a regular examination of her work and life, focusing on both her content and the innovative voice and structural techniques.

As a result of the renewed popularity of the book and author, *Their Eyes Were Watching God* was adapted as a play multiple times and then, in 2005, as a made-for-television film. However, because the movie needed to be appropriate for television viewing, much of the story's content was cut or implied, keeping it from receiving nearly the popularity of the book.

Although the book has regularly been taught in the classroom for decades, it has received a number of challenges. In 1997, for instance, parents in Virginia objected to the inclusion of the book on a reading list, citing the direct discussion of sexuality. As with many such challenges, it is difficult to fully determine whether the core reason for the challenge was the sexual content or if there were issues related to the discussion of race and the portrayal of marriage that were the largest motivating factor. Still, the book remains recognized as a significant (if controversial) work of American literature.

FURTHER READING

Bealer, Tracy L. " 'The Kiss of Memory': The Problem of Love in Hurston's *Their Eyes Were Watching God*." *African American Review*, Summer/Fall 2009, Vol. 43, Issue 2/3, pp. 311–327, 17p.

Beauchamp, Gorman. "Three Notes on Hurston's *Their Eyes Were Watching God*." *Texas Review*, Spring/Summer 2014, Vol. 35, Issue 1/2, pp. 73–87, 15p.

Roberts, Brian Russell. "Archipelagic Diaspora, Geographical Form, and Hurston's *Their Eyes Were Watching God*." *American Literature*, March 2013, Vol. 85, Issue 1, pp. 121–149, 29p.

To Kill a Mockingbird, Harper Lee
(J.B. Lippincott, 1960)

To Kill a Mockingbird is a major novel examining race relations and issues of justice in the American South. While the story stays close to Scout, Jem, and Dill (three children), the major conflict of the novel involves Scout and Jem's father, a lawyer in a town in Alabama during the Great Depression. Their father, Atticus Finch, is defending an African American man who has been accused of raping a white woman. Atticus feels that it is his duty to defend the accused man, Tom Robinson, whom he believes is innocent, but many of the townspeople try to pressure Atticus into stepping away from the case so that they can lynch Tom. The other major strand of the novel involves the children speculating about one of their neighbors, the reclusive Boo Radley, who sometimes will leave small trinkets for the children, but who also never interacts with them directly. Although the children are able to have some pleasant times together, they do feel some of the same pressures that their father feels. At school, they are told that their father is a "Nigger lover," and Scout in particular nearly comes to blows with some of her classmates. Before she can start the fight, though, she remembers her father's advice that violence is never a good answer. Atticus not only gives this advice, he also seems to practice it when he fends off a group of townspeople who are angry about his role in the trial. The kids help to fend the townspeople off by calling them out on their cowardice and lack of commitment to justice. When the trial starts, Atticus tells the kids not to come, but they do anyway. When there are no seats available in the main area of the courtroom, the children are seated in the "colored" section, a hot, stuffy area in the balcony. Sitting there, the children see their father defend Tom by proving that both the woman accusing Tom and her father, a known alcoholic, are lying. In particular, he establishes that the real culprit of the woman's beating is her alcoholic father who caught her making advances upon Tom, and he proves that Tom's physical disabilities would have made it impossible for him to be the perpetrator of the violence committed against her. Despite all of this evidence, the jury find Tom guilty, devastating both Tom and the children. Recognizing his fate, Tom tries to escape from prison, and he is shot. When this news comes in, both Scout and Atticus doubt the effectiveness of the justice system. Although Tom was found guilty and was murdered, the father of the accusing woman has been publicly humiliated by the trial, being identified as both a drunk and a liar. As a result of this humiliation, the father threatens both the judge of the trial and Atticus, going so far as to spit in Atticus's face. Even worse, the father seeks out Jem and Scout, and he attacks them. Although he breaks Jem's arm, someone comes to the rescue of the children, stopping the father from further injuring them. It is only after the altercation that Scout comes to realize that the person saving them is actually Boo Radley. When Boo Radley returns the children to the Finch household, they all discover that the father of the accusing woman died during the fight with Boo. Atticus and the town sheriff argue about what should happen, with Atticus arguing that Jem was likely responsible for the father's death and the sheriff arguing that Boo Radley is likely responsible for the death. In the end, the sheriff agrees to close the case by concluding that the father, who had attacked Jem and Scout, fell on his own knife, essentially dying by misadventure. After Boo is saved from prosecution, he asks Scout to walk him home. When they reach the Radley house, Boo says goodbye, and he leaves Scout alone, pondering what his life must be like.

To Kill a Mockingbird is regarded by both students and teachers alike as a sentimental favorite. In particular, many readers appreciate the struggle for freedom and justice that is seen in the book. The book was also made into a beloved movie, with Gregory Peck starring as Atticus Finch. The film was a huge success, earning quite a bit of money and receiving multiple Oscars, including Best Actor for Gregory Peck and Best Screenplay. Critical reception to the book itself was mixed, though even the negative reviews acknowledged that the story was at least engaging. The book also received multiple major awards, most notably the Pulitzer Prize in 1961. It also was on the best-seller list for many weeks, making it a critical and popular success. The story was also adapted into a play, though the play received less attention and reception than the film.

The author, Harper Lee, has acknowledged that there was notable overlap between the book and her own life. Lee's father did defend two African American men accused of murder. Despite his efforts, not only the men were found guilty, but they were also killed and mutilated. This marked the end of her father's legal career. The other noteworthy element of the book was that the character Dill was based upon Truman Capote, who was a childhood friend of Harper Lee and who would also go on to become a prominent American author. In 2015, many years after the original publication of *To Kill a Mockingbird*, a different book of Lee's, titled *Go Set a Watchman*, was published. There was a good deal of controversy over the release of this book, both about whether or not Lee wanted the book published and also about the order in which the books should have been published. Another major issue was that, in *Go Set a Watchman*, Atticus Finch was portrayed as much less racially sensitive than he was in *To Kill a Mockingbird*. In some ways, though, the controversy over the switch in portrayal of Atticus Finch affirms the stature of the original text, showing the deep emotional commitment that many readers have to the book. The follow-up publication was also particularly noteworthy because of the long break between the books. Although Lee had written a few articles in the interim, it had been over fifty years between *To Kill a Mockingbird* and *Go Set a Watchman*.

Despite the critical and popular success of *Mockingbird*, the book did receive some serious challenges. The first challenge came in 1977 when a school district in Eden Valley, Minnesota, temporarily banned it for the use of vulgar language. In subsequent years, the book was challenged on the basis of both its racial epithets and its discussion of racial barriers and conflicts. Given the book's frank and complex discussion of racial relations, the sort of objection made by these critics brought about some very charged and divisive discussions. Interestingly, a number of the challenges have come from African American parents. In fact, in 1985, the NAACP supported a challenge against the book in a school district in Arizona. Despite the publicity and efforts against the book, this challenge was not successful, though the book was only on the supplemental reading list, not part of the core curriculum. Although the book has been challenged across the country, from Minnesota to Texas, it still has a large following and one that was bolstered with the release of *Go Set a Watchman*.

FURTHER READING

Daniels, Anthony. "Harper Lee's Loving Kindness." *New Criterion*, June 2015, Vol. 33, Issue 10, pp. 16–20, 5p.

Philpot, Chelsey. "The Long Life of a Mockingbird." *Horn Book Magazine*, May/June 2011, Vol. 87, Issue 3, pp. 51–55, 5p.

Watson, Rachel. "The View from the Porch: Race and the Limits of Empathy in the Film *To Kill a Mockingbird*." *Mississippi Quarterly*, Summer/Fall 2010, Vol. 63, Issue 3/4, pp. 419–443, 25p.

2

RELIGION AND CENSORSHIP IN AMERICA

Religion has been a source of controversy and dispute since the early days of European settlement in North America. Settlers would claim to be going into contact with Native peoples in the interest of spreading their religion. The Declaration of Independence referenced God as a justification for the rights of man. At the same time, there was careful work to ensure the separation of church and state, keeping the government from being influenced by religious concerns and keeping the church from being brought into secular battles. As time went on, the lines between religion, culture, and government continued to be blurred and challenged, and the influence of these struggles continued to impact both literature and the challenges that books and films were met with. As America and Russia were rivals, being American and publically declaring a belief in God became intertwined, and there was a real danger to being seen as promoting atheism or communism. Some writers lashed out against this repression. John Steinbeck, for instance, wrote pieces that both championed workers' rights and challenged the beliefs and values that came out of Christianity. Main characters who were not good or pure became sympathetic characters, and justice became something to be dealt out by common people rather than the criminal justice system or supernatural powers. This led to many calling for Steinbeck's works to not only be banned but also even burned. Other writers like Upton Sinclair and William Faulkner also portrayed religion as outmoded or dominated by deteriorating structures.

While these debates and challenges lasted for some time, new forms of censorship and objections emerged after the Cold War. In the 1980s, Christian televangelists and other figures started to speak out against a number of societal trends, from heavy metal music to games like Dungeons and Dragons, claiming that they promoted Satanism. The ensuing paranoia and misinformation led to continued challenges against largely innocuous books like those in R. L. Stine's Goosebumps series and respected works like Madeleine L'Engle's *A Wrinkle in Time*. Some of the works, like L'Engle's novel, even referred to Christianity or Jesus in a positive light, but nearly any discussion of magic that was not portrayed in a negative fashion could be met with harsh criticism and challenges to inclusion within libraries. This new set of challenges may have been most clearly seen with the publication of the Harry Potter series. The portrayal of magic and the use of the term "witches" to describe good characters led to significant and sustained challenges from a variety of Christian groups. As with previous generations, there were calls for removing the books from libraries and burning copies. Despite these challenges, many of the books, the Potter series and *A Wrinkle in Time* in particular, achieved massive critical and commercial success.

The conservative reaction to literature was not unique to Christianity, though. Salman Rushdie's novel *The Satanic Verses* received one of the harshest backlashes in the history of literature. After fundamentalist Muslims declared the book to be blasphemous, the book was banned in India and burned in a number of countries. Beyond these reactions, Ayatollah Khomeini called for both Rushdie and those involved in the book's publication to be killed for their blasphemy. Rushdie went into hiding for over a decade, and a number of people involved in the book's publication and/or translation were injured or killed.

As global communication has increased and America has become more secular, many feel that the controversies over portrayals of religion in literature have diminished. Still, every year graphic novels, literary works, and young adult novels receive challenges from parents and religious groups, expressing concern over the influence of these works over readers.

TIMELINE

1692–1693—The Salem witch trials began, leading to the executions of innocent people

1903—*Call of the Wild*, Jack London, published

1906—*The Jungle*, Upton Sinclair, published

1925—*The State of Tennessee v. John Scopes* (the Scopes Monkey Trial) ended with a decision that the teacher (Scopes) was guilty for teaching evolution in school; the trial was later the inspiration for the play and film *Inherit the Wind* by Jerome Lawrence and Robert Edwin Lee; also, *An American Tragedy*, Theodore Dreiser, published

1930—*As I Lay Dying*, William Faulkner, published

1939—*The Grapes of Wrath*, John Steinbeck, published

1940—*The Grapes of Wrath* adapted into a film, winning a number of Academy Awards

1946—*All the King's Men*, Robert Penn Warren, published

1949—*All the King's Men* first adapted into a film

1963—*Cat's Cradle*, Kurt Vonnegut, published; *A Wrinkle in Time*, Madeleine L'Engle, published, establishing her as a major author

1970—*Are You There, God? It's Me, Margaret* published, helping to establish Judy Blume as a major writer of young adult fiction

1971—*The Exorcist*, William Peter Blatty, published

1972—*Bless Me, Ultima*, Rudolfo Anaya, published, marking a major entry into Chicano literature and increasing the presence of magical realism in the canon

1973—*The Exorcist* adapted into a highly successful film

1974—*The Chocolate War*, Robert Cormier, published

1977—*Bridge to Terabithia*, Katherine Paterson, published

1978—American Indian Religious Freedom Act passed, returning significant religious freedoms to Native Americans

1979—*The Dead Zone*, Stephen King, published

1983—*The Witches*, Roald Dahl, published; *The Wish Giver*, Bill Brittain, also published

1985—*The Handmaid's Tale*, Margaret Atwood, published

1988—*The Satanic Verses*, Salman Rushdie, published

1989—Ayatollah Khomeini declared a fatwa on Salman Rushdie, accusing Rushdie of blasphemy, prompting Rushdie to go into hiding for years

1992–1997—Goosebumps series of books by R. L. Stine established a major presence in horror in the young adult genre

1993—*The Giver*, Lois Lowry, published

1997—First Harry Potter book by J. K. Rowling published in the United Kingdom

1998—Harry Potter first published in the United States

2001—World Trade Center Towers attacked by Muslim fundamentalist terrorists, leading to significant tensions and debates about the nature of Islam in America

2007—*Bridge to Terabithia* adapted into a major motion picture

2014—*The Giver* adapted into a film

All the King's Men, Robert Penn Warren
(Harcourt, Brace and Co., 1946)

All the King's Men follows Willie Stark, a tremendously successful governor, though one whose success depends largely upon his corrupt methods of attaining and maintaining his power. The story is told by journalist Jack Burden, who finds Stark both captivating and frustrating. Jack initially helps Willie to come to power, finding secrets that help to bring down those standing in Willie's way. Jack is good at finding these secrets, but his skills ultimately lead to frustration when Stark asks him to find a secret about Judge Irwin, who had been a sort of role model and guiding figure for Jack when he was young. Despite this connection, Jack does find details about past corruption on Irwin's part. As a result of Stark blackmailing Irwin, Irwin commits suicide. Around the same time, Stark begins having an affair with Anne Stanton, a former love interest of Jack Burden. When the affair is discovered by Adam Stanton, Adam murders Willie, putting an end to what might otherwise have been an impressive rise to power. At the novel's end, Jack has reconnected with Anne Stanton, and the two of them marry. Jack also is working on a book that connects to the dissertation that he had given up prior to working for Stark.

Although Robert Penn Warren was known before the book was published, this novel was to become his most well-known work. The general reception to Penn Warren's novel was positive. Critics praised him for both the timeliness of his examination of American politics and also the rich and varied voices found in the novel.

Still, there was a good deal of debate over the worldview that Penn Warren articulated in the book. Penn Warren himself admitted that Louisiana governor and U.S. senator Huey Long served as partial inspiration for the character of Willie Stark, and there were a number of clear parallels between them, not the least of which was the fact that both Long and Stark were assassinated in the state capitol building. These sorts of overlaps led many critics to read the book as a comment on Long specifically, though there was a great deal of debate over whether the book critiqued Long for his corruption or celebrated Long for his mission to achieve a more equal distribution of wealth and resources. Through these debates, Penn Warren never actively suggested that the book took a clear stance. In fact, in a later edition, Penn Warren acknowledged the inspiration that Long brought but discounted either of the competing interpretations, suggesting, instead, that the book's focus transcended politics, let alone any singular political figure.

Certainly, there were many thematic elements that went outside of the world of politics. In addition to Huey Long, Penn Warren found inspiration in Edmund Spenser's *The Faerie Queene*, and he also examined philosophical and religious themes and schools of thought. These inspirations were the source of objections that some readers took with Penn Warren's work. In 1974, libraries in Texas challenged *All the King's Men*, suggesting that its fundamental nihilism and examination of immoral situations made it unfit for many readers. Some elements of the book, like "the great twitch," do indeed give a dark view of life, implying that people function as automatons rather than pursuing any genuine purpose. And the difficulty that Jack Burden has in removing himself and his life story from that of Stark's does give a sense of bleakness. Still, the challenge was largely unsuccessful, with Penn Warren's literary reputation and following overpowering the efforts of those opposing the work. In fact, the book's impact has been both deep and long-lasting. There have been two film adaptations; the 1949 version received widespread acclaim and won the Academy Award for Best Picture.

Although the book is still widely read and respected, the attempts to censor it represent an important intersection between literature, politics, and cultural arguments. The fact that this text has a very wide variety of ideas examined (politics, religion, social class) makes the true motivation for challenging this book difficult to wade through, which makes the discussion surrounding the text particularly interesting.

FURTHER READING

Mitchell, Mark T. "Theological Reflections on Robert Penn Warren's *All the King's Men*." *Modern Age*, Fall 2006, Vol. 48, Issue 4, pp. 312–319, 8p.

Polk, Noel. "Editing *All the King's Men*." *Southern Review*, Autumn 2002, Vol. 38, Issue 4, pp. 849–860, 12p.

Teachout, Terry. "The Prescience of a Political Novel." *Wall Street Journal—Online Edition*, March 2016, p. 1.

An American Tragedy, **Theodore Dreiser**
(Boni & Liveright, 1925)

Theodore Dreiser based *An American Tragedy* on a major criminal case. Like much of Dreiser's work, the book looks at human frailties and the bad ends that desires can bring. In the actual crime, a man was tried, convicted, and executed for the murder of his lover, who was found in an overturn boat. Dreiser spent well over a decade researching the crime and trial before writing and publishing the book. The book generally keeps a distance from the characters, and the male character's guilt or innocence is left ambiguous. Although the book was met with positive reviews, it also struck many readers as dark and sad. One of the core issues is that the murderous character, Clyde Griffiths, came from a family of street preachers, setting up the contrast between the perceived goodness of religion and the depravity of the realistic world. Although Dreiser achieved a high level of success with this book, it also marked the climax of his career. Although the novel received significant critical praise, it also was challenged not only because of its dark tone but also because of some of the overlaps between the promiscuous behavior found in the book and Dreiser's own behavior. These elements, along with some depictions of desire and sexuality that, for the time, were seen as racy, led to various groups' opposing the work.

Although Dreiser's work did meet with some resistance, it helped to fully establish the Naturalist writing movement in American literature. The Naturalists looked at society as a system, recognizing the structural problems that led to individual failures. While this could lead to sympathetic portrayals of characters that would, in other hands, appear despicable or weak, it also often led to portrayals of society that made readers uncomfortable, because they recognized genuine problems that often lacked a real sense of solution. In the case of *An American*

Tragedy, the gender politics and difficult moral standards presented in the book reflected social problems of the time that provoked a discussion that many readers found uncomfortable. In particular, the ambiguity of the situation (which stood in stark opposition to many true crime novels that clearly condemn the criminal) was perceived by some as encouraging violence or disregard for others.

FURTHER READING

Brevda, William. "The Straw Hat in Dreiser's *American Tragedy*." *Midwestern Miscellany*, Fall 2014, Vol. 42, pp. 56–63.
Pizer, Donald. "Crime and Punishment in Dreiser's *An American Tragedy*: The Legal Debate." *Studies in the Novel*, Winter 2009, Vol. 41, Issue 4, pp. 435–450.
Stoehr, Liz. "Time-Tables, Visual Culture, and the Reconfiguration of Subjectivity in Theodore Dreiser's *Sister Carrie* and *An American Tragedy*." *Lit: Literature Interpretation Theory*, July–September 2015, Vol. 26, Issue 3, pp. 235–254.

Are You There, God? It's Me, Margaret, Judy Blume
(Bradbury Press, 1970)

One of Judy Blume's early books, *Are You There, God? It's Me, Margaret* focuses on a sixth-grade girl who comes from an interfaith family, with her mother being Christian and her father being Jewish. Although to many readers of later generations, this sort of marriage would not seem at all controversial, readers of the time found the material (and the character's reflections on the possibility for deciding on a single religion) quite provocative. The book's core struggle revolves around a year-long project that Margaret does for her school. The project's focus is on people's beliefs, and Margaret's study leads her to discussions with her grandparents, considering whether she views herself as belonging to either religion or if she even believes in God at all. In addition to this material, Blume also included another young female character who brings Margaret to gatherings where they discuss bras, periods, and other material that would have been controversial at the time of the book's writing. Although there is a good deal of potentially provocative material, the book does still have Margaret praying and thinking about God in a way that implies a level of faith.

From early on, the book was successful both commercially and critically. Judy Blume has had a wide variety of works, both simple and realistic books like Blume's Fudge series as well as other difficult topics, from racism to masturbation. But *Are You There, God?* was one of Blume's early books, so she met with more resistance than she might have as an established author. Even with the positive reactions of many readers, the book was challenged or removed from school libraries around the country, from Alabama to Wisconsin to Montana. Although some areas challenged it as profane or immoral (the rationale for these challenges were largely the sexual content or the skepticism shown toward religion), the book withstood the challenge in Montana as well as in Minnesota.

Despite the challenges, the book has cemented itself into mainstream American popular culture. The title alone has been referenced by a number of other works, including Chelsea Handler's book, *Are You There, Vodka? It's Me, Chelsea* and in the TV show *Frasier*. The book itself has also earned numerous honors, including being included on *TIME*'s "Top 100 Books in English Since 1923" list. Although Blume may be better known today for some of her subsequent writing, *Are You There God?* helped to establish her career as a prominent children's and young adult novel writer, and it gave young readers a text to help them navigate the difficult world of interfaith families and relationships.

See Also: *Blubber* and *Deenie*.

FURTHER READING

Brewbaker, James M. "Are You There, Margaret? It's Me, God–Religious Contexts in Recent Adolescent Fiction." *English Journal*, September 1983, Vol. 72, Issue 5, pp. 82–86.
Sommers, Joseph Michael. "Are You There, Reader? It's Me, Margaret: A Reconsideration of Judy Blume's Prose as Sororal Dialogism." *Children's Literature Association Quarterly*, Fall 2008, Vol. 33, Issue 3, pp. 258–279.

As I Lay Dying, **William Faulkner**
(1930)

As I Lay Dying was published in 1930 by William Faulkner himself. The book was the follow-up to his novel *The Sound and the Fury*, and Faulkner claims to have written it in a series of late-night sessions and without real editing. While some of these details might be apocryphal, the stream-of-consciousness style of the book is clear and could easily have come from the type of schedule described by Faulkner. The book's material covers a variety of disturbing and troubling topics. It centers on a family committed to bringing the mother's body to be buried in her hometown. Other storylines include one of the daughters trying to seek out an abortion.

These dark portions of the story, particularly the tension over the deterioration of a family in the South, are quite typical of Faulkner's work, and many readers appreciate the book's complex portrayal of the family. That said, in Kentucky, a school board heard a complaint about the book, with one student's mother claiming that the discussion of religion in the book was often undercutting Christianity.

The principal defended the book at the hearing, but the board originally voted to have the book removed from schools. The ban was quite short-lived, though, with the school board backing down after it came to light that the school board members had voted to ban the book without having read it. That was not the only challenge that the book ever faced, but the lack of success of the challenge was typical of those that the book faced.

Beyond defeating the challenges to it, the book has had a consistent and distinguished life in both literary circles and popular culture. The book has been taught in schools for decades, reprinted by multiple publishing companies and ranked highly in lists of the best novels of the 20th century.

FURTHER READING

Hellwig, Harold. "*As I Lay Dying* and Features of Greek Tragedy." *Explicator*, 2010, Vol. 68, Issue 3, pp. 199–202, 4p.

Hodge, Amber. "The Casket in the Corpse: The Wooden (Wo)man and Corporeal Impermanence in *As I Lay Dying*." *Southern Quarterly*, Fall 2015, Vol. 53, Issue 1, pp. 13–24, 12p.

Kovesdy, Joe. "Dewey Dell in Faulkner's *As I Lay Dying*." *Explicator*, 2010, Vol. 68, Issue 4, pp. 261–263, 3p.

Bless Me, Ultima, Rudolfo Anaya
(TQS Publications, 1972)

Bless Me, Ultima is a coming-of-age story that is one of the first major works by a Chicano American author. It is particularly well regarded not only for its examination of the history of Chicanos in the 1940s but also for its incorporation of many Chicano and Hispanic cultural elements, like magical realism and the figure of the healer. The book was loosely based on Anaya's childhood, though with clear additions and adoptions to interweave the mystical elements and other thematic elements. While the healing figure from the book does incorporate these mystical elements, there is also an interweaving of Catholicism, with one of the early portions of the book focusing on the protagonist and the healer figure, Ultima, removing a demon from the protagonist's uncle, drawing equal parts from magical realism and the ritual of exorcism. This is indicative of the tension and struggle that the protagonist, Tony, feels with his identity, not quite Hispanic and not quite fully American.

When first published, the book was very well received by critics, who recognized Anaya as a new voice shedding light on a culture that had, up to that point, largely been excluded from literary circles. The book was seen as a major

American literary breakthrough. In the late 2000s, the book was adapted first as a play and then as a film. Both received positive critical reactions.

While many readers have appreciated the originality of the work, some readers have found the material and the delivery either confusing or off-putting. While there had already been some major works of Latin American literature that incorporated magical realism and other cultural elements (perhaps most notably, *100 Years of Solitude*, written by Gabriel Garcia Marquez and published in 1967), *Bless Me, Ultima* was one of the first to be written by an American author. In addition, the book faced some challenges from readers and parents who found the material too adult in terms of its language as well as in its portrayals of sex and violence. In addition, the portrayal of Christianity bothered some parents and readers, because Tony was openly skeptical of the religion. Portrayals of the exorcism and Tony's open questioning of Catholicism struck a negative cord with many readers, leading it to be challenged on a number of different fronts. Some were quite virulent, with some parents even suggesting that copies of the book should be burned.

Even with these challenges, the book has established and maintained a reputation as a significant work in a number of ways, and the lasting popularity of the book makes it an important text in American literary history.

FURTHER READING

Black, Debra B. "Times of Conflict: *Bless Me, Ultima* as a Novel of Acculturation." *Bilingual Review*, May–August 2000, Vol. 25, Issue 2, pp. 146–162, 17p.

Holton, Frederick S. "Chicano as Bricoleur: Christianity and Mythmaking in Rudolfo Anaya's *Bless Me, Ultima*." *Confluencia: Revista Hispanica de Cultura y Literatura*, Fall 1995, Vol. 11, Issue 1, pp. 22–41.

Kárai, Attila. "The Postmodern Use of Mythopoeia in the Narrative Temporality of Rudolpho Anaya's *Bless Me, Ultima*." *Hungarian Journal of English and American Studies*, Fall 2008, Vol. 14, Issue 2, pp. 265–285.

The Boy Who Lost His Face, Louis Sachar
(Alfred A. Knopf, 1989)

The Boy Who Lost His Face is a young adult book that follows David, a young boy, as he tries to gain a feeling of popularity. As David begins to lose his friend, Scott, to a group of "cool" but troublesome boys, he helps them to pick on an elderly woman (one the boys refer to as "a witch"), stealing her cane. As the boys all make their escape, David makes an obscene gesture at the elderly woman, who puts a curse on them. David begins suffering from a variety of minor but troubling problems, such as having his pants fall down as he talks to a girl he likes and falling out of his chair in class. Ironically, the boys that David had worked to befriend now turn on him, ridiculing him when these events occur. David is stuck befriending only unpopular misfits. As the pressure increases and even David's younger brother begins to be picked on, David decides that he must go to the old woman and ask her to lift the curse. The old woman says that she will do so only if David returns her cane. David, with help from his brother and some of the other kids from his school, retrieves the cane from the popular, troublemaking boys, and he returns it to the old woman. When he does so, she reveals to him that there never was a curse. Instead, David's own guilt led him to have the problems that befell him. In the end, David's return of the cane purges him of the guilt that led him to have these difficulties. The title of the book refers to David's losing his identity and real sense of morality when he blindly follows others or hides in others' shadows.

Interestingly, even though the curse was psychological rather than "real" magic, the book met with a good deal of resistance simply for referencing occult themes. Of course, this was not the only reason for the book to be challenged. Some of the challenges made against the book, like those in California and Indiana, had to do with a combination of the book's showing children being disrespectful toward their elders and its incorporation of obscene material—namely, David giving the old woman the middle finger. These challenges were unsuccessful, but there were some places, in Red Creek, New York, and Houston, Texas, for instance, where the book was actually removed from library shelves because the material was deemed unsuitable for younger readers.

Defenders of the book point out that David actually does display a positive morality, because it is, in the end, his own conscience that leads him to seek forgiveness rather than an external curse. It also shows David most actively fighting against the herd mentality when he looks to defend his younger brother. Whether the core reason for the book's negative reaction was the disrespect, the references to occult topics, or the gesture and language, it seems that the gesture and obscene language have given its critics the best results in challenging the book, perhaps because they are the clearest details to which someone could object.

In some ways, it is surprising that this, of all Sachar's books, should receive the negative attention that it did. Other works by him, including the Newberry Award-wining novel *Holes*, for instance, also incorporated discussions of curses, and they also touched on charged subject matter like interracial relationships and violent acts.

FURTHER READING

Allen, Nola. "*The Boy Who Lost His Face.*" *Magpies*, May 2002, Vol. 17, Issue 2, p. 37.
Burns, Connie Tyrrell, Trevelyn E. Jones, Luann Toth, and Virginia M. J. Suhr. "*The Boy Who Lost His Face.*" *School Library Journal*, October 1989, Vol. 35, Issue 14, p. 122.
Sachar, Sherre, and Carla Sachar. "Louis Sachar." *Horn Book Magazine*, July/August 1999, Vol. 75, Issue 4, pp. 418–422, 5p.

Bridge to Terabithia, **Katherine Paterson**
(Crowell, 1977)

Bridge to Terabithia was partially inspired by a tragedy connected to author Katherine Paterson's son, David. David's best friend was killed when she was struck by lightning at age eight. The book follows a young boy who is the only male among his siblings. The boy, Jesse, trains hard one summer to become the fastest runner in his class. To his chagrin, he is beaten by a new girl, Leslie. Jesse's frustrations continue as he is teased and bullied, and he eventually strikes up a friendship with Leslie, who is also a bit of an outcast. The pair combine forces to outwit and humiliate a female bully that had taken a dessert from the lunch tray of one of Jesse's sisters. After Jesse and Leslie see the bully crying, they recognize the damage that they have done, and they befriend the former bully. During this time, Jesse and Leslie also invent an imaginary land, Terabithia, where they rule as king and queen. One day, Jesse takes a trip to the museum with his music teacher, on whom he had a crush before he befriended Leslie. Although Jesse very much enjoys the day, he returns to find that Leslie has died while playing in the area that she and Jesse had thought of as their secret portal to Terabithia. Jesse has two major reactions to this event, the first being that he experiences a level of denial, not accepting that his friend is gone. He also is troubled by the possibility that Leslie is not in heaven, because she had doubts about religion. Jesse slowly accepts the loss of his friend, and he decides to build a sort of memorial to her in the area that the pair considered to be the portal to Terabithia. As he does this, he sees his sister (the one that was bullied and that Jesse and Leslie sought to avenge). The pair lay down a log over the small stream where Leslie drowned, and they think of it as the bridge to Terabithia.

Since the novel's publication, it has received a number of challenges for a number of different reasons. One reason was the inclusion of the death of a main character (and child) as a significant part of the book's plot. Some parents saw this as being too disturbing for young readers. While this argument was likely a part of the anxiety that parents felt toward the book, it is also likely combined with the book's open engagement with the religion. The doubts that Leslie discusses and the connection to an imaginary land that was not directly related to Christianity, heaven, or any specific religious backdrop. In particular, Jesse uses the word "Lord" in a way that some readers objected to. This has also led there to be a number of challenges for the book's supposed rejection of religion.

Despite these sorts of objections and challenges, the book has become a successful part of the young adult literary genre. It has often been taught in schools around the world, from South Africa to Ecuador. In addition, the book has twice been adapted for the screen, first for PBS in 1985 and then as a major motion picture in 2007. Even with the challenges to the book, many readers and parents appreciated the way that the book allowed them to discuss difficult topics such as the death of children, bullying, and a desire to escape.

FURTHER READING

Chattaway, Peter T. "Deeper into Terabithia." *Christianity Today*, March 2007, Vol. 51, Issue 3, pp. 64–66, 3p.

Kelly, Patricia P., and Robert C. Small Jr. "Censorship or Selection?" *Virginia English Bulletin*, Spring 1986, Vol. 36, Issue 1, pp. 3–4, 2p.

Thomas, Trudelle. "Crossing the Water: Spiritual Growth in *Bridge to Terabithia* and *Lizzie Bright and the Buckminster Boy*." *International Journal of Children's Spirituality*, August 2011, Vol. 16, Issue 3, pp. 233–248, 16p.

Bumps in the Night, Harry Allard
(Yearling, 1996)

Bumps in the Night is a children's novel that follows anthropomorphized animal characters as they try to figure out how to deal with a haunted house. Dudley the stork has a haunted house, and he tries to find a way to fight the ghosts. After consulting with his friend, Trevor the hog, Dudley decides that a séance will help him to remove the spirits from his home. The séance does, in the end work, with Dudley being able to sleep soundly in his home, but there are many comic misadventures along the way.

The book had faced challenges for multiple reasons. First and foremost, the book was challenged because it portrayed a séance, which many parents saw as promoting the occult, particularly because the séance appeared to be successful. This affirmation of both the existence of ghosts and the skill of the medium conducting the séance made some parents uncomfortable. That said, many readers found that the setting of the conflict in this alternate world where animals behave like people sufficiently removed the book from the real world to make the conflict comic and not truly antagonistic toward religion. Another challenge that some parents labeled against the book was that its spooky events and themes may have made it too intense for some children. Indeed, the book was geared toward readers between the ages of seven and ten, so it was not seen by either its publisher or its author as being appropriate for younger readers.

FURTHER READING

Romanova, A. L., and E. O. Smirnova. "Funny and Scary in Contemporary Children's Subculture." *Cultural-Historical Psychology*, 2013, Vol. 12, Issue 2, pp. 81–87, 7p.

Staff. "Starlight Goes to Town." *Kirkus Reviews*, August 2008, Vol. 76, Issue 15, p. 192, 1p.

Stevenson, Deborah. "Frightening the Children? Kids, Grown-ups and Scary Picture Books." *Horn Book Magazine,* May/June 1996, Vol. 72, Issue 3, pp. 305–314, 10p.

The Call of the Wild, Jack London
(Macmillan, 1903)

The Call of the Wild begins with a dog, Buck, living in California. Early in the book, Buck is kidnapped and taken as a work dog. Unfortunately for Buck, he is worked hard, having to pull a heavy sled and being given little food. In addition to these hardships, Buck is often yelled at and beaten despite his often strong performance. Despite some initial struggles, Buck begins to fall in with his fellow sled dogs, learning to adapt to his new, strange environment. During this time, Buck also begins to have strange dreams about the early days of dogs and men, when survival was a constant struggle that led to fierce competition for food and shelter. In a related development, Buck fights the team's current leader, Spitz, and wins, becoming the dominant male. In another unfortunate turn, the team gets new human owners, and the new owners end up killing themselves and the other dogs due to their incompetence. Buck becomes one of the only survivors, and he is found by a new human, John Thornton, who saves Buck. The two develop an affectionate relationship. In fact, Buck returns the favor of saving his life, once saving him from a river and also attacks a man looking to hurt Thornton. While they develop this positive relationship, Buck continues to have a sense of longing for the wild, as foreshadowed by his earlier dreams. Thornton heads into the wild with a group of friends, looking for gold in an abandoned mine. While Thornton's party looks for gold, Buck makes occasional forays into the wild, hunting and befriending wolves. Eventually, Buck returns from one of these forays to find that Thornton has been killed by natives of the area. Buck seeks to avenge Thornton's death, attacking some of the natives, but he eventually leaves for the wild, joining a wolf pack, which he leads. While Buck stays with the wolf pack, he returns to where he found Thornton's dead body every year, showing loyalty to his former master even as he has made his way into the wild.

The novel *The Call of the Wild* is one of Jack London's most famous books. London had an unorthodox childhood, dropping out of high school at age fourteen to travel the country. He eventually completed high school, then attending Berkeley briefly before heading up to Alaska, where he would have the experiences that would help him to form much of his writing, including *The Call of the Wild.*

Although the book works on a literal level, simply being a story about a dog in the wild, readers and critics of the time perceived it as coming out of the Naturalist literary movement, engaging in a larger debate over the ideas of nature, Darwinism, and cultural expectations. Like much of London's work, the book explored whether harsh, rugged environments would lead people (or animals, in this case) to become more like wild animals, doing anything to survive, even if it means fighting or even killing others. It also considers whether there is a dark, primal quality within all people, simply waiting for the pressure and conflict that would set it loose.

Upon publication, the book was tremendously popular. The immediate success of the book helped to cement London's reputation as a major American writer, and it became one of the touchstones of his career. Still, the book was banned in Italy and other countries for being "too radical." More than just being banned, the book was actually burned in Nazi Germany. Beyond the designation of radical, the book was challenged partially for the socialist views of London. While some of London's critics saw his views as dangerous or problematic, his defenders viewed him as having an authentic voice that helped to establish him as a significant American writer and that helped to revive interest in literature of the Yukon.

FURTHER READING

Axelrad, Nancy S., Charles Livingston Bull, and Jack London. *"The Call of the Wild."* *Saturday Evening Post*, March/April 1998, Vol. 270, Issue 2, pp. 50–53, 4p.

Raskin, Jonah. "Calls of the Wild on the Page and Screen: From Jack London and Gary Snyder to Jon Krakauer and Sean Penn." *American Literary Realism*, Spring 2011, Vol. 43, Issue 3, pp. 198–203.

Yang, Hongyan. "Psychoanalysis of Jack London's *Call of the Wild* and *White Fang*." *English Language Teaching*, 2015, Vol. 8, Issue 11, pp. 42–46.

Cat's Cradle, **Kurt Vonnegut Jr.**
(Holt, Rinehart and Winston, 1963)

Cat's Cradle is a science fiction novel by Kurt Vonnegut Jr. The book is told from the first-person perspective, with the narrator, John, discussing the fact that he was researching to write a book when he came across the children of Felix Hoenikker, a scientist who helped to develop the atomic bomb, as well as Dr. Asa Breed, who worked with Hoenikker. As John continues his research, he finds out about a substance known as "ice-nine." Hoenikker had invented ice-nine, a form of water that stays solid at room temperature, to help the military by allowing them to navigate through muddy territory without being stopped by the moisture and mucky terrain. As John looks into this, he discovers that the children are currently in possession of the ice-nine. John and the Hoenikker children end up on a small, impoverished island run by a dictator. While there, John learns about the local religion, Bokonism, whose tenets include an odd mixture of very cynical, dark observations, peaceful rituals, and the idea of resigning one's self to God's will. When the group of travelers reach the island, John finds that the dictator is weak and ill, and he is looking for a successor, which will likely be Felix Hoenikker's son, Franklin. Although Franklin briefly accepts control, he quickly recognizes that he cannot communicate well with the people of the island, and he decides to hand over control to John, who only accepts begrudgingly. Before he can fully fall victim to his illness, the island's dictator uses the ice-nine to take his own life. The dictator's doctor, upon examining his body, accidentally comes into contact with the ice-nine and freezes as well. John and the Hoenikkers decide that they will burn all of the bodies in order to rid the world of ice-nine before it can accidentally freeze more people. While trying to dispose of the bodies and thereby the ice-nine, John asks the Hoenikkers how the dictator came into possession of the ice-nine, and they tell him that they had only learned of the true nature of ice-nine after their father's death, when they saw a dog lick some of it and freeze instantly. From there, each of the children had carefully taken a small chunk and sold it in order to stay wealthy. During John's inauguration ceremony, an accident occurs that leads the dictator's body to fall into the ocean, where it immediately freezes all of the water touching the spot where the body fell in. The book ends revealing that John had found a few people to escape the freezing with. He had also found Bokonon, who told John that, had he been younger, he would have written a book about the stupidity of humanity and brought it with him to the top of a mountain, then placed the book at the peak and touched some ice-nine to turn himself into a statue.

Cat's Cradle, while perhaps not Vonnegut's most successful novel, has still met with significant critical and popular success. The book was nominated for the Hugo Award (a popular award for works of science fiction) for best novel. From rock groups like the Grateful Dead (who created a publishing company named Ice Nine) and Joe Satriani (the rock guitar virtuoso who titled one of his instrumental songs "Ice 9") to cartoons like *Futurama*, which featured a sight gag about ice-nine, *Cat's Cradle* has shown up in a wide variety of cultural texts. Despite the positive reception, the book met with significant controversy, like a number of Vonnegut's other books, most notably *Slaughterhouse V*. In 1972, the book was challenged in Ohio, though the reasons for the ban were a bit vague, labeling the book "garbage" and "completely sick." The true reasons for the ban are likely related to the challenging portrayal of religion in the book as well as the nihilistic views that came through in the examination of Bokonism. One of the issues with this objection is the difficulty in fully understanding the position that Vonnegut himself might take upon the various elements of the story given that the book is satirical. By 1976, the challenge to the book was overturned. The book was challenged elsewhere but perhaps not with the same level of animosity and coordinated effort that *Slaughterhouse V* met when it was published.

Vonnegut himself stated that the inspiration for the character Felix Hoenikker was Irving Langmuir. Vonnegut had become acquainted with Langmuir when he worked with Vonnegut's brother at GE Labs. Kurt Vonnegut was struck by the fact that Langmuir was driven by scientific progress and discovery, and this search for progress, in Vonnegut's eyes, could lead Langmuir to be blinded to the ethical consequences of what he found. This sort of observation is very much in keeping with the larger tradition of satire, in which writers question whether change is generally for the better or if it is simply a new kind of problem and dysfunction. Still, this sort of challenging of norms and conventions leaves the door open to a variety of attacks because of the ambiguous presentation of various characters and ideas within the novel.

See Also: *Slaughterhouse V.*

FURTHER READING

Bland, Michael. "A Game of Black Humor in Vonnegut's *Cat's Cradle.*" *Notes on Contemporary Literature*, September 1994, Vol. 24, Issue 4, pp. 8–9.

McNamee, Gregory. "On Vonnegut's Harass vs. Granfalloon." *Virginia Quarterly Review*, Spring 2016, Vol. 92, Issue 2, p. 207, 1p.

Weiner, Jesse. "Mapping Hubris: Mapping Vonnegut's *Cat's Cradle* and Odysseus' Apologoi." *International Journal of the Classical Tradition*, April 2015, Vol. 22, Issue 1, pp. 116–137, 22p.

The Chocolate War, Robert Cormier
(Pantheon Books, 1974)

The Chocolate War is a young adult book focusing on conflicts revolving around identity and the pressure to fit into social expectations. The book follows Jerry, a high school boy who is attending a Catholic school. Jerry is suffering from depression and anxiety in the aftermath of his mother's death. Shortly after his entry into the school, Jerry is recruited into the football team. While he participates on the team, Jerry meets and befriends a freshman whose nickname is "The Goober." In addition to working as a student and athlete, Jerry begins to feel the pressure of the Vice Principal, who has committed the school to selling double the amount of chocolate as the previous year for the school's fundraiser. In particular, the Vice Principal tries to enlist a group of school troublemakers to help him to motivate students to sell extra chocolate. The ringleader of the troublemakers decides that he will sometimes help the Vice Principal, just enough to give him power within the school, thanks to the favor of the Vice Principal, and sometimes defy the Vice Principal. One of the early attempts at defiance is to convince Jerry not to sell any chocolate for ten straight days. However, after the ten-day stretch is done, Jerry decides to continue not selling any chocolate. This leads both the Vice Principal and the troublemakers to antagonize Jerry, trying to make him the target of the whole school's aggression and anger. Jerry gets emotional support from "The Goober," but "The Goober" is not able to make much difference in the level of teasing and antagonism that Jerry experiences. As things escalate, the ring-leader of the troublemakers convinces the school bully to beat up Jerry. Despite all of this, Jerry continues to resist the pressure from both the Vice Principal and the bullies. In the end, he is pushed to agree to a boxing match with the school bully, orchestrated by the ringleader of the troublemakers. The bully brutally beats Jerry until one of the teachers of the school turns out the lights, trying to stop the match. Unfortunately for Jerry, the darkness only further allows the bully to beat him up. Lying down after the severe beating, Jerry tells The Goober that he should have just given in, working to cooperate with both the troublemakers and the Vice Principal. While there is a move to punish the ringleader of the troublemakers, the Vice Principal steps in to protect the ringleader. In fact, he indicates that, in the coming years, he will continue to support the troublemakers because the sales of chocolate had been so successful.

Upon publication, the book was very well received, earning strongly positive reviews from both the *New York Times* and the Children's Book Review Service. In addition to these positive critical reactions, the book was also adapted into a film in 1988. Today, the book retains a powerful and positive reputation within young adult literature.

Despite the positive reaction that many readers have had, the book has been challenged for multiple reasons. One of the first issues that was raised was that the book has frank and direct discussions of sexual desire. In particular, there is a scene where a high school boy masturbates in a restroom stall. There are also discussions of wet dreams. While these issues are both realistic and common for many adolescents, at the time of the book's publication, they were taboo topics, particularly for works in the young adult genre. Also, the level of violence in the book has made some parents uncomfortable. Perhaps even more problematic, though, was the portrayal of corruption and cruelty within the Catholic high school. Some critics point to the fact that many of the challenges toward the books have come from church groups, supporting the notion that one of the driving reasons for challenges to the book has come from the negative portrayal of authority figures, particularly ones associated with the church. In addition, the book's dark themes and general cynicism (Jerry's final conclusion that trying to make a difference is fundamentally not worth it) run counter to traditional thought within a number of religions.

Although the book received challenges and was indeed banned in isolated times and places, it remains a favorite of many readers for the ground that it broke in young adult literature. Cormier also wrote a sequel to the book, *Beyond the*

Chocolate War, in 1985, though the sequel did not receive the significant attention that the original did.

FURTHER READING

Junko, Yoshida. "The Quest for Masculinity in *The Chocolate War*: Changing Conceptions of Masculinity in the 1970s." *Children's Literature*, 1998, Vol. 26, Issue 4, pp. 105–122, 18p.

Keeling, Kara. " 'The Misfortune of a Man Like Ourselves': Robert Cormier's *The Chocolate War* as Aristotelian Tragedy." *ALAN Review*, Winter 1999, Vol. 26, Issue 2, pp. 9–12.

Tarr, C. Anita. "The Absence of Moral Agency in Robert Cormier's *The Chocolate War*." *Children's Literature*, 2002, Vol. 30, Issue 10, pp. 96–124, 29p.

Cross Your Fingers, Spit in Your Hat, Alvin Schwartz
(HarperCollins, 1974)

Cross Your Fingers, Spit in Your Hat is a children's book that examines superstitions and charms. The book is nonfiction, not presenting the superstitions as legitimate or plausible but rather presenting them as interesting pieces of history and folklore. Despite this, the book was met with challenges from parent groups because it was viewed as giving attention to or validating occult beliefs. The book was one of several of Alvin Schwartz's to receive a challenge. While others were sometimes viewed as simply not being age appropriate, *Cross Your Fingers* was challenged on general principle rather than as needing to simply be restricted in who had access to it. While some of the superstitions were perceived as dark or spooky by readers, many of them were relatively mundane.

Despite the relatively neutral portrayal of the superstitions found within the book, it did receive some challenges from various parent groups.

See Also: Scary Stories to Tell in the Dark Series

FURTHER READING

Allen, B. "After Losing the Challenge, Parents Ask for Selection Input." *American Libraries*, April 1992, Vol. 23, Issue 4, pp. 276–277, 2p.

Blue, Margaret. "*Cross Your Fingers, Spit in Your Hat*, Book Review." *School Library Journal*, September 1974, Vol. 21, Issue 1, p. 91.

Marcus, Leonard S. "Night Visions: Conversations with Alvin Schwartz and Judith Gorog." *The Lion and the Unicorn: A Critical Journal of Children's Literature*, June 1988, Vol. 12, Issue 2, pp. 44–62.

The Dead Zone, **Stephen King**
(Viking, 1979)

The Dead Zone is one of Stephen King's early novels. It focuses on a young man who experiences precognition, which leads him to try to fight what he perceives as evil. The book opens with the precognitive character, Johnny Smith, hitting his head while ice skating. While he is still regaining consciousness, Smith gives a warning not to "jump." A few days later, while trying to jump a car, the person who heard Smith give the warning is injured. The book then jumps to a separate character, Greg Stillson, who is deranged and sadistic, kicking a dog to death in a fit of rage. The book's narrative then returns to Johnny, who is now an adult teaching high school. Johnny goes to a fair with his girlfriend and is uncannily good at playing the "wheel of fortune" game, again suggesting his abilities. Shortly thereafter, Johnny is involved in an auto accident that leaves him in a coma. When he wakes from the coma, four and a half years later, Johnny finds that when he touches certain people, he can tell them urgent information, such as future events or secrets of which they were unaware. There is some minor local coverage of Johnny's abilities, but he attempts to downplay them, choosing to return to teaching. After a story in a national tabloid claiming that Johnny is a fake, he gets a brief respite from all of the attention. Unfortunately for him, a sheriff comes to him, asking for help in an investigation into a string of murders. Johnny successfully discovers the identity of the killer, who kills himself before he can be taken in. The book then returns to Stillson's story, showing that he has become successful as a businessman and has also been elected mayor of a city in New Hampshire. Despite these successes, Stillson is still sadistic and psychologically unbalanced. His drive for power and success leads him to run for a seat in the U.S. House of Representatives, which he gains through blackmail and other nefarious dealings. Meanwhile, Johnny has been forced to move from his hometown after the school district deems him too much of a distraction to work in the classroom. Johnny moves to New Hampshire, and he becomes interested in politics. After meeting Jimmy Carter and successfully predicting Carter's election to the presidency, Johnny decides to meet various politicians to see their futures. In pursuing this interest, Johnny attends a rally for Stillson, and, upon shaking Stillson's hand, he has a vision of Stillson becoming U.S. president and leading the world into a nuclear war. After having the vision, Johnny begins to seriously contemplate killing Stillson in an effort to avert nuclear war. Johnny is very hesitant to pursue this possibility because of the evil inherent in killing and also because his health has worsened, making him uncertain of his potential for success. Part of what pushes Johnny over the edge comes when he learns that an FBI agent investigating Stillson died from a car bomb. When Johnny finally decides to fully pursue the assassination of Stillson, he actually fails. While

Johnny seeks out a position from which he could shoot and kill Stillson, he misses on the initial shot. However, before he can take a second shot, Stillson picks up a child from the crowd and holds the child up in order to prevent himself from being shot at again. Once Johnny hesitates, Johnny is shot and killed by Stillson's bodyguards. Although Johnny dies, he is able to touch Stillson once more, and he recognizes that, given Stillson's cowardly actions of holding up the child to prevent injury to himself, Stillson no longer represents any genuine threat to the world. The book closes with an epilogue, explaining that Johnny's abilities were at least partially the result of a brain tumor. The book also closes with Johnny's wife feeling a brief moment of connection with him even after Johnny dies.

The book was met with a striking interest. It was adapted twice, first into a film directed by David Cronenberg and starring Christopher Walken and Martin Sheen and second into a television series starring Anthony Michael Hall, though the latter took much more significant departures from the book's core plot than the original film did. Still, the book sold well, and its popularity only increased after the production of the motion picture, which generated many positive responses.

Although there was significant objection to the book, it is hard to pinpoint what raised the most significant objections. Part of this issue is the fact that Stephen King's novels have consistently been challenged by a wide variety of parent groups and school administrators. Of course, *The Dead Zone* was a relatively early entry in King's body of work, so it did not immediately carry the stigma that some of his later works did. All of this said, the book did confront some clear moral issues, like whether or not assassination is ever justified. The continuing question with the book—if you could kill Hitler to avoid the Holocaust, then should you?—is likely meant to be treated as a legitimate question (after all, if someone agrees to assassination, then the question of when killing is acceptable and when killing is not naturally follows). Moreover, who has the authority or moral right to decide who should live and who should die can make many readers uncomfortable. Still, the violence may not be the core cause of the challenges. The incorporation of supernatural elements and some language and sexual content likely led objectors to challenge the book's presence in schools and libraries.

Whatever the genuine cause of the challenges for *The Dead Zone*, the effect has been uneven. Although there have been challenges, King's overall popularity and the general popularity of the Cronenberg film have helped the book to overcome many of the hurdles that attempts at censorship have presented to other texts.

See Also: *Christine, Cujo,* and *It.*

FURTHER READING

Cooney, Eleanor. "Gore Wins!" *Mother Jones,* May/June 2006, Vol. 31, Issue 3, pp. 73–77, 5p.
Hemesath, James B. *"The Dead Zone* (Book Review)." *Library Journal,* July 1979, Vol. 104, Issue 13, p. 1485.

Turner, Charles C. "Political Assassination in Popular Fiction and Political Thought: Trotsky, Arendt, and Stephen King." *Conference Papers—American Political Science Association*, 2008 Annual Meeting, pp. 1–16, 17p.

The Exorcist, William Peter Blatty
(Harper & Row, 1971)

The Exorcist is a novel examining the practice of exorcism and the philosophical and theological concerns that come out of this practice. The book begins on an archeological dig in the Middle East with Father Lankester Merrin, an elderly priest. During the dig, the party finds a statue of an ancient demon, which is only the first in a series of dark omens that Father Merrin comes across. Meanwhile, a famous actress moves to Washington DC with her daughter, Regan. While Regan's mother works on a film, Regan becomes sick with a condition that doctors find difficult to diagnose. Also inexplicable are the odd events happening around Regan's home, such as objects moving without direct touch. Although Regan's mother is not religious, she eventually reaches out to Father Damien Karras, a Catholic priest who is struggling with his faith after the loss of his mother. Regan's mother is partially hoping that the act of the exorcism might give Regan a psychological cure for what is leaving her daughter unsettled. After some persuasion, Karras agrees to seek out permission to conduct an exorcism. When Karras seeks out permission, the Bishop with whom he speaks tells Karras that he should have help in conducting the exorcism, and so Father Merrin is brought in to manage the process. It is at this point that the reader discovers that Father Merrin had overseen an exorcism in Africa. The two priests work through the exorcism, though Merrin eventually dies from a preexisting heart condition. Karras is left to complete the exorcism on his own, and he asks the demon to come into him, leaving the child safe. After being possessed, Karras jumps from the window, falling to his death, though he is able to receive his last rites before he dies.

William Peter Blatty took his inspiration for the novel from a combination of real-life exorcisms. In fact, part of the inspiration for Blatty's choice of Washington DC for the setting of the novel is that one of the exorcisms that he used as a point of reference took place near Georgetown University. The novel's publication met with great success and was adapted into a feature film in 1973. The film's screenplay was written by Blatty, and it earned him an Oscar for the best screenplay. In 2010, the book was republished by a different publishing house. This new edition featured a few revisions and a new scene.

While the book enjoyed significant commercial success, it did receive a significant number of challenges as well. The occult content made it a lightning rod for criticism, and the fact that both priests involved in the exorcism died led many religious groups to strongly oppose the inclusion of the book in libraries. The book also faced difficulties because exorcism had largely fallen out of widespread practice even by the time of the book's publication. As with other books, such as Anthony Burgess's *A Clockwork Orange*, *The Exorcist* received greater attention because of the adaptation of the book to film. Particularly with the film's commercial and critical success, the book faced additional scrutiny. Some of the scenes in the film, such as the scene where a possessed Regan uses a crucifix to masturbate, were also seen as particularly disturbing because of the violence and sexual connotations that were being applied to a child.

FURTHER READING

Dudenhoeffer, Larrie. " 'Evil against Evil': The Parabolic Structure and Thematics of William Friedkin's *The Exorcist*." *Horror Studies*, 2010, Vol. 1, Issue 1, pp. 73–88.
Laycock, Joseph. "The Folk Piety of William Peter Blatty: *The Exorcist* in the Context of Secularization." *Interdisciplinary Journal of Research on Religion*, 2009, Vol. 5 Special section, pp. 1–27, 27p.
Wetmore, Kevin J., Jr. "Colonial Possessions: A Fanonian Reading of *The Exorcist* and Its Sequels." *Social Research*, Winter 2014, Vol. 81, Issue 4, pp. 883–896, 14p.

Final Exit, Derek Humphrey
(Dell, 1992)

Final Exit: The Practicalities of Self-Deliverance and Assisted Suicide for the Dying is a nonfiction book, frankly discussing the issues surrounding patients suffering from terminal illnesses and seeking to end their lives. The book covers not only the actual act of aiding someone in ending his or her life but also the many practical issues surrounding the act, ranging from making legal and financial preparations to deciding what method of suicide would be most comfortable and empowering for the individual.

The author, journalist Derek Humphrey, had watched his wife suffer from cancer for some time before helping her to overdose. After this experience, Humphrey decided to write a book that discusses the very practical concerns that surround the ending of one's or a loved one's life. The book was met with both success and challenges. The success was shown in a variety of ways, from being translated into twelve languages to being named "One of the 25 most memorable books of the last quarter century" by *USA Today*. It also helped to spawn a number of other books and resources for helping people to seek out methods of euthanasia. The challenges also came in a variety of ways. The book was banned outright in France, and it had received a number of challenges in libraries across America.

Ironically, when the book was included in a display of commonly challenged books at Lethbridge Public Library in Alberta, Canada, a patron complained that the book should be removed, thus making it a book that was challenged during part of a celebration of the freedom to read. Even with these challenges, the book has often received support from advocates of the right to die. In fact, the book has become a prominent part of the debate about euthanasia, being praised by members of the right-to-die movement and being a lightning rod for criticism of opponents of euthanasia. Interestingly, the facts and study within the book generally are not disputed; it is the more general stance on the content that typically determines readers' reactions.

FURTHER READING

Altman, L. K. "A How to Book on Suicide Surges to Top of Bestseller List in a Week." *New York Times*, August 1991, Vol. 140, Issue 48687, p. A1.

H.L.N. "Shuffling off This Mortal Coil." *Hastings Center Report*, July/August 1992, Vol. 22, Issue 4, p. 3.

Zucker, Arthur. "Suicide by Hemlock." *Death Studies*, March/April 1994, Vol. 18, Issue 2, pp. 216–217, 2p.

The Giver, **Lois Lowry**
(Houghton Mifflin, 1993)

The Giver is a young adult, dystopian science fiction novel. At the book's opening, Jonas, an eleven-year-old boy is thinking about the ritual that he must undergo at age twelve and where he will be assigned a line of work, as happens to everyone at age twelve. The reader also learns that the members of this community have little privacy and that everyone in the community readily accepts their fate. While Jonas is thinking about this, he meets with the Receiver, a man whose eyes look like Jonas's. As they meet, Jonas begins to feel happiness, something that is generally absent from the members of the community. However, with the happiness come memories, which are unhappy as well. Jonas recalls seeing rainbows and snow, but he also learns about war and death. From these memories, Jonas comes to understand the nature of his community. They have given up individuality and strong emotions in order to preserve a sense of safety. After coming to this realization, Jonas wants to leave his community, and he asks the Receiver if there is a way to escape. The Receiver then changes his title, being called the Giver, and he promises to show Jonas "the Release." The Release turns out to be a lethal injection, and Jonas sees his father performing a Release on a twin, because twins are deemed unfit by the rulers of the community. Jonas and the Giver plot to help

Jonas escape and to return all of the memories to the people who have lost them. Jonas asks the Giver to come with him, but the Giver indicates that he must stay to help people manage the sudden return of their memories. He also reveals that he had tried to help a girl (his daughter, in fact) in the way that he had helped Jonas, and the Giver wants to stay to be with her. Jonas and the Giver's plan involves faking Jonas's death, but, before they can carry it out, Jonas finds out that a baby that has been staying with his family has been scheduled for a Release, and he feels that he cannot allow that to happen. Complicating matters is the fact that the infant has the same unusual eyes as Jonas, the Giver, and the Giver's daughter have. Jonas takes the infant (named Gabriel) and his father's bike, and he strikes out, trying to find the area outside of the community that the Giver had discussed with him. Eventually, they reach an area that Jonas believes to be the edge of this place, though both he and the infant are weak and cold by the time that they reach it. Using his unique vision, Jonas is able to find a sled, and he and Gabriel use it to head down a hill, finding a house with lights and a Christmas tree. Though the ending is somewhat ambiguous, the author indicated that Jonas survived his ordeal in both interviews and in the follow-up novel, *The Messenger*.

The book quickly gained a good deal of success, both critically and commercially. In 1994, the book won two major awards, including a Newberry Medal, and it continued to receive honors from both library associations and other organizations and publications. It also became part of "city reads" programs in which various groups within a given city read and discuss the book, most notably in San Diego, California. Not all critics were positive in their reception, though. A number of critics indicated that they found the book's plot to lack originality and to feel overly moralizing, not creating characters who were fully fleshed out and dynamic. Still, the book has maintained a consistent and broad readership, and it also has been adapted a number of times into different media. From stage plays to video games, it has continued to be explored by new audiences. Most notably, the book was adapted as a major motion picture, starring Jeff Bridges, Meryl Streep, and Taylor Swift.

Despite its popularity, the book has been challenged frequently. In fact, since its publication, the book has been challenged over 10,000 times, and it has been removed from schools many times as well. In fact, it has been in the American Library Association's top one hundred "Most Challenged Books" for both the 1990–2000 and 2000–2010 lists. Some of the challenges have been based on specific complaints like violence and sexual content, but the most frequent complaint has been the relatively vague one that the material is unsuitable for the age group. Some of the anxiety for parents is clearly the suggestion that young people should avoid conformity and should be antagonistic to power structures. In addition, there have been claims that the book promotes suicide, because Jonas puts his life and the infant's life in danger in order to escape from the world that he inhabits. There also have been claims that the book challenges Christianity. Despite these challenges, *The Giver* is often included on reading lists in classrooms (though teachers are sometimes required to alert parents if they are using the book).

FURTHER READING

Brugar, Kristy A. "Empowering Students through History: *The Giver* as a Metaphor and Preparation for Studying History in the Secondary Classroom." *History Teacher*, November 2012, Vol. 46, Issue 1, pp. 85–94, 10p.

Hubler, Angela E. "Lois Lowry's and Suzanne Collins' Dystopian Fiction Utopia and Anti-Utopia." *Against the Current*, July/August 2014, Vol. 29, Issue 3, pp. 23–27, 5p.

Wend-Walker, Graeme. "On the Possibility of Elsewhere: A Postsecular Reading of Lois Lowry's Giver Trilogy." *Children's Literature Association Quarterly*, Summer 2013, Vol. 38, Issue 2, pp. 137–158.

Goosebumps Series, R. L. Stine
(Scholastic Publishing, 1992–1997)

Goosebumps was a popular series of middle-grade books published during the 1990s. The books focused on monstrous creatures and the children or young-adult characters who confronted these terrors. They also led to a number of spin-offs, including Goosebumps Series 2000, Give Yourself Goosebumps, and Goosebumps Most Wanted. Though the books had elements of horror in them, familiar monsters like vampires and werewolves, they also were generally funny, looking at the zany misadventures and wild romps of the children in the stories. Stine himself has indicated that he made an effort not to incorporate death into his stories or to show elements like drugs or depravity. Stine has stated that he believes this decision has helped him to achieve the success that he has enjoyed, as it has ensured that parents and children alike are satisfied with his books. The books were, indeed, popular, selling millions of copies regularly and making a number of bestseller lists throughout the 1990s. The series received mixed reviews from critics, with some claiming that the plotting was sloppy and the characters were flat, while others found the books to be fun, engaging texts that got children reading. Despite the arguments about the literary quality of the series, nobody denies the significance of the series' commercial success.

Although many critics and readers found the Goosebumps series to be generally tame, it has met with multiple challenges. One of the most notable complaints was that the books contained satanic themes. The complaints tended to make up a minority of the children and parents represented in the hearings, with many defenders coming out for the books. Still, the books met with a number of challenges. One such hearing that took place in Anoka-Hennepin, a town near Minneapolis, Minnesota, was even broadcast by C-SPAN. The hearing concluded with the books being kept.

FURTHER READING

Bubar, Joe. "Getting Goosebumps." *Scholastic News*—Edition 4, October 2015, Vol. 78, Issue 6, p. 2.

Hill, David, and Glynis Sweeny. "Who's Afraid of RL Stine?" *Teacher Magazine*, March 1996, Vol. 7, Issue 6, pp. 38–41, 4p.

Stern, Marlow. "Goosebumps Forever." *Newsweek*, August 2012, Vol. 160, Issue 6, p. 54.

The Grapes of Wrath, John Steinbeck (Viking, 1939)

The Grapes of Wrath is one of the most celebrated novels in American literature. The novel follows Tom Joad, who, at the beginning of the book, is being released from prison. Joad has been paroled after serving time for homicide. Joad begins the trip back to his hometown in Oklahoma, and, on the way, he meets a familiar face in Jim Casy. Casy had been a preacher when Joad knew him, but he has left that behind. When Joad and Casy return to Joad's family home, they find it deserted. They search to find what has happened, and they are told by a neighbor that the banks have kicked all of the farmers off of the land. The neighbor appears to be the lone person holding out against the banks. Joad and Casy then go to Joad's uncle's home to find his family. They see them loading up all of their remaining possessions for a trip to California, where the family hopes to remake their lives. Joad finds out that the Dust Bowl had destroyed the family's crops, and the combination of this and the Great Depression left the family unable to keep up payments on their land. Tom Joad decides that he will accompany his family on the trip to California, even though it means that he could be sent back to prison for breaking parole by leaving the state of Oklahoma. He invites Casy to come with his family, and Casy agrees. As the family travels toward California, their hopes begin to dwindle as they talk to other families making the same trip. Seeing the large number of people traveling west, they recognize that not everyone who arrives will receive the high paying jobs that they have been promised. In addition, other misfortunes befall the family, including the death of both grandparents and the abandonment by two of the Joad children. Still, the remaining members of the family (and Casy as well) recognize that they have come too far to turn back to Oklahoma, and so they press forward. When they arrive at California, their fears of not having enough jobs are realized. While there are some farms that offer jobs as part of the federal government's New Deal, there are too many people vying for those jobs for any one family to be totally supported by them, and positions on other farms and in other places exploit the surplus of workers, giving them very low pay and expecting a very high workload. Casy and the Joads split when Casy decided to take work as a union organizer and the Joads take work breaking up strikes, putting them in direct conflict. Things come to a head when the Joads are at a strike that Casy helped to organize. Tom Joad witnesses Casy not only being attacked but being beaten to death. Tom kills Casy's attacker in retaliation, but he now must flee, because he is at risk for arrest for both violating parole and killing a man. The Joad family goes with Tom, finding work on a cotton plantation. The book concludes on mixed notes. Tom's sister gives birth to a baby, but it is stillborn. Tom promises his mother that he will work to help others rather than taking work like their position as strikebreakers earlier in the novel. The family's home is flooded, forcing them to seek higher ground. When they find a barn in which they can stay, the family also finds a young boy and an old man. When they realize that the old man is dying of starvation, Tom's sister (who is still lactating from her pregnancy) offers him her breast so that he can have some form of sustenance.

Almost immediately after its publication, the book became a literary and popular sensation for its portrayal of the hardships experienced by working-class Americans during the Great Depression. Steinbeck had directly stated that he wanted the book to shame the people who profited from the suffering and hardships of those years. The book was at least partially inspired by journalism focusing on the problems with issues stemming from corrupt bankers and corporate farmers, and Steinbeck drew on some of the personal stories found in a series of articles that had originally appeared in the *San Francisco News*. The book was very well received by many readers, and it earned a variety of honors, both commercial and critical. It was the bestselling book of 1939, and it also was honored with a Pulitzer Prize and a National Book Award. It also went on to help earn John Steinbeck the Nobel Prize in Literature. Not all readers were so quick to praise the book, though. Many claimed that Steinbeck exaggerated the conditions of the working poor in order to make a political point, and some conservative readers complained that Steinbeck's sympathies for union members were anti-American. Still, the book's reputation has been largely positive, and it has been studied and taught for decades.

The book has been an inspiration for a variety of other pieces of art, including a film adaptation in 1940. The film was almost universally seen as a great work, and it won three Academy Awards. In 1990, the novel was dramatized as a play by the prestigious Steppenwolf Theatre Company. Beyond these direct adaptations, the book has served as inspiration for many songs and albums, with artists ranging from folk heroes like Woody Guthrie to mainstream performers like Bruce Springsteen to punk groups like Rage against the Machine and Bad Religion.

With such a major reception and such charged political content, it is not surprising that *The Grapes of Wrath* was met with many challenges. In Kern County, California, the book was not only challenged, but it was burned at a number of events. Kern County was particularly significant as it was the final destination of the Joad family as they searched for a brighter future. In addition to the burning done by independent groups, the board of Kern County voted to ban the book, complaining that its factual inaccuracies were too severe to allow people to read the book. While there were also complaints that the book portrayed Tom Joad, a murderer, in too positive of a light, it is hard to say what the true motive of the ban was. Many critics and scholars have examined the role of wealthy landowners in the efforts to ban the book. In addition to funding legislative efforts to keep the book out of libraries and off of shelves, many believe that the landowners also used strikebreakers and other agents to physically intimidate proponents of the book. Kern County was hardly the only place that saw groups challenging the book. Kansas saw a decision to have the book removed from libraries, and libraries in Illinois and New York actually burned the book. Still, many librarians (even one in Kern County) fought to keep the book in reader's hands, believing it to be an important social text. In fact, the book became a central one in the creation of the Library Bill of Rights, a statement that was used in many subsequent fights about censorship and the banning of books. Although the book was not banned in every state, it was challenged in as many (if not more) states than it was not, and it also received challenges internationally, being banned or challenged in both Ireland and Turkey. Despite these many challenges, the book has maintained an important position in American literature, often being called "the great American novel," for its craft, its social importance, and its loyal readership.

See Also: *Of Mice and Men.*

FURTHER READING

Dalmaso, Renata Lucena. " 'Modern Monsters,' Old Habits: Nature, Humans, and Technology in John Steinbeck's *The Grapes of Wrath.*" *Steinbeck Review,* 2015, Vol. 12, Issue 1, pp. 26–38.

McCoppin, Rachel. "The Many Faces of Jesus in Steinbeck's *The Grapes of Wrath.*" *Studies in the Literary Imagination,* Fall 2013, Vol. 46, Issue 2, pp. 35–50, 16p.

Yee, Kristine R. "John Steinbeck's *The Grapes of Wrath*: A Call to Action." *Explicator,* 2013, Vol. 71, Issue 4, pp. 255–258, 4p.

The Handmaid's Tale, **Margaret Atwood**
(McLelland and Stewart, 1985)

The Handmaid's Tale is a science fiction novel written by Margaret Atwood. The book is set in a military dictatorship in a fictional land known as the Republic of Gilead, a future space that occupies the land formerly known as America. Within the fictional universe of the book, many prominent members of the American government were assassinated in an attack. After the attack is blamed on Islamic extremists, a movement known as "the Sons of Jacob" begins to take control of the country, initially promising to keep the country safe but quickly moving beyond this stated goal, taking problematic and authoritarian measures like curtailing women's rights and forcing Christianity upon all of the citizens. In order to help maintain these forms of domination, most women are forbidden to learn to read. Within this world, the book comes from the perspective of one of the dominated women, Offred, who is seen as being useful for reproduction only, putting her in a class known as "handmaids." Although oppressed, these women are actually vital to the society, because pollution and sexually transmitted diseases have rendered much of the population sterile. At the book's opening, Offred is handmaid to a high-ranking government official, though she has been handmaid to others prior to this. As the book progresses, Offred's male "owner," Fred, begins to give her gifts and talks to her regularly. In the world of Gilead, this kind of contact is forbidden, as men are only supposed to interact with their handmaids for purposes of sex and reproduction. Fred also allows Offred an unusual amount of education and awareness, letting her see a brothel and allowing her to read. Even more unusual, Fred's wife, Serena Joy, begins to interact socially with Offred. Serena Joy wants Offred to have a child that can be attributed to Fred, so she arranges for Offred to have sex with Nick, Serena Joy's driver. As a reward for going through with this arrangement, Offred is given news of a daughter that she had in a previous relationship, but who was taken from her when Offred tried to flee Gilead for Canada. Things seem to be going well, as Offred finds that she enjoys sex with Nick, and she arranges to meet with him more often after their first time together. Around the same time, another handmaid, Ofglen, tells Offred of a secret resistance to the Sons of Jacob. The band of rebels is called the Mayday resistance, but before Offred can learn much more, Ofglen goes missing. Shortly thereafter, Offred is taken away by the secret police after Fred's wife becomes jealous. As the secret police are taking Offred away, Nick appears, telling her that she is actually being taken away by rebels rather than government operatives. The reader never finds out whether or not Nick is telling the truth. After the close of the central narrative of the book, there is a fictional epilogue, claiming that the story was put together from transcripts of tapes made by Offred. It also states that these transcripts were from the period shortly before

Gilead collapsed and a new, more egalitarian and open society was forged out of the ashes of Gilead.

The Handmaid's Tale was been very well received, earning high praise from many critics and being nominated for major literary and science fiction awards. It was awarded the Arthur C. Clarke Award (a major prize for literary science fiction) in 1987. It has also been adapted into a number of forms, from a film in 1990 to an opera and even to a one-woman show. In addition, the book has helped to push the science fiction genre into new areas, with Margaret Atwood herself referring to the book as "speculative fiction," meaning that it deals less with scientific innovation and more with hypothetical situations, like the Sons of Jacob dominating society, that help the reader to understand certain aspects of the existing society.

Of course, given the story's focus on sex and depictions of religion, it has come under significant fire from a number of groups. A number of times during the 1990s, the book was challenged for having sexually explicit material and other forms of obscenity. While there were some concessions, such as moving the book from a "required" reading list to a "suggested" one, most of the challenges did not result in the book's removal from the curriculum. There were also other challenges to the book, like one in Richland, Washington, in 1998, where the challenge was based on the grounds that the book was too hopeless and promoted suicide. In Waterloo, Iowa, in 1992, the book was challenged partially based on its depiction of religion as an oppressive force, though the book was not ultimately removed. Not every challenge failed, though. In Chicopee, Massachusetts, the book was removed from a class-reading list, and in 2006, the book was temporarily banned in Judson, Texas. In Canada, there was a significant struggle over the book, with a parent objecting to the book for a variety of reasons. Interestingly, one of these reasons was that the book showed poor treatment of women, which took aback many of the book's defenders who had seen the novel as being a strong feminist text. The book was reviewed by the Toronto School District Board, but it was not banned.

The Handmaid's Tale will always be considered one of Atwood's major books, and it continues to be both celebrated and challenged.

FURTHER READING

Beauchamp, Gorman. "The Politics of *The Handmaid's Tale.*" *Midwest Quarterly*, Autumn 2009, Vol. 51, Issue 1, pp. 11–25, 15p.

Devi, C. Nandhini, and Sumathy K Swamy. "Dystopic Vision of Margaret Atwood in *A Handmaid's Tale.*" *Language in India*, December 2015, Vol. 15, Issue 12, pp. 129–134, 6p.

Thirunavukkarasu, K. S., and R. Saravanan. "Sexual Overtones and Explicit Sexuality in Margaret Atwood's *A Handmaid's Tale.*" *Language in India*, June 2011, Vol. 11, Issue 6, pp. 248–253, 6p.

Harry Potter Series, J. K. Rowling
(Arthur A. Levine Books, 1997–2007)

The Harry Potter books are a series of middle-grade and young adult books center-ing around a young British wizard, Harry Potter, learning to master magic. The first book, *Harry Potter and the Sorcerer's Stone* (called *Harry Potter and the Philosopher's Stone* in the United Kingdom), opens with Harry Potter being raised by his aunt and uncle and treated quite poorly. Harry is forced to prepare meals for them, and he sleeps in a closet under the stairs. Despite this, Harry is generally a good boy who is largely unremarkable except for a few strange events, like his hair growing abnormally quickly every time that his aunt cuts it. Shortly before Harry's eleventh birthday, he begins to receive letters (always delivered by owl). The let-ters indicate that they are from Hogwarts, a school for magic, but Harry's uncle tries to destroy them all before Harry can read them. Harry's uncle takes the family to a remote island, and, at midnight on Harry's eleventh birthday, they are visited by Hagrid, a half giant who works at Hogwarts. Hagrid tells Harry that Harry's parents were powerful wizards, and Harry is invited to attend Hogwarts School of Witchcraft and Wizardry. While there, Harry befriends a wizard, Ron Weasley, who is also in his first year at the school, and who comes from a long line of witches and wizards. He also befriends a first-year witch named Hermione Granger, whose parents are "muggles," or people who are not part of the wizard-ing world. Harry also begins to make enemies with some students, most notably Draco Malfoy, a "pureblood" wizard who belittles wizards and witches like Hermione Granger. Harry also catches the ire of Severus Snape, one of the teachers at Hogwarts. During his years at Hogwarts, Harry discovers a number of pieces of his past. First, he finds out that his parents were murdered by an evil wizard named Voldemort, or "You Know Who" (many witches and wizards remain so terrified of Voldemort that they will not utter his name, even after he disappeared). Harry was mysteriously spared on the night that his parents died, and this has earned him the nickname, "the boy who lived," because he was the only wizard in history to survive the killing curse. The fact that Voldemort's curse failed and that Voldemort disappeared after trying to kill Harry makes him all the more mysterious to everyone. At the end of Harry's first year, he faces off with one of the professors at Hogwarts, who has been keeping a weakened Voldemort alive.

In the second book, *Harry Potter and the Chamber of Secrets*, more characters are introduced (perhaps most notably Ginny Weasley, Ron's younger sister). A number of strange events again occur, and Harry learns more about himself, like the fact that he is a "parselmouth," or can speak to snakes, just as Lord Voldemort could. We also learn that Lord Voldemort was once a wizard named Tom Riddle, before he completely turned to a life of evil. At the end of this book, Harry once again is confronted by Voldemort, though this time in a more ghostly form than in the first book.

In the third book, *Harry Potter and the Prisoner of Azkaban*, the reader learns still more about the wizarding world and about Harry's past. In particular, the reader leans about Azkaban prison (first mentioned in the second book when Hagrid has to take a brief stay there). The guards there are known as dementors, dark, ghostly creatures that take away people's happiness and, if left to their own devices, will devour a person's soul. In addition, we find out that Sirius Black, initially a good friend of the Potters, is in Azkaban, as he is suspected of being part of the plot to kill the Potters and for the murder of Peter Pettigrew, another of the Potter's friends. After a major revelation within the book, Harry befriends Sirius, even taking him as a godfather, though Sirius must remain in hiding, so Harry cannot live with him.

In the fourth book, *Harry Potter and the Goblet of Fire*, Harry, Ron, and Hermione attend the Quidditch World Cup (quidditch being a wizard sport that Harry plays at Hogwarts). After the championship game, Voldemort's followers, the death eaters, ruin the camps of fans near the tournament, causing a major panic. When the students return to Hogwarts that year, they find out that there will be an interschool competition known as "The Triwizard Tournament." Although there are supposed to be only three "champions" participating in the tournament (one from each school), Harry Potter's name mysteriously emerges as one of the participants. This causes friction between Harry and his good friend Ron, and it also casts a close eye on Harry from more than one of the professors at Hogwarts. Harry ends up winning tying for first place in the tournament, but he and the classmate who tied with him quickly find out that the much of the tournament was manipulated by a follower of Voldemort. The two are transported to a graveyard where Harry's classmate dies, and Voldemort is brought back to life after another of his followers uses Harry's blood and another major sacrifice to bring Voldemort back to life. Harry manages to escape. When he returns to Hogwarts, some people believe that he saw Lord Voldemort, but the Headmaster, Albus Dumbledore, sides with Harry, trying to convince people that Lord Voldemort has not only returned but is also a major threat. The book ends with Harry and his friends feeling deeply unnerved.

In the fifth book, *Harry Potter and the Order of the Phoenix*, Harry is living in a very different world from the world of the first book. Hogwarts's Headmaster, Albus Dumbledore, has gone from being a much respected member of the wizarding community to someone seen as a crackpot for his continued assertions that Lord Voldemort is assembling forces to try to take over the world. Harry himself has shifted from a popular hero among wizards to someone who has a dark past and an unstable future. Near the beginning of the book, dementors attack Harry at a park near his muggle aunt and uncle's house. Harry's cousin is also there, and Harry narrowly helps them both escape. This is particularly unusual, because the dementors are not supposed to leave their posts as guards of Azkaban prison unless they are specifically instructed by the Ministry of Magic. Although Harry helped to save his cousin with a magical spell (he also receives help from one of Harry's neighbors, who he discovers knows about the wizarding community), his aunt and uncle only blame Harry for there being any trouble at all. Shortly after he returns home, Harry receives a communication from the Ministry of Magic indicating that he has been expelled from Hogwarts for using magic while being underage, which is strictly forbidden by wizarding law, though it is technically not the first time that Harry has used magic while underage and off school grounds. Harry is taken to the house of his godfather, Sirius Black, where he learns that he will be able to appeal the decision to expel him from Hogwarts. Dumbledore shows up to testify on Harry's behalf, and, despite the efforts of the Ministry of Magic and some other folks, Harry is allowed to return to Hogwarts, though Dumbledore does not speak to Harry immediately after the hearing. Although Harry is initially happy to be returning to school, he quickly finds that the school has fallen under the watch of the corrupt and incompetent view of the Ministry of Magic, most particularly an underling of the Ministry of Magic. This underling, Dolores Umbridge, has been given the post of "Defense Against the Dark Arts" professor, a position that is rumored to be cursed, because every year, the professor occupying the position ends up leaving or being chased out. Umbridge quickly works to undermine Dumbledore and the other professors, intimidating people into publicly agreeing with the Ministry of Magic's positions whether they do agree with them in private or not. During this time, Harry also has nightmares, which turn out to be glimpses into Voldemort's mind. Also during this time, Harry, Ron, and Hermione try to get reports from the Order of the Phoenix, a band of wizards and witches devoted to stopping dark wizards in general and Lord Voldemort in particular. Harry learns that both of his parents, along with Sirius Black, opposed Voldemort. Umbridge reaches a position of power that allows her to sack some of the professors. Harry and his friends form a group of wizards who begin training on their own to learn to defend themselves in ways that Umbridge does not encourage or even allow in her classes. The group is jokingly known as "Dumbledore's Army," because they all know of Dumbledore's disdain for Umbridge and the rest of the Ministry of Magic. When Umbridge discovers this group, she begins to go after Harry, but Dumbledore claims responsibility, even acknowledging the fact that the group has dubbed themselves Dumbledore's Army. Dumbledore goes on the run rather than being taken to prison by the Ministry of Magic for being subversive, and Umbridge takes control of Hogwarts. As things become bleak, with Umbridge chasing off Hagrid, Harry has a vision of Sirius Black being tortured. He insists that he and the other kids go to save him, but they are intercepted by Umbridge, supported by Draco Malfoy and other students whose families were affiliated with Lord Voldemort. Harry, Ron, and Hermione first tip off one of the professors that something bad is happening, and then they manage to escape. Harry, his friends, and the Order of the Phoenix face off with Voldemort and his death eaters, with members of both sides dying, and Voldemort eventually being fought off by Dumbledore and Harry. Harry also gets to hear a prophecy linking him and Voldemort. After the fight between the two groups, the Ministry of Magic can no longer deny that Voldemort is both alive and active. The book ends with an even greater sense of foreboding than in book four.

The sixth book, *Harry Potter and the Half-Blood Prince*, increases the sense of serious danger that Harry and his friends face. Near the book's beginning, Dumbledore takes Harry to meet a former professor from Hogwarts. Harry comes to understand that he will be expected to help persuade the former professor, Horace Slughorn, to return to his post. Harry is successful, but before he can press Dumbledore on too much more, Dumbledore brings Harry to the Weasley's home, and he disappears. When Harry and the other students return to school, they find that Professor Slughorn has taken over the position of potions professor and Severus Snape, the former potions professor and someone who is openly hostile to Harry, is now in charge of teaching classes on defense against the dark arts. Harry gets a used potions textbook that has an inscription from someone calling themselves "the half-blood prince." Using the notes that this former student made in the margins of the book, Harry finds himself being tremendously successful. Because of this success and Harry's fame, Professor Slughorn takes a keen interest in Harry, and Dumbledore tells Harry that he will need to cultivate this relationship in order to gain something from Slughorn. To prepare him for this, Dumbledore begins showing Harry memories of Lord Voldemort. Harry finds out that Lord Voldemort was, like Harry, an orphan, and that Dumbledore himself sought a young Voldemort, then named Tom Riddle, out, hoping to train him to control his powers. Other revelations include that Voldemort's father was a muggle who left the family, perhaps creating Voldemort's hatred for muggles, and that Voldemort was a student of Horace Slughorn. After this revelation, Harry is able to get the memory from Slughorn, and he discovers that Voldemort has created seven horcruxes, magical objects that help to make the creator immortal. However, for each horcrux, the creator must commit a murder, thereby losing part of his soul. Dumbledore then reveals that he has been searching for the horcruxes, hoping to destroy them, thereby rendering Voldemort mortal once again. Dumbledore reveals that he has destroyed one already, but there are still six to find. During the course of these events, Harry and Ron's sister, Ginny, develop a romantic interest, as does Hermione for a foreign quidditch player, which creates friction between Hermione and Ron. Near the end of the book, Dumbledore takes Harry to find a horcrux. They successfully locate it, but when they return from the errand, they find Voldemort's mark above Hogwarts. The pair race back to the school, and they find that the signal was a trick. Dumbledore freezes Harry, who is safely hidden under his invisibility cloak. Draco Malfoy finds Dumbledore, and he uses a spell to take Dumbledore's wand from him, but he hesitates before casting the killing curse on Dumbledore. Instead, Professor Snape arrives at the scene and delivers the killing curse. Harry chases after Snape, but Snape easily evades him, inadvertently revealing that he is the half-blood prince who has left the notes that Harry has been using. Even worse, Harry discovers that the horcrux that he and Dumbledore found was a fake.

In the final book of the series, *Harry Potter and the Deathly Hallows*, the three primary characters, Ron, Hermione, and Harry, decide that rather than continuing their studies at Hogwarts that year, they will spend the year hunting for horcruxes. Harry also finds that he is under almost constant threat, since Lord Voldemort's followers have infiltrated the Ministry of Magic. When the Order of the Phoenix decides to transfer Harry from his aunt and uncle's house to the Weasley house, the death eaters attack the party, killing some of the crew. Professor Snape, who still teaches at Hogwarts, was responsible for letting Voldemort know the time and location of Harry's transfer. One of Ron's brothers is getting married at the Weasley's home, and immediately after the wedding, the death eaters attack again. Harry, Ron, and Hermione leave to the muggle world, and they hide in Sirius Black's house. The trio develop plans and try to find information about what is going on in the wizarding world, eventually sneaking into the Ministry of Magic to get the real version of the horcrux that Dumbledore found shortly before his death. Although they do find the horcrux, they have to flee and cannot return to Sirius Black's house. Instead, they hide out in a forest. Things begin to unravel, and Ron leaves the expedition. He does return, and he uses the sword of Gryffindor, the object that Harry used to destroy the monster in *Harry Potter and the Chamber of Secrets*, to destroy the horcrux. The trio continue on, getting captured by some death eaters, and escaping from the Malfoy family manor, then breaking into Gringotts, the wizarding world's largest bank in Europe, in order to find another horcrux. All the while, Harry continues having flashes into Lord Voldemort's mind, and he is able to piece together Voldemort's strategy. The trio decide to try to go to Hogwarts to find the final horcruxes, and this leads to a final confrontation between the wizards and witches loyal to Dumbledore's memory and those siding with Voldemort. Harry learns the true nature of Snape, who had been pretending to be a supporter of Voldemort in order to help defeat him. Harry makes a number of sacrifices, and, in the end, he is able to defeat Voldemort. The book ends with a postscript with Harry and his friends all sending their own children off to Hogwarts. In the final lines, Harry tells his son that divisions between wizards and witches are less important than what is in the heart of each person.

J. K. Rowling, the series' author, was unemployed for a good portion of the first book's writing. She had a good deal of education, having studied and taught Latin and other subjects that often informed the terminology and names that she used in the books. The book was published in Britain and, after its success, was published by Scholastic in America, quickly becoming a major commercial success. Each subsequent book was also a major success, with many bookstores having midnight sales on the dates of the books' release. The books also received major critical acclaim, winning awards and honors like the Hugo Award for science fiction and an honor from the American Library Association. The books were also adapted into a series of eight movies, many of which set sales records and were generally positively received by fans.

The books have also been studied for their impact on popular culture. Rowling was recognized for blending Greek mythology, Christian iconography, and contemporary British culture. Other writers had a variety of reactions, with some writers, like Ursula K. LeGuin, dismissing much of the work, but other major writers, perhaps most notably Stephen King, hailed the entire series as being particularly impressive. The books' impact is distinctive and remarkable, even having tourist attractions built in both Florida and California to continue to bring in fans.

Because of the massive success and attention that the series has received, it has also been a focal point for a number of groups looking to censor or challenge books. In fact, the Harry Potter series was named as the most challenged series of the 21st century by the American Library Association in a 2006 press release. The books have been challenged on both sides of the Atlantic, with different church-affiliated organizations in England saying that the Bible is consistent in its negative portrayal of witches and wizards. In fact, many of the challenges to the series in both England and America came from conservative Christians, claiming that the book portrays witchcraft and magic in a positive light, possibly corrupting children. In New Mexico, some groups went so far as to call the books "satanic" and host book burnings. However, not every challenge was purely rooted in religious arguments. Some readers indicated that the books, particularly the volumes later in the series, were too violent and disturbing for some readers. With multiple murders and a variety of curses and examples of violence, these charges may well have had more legitimacy than the complaints upon religious grounds. In addition, some groups pointed out that Harry and his friends regularly broke school rules and either distrusted or undermined adults in positions of authority, leading them to challenge the books because they are perceived as a bad influence on children.

Although these challenges have been widespread (in addition to challenges in America and Britain, the books have been challenged in Australia and other countries), along with the merchandising, book publications, and spin-off products and books, the entire series is a major cultural touchstone that is not likely to be squelched.

FURTHER READING

Dorigato, Laura, Gill Philip, Ramona Bongelli, and Andrzej Zuczkowski. "Knowing, Unknowing, Believing Stances and Characters' Dialogic Identities in the Harry Potter Books." *Language & Dialogue*, 2015, Vol. 5, Issue 1, pp. 62–89, 28p.

Stojilkov, Andrea. "Love (and) Death in Harry Potter: The Immortality of Love and the Soul." *Mosaic: A Journal for the Interdisciplinary Study of Literature*, June 2015, Vol. 48, Issue 2, pp. 133–148.

Vezzali, Loris, Sofia Stathi, Dino Giovannini, Dora Capozza, Dora, and Elena Trifiletti. "The Greatest Magic of Harry Potter: Reducing Prejudice." *Journal of Applied Social Psychology*, February 2015, Vol. 45, Issue 2, pp. 105–121, 17p.

The Jungle, Upton Sinclair
(Doubleday, 1906)

The Jungle was a major novel exposing major problems with both food safety and treatment of workers in manufacturing. The book follows Jurgis Rudkus, a worker in Chicago who was originally born in Lithuania. Rudkus struggles to earn a living and support his family. As the book opens, Rudkus and his wife are celebrating their wedding. They have high hopes for their future, but they come to find that America does not offer them the opportunities that they had believed it would. To support him and his wife, Rudkus takes a job in a slaughterhouse. Despite his working, Rudkus and his wife are often taken advantage of by others. They are particularly targeted because they are immigrants who have difficulty speaking English. In one example, Rudkus makes a down payment on a home, only to find that it is dilapidated. Even beyond this problem, he soon finds that he cannot afford to keep up with the payments on the home, and Rudkus and his wife are evicted. This is a particularly major blow, because Rudkus had hoped to offer a home to his wife's family. Instead, all of them find that they have to work, including the children and Rudkus's ill father-in-law. All of the jobs are very strenuous, and the family members experience health problems as they are slowly being worked to death. In addition to the long hours, the family members begin to suffer after accidents in their various workplaces. After one accident on the job, Rudkus loses his job. Rudkus then is forced to take a job in a fertilizer factory. Making matters worse, his wife tells him that her boss is forcing her to perform sexual favors for him or else she will be fired. Rudkus snaps and kills his wife's boss. Rudkus goes to jail for the killing. When he gets out, he finds that his family has once again been evicted. Rudkus's suffering continues when his wife dies in childbirth and his first child dies in the street. Rudkus's wife's death came largely because the family could not afford a doctor. After losing most of his family, Rudkus begins drinking heavily, though he still tries to work. In particular, he becomes an itinerant worker, taking field jobs in the South. However, at the end of the season, the farmers that Rudkus worked for turn him away without any support or offer of a job. Eventually, Rudkus returns to Chicago, where he falls even deeper into depravity, practicing scams like the people who took advantage of his family earlier in the novel. As things begin to look bleak, Rudkus finds himself attending a socialist lecture, and he feels a spark of hope. After becoming part of the socialist movement, Rudkus finds regular work and a support system. He is able to take care of his wife's family members again, and the book ends on a sense of hope for the future.

In addition to being a novelist, Upton Sinclair, the book's author, was a journalist. As part of the "muckrakers," Sinclair helped to uncover corruption in large systems and mistreatment of the oppressed. Although Sinclair was able to publish the book in serial form in a socialist newspaper, he had some difficulty finding a publisher for the book as a whole. In the end, Sinclair paid for the first run of the book himself, but it was quickly picked up (although in a condensed form) by Doubleday, Page and Company. In 2003, a full version was published by See Sharp Press, with an introduction claiming that earlier publishers had found the unedited version too shocking and too disturbing for most readers.

Although Sinclair had intended the book to be an expose that made the public fight mistreatment of workers, the thing that seemed to captivate the public most was the descriptions of the manufacturing of food. While there were shocking parts, like workers falling into vats and simply being ground up into meat (implying that the meat that the public was eating had elements of human meat in it), there was also a good deal of discussion of how food was prepared in an unsanitary environment. One reason why the issue of workers' rights did not get more attention is likely that Sinclair's celebration of the Socialist Party left many readers uncomfortable. In fact, President Theodore Roosevelt criticized the book and Sinclair as being overly sensationalist and not being grounded in fact. However, the attention paid was significant enough that Roosevelt had to send some investigators to meatpacking plants in Chicago. The owners of the plants tried to have them cleaned up before the investigators could arrive, but the conditions were still poor enough to require legislation and oversight by the government. Roosevelt never released the report generated by the investigators to the public, suggesting that there was alarming content that would have shocked the public. After Congress read the report and heard testimony from the investigators, they passed the Pure Food and Drug Act of 1906. Despite this success, Sinclair was not satisfied with the reaction, because it focused only on food issues, not doing anything to address the mistreatment of the workers. Still, the book established Sinclair as a major literary and social figure in American history.

Not surprisingly, the book has met with a number of challenges, both in America and abroad. While it did receive some international support (Winston Churchill, for instance), it faced negative reaction in Lithuania, and it was burned by the Nazis because of its support for socialist views. It was also banned in South Korea. Despite these challenges, the book is regularly read and taught as both literature and a historical text. Although the book's positive reception was not what Sinclair had hoped for, it is widely regarded as one of the most important books in American history.

FURTHER READING

Connery, Thomas. "Fiction/Nonfiction and Sinclair's *The Jungle*." *Journalism History*, Fall 2008, Vol. 34, Issue 3, pp. 167–170, 4p.

Coodley, Lauren Lincoln. *Upton Sinclair, California Socialist, Celebrity Intellectual*. Lincoln: University of Nebraska Press, 2013, pp. xvi, 237.

Valiunas, Algis. "The Blood of Upton Sinclair." *Commentary*, May 2008, Vol. 125, Issue 5, pp. 45–49, 5p.

Moby Dick, Herman Melville
(Harper & Brothers, 1851)

Moby Dick is one of the most significant novels in American literature. It is told from the perspective of Ishmael, a crew member of a whaling ship, the *Pequod*, which is overseen by Captain Ahab. As the crew sets out, a man named Elijah warns Ishmael and another crew member, Queequeg, that they will suffer an awful fate if they accompany Captain Ahab. When the crew (a mix of characters of European descent, an African American, and a Polynesian, Queequeg) has made it out to sea, Captain Ahab tells them that he is looking not just for whales in general but for a particular whale, upon whom he wants revenge. He pledges to give a gold coin to the first person to spot the whale, Moby Dick, who bit off the lower half of one of his legs. While some of the crew object to this single-minded approach, Ishmael finds himself compelled to aid in Captain Ahab's hunt. The crew has various adventures, occasionally meeting other whaling crews, though Captain Ahab generally avoids genuine social interaction with them, only asking them if they have seen the white whale. Melville also uses many of the body chapters to include discussions and descriptions of marine life and details from sailing. The crew of the *Pequod* does, eventually, meet another crew who has encountered Moby Dick. Some of the crew died during the encounter, and the survivors feel like they have been cursed despite their survival, because many of them have fallen ill.

The crew of the *Pequod* also finds whales and whale carcasses, and, despite Captain Ahab's quest, they do take valuable pieces from these whales. They continue to find whales and whaling crews, sometimes finding news of Moby Dick, often hearing tales of disaster from those who have crossed paths with the whale. They also do typical whaling work, rendering whale blubber and otherwise harvesting their catches. The crew also loses members as they fall overboard or otherwise expire. As the *Pequod* closes in on where the crew assumes Moby Dick to be, Captain Ahab remains above board constantly, watching for the whale. When he believes that he smells Moby Dick, he looks out to the sea, and he gets sight of the white whale. They pursue the whale in a violent and fearful chase. Moby Dick smashes the smaller boats that the crew uses to pursue him. Multiple members of the crew plead with Captain Ahab to give up the chase, but he refuses, eventually taking one last stab at the whale. While Captain Ahab is able to do severe damage to Moby Dick, the *Pequod* is eventually destroyed, and almost all of the crew (Ahab included) are killed. The only survivor is Ishmael, who rides an empty coffin until another whaling ship (one that had also lost crewmen to Moby Dick) find and rescue him.

Melville worked on the book for some time, taking over a year between the time the book was tentatively accepted for publication and his final revisions.

Interestingly, the book was not much of a success at its first publication. Melville's reputation had already been declining before the publication of *Moby Dick*, and after early reviews from Britain, *Moby Dick* fell out of favor, being seen as indulgent and lacking coherence due to Melville's extensive nautical lore. While the criticism of Melville's research making the plot drag has persisted over the years, after his death, Harper & Brothers published a revised edition in America, and it began to take hold within the literary underground in New York. In the late 1910s and 1920s, the book found some well-respected champions, including Carl Van Doren and D. H. Lawrence. In 1926, Lakeside Press published an illustrated version, pulling in a new generation of readers. Since then, the book has been adapted into movies, graphic novels, and a variety of other media. The book has also become a mainstay within American literature courses, and its focus on a single-minded pursuit of a difficult and ill-guided goal has led it to be regarded as one of the major works of American literature.

As stated previously, the book received challenges and censorship from even before its publication. The British publisher hired editors to cut any material that could be deemed as too sexual, that could be perceived as sacrilegious, or that could be seen as derogatory to the British Empire. They also had requested a different title. The British edition also cut out the passages that indicated that Ishmael survived. Despite these changes, the book still received challenges after its publication. As recently as 1996, the book was challenged in Texas, where parents complained that the book went against family values. This challenge did not result in a ban of the book, and the book has remained popular both within and outside of literary circles.

FURTHER READING

Kaloyanides, Alexandra. "America's God and the World: Questioning the Protestant Consensus." *Church History*, September 2015, Vol. 84, Issue 3, pp. 625–629, 5p.

Noll, Mark A. "The Republican Character of Antebellum American Religion." *Church History*, September 2015, Vol. 84, Issue 3, pp. 637–643, 7p.

Satalino, Kelsey. "Ahab's Failed Godhood: Thor and the Midgard Serpent in Moby-Dick." *Sigma Tau Delta Review*, 2015, Vol. 12, Issue 1, pp. 72–80.

Of Mice and Men, John Steinbeck
(Covici Friede, 1937)

Of Mice and Men follows two migrant workers, George and Lennie, as they look for work during the Great Depression. Lennie is a strong but mentally challenged man, and George tries to take care of him. Because of Lennie's inability to fully control himself, and because he derives pleasure from stroking soft things, a group of people in Weed, California, mistake Lennie's petting of a woman's head for an attempted sexual assault. After this, George and Lennie must flee the area, leading them to look for work elsewhere. As they go, George tries to comfort Lennie by letting him talk about his dream of owning a farm with George where Lennie can care for the rabbits, which he likes because of their soft fur. The pair do eventually find work, but George quickly recognizes that there will be problems at the new ranch as the ranch's owner has a son, Curley, who likes to antagonize the workers, trying to compensate for his short height and small stature. To make matters worse, Curley's wife enjoys flirting with the workers, triggering Curley's jealousy and cruelty. Still, George and Lennie do strike up friendships with some of the other ranch hands, most notably Candy, an older worker who is missing a hand, and Slim, a young but bright worker. Slim's dog has puppies, and he gives one to Lennie to care for. As their friendships build, Candy offers to give George and Lennie money to start their farm, as long as he is able to live on it as well. Before they can realize their dream, though, trouble strikes. Curley begins to berate Lennie, and then he becomes violent. George tells Lennie that he has to defend himself, and Lennie catches Curley's fist, squeezing it and severely hurting Curley. Still, George is hopeful for the group's future, and he attempts to find an area that could serve as their farm. When he is away from the ranch, looking for this area, Lennie accidentally kills the puppy that he has been given. Lennie is depressed, and he finds some solace in Curley's wife, who tells him of her own dreams to be a movie star. She lets Lennie stroke her hair, but when she starts to fear for her safety, Lennie tries to quiet her, and he accidentally breaks her neck. Lennie panics and tries to hide her body, and he leaves for a spot where he knows that George will find him. When George discovers that Lennie has killed Curley's wife, he goes to Lennie. When they meet, George has Lennie tell him about the dream of their farm. As Lennie is doing so, calming himself after the death of Curley's wife, George shoots Lennie, killing him as quickly and painlessly as he can so that Curley and the other ranch hands will not be able to beat and torture Lennie before his death. Curley and the ranch hands find George with Lennie's body. While most of them think that George killed Lennie simply for vengeance or justice, Slim realizes that George did it to protect Lennie from an even worse fate.

Of Mice and Men was extremely successful, becoming a "Book of the Month Club" selection before it was even officially published, and it received high praise from a wide variety of critics. It has also been taught in schools for decades and has been adapted to a variety of media a number of times. Steinbeck had structured the book like a play, hitting the various acts typically scene in drama, and it has been produced as a play for decades. It also has been made into films multiple times, and it has been nominated for major awards in both its stage and screen adaptations. The book's influence can also be seen from its use in debates over capital punishment. In Texas, the line between being mentally competent to be prosecuted and having too low of an IQ to stand trial has sometimes been referred to as "the Lennie standard."

Like many of Steinbeck's works, *Of Mice and Men* portrayed the working class as victims of a cruel and harsh upper class. In particular, Curley was shown to be a cruel and petty man who relied on his father's wealth to hold power over the workers. In addition, Curley's wife used her position to put the workers in difficult positions, even going so far as to tell an African American worker that she could easily accuse him of trying to rape her, resulting in a lynching. While many readers appreciated the validation of the working class, some found the cruel figures in the upper class and the death at the end of the book to be melodramatic. Still, the portrayal of an innocent and hardworking working class during the Great Depression was one of the core reasons for the book's widespread popularity.

Despite this popularity, there were challenges to the book. In fact, the book has been challenged more than fifty times since its original publication, making it one of the most challenged books on record. The challenges also have come for a variety of reasons. In addition to the violence and obscenity in the book (many groups have disapproved of characters saying, "Jesus Christ" as an expression of shock or frustration), there has been an ongoing challenge to the book based upon its ending. Some groups see the validation of George's decision to take Lennie's life as supporting assisted suicide. Challenges have also come because of the use of racial slurs in the book, though the people using the racial slurs often were the more despicable characters in the play. It also has received challenges based upon more vague complaints, such as not representing traditional values. Because the book has been challenged for so long and in so many places (from Alaska to Florida and even in Ireland) and for so many different reasons, the challenges have met with varying degrees of success.

See Also: *The Grapes of Wrath*.

FURTHER READING

Brady, Monica. "On Being (And Not Being) Mrs. Curley's Wife." *Changing English: Studies in Culture and Education*, December 2014, Vol. 21, Issue 4, pp. 334–347.

Leaf, Jonathan. "Of Mice and Melodrama." *New Criterion*, December 2007, Vol. 26, Issue 4, pp. 84–87, 4p.

Owens, Louis. "Deadly Kids, Stinking Dogs, and Heroes: The Best Laid Plans in Steinbeck's *Of Mice and Men*." *Steinbeck Studies*, Fall 2002, Vol. 25, pp. 1–8.

The Power of One, Bryce Courtenay
(Heinemann—Australia/Random House—America, 1989)

The Power of One is a novel examining the issues of colonization in South Africa. The book takes place from the late 1930s to the early 1950s in South Africa. The principal character is a young boy who goes by the name of Peekay. At the book's beginning, Peekay's mother suffers from a nervous breakdown, leading him to be raised more by his nurse, Mary, who is a native African. When Peekay is old enough, he is sent to a boarding school, where he is picked on by many of the other boys. His harshest attacker is a boy known as The Judge. The Judge speaks highly of the Nazis, and this deepens his dislike for Peekay, who speaks English and, therefore, is associated with the opponents of the Nazis. Unfortunately, Peekay gets little help from the people running the boarding school, leaving him feeling fundamentally alone. In addition to his English heritage, Peekay gets teased and abused because he wets the bed. When he returns home after his first year at the boarding school, Mary consults a medicine man, hoping that he will be able to cure Peekay of his bed-wetting problems. The medicine man, Inkosi-Inkosikazi, does cure Peekay of his bed-wetting, and he also teaches Peekay to go to a peaceful place in his mind, telling Peekay that he will be able to find him there when Peekay needs him. When Peekay returns to school the following year, he approaches it with a belief in "the power of one," a sense of keeping out of the way of people who will otherwise be cruel to him, and he is able to do well in his studies without receiving the abuse and humiliation that he had in his first year. Although it helps for much of the year, he does continue to suffer at the hands of The Judge. Peekay attempts to gain favor by doing The Judge's math homework, and it helps for a time, but at the end of the year, The Judge kills Peekay's pet chicken (a gift from Inkosi-Inkosikazi) and even makes Peekay eat human waste. Peekay wants to return to Mary to feel safe again, but he discovers that he will be spending the summer with his grandfather. On the train to see his grandfather, Peekay meets a boxer. When Peekay sees him fight, he becomes inspired to become a boxer himself. As Inkosi-Inkosikazi did, the boxer gives Peekay advice, teaching him the phrase, "First with your head, then with your heart" to keep him from making any rash decisions. When Peekay reaches the town where his grandfather lives, he sees his mother, who has recently been released from a mental institution. She has become a born again Christian, and she has fired Peekay's former caretaker, Mary, for not following suit. Peekay resists his mother's attempts to make him convert as well. Alienated from his mother, Peekay befriends a German professor who grows cacti and studies botany. He also begins to teach Peekay piano. Unfortunately, when the conflicts of World War II begin, he is taken away for being an unregistered German. While Peekay visits the professor in jail, he continues to learn to box, befriending an inmate. While Peekay is able to temporarily brighten the days of a number of prisoners, his visits bring him more heartache when he discovers that the inmate who has been teaching him how to box has been murdered in the prison. When World War II ends, the professor is released from prison. He and a small group of other adults (a local librarian and a school teacher) help to mentor Peekay. Peekay comes into his own under their supervision, becoming a gifted boxer and musician, leading to his admittance to a prestigious South African school, Prince of Wales. Peekay excels as a boxer and befriends a wealthy boy who acts as Peekay's manager. After graduating, Peekay takes a hard job in the copper mines, strengthening himself and earning enough money to enroll in Oxford. After an accident in the mines kills one of Peekay's friends, he goes to a bar where he runs into The Judge, who is now fully grown like Peekay. The Judge picks a fight with Peekay, but after his extensive training, Peekay is able to fully defeat The Judge. At the book's close, Peekay carves the initials PK into a tattoo of a swastika on The Judge's arm.

The book achieved significant commercial success, selling millions of copies and being translated into a number of languages. It has also been adapted as a film, though the film achieved less favorable critical response than the book did. Courtenay, the author, has said that the book's events were partially inspired by his observations of life in South Africa as a child. Interestingly, he has also acknowledged that his writing is geared more toward a popular audience than an audience of critics and literary readers, though he typically makes this point as a validation of his popularity rather than purely as an admission of inferiority.

Although the book was seen as inspirational by many readers and critics, it does contain a large number of events and themes that have troubled some parents. With discussions of race, violence, and a positive portrayal of prisoners, there are any numbers of issues that parents could take with the book. However, the two core causes for objections were the cruelty that the other students inflicted upon Peekay and the issues with religion that the book had. In particular, the derogatory characterization of Peekay's mother, who had become a Christian after her bout of mental illness, bothered many parents, particularly if they saw the portrayal of the medicine man as validating magic above Christianity. Still, with its global focus and focus on an individual overcoming challenges, the book has maintained a strong readership over the years.

FURTHER READING

Giffard, Sue. "*The Power of One.*" *School Library Journal*, November 2005, Vol. 51, Issue 11, pp. 130–131, 2p.

Glantz, Shelley. "The Power of One." *Library Media Connection*, January 2006, Vol. 24, Issue 4, p. 73.

Gwynn-Jones, Bronwen. "Older Readers." *Australia's Parents*, October/November 1999, Issue 113, p. 24.

The Satanic Verses, Salman Rushdie
(Viking, 1988)

The Satanic Verses is a magical realist novel that is famous for one of the most severe reactions in the history of modern literature. The book follows two protagonists, Gibreel Farishta and Saladin Chamcha. Both of them are Muslims of Indian descent. The novel opens with both actors on a plane that has been hijacked. Before the plane can reach its new destination, it explodes. The book starts to move away from realism when the two actors are the only members of the flight to survive, and both have been transformed, Gibreel into an angel and Saladin into the devil. When Saladin makes his way to civilization, he is arrested after being suspected of trying to illegally enter England. Gibreel also suffers, developing schizophrenia. The pair try to return to a sense of regularity, but they continue to struggle. Saladin eventually is released after he loses his demonic form, but he is embittered that Gibreel did not come to his aid after their common tragedy. To seek revenge, Saladin ruins Gibreel's attempts to reconnect with his former love interest. Despite this, Gibreel forgives Saladin. The pair return to India, though with much different experiences. Gibreel once again is overtaken by psychosis. He kills his former love, then he also kills himself in despair. Saladin, by contrast, reconnects with his estranged father, beginning to rekindle his sense of belonging within his culture. Interspersed with this larger narrative are a series of dream sequences rooted in Gibreel's perspective. These dream sequences retell parts of the Quran, portraying moments from the life of the Prophet Muhammad. It is these sequences that led to much of the negative reaction to the book.

The Satanic Verses was Rushdie's fourth book, and he had already established his literary reputation with *Midnight's Children* and *Shame*. However, it was *The Satanic Verses* that put Rushdie into a larger, mainstream cultural conversation. The book was very well received by critics, recognizing the wide variety of contexts that Rushdie was able to incorporate into a coherent text. Many critics also saw it as a critique of British exploitation of its colonies and former colonies, and Rushdie himself validated this interpretation in interviews.

However, the response from outside of the literary community was mixed. Many Muslims felt that Rushdie's use of the Quran was blasphemous, and the book was banned in India. In addition, the book was burned a number of times in the United Kingdom. In Pakistan, there were riots as different groups either supported the book, with Rushdie supporters advocating for his right to freedom of speech, and other groups fighting the sale and reading of the book. Things developed so far that Ayatollah Khomeini, the top religious figure in Iran and a prominent Muslim, called for Rushdie's death. British Prime Minister Margaret Thatcher pledged to give Rushdie constant protection to ensure that he did not fall victim to the threats. Despite this support, many politicians actually resented the amount of attention that Rushdie required, and some felt like the text was unnecessarily provocative, creating more trouble than it merited. Some authors, Fay Weldon, for instance, supported Rushdie's rights, and many prominent speakers and thinkers weighed in on the controversy. Surprisingly, Rushdie seemed relatively unshaken and, after a time, declared that he would not stay in hiding, because he felt that it was important to not remain intimidated by fundamentalist religious zealots. Unfortunately, not all of the people involved with the publication of the book escaped harm. Two translators were stabbed for their involvement, with Hitoshi Igarashi, the Japanese translator, dying as a result. There was an unsuccessful attempt upon the life of the Norwegian publisher, and, in Turkey, there was a massive attack on the Turkish translator that resulted in dozens of deaths. In 1998, Iran finally offered an apology for the demand for Rushdie's death, though they also indicated that such threats can never be officially called off. Although Rushdie himself has remained a respected figure within the literary community, *The Satanic Verses* is one of the most controversial texts in the history of English literature.

FURTHER READING

Gill, Josie. " 'Under Extreme Environmental Pressure, Characteristics Were Acquired': Epigenetics, Race and Salman Rushdie's *The Satanic Verses*." *Textual Practice*, May 2015, Vol. 29, Issue 3, pp. 479–498.

Mazrui, Ali A. "Satanic Verses or a Satanic Novel? Moral Dilemmas of the Rushdie Affair." *Third World Quarterly*, January 1990, Vol. 12, Issue 1, pp. 116–139, 24p.

Taylor and Francis. "*The Satanic Verses*: A Chronology." *Index on Censorship*, 2008, Vol. 37, Issue 4, pp. 144–147, 4p.

Scary Stories to Tell in the Dark Series, Alvin Schwartz
(Harper & Row, 1981–1991)

Scary Stories to Tell in the Dark is a series of books published for children. They generally are made up of folk tales, urban legends, and illustrations. The stories vary in gruesomeness and graphicness, sometimes being more playful and short and other times describing ghouls desecrating graveyards. Still, most of them were relatively simple and tended to focus on imaginary monsters rather than realistic violence and threats.

The books were a significant commercial success, selling well and being very popular with younger readers for years. Though critical response was less consistently positive, many critics did appreciate the work done by Schwartz, assembling folktales. The series also was, in some ways, an inspiration for a television series that ran for one season from 2012 to 2013.

The books also received a significant amount of challenges, despite their popularity. In particular, the books were criticized for being too violent and disturbing for young readers, with people citing some violent content as well as issues that might be seen as related to the occult. The books were challenged so often that they topped the list of "Most Challenged Books" from 1990 to 2000 as ranked by the American Library Association. While some of the challenges ended in removal, many of them were unsuccessful, and many fans of the series were actually surprised to find that the books were challenged at all, given that their memories of the books were positive. Like other horror books for younger readers, such as the Goosebumps series, Scary Stories to Tell in the Dark has maintained its popularity over the course of the years.

See Also: *Cross Your Fingers, Spit in Your Hat.*

FURTHER READING

Chamberlin, Leslie Burk. "Scary Stories to Tell in the Dark (Book Review)." *School Library Journal*, January 1982, Vol. 28, Issue 5, p. 81.
Goldberg, Beverly. "Censorship Watch." *American Libraries*, March 2002, Vol. 33, Issue 3, p. 25.
Vermont, Ariana V. "Scary Stories to Tell in the Dark." *Scholastic News*—Edition 4, October 2013, Vol. 76, Issue 7, p. 7.

Slaughterhouse V, Kurt Vonnegut Jr.
(Delacorte, 1969)

Slaughterhouse V is a science fiction novel written by Kurt Vonnegut. A strict plot of the book is difficult to give, because part of its construction relies upon the flashbacks and time travel experienced by the central character, Billy Pilgrim. Even before this fractured narrative (described as "schizophrenic" by Vonnegut himself) begins, the first chapter is a metafictional discussion by Vonnegut of the writing of the book. Vonnegut talks about the difficulties that he has in putting together a logical story about World War II (of which Vonnegut was a veteran), and he also writes of visiting a fellow veteran's home to try to comb through memories. During the visit, the veteran's wife chastises Vonnegut for trying to write the book, assuming that he will write a book that makes all of the soldiers look like heroes and the war look just. Vonnegut promises her that he will not write such a book, and she warms up to him. The first chapter also quotes from historical and literary texts that deal with war, time, madness, and spirituality. At the end of the first chapter, Vonnegut tells his reader what the first words and the last words of the book will be, though the closing words of the book are a birdcall that does little to help the reader to understand the plot. Once the book properly begins, the reader meets Billy Pilgrim who has "come unstuck in time," meaning that he has no control over where he ends up, but he always occupies his own body at that point in time so that he might be a child for a brief period, then he might be in the war, then he might be home and safe, married and with children. The book follows Billy as he struggles in the war, not seeming to want to survive. Despite Billy's repeated insistence that he wants to be left alone to die in the German wilderness, another soldier, Roland Weary, tries to keep Billy going, though he does so through cruel means, punching and kicking Billy. When the pair are captured by German soldiers, Weary has his boots taken from him, and on the march to the trains that will take them to prison, Weary falls ill. As he dies from this illness, he makes other captured soldiers pledge to kill Billy Pilgrim when they get the chance. A particularly vicious soldier, Lazzaro, agrees to take this task on, even meeting Billy in the prison and letting him know that, one day, Billy would die at his hands. In the later storyline (though, again, the storylines are interspersed and interwoven), Billy Pilgrim is a successful optometrist who is married to Valencia Merble, a woman whom he does not love, but who has borne him two children. One child, their son, is a Green Beret fighting in the Vietnam War, and the other, their daughter, has gotten married. The night of her wedding, Billy Pilgrim believes that he is abducted by an alien race known as the Tralfamadorians. On their home planet, Billy is kept in a kind of zoo, where they eventually bring a female adult film star so that they can watch a pair of humans have sex and reproduce. The Tralfamadorians also tell Billy that time is not linear, as human beings experience it. Instead, from their perspective, everything happens simultaneously, meaning that there is no free will, because everything has already happened, and we can only notice different events and eras. When Billy returns to Earth, he tries telling people this, but his daughter tells him that he is insane. In the midst of these events, Billy also befriends science fiction author Kilgore Trout. The book frequently describes the books that Trout has written, and many of them have to do with either time travel or religion. In the most recent timeline of the book, Billy is part of a plane crash. He survives, but his wife, Valencia, dies on the trip to the hospital to see him. After this, Billy starts discussing the Tralfamadorians in earnest, eventually going to New York City and getting on a radio program, where he talks about his experience with the aliens before being kicked out of the studio. The book ends by flashing back to the war and seeing a mixture of devastation of the German cities after being bombed by America and the nonsensical nature of the birdcall in the opening chapter. Over the course of the novel, we see that the vengeful soldier Lazzaro does actually get to have Billy Pilgrim killed. Billy Pilgrim is giving a speech and, at the outset, tells the audience that he will be assassinated by the end of the speech. If this is correct, then it proves that Billy Pilgrim has correctly seen the future, though it also means that, from that point on, Billy Pilgrim is not able to present his message to others. Also over the course of the book, Vonnegut directly addresses the reader, sometimes sharing strange facts, like the IQ of characters in the book or the history behind the first pornographic photograph, and sometimes discussing where Vonnegut was during the scenes with Billy Pilgrim in the World War II scenes.

The book was very well received in a number of quarters. It was nominated for a number of major science fiction awards, and it garnered some very positive reviews from critics. Still, some critics dismissed it, saying that science fiction was not the genre to use for serious inquiry and reflection on moral issues like the ones discussed in *Slaughterhouse V*. Interestingly, Vonnegut hinted at this criticism in the book, and he directly addressed the criticism in later works, like in the introduction to his collection of short stories, *Welcome to the Monkey House*. Although some critics dismissed the book because of its genre at the time of its publication, the reputation of the book has only grown more positive over the decades. The book was adapted into a film in 1972. It also has been adapted as a play and a radio play.

Slaughterhouse V has met with both criticisms and significant challenges, sometimes resulting in outright banning. Some of the criticisms have been about the book's ambiguous morality. The skepticism of free will in particular has been seen by some as a tacit endorsement of hedonism and amorality. Of course, not all readers interpret the book this way, and many of the objections lodged against the book are about more literal than thematic issues. In particular, a number of groups have complained about the book's direct portrayal of sex and pornography with both the character of Montana Wildhack and the discussion of the first pornographic photograph as well as a pornographic bookstore where Billy Pilgrim finds a Kilgore Trout novel. It also was criticized for a sympathetic discussion of gays and lesbians. In addition, the book has been challenged for being antagonistic to the ideals of America and Christianity. The book was successfully banned in 1972, being removed from school libraries in Oakland County, Michigan. This and other challenges to the book led *Slaughterhouse V* to be one of the texts included in the *Island Trees School District v. Pico* case heard by the Supreme Court. Other books included on the list were *Black Boy* by Richard Wright and *Soul on Ice* by Eldridge Cleaver. The Supreme Court found that these books, often challenged because of the ideas with them rather than specific examples of obscenity, could not be banned from school libraries, because the banning would interfere with the right to free speech. Despite this ruling, multiple dissenting opinions were issued by some of the justices who felt that the school board should have local authority to ban or allow books or that the school is an educating agent, not a governing agent, and so the banning of books from school libraries is fundamentally different from banning them in stores. Despite these dissenting opinions, the Court ruled to allow *Slaughterhouse V* and the other books on the list in school libraries. This court case helped to make the book a landmark text for its impact upon freedom of speech, how it helped the science fiction genre to evolve, and its innovations in style and structure of the novel. The book is one of few of Vonnegut's that he continued to hold in high esteem at the end of his career, and it is considered by many to be Vonnegut's best work of all.

See Also: *Cat's Cradle*.

FURTHER READING

Jensen, Mikkel. "Janus-Headed Postmodernism: The Opening Lines of *Slaughterhouse-Five*." *Explicator*, January–March 2016, Vol. 74, Issue 1, pp. 8–11, 4p.

Kavalir, Monika. "Modal Structure in Kurt Vonnegut's *Slaughterhouse Five*." *Acta Neophilologica*, 2011, Vol. 44, Issue 1–2, pp. 103–111, 165.

Wicks, Amanda. " 'All This Happened, More or Less': The Science Fiction of Trauma in *Slaughter House Five*." *Critique*, 2014, Vol. 55, Issue 3, pp. 329–340, 12p.

The Wish Giver, Bill Brittain
(Harper & Row, 1983)

The Wish Giver is a young adult novel coming out of a larger tradition of stories for moral instruction. The book follows a boy named Stewart Meade. While at a carnival, Stewart (nickamed "Stew Meat" in a play on his name) sees three children whom he knows. They are in a tent, where they are buying cards from a man named Thaddeus Binn. Binn tells them that if they make a wish and touch a red dot on the cards they have received from him, they will each be granted their wish. The first of the friends to make her wish is Polly, a tomboy who is envious of the popular girls at school. When she wishes to be invited to a tea party, she begins croaking like a frog. Polly does get the invitation to a tea party, but it is disappointing, as she is stuck croaking for much of the party, and she finds the popular girls that invited her to be shallow and petty, ridiculing other children and revealing that they only invited Polly to belittle her for croaking. Although Polly is disappointed, she does realize that she could have friends more easily than she had originally thought and the friends would likely be better to her than the popular girls. The second wish is made by Rowena, who wishes for a traveling salesman with whom she is smitten to "put down roots" in town. As with Polly, Rowena's wish is fulfilled in a literal way, with the salesman becoming rooted to the ground like a tree. As she tries to help him, Rowena realizes that she never should have been interested in the salesman, and she ends up starting a romance with a boy who works with her family. The final wish comes from Adam, who wishes that his family's farm could have all the water that it ever needs. Like the other two wishes, Adam's wish goes awry when the family gets not only enough water for a short period of time but a flood of water that ruins the farm. Each of the children visits Stew Meat looking for help. With some work, Stew is able to help them undo their wishes, and each child is left the wiser for their misadventures.

The book was generally well received, gaining very positive reviews and being listed as an honoree by the prestigious Newberry Award committee. It was a modest commercial success, and one of Britain's many books set in a small town in New England. Although many readers appreciated the wholesome setting of New England, the book opens with a brief reference to the history of witchcraft associated with Salem and the region in general. This, along with the partially sinister magic of the carnival worker, led some parents to object to the book, though the entirety of the novel does examine progress and growth from the three principal children. Although there were some challenges (the book was listed as number 99 out of the one hundred "Most Challenged Books" of the 1990s), the book overall did not receive major bans or hits to its popularity, and it is generally appreciated as a minor but enjoyable entry in the young adult canon.

FURTHER READING

Gerhardt, Lillian. "*The Wish Giver*." *Reading Time*, May 2009, Vol. 53, Issue 2, p. 19.

Gleason, George, and Lillian N. Gerhardt. "*The Wish Giver* (Book Review)." *School Library Journal*, April 1983, Vol. 29, Issue 8, p. 110.

Jones, Trevelyn E., David J. Gale, and Lillian N. Gerhardt. "*The Wish Giver* (Book Review)." *School Library Journal*, May 1983, Vol. 29, Issue 9, p. 31.

The Witches, Roald Dahl
(Jonathan Cape, 1983)

The Witches is a children's book written by Roald Dahl, author of other classics such as *The BFG* and *Matilda*. The story follows a young boy who is forced to live with his Norwegian grandmother after his parents die in a car crash. The grandmother tells the boy about witches, focusing in particular on ways that he can recognize witches by their telltale signs. Although the grandmother lives in Norway, the boy's parents' will indicates that they must return to his home in England, and the grandmother obliges, though she warns the boy that he must be wary so that he is not cursed himself. She warns him that the witches in England are particularly cruel and effective. The boy quickly suspects that he is being watched by a witch when he sees a strange old woman watching him as he works on his tree house. The old woman tries to coax the boy into coming with him, but he refuses, and he becomes even more convinced that his grandmother is right to warn him. The boy's grandmother falls ill, forcing her to cancel a trip to Norway, and she and the boy end up taking a smaller vacation in England. While on vacation, the boy finds that a convention advertising itself as advocating for children is actually a national convention of British witches. A seemingly young woman takes the stage as the boy secretly watches. When she takes off her mask, he realizes that she is the Grand High Witch, a figure that visits every nation to oversee its witches. The Grand High Witch shows herself to be exceptionally cruel, chastising the witches for not killing enough children and burning one of the witches in attendance. She tells the remaining witches that they need to take over area candy shops so that they can distribute free candies that have been filled with a secret formula that turns children into mice. Shortly after demonstrating that the formula works by giving it to a child that she has lured into the convention, the witches smell the protagonist, and they trap him. The Grand High Witch gives him the secret formula, and the boy is turned into a mouse himself. Surprisingly, the boy can still speak. He finds the first boy who was turned into a mouse, and, together, they find the protagonist's grandmother, telling her what has happened. The grandmother tries to return the first boy to his parents, while the protagonist tries to find the secret formula so that he can give it to the witches themselves. While the grandmother fails, the boy succeeds, and the grandmother takes both boys, along with a bottle of the formula, to a dining area in the hotel hosting the witch convention, hoping that they can slip it to the witches. They do manage to pour it into a soup that the witches are having for dinner, but a cook spots the narrator and cuts off part of his tail. The narrator gets away, and the witches are all turned into mice. Thinking that their hotel is being overrun by mice, the hotel staff end up killing all of the witches, including the Grand High Witch. Still angered, the boy and his grandmother decide that they will return to Norway to find the witch who will replace the dead Grand High Witch, giving her and her followers the secret formula so that they can rid the world of witches. Near the end of the book, the protagonist is still a mouse, and the grandmother points out that he will likely live less than ten more years, but the boy says that he can accept this, because he and his grandmother will live to about the same date.

The book was largely well received, selling well and earning the Whitbread Book Award in 1993. It also was adapted to a movie and a radio drama. Although the book is not necessarily one of Dahl's major works, it does have a significant readership.

Many of Dahl's books have been challenged for a variety of reasons, including the portrayal of adults, magic, and violence. Surprisingly, the portrayal of witches was not the only or even the primary reason for *The Witches'* challenges. Instead, some readers have challenged the book based upon its perceived hatred toward women. Despite the role that the grandmother plays in trying to protect the protagonist, some readers have argued that it teaches young boys to be suspicious of or hostile toward women. While there certainly were some more conventional challenges (such as in Iowa, where there were objections to words like "slut," or in Oregon, where some parents argued that the book could give children too much interest in the occult), the book elicited a more complex set of challenges than many other texts because the political leanings of the challenging groups run over a broader spectrum. While some of the challenges did result in children needing parents' consent to check the book out, the book was generally not banned outright, and it has maintained a steady readership as part of Dahl's larger body of work.

See Also: *James and the Giant Peach*.

FURTHER READING

Basbanes Richter, Barbara. "Roald Dahl and Danger in Children's Literature." *Sewanee Review*, Spring 2015, Vol. 123, Issue 2, pp. 325–334, 10p.

Curtis, James. " 'We Have a Great Task Ahead of Us!': Child-Hate in Roald Dahl's *The Witches*." *Children's Literature in Education*, June 2014, Vol. 45, Issue 2, pp. 166–177, 12p.

Flegar, Željka. "The Alluring Nature of Children's Culture: Fairy Tales, the Carnival and the World Wide Web." *International Research in Children's Literature*, December 2015, Vol. 8, Issue 2, pp. 169–184.

A Wrinkle in Time, Madeleine L'Engle
(Farrar, Straus & Giroux, 1963)

A Wrinkle in Time is a science fiction book that is particularly notable for being one of the first in its genre to feature a female protagonist. In fact, it had received a number of rejections because some publishers were skeptical of whether or not a readership would support a science fiction book with a female protagonist. The book follows thirteen-year-old Meg Murry. Here Meg is generally seen as a troublesome student, not popular with her classmates and seen by even her family as immature. This is particularly problematic within her family, because her family is seen as overachievers, with her two twin brothers being great athletes and her youngest brother being a genius. In addition, both her parents are intelligent scientists, though her father is generally absent from her life. At the book's opening, Meg is awakened by a thunderstorm. When she goes down from her bedroom to the kitchen, she finds her youngest brother, Charles Wallace, having a snack and drinking milk. After they talk a bit, their mother comes down as well, and then their neighbor, the eccentric Mrs. Whatsit, also comes to visit. She reveals the existence of tesseracts. While the reader does not know, at this point, what a tesseract is, Meg's mother nearly faints at this news. The family goes to bed, and, the next morning, Meg begins to discover what this term refers to and that it is related to a project that her father was working on before he disappeared, a project related to tesseracts. Not long after, Meg and Charles Wallace join a popular high schooler in exploring what they believe to be a haunted house. It turns out that the house belongs to Mrs. Whatsit, and her assistant, Mrs. Who, meets the children. She assures Meg that she will help her to find her father. Charles Wallace agrees that they should go on a mission to find him. At this point, another associate of Mrs. Whatsit, Mrs. Which, materializes out of thin air. At this point, the children discover that all three Mrs. W's are supernatural beings. They reveal what a tesseract is when they use one to transport the children to the planet Uriel. The tesseract is described as somehow folding the universe by means of elements of the fifth dimension. On Uriel, the children find an idyllic world where half-horse-half-human beings exist in a state of peace. The three Mrs. W's tell the children, at this point, that they are actually members of the same race as the inhabitants of Uriel and that their world is threatened by a malevolent force known as "The Black Thing." From Uriel, the Mrs. W's take the children to speak with The Happy Medium, who uses a crystal ball to show the children a vision of the Earth partially covered in darkness. The children also gain further knowledge of the Mrs. W's, discovering that Mrs. Whatsit was, at one point, a star, but that she had sacrificed herself in a battle. After these revelations, the children are transported to a planet known as Camazotz, which is dominated by The Black Thing. The beings on Camazotz appear to be automatons to the children, and they are, indeed, controlled by a central station on the planet. While on this planet, the children find a red-eyed man who claims to know where their father is. Charles Wallace allows himself to be influenced by this man, who turns out to have telepathic abilities, in hopes of finding his father. Charles Wallace does, indeed, take Meg and the popular high schooler, Calvin, to the place where their father is being kept. The children find out that the planet is controlled by an evil brain, which is close to where their father is being held. When they are brought close to it, the children nearly all fall under its control, but Dr. Murry is able to transport Meg, Calvin, and himself away. Dr. Murry gets the children to a nearby planet, Ixchel, but the difficult journey nearly kills Meg, and she is frozen when they reach the new planet. The inhabitants of Ixchel initially appear to be threatening, as they have no eyes and four tentacles, but they turn out to be kind and intelligent. These creatures help to cure Meg of her frozen state, and Meg and her father connect, emotionally. At this point, the three Mrs. W's return, and they tell Meg that she needs to save her brother. Meg agrees, and she accepts gifts and advice from the Mrs. W's. When Meg returns to Camazotz, she sees that love will be able to overpower the evil brain controlling Charles Wallace. Meg focuses her feelings of love on Charles Wallace, and it does remove him from the evil brain's control. The three Mrs. W's then transport all of the Murry's and Calvin back to Earth, where they reunite with Meg's mother and other two brothers. The three Mrs. W's show their appreciation, but they then disappear, claiming that they are needed elsewhere.

Despite the book's initial struggles to find a publisher, it has been tremendously successful, never going out of print, and going through a number of editions. It also was a finalist for a number of awards and won many prestigious awards, including the Newberry Medal. Upon the success of this book, L'Engle continued the story, creating a series of books centering around the Murry family. As stated previously, the book also was noteworthy for bringing a female protagonist into a series with science fiction and fantasy elements, paving the way for many subsequent science fiction series, like *The Hunger Games* or *Twilight*. The book was also adapted into both a made-for-television movie and a play. It also has been the inspiration for an opera and a graphic novel adaptation.

Despite these successes, the book has been met with challenges. Like many challenged books, it is hard to say whether the reasons for the challenges lodged against this book were the ones stated or if there were other reasons. Some parties challenged the book feeling that there were themes contained in the book that could have been perceived as favoring Communism, and this would have been a source of significant resistance during the book's first publication. More directly, parties challenging the book have cited the portrayal of religion. Conservative Christian Jerry Falwell led a movement against the book, claiming that the book did not portray religion in a positive light. Many critics disagreed, citing the fact that one of the three Mrs. W's quoted a Bible verse to Meg before she made the final trip to rescue her brother. In addition, L'Engle has clear ties to the Episcopal Church, albeit to a more liberal wing, serving for a time as writer-in-residence at New York's Cathedral of St. John the Divine. L'Engle herself feels that there is a sense of belief in her books, but that the themes and views of the books are not specific to Christianity. To add to the confusion, although Falwell's followers have fought to ban the book (and have been unsuccessful), other Christian groups, most prominently Zondervan Publishing House, have listed the book as a positive Christian story for young readers. Still others have argued that the book's use of the evil force in the universe actually demonstrates satanic themes, particularly claiming that the three Mrs. W's were actually witches who were trying to indoctrinate the children in the book and, by extension, young readers as well. In 1990, the book received a challenge in Anniston, Alabama, when some students and parents objected to the fact that Jesus was mentioned not as a purely divine being but as a thinker in the same category as Shakespeare or various philosophers. They saw this sort of categorization as being offensive to practicing Christians. Families in Waterloo, Iowa, made similar accusations, requesting that the book be removed. The direct discussion of Christianity, the use of a female protagonist, and other aspects of the book will likely make this book continue to be both a draw for many readers and a lightning rod for others.

FURTHER READING

Barron, T. A. "Why Fantasy Must Be True." *Horn Book Magazine*, July/August 2012, Vol. 88, Issue 4, pp. 85–89, 5p.

Maloney, Jennifer, and Ben Fritz. "A New Wrinkle in Time." *Wall Street Journal—Eastern Edition*, April 2015, Vol. 265, Issue 89, pp. D1–D3.

Staff. "*A Wrinkle in Time*." *Publishers Weekly*, April 2012, Vol. 259, Issue 18, pp. 132–133, 2p.

3

SEX AND CENSORSHIP IN AMERICA

While there have been innumerable cases of writers and artists being silenced because of their political views or discussions of authority figures, some of the earliest censorship in modern legal systems have come out of concerns over the portrayal of sex and sexual desire. One early and significant figure in this category is D. H. Lawrence, whose controversial novels caused major scandals at the time of their original publication. The sources of concern ran from the actual descriptions of sexual acts to which characters were having relations with each other. In Lawrence's *Lady Chatterley's Lover*, for instance, the fact that a woman from the upper class was not only engaging in an affair but was also engaging in an affair with someone beneath her station led some readers to be alarmed by the book's material. Lawrence's own feelings toward the British class system no doubt fed into his portrayal of the hypocrisies and dissatisfaction within the upper-class marriage.

Lawrence was not the only one to receive criticism for his romantic pairings. One of the most shocking examples involved the portrayal of pedophilia in *Lolita*, by Vladimir Nabokov. Many critics' writing around the time of the book's release saw it as dangerous and referred to it as "pornography." In the case of *Lolita*, the reputation of the publisher may well have added to the reactions to the novel. Many of the other novels published by Olympia Press were considered erotica, and so leading opponents of *Lolita* characterized it as cheap and dirty rather than truly literary and artistic. Of course, some publishers found an interesting middle ground between respected artistic work and more edgy, erotic material. Grove Press published some of D. H. Lawrence's work, and it also became the center of not only a controversy but also a number of legal challenges after publishing William S. Burroughs's book, *Naked Lunch*.

As with other areas of controversy like drugs and alcohol or sexual orientation, what has been deemed as too sexually provocative in the past has changed quite a bit over the years. While *Lady Chatterley's Lover* seemed highly graphic and transgressive at the time of its first publication, many contemporary readers might find it relatively tame, particularly compared to the graphic and shocking matter found in *Naked Lunch* or *Lolita*. While it is easy to argue that Lawrence's and Nabokov's works had sex or sexual desire as an integral part of the story, other works, like Stephen King's *It*, for example, have been attacked for including gratuitous sex scenes that had nothing to do with the main story. Some of the biggest objections to *It* revolve around a scene in which a number of boys all have sex with a young girl. While defenders of the book claim that the scene is meant to show the corruption of innocent youth and the dark influence of the town in which they are raised, even some of King's usual defenders felt that this book was going too far, particularly because the act involved children. In general, books that combined young characters and sexual desire face consistent challenges.

Beyond the parties involved in the sexual relations, critics often cite the nature of the sexual acts as being problematic. While many advocates have argued that it is important for younger readers to understand the dangers that come along with relationships as well as how to deal with issues of sexual assault, many parent groups have stated that they are uncomfortable with direct portrayals of this material. Books like *The Perks of Being a Wallflower* by Stephen Chbosky take on the issue of sexual assault from multiple angles, and they also look at incest and sexual assault, making the material even more charged and heightening the discomfort for some readers and parents. Often, these challenges can be unsuccessful, because their basis can be perceived to be a matter of comfort with ideas rather than a matter of how graphic the descriptions of sex acts are, giving defenders of the books a stronger argument when invoking the First Amendment.

That said, even seemingly clinical or innocuous descriptions of sex or sex organs have led to banning. Books like Maurice Sendak's *The Night Kitchen* and even Martin Handford's *Where's Waldo* have been met with challenges simply for the visual portrayal of the human body. While *The Night Kitchen* upset some parents because there was an illustration of a naked child, *Where's Waldo* was challenged simply for having an illustration of a bare-chested woman at a topless beach. Susan Patron's *The Higher Power of Lucky* was challenged for having the word "scrotum" in it, even though the term was not put into a context where readers could fully understand what the term meant. A simple reference to sex organs was enough to bring challenges to the book. Handbooks about sex and puberty have often been challenged by parent groups who claimed that discussions of sex and sexual development should be covered by parents rather than schools. Proponents of these manuals regularly argue that many parents are uncertain of how to approach these topics with their teenaged and preteen children, making the books as much for parents as for children.

While these challenges have sometimes led to major debates about school libraries and even legal proceedings, the rise of the Internet has begun to shift the access that young people have to sexual slang, terminology, and knowledge, and there has been a shift in what has been seen as acceptable as well. In addition to online sources like the Urban Dictionary, which define slang terms (many of them sexual in nature), fan fiction groups often explore sex and sexual desire between characters in clear and direct ways. Fan fiction communities have entire genres dedicated to sexual encounters between established characters, often shifting sexual orientation of the characters. While these are not considered legitimate works of art by most of the literary community, the easy access of images and writing dealing with sex and sexual desire has led to an erosion of some restrictions held by previous generations.

Of course, that does not mean that challenges to texts have completely died down. Every year challenges come in against both books that have been recently published and old standards that are being used on class-reading lists, but that some parents are encountering for the first time. While the larger cultural discussion about sex in America may be opening up in many ways, it is not likely that some degree of resistance toward books that portray or even discuss sex will disappear any time soon.

TIMELINE

1855—*Leaves of Grass*, Walt Whitman, published

1885—D. H. Lawrence born

1913—*Sons and Lovers*, D. H. Lawrence, published

1915—*The Rainbow*, D. H. Lawrence, published

1922—*Ulysses*, James Joyce, published

1927—The film *Wonders of the Unseen World* was released, helping to establish the "stag" film genre

1928—*Lady Chatterley's Lover*, D. H. Lawrence, published

1931—*Brave New World*, Aldous Huxley, published, helping to establish the legitimacy of science fiction in the literary canon

1934—*Tropic of Cancer*, Henry Miller, published

1938—Judy Blume born

1947—Kinsey Institute for Research in Sex, Gender and Reproduction founded

1948—*Sexual Behavior in the Human Male*, Alfred Kinsey, Wardell Pomeroy, and Clyde Martin, published, opening up a new line of research

1949—*1984*, George Orwell, published

1953—*Playboy* magazine founded, also *Sexual Behavior in the Human Female*, Kinsey et al., published

1956—Elvis Presley was shown dancing only from the waist up on the *Ed Sullivan Show*, with censors claiming that his dancing was too suggestive

1958—*Lolita*, Vladimir Nabokov, published in America

1964—Masters and Johnson research team founded the Reproductive Biology Research Foundation

1964–1966—Female TV characters like Gidget and Jeannie were forbidden from showing their navels on television

1968—*Boys and Sex*, Wardell Pomeroy, published

1969—*Midnight Cowboy* becomes the only X-rated film to win Academy Awards; *Penthouse* magazine first published; Andy Warhol releases *Blue Movie*, arguably establishing a new wave of pornographic films

1970—*Girls and Sex*, Wardell Pomeroy, published

1973—*Playgirl* magazine first published, establishing a widely published magazine showing nude and seminude men

1974—*Blubber*, Judy Blume, published; *Carrie*, Stephen King, also published; *Hustler* magazine founded

1980—*The Clan of the Cave Bear*, Jean M. Auel, published

1982—The Playboy Channel launched

1988—*Asking about Sex and Growing Up*, Joanna Cole, published; *Fade*, Robert Cormier, also published

1990—The X rating for films was changed to NC-17 in an effort to separate out violent and pornographic films

1991—*Women on Top*, Nancy Friday, published

1993—*Private Parts*, Howard Stern, published

1997—*Blood and Chocolate*, Annette Curtis Klause, published

2004—Janet Jackson's breast was accidentally shown during the Super Bowl halftime show, leading to many calls for censorship as well as a number of send-ups about people outraged over the perceived impropriety

2005—*Twilight*, Stephenie Meyer, published

2007—*The Absolutely True Diary of a Part-Time Indian* published, marking Sherman Alexie's entry into young adult fiction

2008—*Twilight* adapted into a major motion picture

2011—*50 Shades of Gray* by E. L. James published, leading to long debates over sexual propriety and sadomasochism

1984, George Orwell
(Secker & Warburg, 1949)

1984 is a seminal and respected work of science fiction. The book follows Winston Smith, who lives in a London that was, at the time of the book's publication, set in the future. This world is a dystopia ravaged by war, where supplies are limited and the government is strict, supporting only a small portion of the population. Winston lives a modest life, subsisting on black bread, gin, and what little rations he is given by the government. He also lives in fear, knowing that the government has placed cameras everywhere so that the Thought Police can take away anyone who might work to overthrow the government. Even children are told to inform the government if they believe that their parents might be working against the government. Winston works for the Ministry of Truth, an office of the government that changes photos and speeches to adhere to the narrative that the government wants the population to receive. It also disposes of documents and records of individuals that might undercut the news and stories that it gives to the citizens. After becoming disenchanted with his work, Winston decides to research some of the hidden history. He also begins writing documents that criticize Big Brother, the secretive leader of the government. Winston has to do this in secret, because he knows that the penalty will be death if he is caught.

A fellow worker for the government, Julia, secretly lets Winston know that she is interested in him. Although Winston was not interested in her prior to her letting him know, he comes to realize that she feels the same disdain for the government that he does. The two begin having a secret affair, first in the country and then at an apartment that they believe is safe from any cameras. Winston approaches a member of the government whom he believes is part of an underground movement known as the Brotherhood. The Brotherhood is believed to be gathering resources to overthrow the government. The member, O'Brien, gives Winston a book that explains how the government maintains its control and how it could be overthrown by the vast population of oppressed people in the country.

Not long after this, Winston and Julia are taken in by the Ministry of Love, who have discovered their affair. Winston discovers that both the person who rented them an apartment and O'Brien are members of the Thought Police, and they have set him up as part of a sting operation to find people who might become part of the Brotherhood. O'Brien tortures and tries to brainwash Winston, first using electrical shocks to wear him down and then telling him that any opposition to the government is insanity. He also says that the government works not for the people but to achieve absolute power over the people, making it a very dangerous body to try to oppose. Winston is partially worn down, confessing to crimes and implicating some of his associates, but he refuses to implicate Julia in any real wrongdoing. Not satisfied with this, O'Brien straps a cage with rats over Winston's head, making him confront his worst fear. Winston breaks, turning on Julia, and O'Brien is satisfied. Winston is released, believed to no longer be a threat. He does, alter, run into Julia, and they both share stories of their tortures and admit to turning on the other. After a time, Winston becomes an alcoholic, and he wonders how much of his memory is true and how much is delusion. By the end of the book, he has become fully dominated, drinking along to a celebration after an announcement that the government has achieved a military victory, the type of story that Winston himself would have helped to falsely craft earlier in the book.

The book was generally well received at the time of its publication. Many critics stated their admiration for Orwell's carefully crafted world, which included not only characters and a fictitious government but also slang and political parties that helped to highlight the social and political commentary that he meant to give. Orwell's famous essay "Politics and the English Language" set up the ideas that he used in the construction of Newspeak, the system of language that was crafted to limit the thought and freedom of citizens under Big Brother. This helped to make a world that seemed not only inventive but also grounded in the reality of subtle forms of domination. Not all reviews were entirely positive, though. Prominent writers like C. S. Lewis said that the book was too cynical and dark to give an accurate view of the world. Even some of the book's positive reviews acknowledged its dark and depressing view of humanity and systems of government. The book also was sometimes compared negatively to Aldous Huxley's novel *Brave New World*, which had also looked at an authoritarian government and a dystopian future and had been published over a decade prior to *1984*.

The book and its Newspeak slang have had a long-lasting impact upon the culture at large. In addition to two significant adaptations, once as a radio play and once as a film, the book's language has infiltrated popular culture in both direct references and indirect references. The reality television show *Big Brother* took its name from Orwell's work, and it followed members of a house who were constantly being watched by video cameras. In fact, the term "Orwellian" comes largely from his portrayal of the government in *1984*, meaning a totalitarian political structure or system that is built to control people rather than to keep a government open to its citizens. A host of memes, bumper stickers, and other references to the book have also been used in both serious and satirical ways over the years since the book's publication.

While the book has been acknowledged as one of the most influential in the history of science fiction, it has also received a number of challenges. In fact, it made a "top ten" list of "Most Challenged Books" published by *Time* magazine. Almost immediately after it was translated into Russian, the book was banned in Russia, largely for its perceived critique of the Stalin regime and its harsh portrayal of governmental controls. The challenge that the book faced in the Union of Soviet Socialist Republics (USSR) is ironic, given that it was also challenged in Florida in 1981, with the challenging group claiming that the book was pro-communist, though the group also cited the explicit sexual material as a reason for objection. Because of its skepticism of the government and its antiwar sentiment, the book was frequently challenged in both America and Europe through the 1960s and 1970s. Beyond the concerns about how it portrayed the government, challenging groups also cited the sexual material, and they claimed that the book was too dark or depressing for young readers. However, even with these challenges (and perhaps even because of them), the book has had a consistent following for decades, and it has been the inspiration for a variety of social critiques and pop culture references. In fact, after the election of Donald Trump in 2016, the book sold out in many bookstores as people looked for sophisticated criticism of authoritarian regimes that regularly turned to doublespeak to justify their actions.

See Also: *Brave New World*.

FURTHER READING

Beauchamp, Gorman. "Of Man's Last Disobedience: Zamiatin's 'We' and Orwell's '1984.'" *Comparative Literature Studies*, 1973, Vol. 10, pp. 285–301.

Dilworth, Thomas. "Erotic Dream to Nightmare: Ominous Problems and Subliminal Suggestion in Orwell's Nineteen Eighty-four." *Papers on Language & Literature*, Summer 2013, Vol. 49, Issue 3, pp. 296–326, 31p.

Kuppig, C. J. (ed.) *Nineteen Eighty Four to 1984: A Companion to George Orwell's Classic Novel*. New York, NY: Carroll & Graf, 1984, p. 316.

The Absolutely True Diary of a Part-Time Indian, Sherman Alexie
(Little, Brown Books for Young Readers, 2007)

The Absolutely True Diary of a Part-Time Indian is a young adult novel written by prominent Native American author Sherman Alexie. Like many of Alexie's works, it follows a Native American character living on the Spokane Indian Reservation in Washington. The narrator goes by the name of Junior, and he is a high school boy who enjoys basketball and drawing. Like many families on the reservation, his family struggles with poverty, leading his sister to leave the family after she gets married. Although the family struggles run throughout the book, the principal narrative follows Junior as he makes the decision to attend a nearby high school that has mostly white students. This move initially angers Junior's good friend, Rowdy, who sees Junior as betraying his culture, though some people support Junior's desire to find a better life. The fallout with Rowdy is particularly troubling with Junior, because he has a number of medical issues stemming from his having been born with hydrocephalus (a condition that Alexie himself had at birth), and these conditions (including needing glasses and having seizures) lead other kids to view Junior as weak. Because of this, Rowdy was Junior's only real friend and his protector, and Junior does not have a similar figure at his new school, nor does he feel like he can fully count on Rowdy after he begins attending the new school. Junior does not immediately make close friends at the new school, but he does develop a basic friendship with Gordy, a smart but quirky boy, and he also becomes attracted to Penelope, a kind white girl at the school. Junior does face his share of hostility from some of the other students. This results in a fight between Junior and Roger, a star athlete. Junior punches Roger during the fight, and he is shocked when Roger does not fight him back. He comes to realize that the white students at his new school are not as used to aggression and physical confrontation as Junior is from living on the reservation. He also comes to see that the families of these students do not have the type of strong bonds that families on the reservation have. After the fight with Roger, Junior becomes more popular, with even Roger himself showing Junior a good degree of respect. Encouraged at the turn of events, Junior joins the basketball team at his new school. He plays well, but when Junior's new school plays his old school, he finds that the other kids from the reservation play in a very aggressive, physical way, specifically targeting Junior himself. Junior's old school wins the game, with Rowdy playing a key role and even knocking Junior out during the game. The teams play again later in the season, and, this time, Junior outplays Rowdy, and his new school wins. Initially, Junior is ecstatic, but he quickly loses that excitement when he realizes what it has meant to help beat his old team. Feeling like he has added to the feelings of hopelessness that the other boys feel, Junior runs into his own locker room and breaks down crying and even throwing up. Junior's own feelings of hopelessness are added to by many of the problems that he encounters over the course of his first year at the new school. His sister dies in a fire, his grandmother is hit by a car, and a host of other tragedies befall people on the reservation. He also sees that some of the students at the new school have difficult times, being ignored or mistreated by their parents. Junior is able to get a date with Penelope, but he comes to recognize that the likelihood of a long-term relationship is low, particularly because her father is racist, and she dreams of leaving the area to see the larger world. Instead, Junior ends the year feeling a renewed connection to his family and especially to Rowdy. Rowdy tells Junior that his time at the new school actually makes him a nomad, which, ironically, makes him a more traditional Indian than most of the people living on the reservation. The pair play basketball together as well, showing a full reconciliation.

The book has been very well received, being a relatively rare example of a novel that has been able to gain positive reception from both literary and popular circles. The book received a number of very positive reviews from prominent publications like the *New York Times* and *San Francisco Chronicle*. In addition, it won the National Book Award for Young People's Literature and the Boston Globe-Horn Book Award, and it was named to a number of "best of" lists. The entry into young adult literature also marked one of Alexie's most commercially successful books, tapping into a market for new readers while maintaining a loyal following with his established readership.

Not long after *The Absolutely True Story of a Part-Time Indian* was published, the book became a lightning rod for censorship and challenges. In 2010, the book was challenged in Stockton, Missouri, with a parent complaining about the portrayal of teenaged sexual desire and alcohol abuse. The school board voted to ban the book. When the American Library Association requested that the school board reconsider, it maintained its initial position, keeping the book out of the classroom and school libraries. The following year, the book was challenged in Richland, Washington. The initial vote banned the book from the classroom and the library. Interestingly, at the time of the ban, all of the copies of the book were not only checked out but also had a wait list for other students. Despite this initial banning, the school board actually reversed its decision after members of the board read the book and found it to have legitimate social and literary merit. The book continued to face challenges that received both local and national attention. Alexie responded to these challenges in two ways. He often would give flippant responses, particularly on his blog and in other social media venues. These primarily focused on the fact that the challenges to and bans of the book often gave the book publicity, which translated into greater sales. Seeing this, Alexie satirically suggested that he should thank the people bringing challenges against his book. But Alexie gave a more thoughtful, serious response as well. In 2011, Alexie wrote a piece published in *The Wall Street Journal* in which he discussed that his own childhood was sometimes influenced by rock bands and other figures that people had claimed would warp and corrupt him. He also claimed that he often received letters from young readers telling him that reading his works had helped them work through their own issues, and he claimed that he had never received a letter from young readers saying that his book had traumatized them. This claim fit with Alexie's discussions of how his own experience as a young man influenced the writing of the book. Not surprisingly, the piece that Alexie wrote was fairly divisive, leading both the book's attackers and defenders to claim it as evidence for their respective sides. This discussion helped to make the book a significant text not only for its content but also for the debate that has surrounded it.

FURTHER READING

Alexie, Sherman. "Fiction and Poetry Award Winner: *The Absolutely True Diary of a Part-Time Indian*." *Horn Book Magazine*, January/February 2009, Vol. 85, Issue 1, pp. 25–28, 4p.

Burner, Joyce Adams. "Finding Common Ground." *School Library Journal*, May 2010, Vol. 56, Issue 5, pp. 46–50, 5p.

Kertzer, Adrienne. "Not Exactly: Intertextual Identities and Risky Laughter in Sherman Alexie's *The Absolutely True Diary of a Part-Time Indian*." *Children's Literature: Annual Publication of the Modern Language Association Division on Children's Literature and the Children's Literature Association*, 2012, Vol. 40, pp. 49–77.

Angus, Thongs and Full-Frontal Snogging, Louise Rennison
(Piccadilly Press, 1999)

Originally published in the United Kingdom, *Angus, Thongs and Full-Frontal Snogging* caught significant attention for its frank and playful discussion of teenage desire and its focus on a young woman's discussion of her body. Moving beyond more innocent fare, this book directly discussed wearing thongs and padded bras and used language that implied a genuine knowledge of human sexuality (the main character referred to a male character as a "sex god"). That said, the book does not portray explicit scenes or acts, and much of the discussion of romantic interaction is discussed in the abstract (Georgia Nicolson, the first-person narrator of the book, discusses the awkwardness of figuring out how to hold your head while kissing). In addition, much of the book focuses on things other than desire, including her wild cat, her struggles with her younger sister, and other elements familiar to female teenage narrators.

Although the book did meet with some resistance, it was a launching point for Rennison's career, as she went on to write a number of other young adult books following Georgia Nicolson. The playful use of the diary or "confessions" format and the time period it came from led many readers to compare *Angus, Thongs and Full-Frontal Snogging* to the successful adult series that began with *Bridget Jones's Diary* by Helen Fielding. Still, the book did receive significant challenges, landing at number 35 on the list of "Most Challenged Books" for the period from 2000 to 2009.

FURTHER READING

Nicolson, Georgia. "Milestones." *TIME*, March 14, 2016, Vol. 187, Issue 9, p. 13.
Roback, Diane, Lynda Brill Comerford, Sally Lodge, and Kate Pavao. "Spring Attractions." *Publishers Weekly*, April 1, 2002, Vol. 249, Issue 13, pp. 24–26, 3p.
Rosenberg, Eli. "Louise Rennison, 64, Young Adult Author." *New York Times*, March 5, 2016, Vol. 165, Issue 57162, p. D8.

Asking about Sex and Growing Up, Joanna Cole
(Harper Collins, 1988)

Asking about Sex and Growing Up was an illustrated book of question and answers meant to support preteens in their curiosity about sexuality, puberty, and other struggles that they might be facing. Meant to be a simple and honest discussion of these topics, the book caught resistance because it discussed issues like homosexuality and sexual desire. While the book covered a wide variety of topics, it did keep a relatively consistently factual approach to the examination of these topics.

Not surprisingly, the frank and direct discussion of sex was met with a wide variety of objections in a number of places. Like many of the books receiving challenges, *Asking about Sex and Growing Up* had not only struggles and challenges but also support for its significance. While many parent groups claimed that the book gave too graphic of presentations or material that was not appropriate for children, there were supporters from parents to guidance counselors to teachers who championed the book's use for talking to children about topics that might otherwise make both parents and children uncomfortable.

FURTHER READING

Brodie, Carolyn S. "Get on Board with Joanna Cole." *School Library Media Activities Monthly*, January 2000, Vol. 16, Issue 5, pp. 45–48, 4p.

Piehl, Kathy. "*Asking about Sex and Growing Up*: A Question and Answer Book for Kids." *School Library Journal*, February 2010, Vol. 56, Issue 2, pp. 128–129, 2p.

Scarpellino, Ann, and Trevelyn E. Jones. "*Asking about Sex and Growing Up* (Book)." *School Library Journal*, August 1988, Vol. 34, Issue 11, p. 101.

Blood and Chocolate, **Annette Curtis Klause**
(Random House, 1997)

Blood and Chocolate is a young adult novel portraying shape-shifting, werewolf characters. Although the events of the novel are fantastic, many of the most basic themes and conflicts of the book draw from anxieties and tensions that young adults might well be feeling. The main character, Vivian, must defend her friends to her father after they take a human life. They do so in order to protect one of their pack, but the tension of negotiating the parent-child conflicts is familiar, even if the specifics of the novel are fantastic. Another theme common to young adult writing that is explored in the book is that of the main character coming into one's own. After human neighbors become suspicious of Vivian and her friends (largely because of the actions that they took to defend the member of their pack), the neighbors set fire to some of their houses, killing Vivian's father. The pack must then move to a new place to avoid further persecution, and Vivian must carry on without her father's guidance, all while maintaining her secret. These themes of feeling like an outsider and discovering one's identity are, again, familiar young adult tropes. In particular, the idea of changing into a werewolf, of determining what one's "true self" is, and of belonging to a group is very much in keeping with other young adult literature, just put into a different context than what many readers might typically see. (Interestingly, though, Stephenie Meyers's Twilight series came out in 2005, nearly ten years after *Blood and Chocolate*, and it would become quite popular, building on the teen-monster genre.)

Blood and Chocolate had very direct portrayals of sexual desire and intense violence. For this reason, the book often faced significant challenges from parents. In Texas, South Carolina, Oklahoma, and other states, there were requests to take the book off of shelves or off of award ballots. Some of these requests were successful, but many were not. Some of the claims about the book's content were not fully substantiated. Challenging parties would claim that there were graphic portrayals of sex when there were really only discussions of desire, not direct portrayals of actual sex acts. This led to significant controversy, whether it was deserved or not.

Despite the controversy, the book did well commercially. It had a large readership and was adapted into a film in 1997. Although it never hit the level of widespread success that the Twilight series did, many critics see *Blood and Chocolate* as laying the groundwork for teenage monster books and films that would follow it.

FURTHER READING

Adams, Lauren. "*Blood and Chocolate*." *Horn Book Magazine*, July/August 1997, Vol. 73, Issue 4, pp. 459–460, 2p.

"Freaks: Alive on the Inside." *Library Media Connection*, October 2006, Vol. 25 Issue 2, p. 74.

Klause, Annette Curtis. "A Hitchhiker's Guide to Science Fiction." *School Library Journal*, September 1988, Vol. 35, Issue 1, pp. 120–123, 4p.

Blubber, **Judy Blume**
(Bradbury Press, 1974)

Blubber is a young reader's novel that looks at a variety of struggles and conflicts that children face. The main character, Linda, is bullied by some of the other girls in her class. Although Linda is not the heaviest girl in her class, she gets picked on by Wendy, Jill, and Caroline, being called "Blubber" and being bullied into referring to herself as "Blubber." While these incidents are troubling enough, the bullies go further, trying to take her clothes off in the bathroom to further intimidate and shame Linda. In addition to these struggles, Linda gets caught in the middle of a conflict between the mean girls and a grouchy elderly neighbor, Mr. Machinist. Through the various tensions and conflicts, the friendships among the mean girls begin to crumble, with Jill starting to receive taunts and insulting nicknames while Linda begins to become part of the mean girl group. All of this ends in a sort of standoff, where the girls in the class are in a mild conflict but not able to single any one individual out as the most vulnerable girl to pick on.

While many readers applaud the book for its examination of the tension created by bullying in school, not everyone was so appreciative. For instance, the book was banned in Montgomery County, Maryland. Still, Blume noted in an essay (one which was included with the book in some later editions) that the events were roughly based upon a conflict in her daughter's school. However, that level of realism made some readers uncomfortable. The fact that the bullying persisted throughout the book, and the fact that the primary instigator went largely unpunished by any adult or authority figure, made some critics feel that the book did not give a strong sense of morality. In addition, there were some terms that made readers feel uncomfortable. Of course, Blume was no stranger to challenges. As with her book, *Are You There, God? It's Me, Margaret*, Blume had set out to give what she saw as a realistic presentation of what preteen girls faced, and so a simple solution coming from an adult authority figure would have run counter to her purpose for the book. Also as with her other books, *Blubber* was quite commercially successful, often giving a sense of voice to experiences of young women who were teased for being overweight or otherwise unpopular.

See Also: *Are You There, God? It's Me, Margaret* and *Deenie*.

FURTHER READING

Blume, Judy. "Judy Blume on Being Banned." *Index on Censorship*, September 23, 2013. https://www.indexoncensorship.org/2013/09/judy-blume-banned-books/.

Goldberg, B. "Censorship Watch." *American Libraries*, March 1999, Vol. 30, Issue 3, p. 17, 1p.

James, Helen Foster. "Bullies and Bullying." *Book Links*, February/March 2002, Vol. 11, Issue 4, pp. 41–44, 4p.

Ralston, Jennifer. "*Blubber*." *School Library Journal*, May 2005, Vol. 51, Issue 5, p. 50.

Boys and Sex, Girls and Sex, **Wardell Pomeroy** **(Delacorte, 1968 and 1970)**

Boys and Sex and its counterpart, *Girls and Sex*, are nonfiction books intended for adolescent readers. They were written by Wardell Pomeroy, who participated in and helped to write the Kinsey reports, which looked at interviews done with a large number of adults, discussing their sexual habits and interests. While the

Kinsey reports were largely meant for an adult, educated audience, their findings did help to shape Pomeroy's presentation of ideas regarding sex and desire in these two books. Like other books of the era, such as *Everything You Always Wanted to Know about Sex (But Were Afraid to Ask)* by David Reuben, Pomeroy's book is meant to provide readers with a frank and factual discussion of sexual desires and the biological mechanisms of sexual desire and the human body. The topics are quite wide ranging, covering both normal bodily development through puberty and also taboo topics and "deviant" sexual interests. It also clearly and directly discusses topics like masturbation, which teenagers might be both interested in and also uncomfortable in discussing with adults or in any public forum.

Not surprisingly, the books quickly and consistently faced scrutiny and challenges because of its direct discussion of sexuality. In particular, its impartial discussion of topics like homosexuality and masturbation (the book actually encourages masturbation as healthy and a natural outlet) made it a lightning rod for critics. Both books were quickly challenged regularly. In 2000, a challenge came in Charlotte, North Carolina, with strong concerns that the content of the books would actually encourage young children to explore sexuality before they were ready and to take up sexual practices that parents and other adults might find problematic. Because the book was nonfiction, and because it was presented as scientific and educational, the nature of the battle over this book was quite different than the battles over other books that portrayed or examined human sexuality. Rather than having questions about what might be essential to a plot or a theme, the debate over this book focused entirely on what was appropriate for children to be exposed to.

FURTHER READING

Benoff, Symme J. "*Boys and Sex/Girls and Sex* (Book Review)." *School Library Journal*, December 1981, Vol. 28, Issue 4, p. 72.

Gebhard, Paul H. "In Memoriam: Wardell B. Pomeroy." *Archives of Sexual Behavior*, April 2002, Vol. 31, Issue 2, pp. 155–156, 2p.

Goldstein, Irwin. "Looking at Sexual Behavior 60 Years after Kinsey." *Journal of Sexual Medicine*, October 2010, Vol. 7, Supplement 5, pp. 246–247, 2p.

Brave New World, Aldous Huxley
(Chatto & Windus, 1932)

Brave New World is a science fiction novel examining a number of social issues, from promiscuity to fascism. By the time that Huxley wrote *Brave New World*, he had already established a reputation as an effective writer and a satirist with a keen eye for critiquing systems and structures. The novel is set far into the future

(AD 2540) in London. Within the world, there is a clear social structure that leads people to be shaped (both figuratively and literally) to fit into certain social classes and jobs. The idea of genetic engineering runs throughout the novel, impacting the birthrates, the way that fetuses are prepared for life, and the appearance of people. Children are also educated hypnotically, programming them rather than giving them a chance to ask questions or assert any type of independence or curiosity. In addition to the hypnotic programming, people are fed canned phrases and ideas, much in the way that the masses are in George Orwell's *1984*.

The type of programming done in *Brave New World* very much drives the population to value buying and consuming drugs that allow people to spend their time intoxicated rather than pursuing any genuine social movement or personal development. The population is also kept from performing any meaningful rebellion or progress by the government encouraging casual sex. In fact, if people do not participate in recreational sex and drug use, they are regarded with great suspicion. Although most of the population seems happy with these arrangements, the book focuses on Bernard Marx, a psychologist who finds the state of affairs to be problematic, and who seeks to think beyond the boundaries of the established society.

Bernard goes on a trip to New Mexico to visit a "savage" reservation, where he encounters a woman who had given birth to a child who was fathered by Bernard's boss. As Bernard talks more with the woman, Linda, and her son, John, he discovers that they are treated poorly on the reservation, but they are also not allowed to return to mainstream society. Interestingly, this arrangement has allowed John to have access to things that Bernard had never known, most notably some of Shakespeare's works (in the main society, Shakespeare had been banned for appearing too subversive). Bernard decides to work to bring Linda and John back to London with him. John also develops a romantic interest to Bernard's travelling companion. When Bernard returns to mainstream society with Linda and John, Bernard briefly enjoys a sense of fame and power, seeing his boss have to step down in disgrace when it is revealed that he had fathered a son with Linda. Linda and John both find the society hollow, with John turning from Bernard and Linda remaining intoxicated until she dies.

Shortly after this, John's rage and despair over his mother's death leads him to go berserk, eventually causing a riot. After the riot is quelled, Bernard and John talk to Mustapha Mond, who, in his position in the fascist world government, has access to all of the history that explains how the world came to its present state. Bernard and John learn many of the world's secrets, and John and Mond debate each other over the political system and the value and nature of religion. Eventually, Bernard is exiled. John also wants to be exiled, but he is instead forced to remain part of the mainstream culture. He is watched closely, and he commits a number of strange acts, twice whipping himself. Eventually, John hangs himself, angry with the state he devolved into after being thrust into the mainstream society.

The book had a positive reception overall. It was hailed by some critics as astutely critiquing the hopeful nature of "the Age of Utopias," when many people believed that mankind would correctly solve all of the world's problems, evolving into a perfect society. The society of the book was perceived by some of the characters, Mustapha Mond, for instance, as a perfect world because everyone was correctly matched to their work and also kept satisfied with a mixture of sex and drugs. Readers in the real world also appreciated the imagination and fully realized world of the book's universe. Still, from the first year that it was published, the book was met with challenges and bans. In Ireland, the book was banned in 1932 after being labeled as antireligious and undermining the value of families. By the middle of the 1960s, the book was challenged in America as well. In Maryland, a teacher who lost his job attributed his firing to his use of the book in a class, though the school board never confirmed that as the specific reason for his firing. The book continued to be challenged in America, in India, and in many other parts of the world. In addition to the challenges and bans that the book faced, there were also accusations of plagiarism leveled against Huxley. In addition to accusations that he may have intentionally borrowed a number of ideas and plot points from Polish author Antoni Smuszkiewicz, George Orwell suggested that Huxley may have been strongly influenced by the novel *We*, by Yevgeny Zamyatin. While these accusations have not stopped the book from maintaining a strong position of literary significance for decades, they did cause minor blemishes around the time of the book's first publication.

Despite these blemishes and the challenges the book faced, it has had a deep impact upon the realms of science fiction and political discourse. From later science fiction works like Kurt Vonnegut's *Player Piano* and Ray Bradbury's *Fahrenheit 451* to films like *Demolition Man*, *Brave New World* had been borrowed from or directly referenced. The book has also twice been adapted for both radio and film.

See Also: *1984* and *Fahrenheit 451*.

FURTHER READING

Boone, N. S. "D. H. Lawrence's 'Men Must Work and Women as Well' in Aldous Huxley's *Brave New World*." *Notes and Queries*, March 2014, Vol. 61 (259), Issue 1, pp. 133–135.

Buchanan, Brad. "Oedipus in Dystopia: Freud and Lawrence in Aldous Huxley's *Brave New World*." *Journal of Modern Literature*, Summer 2002, Vol. 25, Issue 3/4, pp. 75–89, 15p.

Congdon, Brad. " 'Community, Identity, Stability': The Scientific Society and the Future of Religion in Aldous Huxley's *Brave New World*." *English Studies in Canada*, September 2011, Vol. 37, Issue 3/4, pp. 83–105, 23p.

Carrie, **Stephen King**
(Doubleday, 1974)

Carrie was Stephen King's first novel to be published. It focuses on teenager Carrie White, a misfit raised by an unbalanced mother. Because White is raised solely by her fundamentalist Christian mother, she is largely unaware of certain topics that her classmates know. This comes out early in the book, when White has her period while showering after gym class. White believes that she is bleeding to death, and her classmates respond by ridiculing her. White's home life offers her no relief. Her mother locks her in the closet for even minor mistakes and transgressions. The gap between Carrie's home life and her school life also leads to tension when the outdated and unbecoming clothing that she is forced to wear leads to her being mercilessly teased by her classmates. During one of the teasing episodes (the one that is related to her menstruation after gym class), a lightbulb explodes above Carrie's head. This is the first suggestion of her telekinetic powers that will become the core of the book's narrative. The conflict over this event leads some of the popular girls to be suspended from school and banned from the prom. One of the popular girls, Sue Snell, takes pity on Carrie and befriends her, encouraging Carrie to attend prom. In the meantime, one of the popular girls convinces her boyfriend to help her humiliate Carrie at the prom. They kill two pigs, taking the pigs' blood to dump onto Carrie. A popular boy, Tommy, agrees to take Carrie to prom, and he begins to be legitimately attracted to her. Unfortunately for Carrie, some of the other popular kids take the pig blood and, when Carrie and Tommy are elected prom king and queen, the popular kids dump the blood on the pair. At this point, Carrie decides to use her telekinetic powers to seek vengeance upon the people who shamed her. She uses her powers to lock the doors to the gym where prom is being held, and she also sets fire to the gym, leaving most of her classmates to be killed. Carrie then returns home, where she confronts her mother. Carrie's mother tells Carrie that she was the product of a rape, and then she stabs Carrie. Carrie uses her powers to stop her mother's heart, and then she seeks out the popular kids who dumped pig's blood on her. After continuing to terrorize the town, Carrie kills the popular kids, then drops dead from blood loss. The book closes with first Susan Snell reflecting upon events, recognizing the unfortunate nature of things and then a letter from a mother whose daughter is developing telekinetic powers not unlike that of Carrie.

King's book tapped a nerve with many readers who had felt like outsiders in high school. Although the hardcover sold modestly, the paperback very quickly sold one million copies. It also was made into a film in 1976, earning two Academy Award nominations. In 1999, a sequel was filmed, though it met with much less critical acclaim than the original. There have also been stage adaptations of varying levels of success.

The many challenges met by *Carrie* have been of varied logic and viewpoint. As early as 1975, the book was challenged for being considered "trash," a vague and hard to argue point. Later, the book was challenged for a number of reasons, particularly for the assumption that the murder of the pigs for their blood had an undercurrent of satanic beliefs as well as the assumption that the negative portrayal of Carrie's mother undercut Christian belief and practice in a general way.

King has openly discussed the nature of literature and challenges, acknowledging that there are some texts (his own and others, such as Bret Easton Ellis's *American Psycho*) that are simply inappropriate for younger readers. And yet, King has also maintained that if one person or group of people cannot handle a book, that does not automatically mean that all readers should have the book removed from their access. For *Carrie* in particular, the book's themes and literal content (from the violence of the climax to some of the discussions of menstruation and sexual desire) were seen by King as appropriate for adult readers and not worthy of outright banning. That said, some readers have argued that the themes of feeling like an outsider and being bullied actually make it a good text for adolescents to read. Of course, the violent nature of the conclusion makes it a very controversial text.

See Also: *Christine*, *Cujo*, and *It*.

FURTHER READING

Dollard, Peter. "The Science of Stephen King: From *Carrie* to *Cell*, the Terrifying Truth behind the Horror Master's Fiction." *Library Journal*, September 15, 2007, Vol. 132, Issue 15, p. 61.

Dymond, Erica Joan. "An Examination of the Use of Gendered Language in Stephen King's *Carrie*." *Explicator*, 2013, Vol. 71, Issue 2, pp. 94–98, 5p.

King, Stephen. "The Book Banners: Adventure in Censorship Is Stranger than Fiction." http://stephenking.com/library/essay/book-banners:_adventure_in_censorship_is _stranger_than_fiction_the.html.

Korinna, Csetényi. "Fairy Tales in Stephen King's *Carrie*." *Gender Studies*, 2008, Vol. 1, Issue 7, pp. 165–170.

Christine, **Stephen King**
(Viking, 1983)

Christine is a horror novel written after Stephen King had already become a significant figure in popular American writing. The novel follows the strange relationship between teenager Arnie Cunningham and a vintage car, "Christine." Arnie buys the car for a low price from an elderly man. Arnie's plan is to fix the car up, but

Arnie's friend, Dennis, has an eerie feeling about the car. As Arnie works on Christine, he becomes aloof from Dennis, but Arnie also takes on a greater level of confidence than he had experienced prior to working on Christine. In addition to a greater level of confidence, Arnie seems to become in better physical shape as he repairs Christine, despite the fact that he has not radically changed his eating or exercise routines. Similarly, some of the repairs that Christine experiences seem to go unusually easily for someone of Arnie's experience level. When the elderly man who sold Christine to Arnie dies, his brother speaks to Arnie's friend Dennis. Dennis finds out that Christine's former owner had many sadistic tendencies, and there were a number of disturbing events associated with Christine, perhaps most notably that his daughter died in Christine, choking on a hamburger, and his wife had used Christine to commit suicide, dying of carbon monoxide poisoning. Given this backstory and the burgeoning relationship between Arnie and Will Darnell, a garage owner who is believed to be responsible for running an illegal business, Dennis becomes worried for his friend. During this time, a new girl, Leigh, moves into the town and strikes up a relationship with Arnie, to everyone's surprise. Although things go well in the early going, the relationship eventually sours. When Leigh and Arnie are eating hamburgers in Christine, she begins to choke, recalling the death of the original owner's daughter. Rather than correctly helping her, Arnie pounds Leigh on the back, which actually brings her closer to death. After the event, Leigh feels that Christine was somehow responsible for the choking and Arnie's mistaken course of action. As suspicion toward Christine increases, Arnie's mother tells him that he may no longer keep Christine at their home. In an effort to prevent a major fight, Arnie's father buys a pass for Arnie to keep Christine at the airport's long-term parking lot. While Christine is parked there, bullies from school break into the lot and do serious damage to Christine. Arnie is furious, and he tries to take Christine to Will Darnell's repair lot. Inexplicably, Christine repairs herself, though as Arnie was pushing Christine, he strained his back, leaving him wearing a back brace just like the one worn by Christine's original owner when Arnie bought the car. Shortly after these events, the bullies die from injuries at the hands of a car. Although there is no evidence tying Christine to the accidents and although Arnie can produce alibis for the times that each of the crimes were committed, both a police detective and also Dennis are suspicious of Christine. Dennis and Leigh look further into the deaths, and, during the time that the pair look into this, they become romantically involved. After both Will Darnell and the police detective investigating the car-related deaths also die, Leigh and Dennis realize that they are in serious danger. They go to the repair yard where Arnie had fixed Christine, and Christine appears. The pair eventually destroy the car, though, as they do so, they recognize the spirit of the original owner, who had been possessing the car and leading it to commit the crimes. The book ends four years after the core events of the book. Dennis and Leigh have parted ways, and Dennis finds a newspaper story of a freak car accident that took the life of the last of the bullies. Dennis speculates that Christine might well have repaired or rebuilt herself, and he may be hunted soon.

The book was very successful commercially, spawning a film adaptation the same year that the book was released. Like the book, the film was commercially successful too. Not surprisingly, the book was challenged in a number of places. In Alabama, Montana, and Iowa, the book was challenged on the basis of having graphic portrayals of sex. In other places, the book was challenged for containing obscene language. In Illinois and North Dakota, *Christine* was one of several of King's books receiving challenges (nine books in North Dakota and all of King's novels in Bluford, Illinois). Though the challenges were successful in places, the easy availability of King's work in bookstores and through parents or older siblings has made it difficult for groups to fully keep the book out of the hands of minors. In fact, some argue that the moves to keep King's books out of schools might be one of the driving factors in King's continued popularity among young adult readers. Interestingly, the occult material regarding a car possessed by a ghost was not frequently cited as a reason for challenging the book. Instead, the focus was more typically upon the actions and words that could be realistically imitated by readers. While *Christine* was not one of the major works of King's career, it definitely contributed to his reputation as both a significant American cultural figure and also as a target for bans and challenges from school districts and parent groups across the country.

See Also: *Carrie*, *Cujo*, and *It*.

FURTHER READING

Kelso, Sylvia. "Take Me for a Ride in Your Man-Eater: Gynophobia in Stephen King's *Christine*." *Paradoxa: Studies in World Literary Genres*, 1996, Vol. 2, Issue 2, pp. 263–275.

Power, Brenda Miller, Jeffrey D. Wilhelm, and Kelly Chandler. *Reading Stephen King: Issues of Censorship, Student Choice and Popular Literature*. New York, NY: National Council of Teachers of English, 1997, p. 246.

Schopp, Andrew. "From Misogyny to Homophobia and Back Again: The Play of Erotic Triangles in Stephen King's *Christine*." *Extrapolation: A Journal of Science Fiction and Fantasy*, Spring 1997, Vol. 38, Issue 1, pp. 66–78.

Cujo, Stephen King
(Viking, 1981)

Cujo is one of Stephen King's horror novels to be set in the fictional town of Castle Rock, Maine. The book follows two families, the Trentons, who have moved from New York to Castle Rock, and the Cambers. The Trenton family is facing difficulties, with the father, Vic, discovering that his wife, Donna, had recently had an affair. Adding to the tension, Vic's business is struggling. In an effort to help his family financially, Vic is forced to travel out of town for a time, leaving Donna alone with their son, Tad. The Cambers are also struggling as a family, with the father, Joe, being abusive to both his wife, Charity, and his son, Brett. When Charity wins a small lottery prize, both parents develop separate plans for how to spend the money. During this time, the Cambers's dog, Cujo, is bitten by a rabid bat. Cujo develops rabies himself, turning violent and killing first one of the Cambers's neighbor and then Joe himself. This was particularly shocking to the family, because Cujo had previously been known for being a well-behaved, friendly dog. Donna and Tad Trenton take their car to the Cambers for repairs, not knowing that Cujo is rabid. Charity and Brett are out of town, leaving nobody in the home to save Donna and Tad. When the pair arrive at the Cambers home, the car breaks down. While Donna searches for Joe, she finds Cujo. Recognizing that something is wrong, Donna runs back to her car and locks herself and Tad in. The situation worsens as the heat in the car's interior rises. Donna makes an attempt to escape, but she is bitten twice by Cujo before returning to the inside of the car. In the meantime, Vic has tried calling his home a number of times, never hearing an answer. He panics and returns to Castle Rock, also alerting the police. The police assume that Donna's former lover had kidnapped her and Tad. The one officer who does go to the Cambers home is also killed by Cujo. Donna realizes that her son will die from the heat of the car if she does not get them out, so she exits the car and begins to fight Cujo, eventually killing him. Unfortunately, by the time that she finishes Cujo off, Tad has died. The book then jumps ahead in time, giving an update on both families. Despite the affair and the loss of their child, the Trentons have reconciled and are still together, with Donna having successfully completed treatment for rabies. Charity has given Brett another dog, and the families are relatively happy.

Cujo stands out from many of King's works in that the monstrous presence is relatively realistic. Rather than a demonic presence or a supernatural threat, the rabid dog represents a danger that could exist. The book came after King had broken through into national prominence with books like *Carrie*. Still, it was a significant work for him, receiving the British Fantasy Award in 1982 and being made into a film in 1983. Another distinction for *Cujo* is that it reached the highest ranking of King's works on the American Library Association's list of "Most Challenged Books." Interestingly, the violence within the book was often not listed as a reason for its being challenged or banned, and it was never the sole reason. While some places did reference the violence as a contributing factor (Sparta, Illinois, and Durand, Wisconsin, for instance), the most frequently cited reasons for its challenge was its vulgar language and obscene references to sex. The discussion of Donna's affair, in particular, was the grounds for many people's objections.

That said, there were also some challenges that did not seem to give a clear rationale for objections that were based in specific details within the book. In Bismarck, North Dakota, the book was challenged as part of eight works by King that were being attacked for generally not being "age appropriate." Even more striking, in Prineville, Oregon, parents and the principal threw the book in the garbage, and one parent even wanted all horror books removed from the library. Some challenges toward the book were successful. In Peru, Indiana, for instance, the book was banned from schools. However, other places had mixed success with their challenges. Often, the book was placed in a "restricted" section in schools rather than outright banned. In other areas, like South Portland, Maine, the book was challenged, but ultimately kept in schools.

While the book is not necessarily seen by many as one of King's best works, it did include many hallmarks of King's works. Like many of his books, the personal anxieties and struggles of the characters (Donna's affair, Joe's abusive nature, and Vic's struggles with his business) take up much of the narrative, sometimes moving away from the central threat itself. In addition, the portrayal of working-class characters and examination of sexual lives and desires of the characters are typical of King's books. The book is also representative of King's works in that it was met with enthusiasm by many readers and a great degree of suspicion and resistance from teachers, administrators, and parents.

See Also: *Carrie*, *Christine*, and *The Dead Zone*.

FURTHER READING

Pascal, Sylvia, and Ron Brown. "*Cujo* (Book Review)." *School Library Journal*, October 1981, Vol. 28, Issue 2, p. 162.
Rozen, Leah. "Spooked by Stephen King." *People*, December 3, 2007, Vol. 68, Issue 23, p. 32.
Stanton, Ryan. "*Cujo*." *Teen Ink*, November 2012, Vol. 24, Issue 3, p. 31.

A Day No Pigs Would Die, **Robert Newton Peck**
(Alfred A. Knopf, 1972)

A Day No Pigs Would Die gives a clear and descriptive discussion of farm life and the issues related to it for a generation of Americans. The book focuses heavily on the relationship between the protagonist, his parents, and one of the family's pigs. In particular, the protagonist discusses his views on his relationship to a particular pig over the course of the novel. As a pig farmer, the father of the protagonist should have a strong impact upon that son's view of livestock and how the family supports itself. In many ways, the protagonist's father does have that role, but the protagonist also struggles in his willingness to adhere to the demands of farm life. In some sections of the book, the narrator is particularly expressive about the pig's rights to live and the trauma of the character's loss of the pig. In the end, the protagonist not only witnesses but also assists in the slaughter of his pig. There are a number of more humorous, episodic components of the narrative, but the core story of the protagonist and his pig provides the bulk of the book's emotional weight. It also serves as the backbone for the coming-of-age story.

Interestingly, it is not necessarily the case that the book was challenged or rejected because of the using of the pig for meat. There were some parents who felt that the book's depiction of the pig's slaughter was graphic, but many readers also agreed that the portrayal was accurate and detailed in a way that reflected Peck's own childhood experiences. Instead of the slaughter, most of the challenges revolved around the depiction of a scene in the book in which the protagonist's pig was forced to mate with another pig. Essentially a rape scene, the portrayal was seen by many as too troubling to be appropriate for younger readers.

More largely, *A Day No Pigs Would Die* taps into some fundamental concerns for young people. The issues of growing up, making moral decisions about the relation between animals and humans, and deciding to submit to or rebel against traditions have led some readers and parents to be uncomfortable discussing the book and its content. Still, its capturing of a particular time and place makes it a favorite of many readers.

FURTHER READING

Brownson, Ann. "A Day No Pigs Would Die." *School Library Journal*, April 2011, Vol. 57, Issue 4, p. 64.

Lucie-Nietzke, Teresa J. "As Simple as Shaker Life: Teaching Metaphor in *A Day No Pigs Would Die.*" *Clearing House*, July/August 1991, Vol. 64, Issue 6, pp. 399–400, 2p.

Morrell, Judy. "Pinkie's Tale: An Appreciate Response to *A Day No Pigs Would Die.*" *Virginia English Bulletin*, Winter 1986, Vol. 36, Issue 2, pp. 21–26.

Deenie, Judy Blume
(Bradbury Press, 1973)

Deenie is a young adult novel written by Judy Blume. The book follows the title character, a thirteen-year-old girl who feels pressured to become a model by her mother. This pressure stands in stark contrast to what her sister faces in that their mother insists that the sister, Helen, keep up her grades so that she can become a doctor or a lawyer. Their mother's desire for Deenie to become a model finds a challenge when Deenie is diagnosed with scoliosis, meaning that she has to wear a body brace to correct her posture. Tensions continue to mount as Helen strikes up a romantic relationship with Joe, a boy who works at the gas station owned by Helen and Deenie's family. Their mother, who was concerned that Joe could be a distraction for Helen, told her that Deenie's medical bills were the reason that the family had to fire Joe. This leads Deenie to worry that Helen will approach her with resentment, but when the topic comes up, Helen tells Deenie that the problem is their mother, not Deenie, and the two deepen their sisterly bond. The subject of the brace comes up regularly over the course of the book, with Deenie worried that it will make boys not like her and, initially, being concerned about the impact that it will have upon her future modeling career. It also leads Deenie to form friendships with other kids who are perceived as having differences, such as the girl who suffers from a skin condition and is therefore ostracized from other kids. As the book progresses, Deenie comes to terms with having to wear the brace, even deciding that she would prefer to be an orthopedist rather than a model, much to the chagrin of her mother. Near the end of the book, Deenie is invited to a party at another girl's house. She wants to go without her brace so that she can wear a nice dress. While her mother gives her permission, her father says that it would not be right, because if they let her take off her brace for this party, then Deenie will regularly look for excuses to not wear it, and she will not get the support that she regularly needs for the brace. Deenie initially brings the dress that she wants to wear to the party in a separate bag, intending to take off her brace and put on the dress once she makes it to the party, but, when she arrives, she has a change of heart and continues to wear the brace for the duration of the party.

At the time of *Deenie*'s publication, Blume had already begun to establish herself as a young adult author, having written works like *Are You There, God? It's Me, Margaret* and *Tales of a Fourth Grade Nothing*. *Deenie* continued her success, selling well and earning praise from critics. In particular, it was one of the first young adult books to take on a chronic condition like scoliosis, giving some readers exposure to the disease and giving children with that or similar conditions a character to look to as they navigated issues of social pressure and identity in their own lives.

As with many of Blume's other books, *Deenie* received challenges a number of times. The challenges came quickly after the book's publication, and they have not subsided since. In fact, the book was in the top fifty "Most Challenged Books" list between the years of 1990 and 2000 as compiled by the American Library Association. The key passages that are cited during the challenges are ones that deal with masturbation and sexual desire. While the mentions of actual masturbation are brief compared to the larger arc of the book, there is a longer scene where a physical education teacher led the girls in class in a discussion of masturbation and menstruation. While some readers applauded what they saw as a realistic portrayal of the concerns and desires of many teenage girls, the discussions were uncommon for the era in which Blume was publishing. While these challenges have not led to widespread banning of the book, they have added to Blume's reputation as a somewhat controversial author within the world of young adult writing. Despite these challenges and controversies, Blume remains a beloved figure for many, and her books continue to be read regularly.

See Also: *Are You There, God? It's Me, Margaret* and *Blubber.*

FURTHER READING

Editors. "Pick Up the Book." *Writing*, September 2004, Vol. 27, Issue 1, p. 4.

Flood, Sarah. "Deenie." *School Library Journal*, August 2011, Vol. 57, Issue 8, p. 54.

Staff. "ACLU Appeals *Deenie* Ban." *School Library Journal*, December 1985, Vol. 32, Issue 4, pp. 11–12, 2p.

Detour for Emmy, **Marilyn Reynolds**
(Morning Glory Press, 1993)

Detour for Emmy is a novel based on a true story about a young girl who becomes pregnant. Emmy, the protagonist, had been successful in middle school, both academically and socially. When she enters high school, she finds herself struggling more than she had in previous years. But, with the support of her two close friends, Emmy does begin to manage the transition from middle school to high school. As part of this transition, Emmy begins dating, and she becomes sexually active. This leads to Emmy's unplanned pregnancy. Emmy carries the child to term, and she begins to work through high school once more, this time trying to balance parenthood with the other challenges and pressures of teenage life. The book shows Emmy navigating many of the hurdles that would have been realistic for a single, teenaged mother of her era. Issues like having a relatively limited social life to balancing her schedule make up the book's core narrative.

Not surprisingly, *Detour for Emmy* was a polarizing book. Proponents of the novel claimed that the book took on a major issue and presented it in an even-handed, realistic way, neither demonizing nor lionizing the protagonist. Challengers of the book claimed that it exposed young readers to too direct discussions of sexual activity and that it might introduce ideas to readers that they might not otherwise explore. In particular, many of the groups advocating for the removal of the book felt that having the protagonist work through school validated or even celebrated teen pregnancy.

The book received challenges in various places, most notably in Illinois and Arizona, where it was removed from schools. The basis of the book in real-life events also made it a bit of a lightning rod, with some readers questioning how faithful the book was to real-life events and others expressing concern over whether or not the book would be exploitative, taking advantage of a young girl's struggles for publishing success. Still, the book received high praise from a number of groups for its careful treatment of difficult material (the author was a teacher, and many readers felt that this brought a level of authenticity and weight to its portrayal of high school life). While some of the discussions and presentations of stereotypes and stigmas toward teen pregnancies might seem a bit outdated for readers of later generations, the book remains an important text, bringing attention to the growing issue of young women trying to care for a child while making it through high school.

FURTHER READING

"Censorship Watch." *American Libraries*, April 2000, Vol. 31, Issue 4, p. 21, 1p.

Roback, Diane, and Elizabeth Devereaux. "Detour for Emmy." *Publishers Weekly*, June 28, 1993, Vol. 240, Issue 26, p. 79.

Smith, Alice Casey. "Book Review: Junior High Up." *School Library Journal*, July 1993, Vol. 39, Issue 7, p. 102.

The Diary of Anne Frank, Anne Frank
(Contact Publishing, 1947)

The Diary of Anne Frank, also called *The Diary of a Young Girl*, is comprised of the writings of a Jewish girl hiding with her family and a few other people during the Nazi occupation of the Netherlands. The subject of the writings ranges from the historical events impacting the lives of Anne Frank and her family to personal observations about the nature of justice, love, and other concepts. The diary is less a series of chronological entries than it is a collection of letters addressed to "Kitty," her name for her diary. For most of the time of Anne Frank and her family's hiding, she was with her mother, her father, her sister Margot, a business associate of Anne's father, and the associate's wife and son along with another man, Mr. Dussel. The book covers the time from when Anne turns thirteen to the end of her life at age fifteen. Anne discusses how the inhabitants of the hiding place (the attic of a house) listen to the radio, hoping to get news of the war and the Nazi occupation. She also discusses her relationships with all of the inhabitants, telling of how she feels very close to her father, but she does not get along with her mother, and she generally does not get along with the other adults. Part of the tension comes from the lack of privacy and freedom within the small space that they all must share. Anne also regularly discussed her feelings of loneliness, and she begins to develop a crush on the boy, Peter, though things fizzle after Anne's father tells her that it is not a good idea to pursue a relationship with him. The final entry of the diary ends in a relatively plain fashion, as Anne did not know at the time of its writing that it would be her last one. Shortly after she wrote the entry, the inhabitants of the attic were betrayed, and they were taken by the Nazis, with Anne's father Otto being the only one to survive the Holocaust.

After the end of the war, Otto Frank was able to find the diary, and, after reading it, he wanted to honor his daughter by seeing it published. The book was first published in Amsterdam after Otto had circulated a transcription among friends. The first draft had been edited, removing some discussion of Anne's feelings for Peter and her ponderings about sexuality and desire. In 1950, efforts began to translate the book into English, and, in 1952, the book was published, this edition with the previously censored portions now restored as part of the book. The book was a tremendous success, not only becoming a bestseller but also being hailed as a tremendously important record of a significant and disturbing part of the world's history as showcased by the fact that it has been translated into over sixty different languages. It has also been adapted in a number of forms. *The Diary of Anne Frank* has become a successful play as well as a film for which Shelley Winters received an Academy Award for Best Supporting Actress.

Despite these accolades and positive receptions, the book has met with a large variety of challenges and obstacles. Some groups claiming that the Holocaust was faked or exaggerated have challenged the book's authenticity. However, in 1980, the Netherlands Institute for War Documentation began a significant and extensive examination of the original manuscript. After a good deal of study, the institute concluded that the book was indeed an authentic text, matching handwriting from it to other writings known to be by Anne Frank and dating the paper to the time of the book's writing according to Anne's records. The book has also been vandalized in Tokyo, Japan, though the responsible party was declared mentally unstable rather than motivated purely by anti-Semitism.

In 2010, schools in Culpeper County, Virginia, declared that the book contained too much overt sexual content and that the portions of the diary in which Anne Frank discusses her feelings about her mother were too unsettling for young readers. This was in the updated version containing the entire text of the diaries rather than the edited version first published by Anne Frank's father. The school system decided that the library would keep copies of the full version, but the original, edited version would be used in the classroom. There have been at least a half dozen challenges to the book, typically with similar results, the book being recognized as a substantial enough historical record that its cultural and social significance outweighs concerns about discussions of sexuality. Still, the book remains one of the most widely read and taught texts around the world.

FURTHER READING

Ivry, Benjamin. "Will the Real Anne Frank Please Stand Up?" *American Theatre*, January 1998, Vol. 15, Issue 1, pp. 42–45, 4p.

Kuitert, Lisa. "The Publication of Anne Frank's Diary." *Quaerendo*, Spring 2010, Vol. 40, Issue 1, pp. 50–65, 16p.

Larson, Thomas. " 'In Spite of Everything': The Definitive Indefinite Anne Frank." *Antioch Review*, Winter 2000, Vol. 58, Issue 1, pp. 40–54, 15p.

The Earth, My Butt, and Other Big Round Things, Carolyn Mackler
(Candlewick Press, 2003)

The Earth, My Butt, and Other Big Round Things is a young adult novel that follows the body insecurities of a young woman in New York. The protagonist is Ginny Shreves, a sophomore attending a private school in Manhattan, New York. Although she has a casual boyfriend, "Froggy," she still feels insecure about her self-image, not wanting anyone to see what she feels is her fat body. As the book progresses, Ginny decides that she wants her relationship to Froggy to become more serious. Ginny's parents do not help matters, as her father continually praises thin women for their looks. Her mother, a psychologist who works with adolescents, also worsens matters by consistently asking Ginny about her weight and her self-image. Ginny loses a partner in her frustration with her parents when her sister, Anais, joins the Peace Corps to get out from under the watch of their parents, their mother in particular. Her relationship with her family is further complicated when her brother, whom she held in very high regard, is expelled from his university after he is convicted of date rape. Amidst all of the familial upheaval, Ginny decides to strike out on her own, secretly buying a ticket to Seattle to visit a friend. When she returns, Ginny continues her efforts to feel independent and strong, changing her hair color and getting piercings. As she feels better about herself, Ginny finds new friends and takes up kickboxing. In the end, Ginny comes to understand that she does not need to be obsessed with her looks, because focusing on her inner life will bring her a greater level of satisfaction and peace.

Critical reaction to the book was varied. Some critics gave it favorable reviews for its ability to catch some of the real anxieties of teens, but others also said that the book left too many strands incomplete, not fully exploring the storylines centered around Ginny's siblings, for instance. Beyond those technical concerns, the book received much support for giving a voice to young women who might feel insecure about their bodies.

While the book has some positive responses, it has also led to challenges. In 2006, the superintendent of the Carroll County schools in Maryland had the book removed from schools. After librarians, students, and even the book's publisher objected, the superintendent allowed the book to be put back in the high school library but did not change his mind about the middle school libraries, citing the book's use of profanity and discussion of adolescent sexuality. The book was again challenged in 2010, though this time it was not removed at all. Despite these challenges, the book has become a well-received entry in Mackler's larger body of young adult work.

FURTHER READING

Gepson, Lolly. "Best Friend Next Door." *Booklist*, September 1, 2015, Vol. 112, Issue 1, p. 143.

Masurat, Anastasia. "Why Not?" *Bitch Magazine: Feminist Response to Pop Culture*, Fall 2008, Vol. 12, Issue 41, pp. 66–71, 6p.

Moore, Emily. "Infinite in Between." *School Library Journal*, September 2015, Vol. 61, Issue 9, pp. 156–160, 5p.

Earth's Children Series, Jean M. Auel
(Crown, 1980–2011)

Set in Europe approximately 30,000 years prior to the present day, the Earth's Children series examines the interactions and rivalries between Cro-Magnons and Neanderthals. The books follow Ayla, a Cro-Magnon girl who is taken in by a family of Neanderthals after she is orphaned. The series of novels follow Ayla and her partner Jondalar (along with the associated family members) as they continue their travels over the land that will eventually become Europe. One of the interesting things that comes from this narrative is that the journey to find a new geographical location is mirrored by the journey to self-discovery, where the characters reach new understandings of themselves, the land that they cover, and new understandings of their species designations. In particular, the interbreeding that occurs within the core narrative arc forms a major and striking part of the overall story of the series. The prospect of miscegenation, though, was not the only problem. Critics often cited the clear depictions of sex as problematic. The books also examined differing cosmologies, often showing relationships to the land and the animals that more closely fit Wiccan or neo-pagan views of the universe than Christian views. This is not to say that the books ever explicitly promoted any given cosmology or set of beliefs, but even the lack of a clear valuing of Christianity seemed daring at the time of the series' first publication. Still, the series was lauded by many as being relatively faithful to discoveries about human development and interspecies breeding.

While the books are hailed by many readers, the treatment of sexuality raised eyebrows for many critics. Some of the objections were rooted in the level of detail involved in the portrayal of sex acts within the book. In 1992, for instance, *Clan of the Cave Bear* was banned from a middle school in Eugene, Oregon, for its portrayal of a rape. Not every challenge was successful, though. In 1993, *Cave Bear* was challenged in a school in Sunnyville, California, but it was retained.

Although the series tends to have more of a cult following than a large, mainstream readership, it has managed to maintain a consistent readership for decades, earning it a significant spot in American literature.

FURTHER READING

Bethune, Brian. "Sex and the Stone Age Woman." *Maclean's*, April 18, 2011, Vol. 124, Issue 14, p. 86.

Lewis, Glenn. "Auel's Epic Saga Back at Last." *Library Journal*, February 15, 2002, Vol. 127, Issue 3, pp. 34–36, 3p.

Wilcox, Clyde. "The Not-So Failed Feminism of Jean Auel." *Journal of Popular Culture*, Winter 1994, Vol. 28, Issue 3, pp. 63–70.

Face on the Milk Carton,
Caroline B. Cooney
(Bantam Doubleday Dell, 1990)

Face on the Milk Carton is a young adult book that is part of the Janie Johnson series. The core character, Janie, sees herself on the side of one of her friend's milk cartons. The picture of her is from when she was younger, implying that she is the victim of kidnapping. As she looks closer, this is confirmed by information on the side of the milk carton claiming that she was kidnapped in New Jersey when she was three years old. While Janie initially disregards this information, she begins to have flashbacks that would correlate to a kidnapping. Although she believes that her parents, Mr. and Mrs. Johnson, are good people, she also begins to have memories of another woman and other children that could be part of another life. Janie becomes curious, so she looks around the house to try to find evidence of a life before her parents. She does find papers with another name, Hannah Javensen, and she also finds the dress that the girl on the side of the milk carton was wearing. Janie goes to Mr. and Mrs. Johnson, asking who she really is. They tell Janie that she is actually their granddaughter and that their actual daughter had become pregnant with Janie after falling in with a cult and being married to another member of the cult. Mr. and Mrs. Johnson tell Janie that they were afraid for Janie's safety if they stayed around Hannah, so they left the area and changed their last name to avoid being found. Janie does a bit of research to find out about the kidnapping incident. While Janie does become skeptical of Mr. and Mrs. Johnson's story, she still feels that they have been good to her, and she forgives them for their actions. However, she still wants to go with her boyfriend to New Jersey (the area from which she was kidnapped) to see the family that she was taken from. When they arrive at New Jersey, they find that the family who lost the child, and they see that the members of the family look much more like Janie than either of the Johnsons do. Janie writes a letter to the family in New Jersey, but she decides not to mail it. However, after the letter goes missing, Janie wonders if her boyfriend has dropped it in the mail for her. She asks Mr. and Mrs. Johnson what she should do, admitting that she had done some looking into her family. After some discussion, Mr. and Mrs. Johnson come to realize that their daughter, Hannah, was the one to kidnap Janie. Instead of being Mr. and Mrs. Johnson's granddaughter, Janie was actually the child of the family in New Jersey. In the end, Mrs. Johnson ends up calling the family in New Jersey.

The book received some positive reviews. It also sold well, leading to a series, following Janie as she goes to live with her biological parents and eventually goes to college. It also was adapted into a made-for-television film in 1995. The book generally received positive reviews, with many critics describing it as entertaining and having an exciting storyline. Some readers also praised the book for having a story that showed a young character searching for the truth in the face of numerous challenges. It also won a number of honors, including several state-based awards like the Iowa Teen Award and the Indiana Young Hoosier Book Award, and it was also nominated for various other awards.

The book did receive challenges for a number of reasons. One of the most common reasons was that it contained material that was not age appropriate, referring partially to the issue of cults and also to the general distrust of adults, which could lead children to be rebellious. Interestingly, there were some complaints toward the book that Janie was a bad role model for children because she seemed emotionally unstable, frequently crying and upset. The initial challenge to the book, though, came from complaints that the book contained sexually explicit material. Although the specifics of these sections were not articulated in the challenge, there was a sense that interactions between Janie and her boyfriend as well as references to Hannah and her life in the cult were the source of concern for the challenging parties. The book had been removed in some cases, though certainly not in all of them. Still, the book has continued to receive a number of challenges, making it onto the one hundred "Most Challenged Books" from 1990 to 1999 and from 2000 to 2009 lists from the American Library Association. Author Cooney herself did not fight or object to the challenges. Instead, her public statements were that the challenges themselves constituted free speech and, although she disagreed with the sentiment behind the challenges, she did not want to work to stop them. The success of the series has led it to be widely read, and many readers were not even aware that the book had been challenged.

FURTHER READING

Hixon, Tara. "No Such Person." *School Library Journal*, October 2015, Vol. 61, Issue 10, pp. 53–54, 2p.

LeMerise, Alissa. "They Never Came Back." *School Library Journal*, May 2012, Vol. 58, Issue 5, pp. 60–61, 2p.

Walker, Meghan. "The Face on the Milk Carton." *Teen Ink*, January 2011, Vol. 22, Issue 5, p. 31.

Fade, Robert Cormier
(Dell, 1988)

Fade is a young adult novel following a young boy who is able to become invisible. The novel is set in 1938 in a small town in Massachusetts. The main character, Paul, is the son of a factory worker. Paul feels insignificant until he discovers his ability. Even once he finds that he can turn himself invisible, he initially uses his ability to commit small actions, such as spying on his Aunt Rosanna, whose promiscuity fascinates Paul. His following of her takes a significant turn when he begins to witness some of the criminal activity that her lover takes part in. The criminal activity becomes even more strongly pronounced when the workers at the town's factory (which includes Paul's father among its employees) go on strike, increasing tension and the potential for violence in the town. As Paul continues to follow around his family members, he makes a number of discoveries that unnerve him. Even his discoveries are something that Paul can largely put behind him (even becoming a successful writer) until he discovers that his nephew, Ozzie, can also fade. Ozzie uses his power to do more than spy, seeking vengeance after being abused. Paul tries to balance confronting and consoling Ozzie, not wanting their shared gift to enable evil. All of this is treated largely as factual or real until the book's final section, in which another relative of Paul, Susan, who is an aspiring writer, discovers Paul's manuscript. Knowing that he was a writer, Susan suspects that this is a story, but something about the overlaps between Paul's life and the events makes her also wonder if it could be a memoir or confession on Paul's part. This third part of the book gives the novel ambiguity, making the disturbing events of the first two questionable in the sense that they may or may not have occurred even within the reality of the novel. Ultimately, the assumption is left up to the reader to make, regardless of Susan's opinions.

Not surprisingly, the themes of incest and violence made the book a target for many groups. In Fairfax County, Oklahoma, in particular, there was a significant struggle over the book's place in the county library. After the group Parents against Bad Books in Schools (PABBIS) challenged a number of books in schools and libraries, the Fairfax County Providence District Supervisor was reported to have said that if some books were banned (and he included *Fade* in this list), then sections of the Bible should also be banned, because the Bible also contains scenes of violence and sexual activity (incest in particular). PABBIS responded by blasting the District Supervisor publically, claiming that scenes of oral sex between an adult man and a thirteen-year-old girl constituted child pornography. They also repeatedly accused the District Supervisor and the schools in general of supporting "smut." The attempt to remove *Fade* from shelves resulted in it being transferred from young reading sections to adult sections, but it did not generally result in permanent removal from libraries.

FURTHER READING

Bodart, Joni Richards. "Some Banned Books worth Talking About." *Book Report*, March/April 1993, Vol. 11, Issue 5, p. 28.

Lees, Cynthia. "In Search of an Invisible Culture in David Plante's *American Ghosts* and Robert Cormier's *Fade*." *American Review of Canadian Studies*, June 2014, Vol. 44, Issue 2, pp. 234–248, 15p.

Stewart, Susan. "In the Ellison Tradition: In/Visible Bodies of Adolescent and YA Fiction." *Children's Literature in Education*, September 2009, Vol. 40, Issue 3, pp. 180–196, 17p.

The Higher Power of Lucky, Susan Patron
(Simon & Schuster, 2006)

The Higher Power of Lucky is a popular children's book. It follows Lucky, a ten-year-old girl, whose mother has been electrocuted. After her mother's death, Lucky's father has called upon a former wife, who currently lives in France, to come to the small town in California to help raise Lucky. Lucky likes her new caretaker, Brigitte, but she is concerned that Brigitte will dislike living in a small town and will leave her. This fear comes to a head when Lucky sees Brigitte's suitcase and passport out, leading her to believe that Brigitte is, indeed, leaving. Lucky decides that she will leave before Brigitte can, and she takes her dog with her, leaving during a storm to help hide her departure. On her way, she finds her friend, Miles, who has injured himself during the storm. They find a place to hide safely during the storm, but they are found by a third friend, Lincoln. Lincoln tells them that the whole town is searching for them. The townspeople find Lucky, Miles, and Lincoln, and Lucky has a type of memorial service for her mother, scattering her ashes. After Lucky returns home, Brigitte tells her that she needed her passport as a type of identification so that she could legally adopt Lucky. In addition, she tells her that she plans to open a restaurant in town, helping Lucky to feel happy and secure.

The book was well received, achieving commercial success and leading to multiple sequels. It also was met with positive critical reviews, even winning a Newberry Award Medal. Although Susan Patron had success prior to *The Higher Power of Lucky*, it did help to cement her career as a successful children's author.

Despite a relatively benign storyline, the book had sparked a significant and lasting controversy. The character Lucky has a habit of overhearing things and misunderstanding what they mean (the title comes from Lucky hearing the phrase "higher power" at a twelve-step meeting in her town and believing that she needs to search for it). Early in the book, Lucky overhears the word "scrotum." This led a number of libraries and schools to ban the book outright for its use of a term referring to genitalia. The author, Susan Patron, defended the use of the word, and multiple other children's authors also came to her defense. The publisher, Simon & Schuster, posted a video on their website with an interview between the author and another author. Accompanying the video was a statement indicating that the book had merit and, despite the use of the word "scrotum," it ultimately upheld family and small-town values. As with several challenged books, the attention garnered over the controversy may have actually helped the book's sales, giving it a high level of attention.

FURTHER READING

Oleck, Joan. "The Higher Power of Patron." *School Library Journal*, March 2007, Vol. 53, Issue 3, pp. 42–45, 4p.

Perkins, Mitali. "No Place like Home." *School Library Journal*, Spring 2007 Curriculum Connections, Vol. 53, Issue 4, pp. 14–17, 4p.

Staff. "The Higher Power of Lucky." *Publishers Weekly*, February 12, 2007, Vol. 254, Issue 7, pp. 88–89, 2p.

In the Night Kitchen, Maurice Sendak
(Harper & Row, 1970)

In the Night Kitchen is one of Maurice Sendak's many popular children's books. In the book, a young boy, Mickey, is sleeping when he suddenly hears a noise coming from the lower level of his house. He floats into a strange world known as "the night kitchen." As he makes this transition, his clothes disappear. Mickey is dumped into a bowl, where he begins to be covered by ingredients for a "morning cake." Three bakers mix the ingredients, not taking any notice of Mickey as he gets more and more covered in the morning cake batter. Eventually, he is able to get out of the bowl, telling the bakers that he is not one of the ingredients. Mickey uses elements of the baking ingredients in the kitchen, building an airplane out of bread dough and flying up to a large bottle of milk. After soaking in it for a bit, Mickey is once again naked. He tips the bottle, pouring enough milk for the bakers to finish making their cake. After he has finished helping them, Mickey slides down the side of the bottle, landing in his bed where he wakes up in the morning.

The book was very successful, earning a number of major honors, including being honored by the Caldecott committee and being listed as a notable children's book by the American Library Association. It also was adapted into a short film in 1987.

Despite these honors and the commercial success of the book, it also received a number of challenges across the country. The fact that Mickey was shown naked both from behind and from the front made many parents uneasy, and it quickly became one of the most challenged (and sometimes banned) books of its time. The presence of the nudity also led some challenging groups to read into the imagery sexual overtones, claiming that the milk poured from the bottle represented ejaculate. The fact that the nudity involved a child led many of these challenges to last and gain support, and *In the Night Kitchen* has met with more concerns than any of Sendak's other works.

FURTHER READING

Adams, Rebecca V. L., and Eric S. Rabkin. "Psyche and Society in Sendak's *In the Night Kitchen*." *Children's Literature in Education*, December 2007, Vol. 38, Issue 4, pp. 233–241, 9p.

Horning, Kathleen T. "The Naked Truth." *School Library Journal*, August 2012, Vol. 58, Issue 8, pp. 32–36, 5p.

Keeling, Kara, and Scott Pollard. "Power, Food, and Eating in Maurice Sendak and Henrik Drescher: Where the Wild Things Are, In the Night Kitchen, and The Boy Who Ate Around." *Children's Literature in Education*, June 1999, Vol. 30, Issue 2, pp. 127–143, 17p.

It, Stephen King
(Viking, 1986)

It is a horror novel written by Stephen King. The book covers two timelines, the first being in the 1950s when a group of childhood friends were fighting an evil force and later, when the group had spread across the country but recognized that the evil force had returned. In the first part of the book, a young boy, George Denbrough, is lured near a sewer by the evil force, at the time, appearing as a clown named Pennywise. When George approached the sewer, Pennywise ripped off George's arms. At the end of the following school year, Ben Hascom, another child, is looking for a place to avoid the bullies who are chasing him, and he finds a group of other children who have been not only bullied, but who have also seen Pennywise in his other forms, each form according to the child's fear. The group works together, trying to find out the history of the evil force. They also discover a ritual that should send the force back. While they are preparing for the ritual, one of the children, Eddie, is attacked by the group of bullies. While Eddie is recovering, one of the bullies is captured by Pennywise, and the groups see a message written to them in the bully's blood. Pennywise then begins to manipulate the head bully, Henry Bowers, to kill his own father and commit other crimes. The group of friends then find a way to banish Pennywise, and they vow that, if it ever returns, they will likewise return to repel him once more.

Years later, Pennywise returns. Although news of the clown is not widespread, Mike Denbrough, George's older brother and the librarian of the town the children grew up in, begins to put the pieces together after a string of child murders. Mike quickly contacts his childhood friends, most of whom have gone on to significant success. Most of the friends return to the town, though one commits suicide. Those who did return find it difficult to remember what exactly they had fought, and Mike works to not only remind them but also to convince them that it truly happened. The group begins to recall what Mike is talking about, and they decide to split up and search the town individually. As the group searches for Pennywise, others also come to the town. Audra, the wife of the horror writer Bill, and Tom, the fashion designer Beverly's abusive husband, come looking for their spouses. While Audra hopes to help Bill, Tom is looking to kill Beverly, believing that she is returning to her old friends to leave him.

In addition, Henry Bowers returns to town after Pennywise helps him to escape from the mental institution that he had been put in. Meanwhile, the group of friends have run-ins with Pennywise as they search for it, but they are unable to stop it. Pennywise retreats to the sewers, and the group decides that the only way to end things is to directly confront Pennywise as a group. When they go into the sewer, they find not only Pennywise but also a set of eggs that Pennywise has laid. One of the members of the group destroys the eggs while Bill, the horror writer, and Richie, the DJ, track down Pennywise. Ultimately, Bill is the one to kill it. Upon Pennywise's death, there is a huge storm in Derry, crushing the downtown, and Mike comes to realize that the town will end without Pennywise's influence. After their success, the friends part company, with their memories becoming hazier as the days go forward. At the book's end, Bill takes his wife, who is still unresponsive, for a ride on the bike he rode on as a child, and she reawakens.

The book was received quite well, earning multiple nominations for horror and fantasy awards and becoming a bestseller. It also was republished in three different editions for its 25th anniversary. In 1990, the book was adapted as a made-for-television miniseries. Reception to the television adaptation was mixed, generally receiving praise but sometimes having some complaints based upon the changes made to the story in order to make it acceptable for mainstream television broadcast.

In addition to the violent content that is to be expected in many horror novels, *It* contained a good deal of frank discussion of sex. This included both relatively typical depictions and also more controversial depictions, including two boys engaging in mutual masturbation, a group sex scene among minors, a hobo offering to perform oral sex on a boy, and the abusive relationship between Beverly and Tom. In addition, by the time that *It* was published, Stephen King had already seen his work challenged a number of times, with books like *Cujo*, *Carrie*, and *The Dead Zone* facing challenges from parent groups. This led to *It* being a target for criticism almost immediately after its release. While few of the challenges were successful in outright banning the book, some of them did lead to changes in who could check the book out and how it was classified. Still, its focus on childhood anxieties and small-town life has made it a dark favorite of a number of King's readers.

See Also: *Carrie*, *Christine*, and *The Dead Zone*.

FURTHER READING

Penny, Karl. "*It* (Book Review)." *School Library Journal*, February 1987, Vol. 33, Issue 6, p. 99.

Rehberger, Dean. "Middle-Class Nightmares and the Structure of Stephen King's *It*." *Studies in Weird Fiction*, Summer 1996, Vol. 19, pp. 2–7.

Staff. "*It*." *Kirkus Reviews*, October 15, 2010, Vol. 78, Issue 20, Special Section, p. 8.

Julie of the Wolves, Jean Craighead George
(Harper & Row, 1972)

Julie of the Wolves is the first book in a series of three children's books. The book itself is broken up into three parts. In the first part, the main character, an Eskimo girl, goes by either Julie or Miyax. This dual name reflects her ambivalence about her position between traditional Eskimo culture and more modern Alaskan culture. Julie loses both of her parents. First, her mother dies, and then, a few years later, her father goes on a fishing expedition and does not return. Julie has developed a strong connection to her natural surroundings, and she seeks comfort in the tundra. After both of her parents die, Julie is sent to live with her aunt, who does not seem to be interested in connecting to Julie. Julie's only option for leaving her aunt is to agree to an arranged marriage with a boy that she has not yet met. So, at age thirteen, Julie is sent to marry the boy, Daniel. However, when she arrives, Julie realizes that Daniel is cognitively disabled, and she does not want to be married to him. Things worsen when Daniel tries to force her to have sex with him after he has been teased that he has not been able to "mate" with his wife. Instead of staying with Daniel and his family, she decides to run away, hoping to make it to San Francisco, where she can live with her pen pal. On the way, Julie is forced to use her knowledge of the natural world in order to survive. In the final section, Julie begins to think of herself as Miyax again. She also begins to make her way south again after strengthening herself with some more food. As she makes her way toward her friend, Miyax is surprised by one of the wolves from the pack, who steals her backpack with supplies. The next day, Miyax backtracks, hoping to find her backpack, even if the wolf who stole it might have taken the supplies. When she finds the backpack, she finds the wolf who stole it as already dead, and she realizes that another of the wolves must have killed him for having stolen the backpack. Though Miyax is grateful, her happiness ends when a plane of hunters shoot down at the wolves, killing several of them. Miyax is able to save one of the wolves, and she then convinces the wolves not to follow her anymore. As she gets a bit further on, Miyax finds a place to build an igloo and live off of the tundra. Miyax eventually finds her estranged father, and they begin to connect, but when she finds out that her father has remarried and that his new wife is white, Miyax is disappointed. This disappointment is exacerbated when she finds out that her father no longer uses Eskimo practices to hunt. After finding this out, Miyax sneaks away and returns to the tundra, where she finds the wolf that she helped to nurse back to health. Unfortunately, the wolf is sick. At the end of the book, the wolf dies, and Miyax buries it, feeling that the wolves and the Eskimos are both dying out.

Julie of the Wolves was very well received. It found a significant readership, and it also won a Newberry Medal and was nominated for a National Book Award in the children's category. The success of the book led it to be adapted into other forms, including a musical play. It also had been targeted for a film adaptation.

The book did generate some controversy. The book was challenged a number of times, making it into the top third of the top one hundred "Most Challenged Books" from 1990 to 2000 by the American Library Association. The core reason for the challenges was that it contained a rape scene, which some parents complained was too graphic. This did result in some removals. In the Pulaski Township in Pennsylvania in 1996, the book was taken off of a sixth grade reading list. It was also challenged in Littleton, Colorado, in 1989 and in Chandler, Arizona, in 1994. Still, the book has maintained its positive reputation and has continued to be widely read and taught.

FURTHER READING

George, Jean Craighead. "Taking Care of Our Planet through Books." *Horn Book Magazine*, March/April 1994, Vol. 70, Issue 2, pp. 170–176, 7p.
Stott, Jon C. "Jean George's Arctic Pastoral: A Reading of *Julie of the Wolves*." *Children's Literature: Annual Publication of the Modern Language Association Division on Children's Literature and the Children's Literature Association*, 1974, Vol. 3, pp. 131–139.
Williams, Karen. "Talking with Wolves, Then Writing about Them." *Christian Science Monitor*, September 25, 1997, Vol. 89, Issue 211, p. B2.

Kaffir Boy, Mark Mathabane
(Macmillan, 1986)

Kaffir Boy is an autobiography exploring the harsh realities of growing up black under South Africa's system of apartheid. The book follow's Mathabane as he begins school on the insistence of his mother, who believes that it will give him a better chance at long-term success. The sense of need for an education and access to social mobility is reinforced by portrayals of going hungry and suffering under poverty. Although Mathabane experiences some challenges as his family has difficulty paying school fees and getting him sufficient school supplies, Mathabane writes about loving learning and the intellectual stimulation fostered by his schooling. His efforts in school pay off when he finishes at the top of his class in primary school, earning him a scholarship for secondary school. Meanwhile, Mark's grandmother works as a gardener for a white family that is sympathetic to the plight of Africans in South Africa. The family lets Mark's grandmother borrow comic books and children's books for him, and he takes great delight in reading them. In addition, they give Mark a tennis racket, and Mark begins to practice, finding that he takes to tennis as quickly as he has taken to school and reading. Mark continues to excel in both tennis and academics as he enters high school, and he joins the school team and also begins to enter tournaments, with a wealthy businessman and owner of the Tennis Ranch sponsoring Mark so that he can afford to enter the tournaments. In these tournaments, Mark ends up playing against Europeans rather than white South Africans, and his perspective on race and belonging changes. Mark continues to make white friends, and he is mentored by Stan Smith, a prominent tennis player who helps Mark enter into a major tournament. At this point, Mark feels that his tennis playing is not only a hobby but also a political act, showing the bigoted white establishment in South Africa that black people can excel at a seemingly elite sport like tennis. However, he also finds out that other black players are boycotting the tournament that he intends to enter, claiming that the white establishment is using them as a symbol without making substantive changes to race relations in South Africa. Mark is skeptical of this complaint, and he tries looking into the situation further, eventually deciding to participate in the tournament despite the complaints of his fellow Africans. This results in Mark's being banned from the black tennis association in South Africa. Despite this negative reaction, Mark's entry into the tournament does earn him a scholarship to play tennis at an American university, helping him to leave the pressures and limitations of South Africa behind.

Upon its publication, *Kaffir Boy* was met with mixed reactions. Many readers and critics applauded it for the ways in which it opened discussion of the oppressive and problematic system of apartheid in South Africa, bringing a focused and meaningful examination of an individual's experience with racism. For these reasons, the book won a number of awards, including the Christopher Award for uplifting literature. It also had commercial success, reaching the number 3 spot on the *New York Times* best-seller list.

Despite this success and critical praise, the book had some significant challenges as well. In Cedar Crest High School in Lebanon, Pennsylvania, the book received a challenge that ended up receiving significant media attention. The root of the challenge came from a scene portraying child prostitution, which was practiced under apartheid. It also portrayed sodomy. These two elements led the challengers to brand the book as being pornographic. Mathabane directly responded to these accusations, saying that he would prefer the book to be banned outright than toned down to be deemed safe for high schools. However, after a number of challenges, Mathabane authorized an "edited" version to be produced. From that point on, the challenges largely stopped, because schools would choose an edited or unedited version rather than remove it from the classroom or library, making it a relatively unique example of a reaction to challenges. Although some authors had allowed their books to be edited (and others, like Ray Bradbury with *Fahrenheit 451*, had their books edited without their knowledge), many shared Mathabane's original stance of wanting the work to remain intact rather than be impacted by forces of censorship.

FURTHER READING

Edmonds, Anthony O. "Kaffir Boy in America: An Encounter with Apartheid." *Library Journal*, June 1, 1989, Vol. 114, Issue 10, pp. 116–118, 3p.

Tembo, Mwizenge S. *"Kaffir Boy: A True Story of a Black Youth's Coming of Age in Apartheid South Africa."* *Journal of Modern African Studies*, December 1990, Vol. 28, Issue 4, pp. 723–725, 3p.

Van Gelder, Lawrence. *"Kaffir Boy* Banned (Again)." *New York Times*, April 13, 2007, Vol. 156, Issue 53913, p. E4.

Lady Chatterley's Lover, D. H. Lawrence
(Tipografia Giuntina—Italy, 1928)

Lady Chatterley's Lover is an erotic novel written by D. H. Lawrence. The novel follows an upper-class, British couple, Constance (the title character) and her husband Clifford Chatterley. Although the couple is well to do and relatively happy at the book's beginning, things begin to deteriorate. Clifford, a veteran, is paralyzed after the war, and he does not emotionally engage with his wife as he once did. While they live in a nice home, Constance (or Connie) also feels alienated by the staff, who are curt and professional rather than truly friendly. She likewise feels bored with and alienated from the people in the village where they live. Connie looks to her father for advice, and he suggests that she takes a lover. Connie eventually follows this advice after she finds herself interested in Michaelis, a playwright who is Irish rather than English. But the affair is short lived after Connie finds herself not fully connecting to Michaelis either. Ironically, after the affair ends, Clifford tells Connie that he would be willing to let her take a lover if it would help them to have a child in their family. With this willingness is a clear demand that she stay committed to the family and close to Clifford. This only serves to make Connie feel even more disconnected from Clifford and her life in general. Connie roams their estate, and she develops a friendship with their gamekeeper, Mellors. As Connie develops her relationship with Mellors, eventually having sexual relations with him, she also hires a nurse to take care of Clifford. Connie and Clifford end up spending more time with the staff than they do with each other. When Connie goes on a trip with her father and sister, Mellors's estranged wife comes back to him, discovering that he has been sleeping with Connie. After his wife spreads rumors in the village, Mellors leaves, writing Connie to tell her that he has gone to London and will not come back. Connie goes to Mellors in London, telling him that she is pregnant with his child. She returns to her home, hoping that Clifford will grant her a divorce. In order to achieve this, she tries lying to Clifford about the affair, claiming that it is with someone else, but Clifford persists, and she eventually admits that it was Mellors. Clifford tells her that he will not grant her divorce, and Connie is forced to go with her sister, living in Scotland. At the book's end, Mellors writes Connie a letter, expressing hope that they both will be able to get divorces so that they can be together.

From the book's publication, it garnered a significant amount of attention for reasons of both literary merit and level of obscenity. Many critics have applauded the book for two principal reasons. The first is that it puts on display the harsh and strict social codes of the class system in Britain, frowning upon the relationships between people from different social classes. The second is the level of examination of the characters' interior lives, something that Lawrence was known for in many of his works. The book has been translated into multiple languages, adapted several times and referenced in a wide variety of media. In some ways, it has become a shorthand for art that is controversial for its sexual content. Interestingly, the adaptations of the book have come from around the globe, not only in England but also in France, India, and the Philippines. The book's publication is also difficult to summarize, because it has appeared in a variety of versions, some with the content edited and some with all of Lawrence's text preserved. In many ways, it is hard to overstate the influence that the book has had, given the way it has been studied and referenced by scholars, historians, and cultural commentators.

Despite this importance, the book has been met with a wide variety of battles, and its challenges have lasted for decades. Although the book was published in America in 1928 and the United Kingdom in 1932, these versions were sometimes edited to avoid controversy. When the full text was published in Britain in 1960, Penguin Books was immediately taken to court for violation of the Obscene Publications Act of 1959. After months of hearings and testimony from major figures of British literature of the day, the book was deemed not obscene, because it had sufficient literary merit. Britain was far from the only place that the book received challenges. In Australia, both the book and transcripts from the trial in Britain were banned for some time. The book was also put on trial in Canada, India, and Japan as well as in the United States. Interestingly, both the book and a French film inspired by the book were banned in the United States. In 1959, in America, the book was part of a major trial in which Grove Books sued the U.S. Post Office for seizing copies of the books. The book was found to have sufficient literary merit to not require banning, and this ruling helped to establish the precedent that would allow texts with sufficient literary merit to be published and sold regardless of the content. In some ways, the trials and attention surrounding the book has overshadowed its literary merit, but both for the precedents that it established and the trends of modernist literature, psychological realism and viewpoints that tapped into the sexual revolution, the book has endured, and its influences have been seen in a wide array of contexts.

See Also: *The Rainbow* and *Sons and Lovers*.

FURTHER READING

Karthikeyan, S. "A Psychoanalytic Study of DH Lawrence's *Lady Chatterley's Lover.*" *Language in India*, April 2013, Vol. 13, Issue 4, pp. 142–145, 4p.

Lehman, Peter, and Susan Hunt. *Lady Chatterley's Legacy in the Movies: Sex, Brains, and Body Guys*. New Brunswick, NJ: Rutgers University Press, 2010, p. 224.
Robertson, Geoffrey. "Trial of the Century." *History Today*, November 2010, Vol. 60, Issue 11, pp. 41–44, 4p.

Leaves of Grass, Walt Whitman
(1855)

Leaves of Grass is a major work of American poetry. It was published in multiple editions. It was, in many ways, the core work of Whitman's career. It covered a variety of subjects, including individualism, people's relationships to the land, and bodily pleasure. The book was met with mixed response. While the book was appreciated by some readers, there was significant backlash. The most immediate and obvious repercussion was Whitman losing his job in 1865 at the U.S. Department of the Interior, after the department's head read Whitman's book and found it so offensive that he did not want any association with Whitman. Some prominent reviewers also declared the book "filthy" and made personal accusations about Whitman, including that he was a homosexual. Despite these challenges, the book has often been referred to by more contemporary critics as one of the most important books of American poetry ever written. It has been cited as an influence by many poets, particularly the Beat poets like Allen Ginsberg. It also is a core part of many American literature courses across the country.

Beyond the immediate bad reviews and the firing of Whitman, the book did face other challenges. In 1882, the district attorney of Boston wrote to James Osgood, who had published a later edition of *Leaves of Grass*, citing complaints from the New England Society for the Suppression of Vice that claimed that the book contained obscene poems. Osgood asked Whitman to remove the poems that were indicated as offensive, but Whitman refused, and Osgood stopped publishing the book. Rather than be censored, Whitman found a new publisher, Rees Welsh & Company, who published an uncensored version of the book. Whitman had claimed that the censorship controversy would only increase his sales (much like Sherman Alexie's stance over a century later when discussing the challenges to his book *The Absolutely True Diary of a Part-Time Indian*), and Whitman was proven correct when the first printing of the book by Rees sold out almost immediately in Boston. The book was also banned by some booksellers in Philadelphia, though, as in Boston, this seemed to increase the publicity and interest for the book. As the years passed, Whitman's innuendo and veiled references to sex and sexual desire have come to be seen as less offensive, and *Leaves of Grass* has become a mainstay in classrooms and libraries.

FURTHER READING

Morton, Heather. "Democracy, Self Reviews and the 1855 *Leaves of Grass.*" *Virginia Quarterly Review,* Spring 2005, Vol. 81, Issue 2, pp. 229–243, 15p.

Schramm, Geoffrey Saunders. "Whitman's Lifelong Endeavor: *Leaves of Grass* at 150." *Humanities,* July/August 2005, Vol. 26, Issue 4, pp. 24–28, 5p.

Smith, Ernest. " 'Restless Exploration': Whitman's Evolving Spiritual Vision in *Leaves of Grass.*" *Papers on Language & Literature,* Summer 2007, Vol. 43, Issue 3, pp. 227–263, 37p.

Lolita, Vladimir Nabokov
(Olympia Press, 1955)

Lolita is likely Vladimir Nabokov's most controversial novel. It follows Humbert Humbert, an academic who has to leave England after a series of problems revolving around his love life. Humbert opens the book by discussing his desire for "nymphettes," or young girls who have something within them that makes them sexual beings. After some trouble in Europe, he moves to America, hoping to start fresh. The family that he moves in with is a single mother and a twelve-year-old girl, Dolores, who also goes by the name "Lo" and whom Humbert calls "Lolita." Humbert believes that Dolores is a nymphette, and he is sexually interested in her. In hopes of eventually bedding her, Humbert becomes close to her mother, eventually agreeing to marry her. Humbert then concocts schemes to be alone with Dolores, and he hopes to kill Dolores's mother. While Lolita is at a summer camp, the mother learns of Humbert's infatuation with Lolita and the plot to kill her. She is so shocked that she runs into the street, and she is struck by a car, dying in the accident. Humbert now finds himself as the guardian of Lolita. He picks her up from summer camp and takes her to a hotel, though he does not yet reveal to her that her mother has died. Humbert then takes Lolita with him on the road, having sex with her as they travel. Eventually, though, the pair have to find a permanent home, and Humbert becomes paranoid, wanting to keep Lolita from forming any meaningful bonds with anyone outside of the home. After some pleading from Lolita, she is allowed to participate in a school play. As she has an activity outside of the home, Lolita becomes more independent, eventually running away for an evening. Humbert finds her in a phone booth, and he is able to coax her back home. Still, Humbert decides that they need to leave town. While they are on the road, Lolita leaves Humbert with Clare Quilty, the director of the high school play that she was in. Humbert eventually finds her again, and he also learns that she is married and pregnant (though only seventeen). Her husband knows nothing of the relationship between Lolita and Humbert. Humbert tries to persuade Lolita to leave her husband to be with him, but she refuses. Humbert gives her the money and leaves to find and kill Clare Quilty. He succeeds in killing Quilty, but he is arrested for driving erratically. At the novel's close, the narrator claims that the story is true, and it is a memoir meant to be published upon his and Lolita's death.

Nabokov knew that the book would likely cause a scandal or a sensation. In fact, he had originally planned to publish the book under an anagrammatic pseudonym rather than under his own name. The book was rejected by a number of prominent American publishers, though Nabokov was well known by the time that he completed the novel. After the many rejections, Nabokov published the novel with Olympia Press in France, a publisher whose catalog was largely comprised of pornographic novels. The book's first publication had a relatively small run, and it went largely unnoticed until author and critic Graham Greene called it one of the best books of the year. This caused a major stir, with some other writers and critics advocating for the book but many others calling the book "filthy" or "trash." Matters were not helped by the fact that the first edition had many printing and editing errors. Upon receiving attention, the book was banned in France, and the British government called for all copies in the United Kingdom to be seized. Other European countries saw releases, and the bans in both the United Kingdom and France were eventually dropped. Surprisingly, the book was not only published without restriction in the United States but also went through three printings shortly after its release.

Lolita has also been adapted or referenced a number of times in popular culture. The first (and one of the most notable) adaptations was Stanley Kubrick's film version in 1962. Nabokov himself helped to write the screenplay, and he earned an Oscar nomination. The book has also been adapted as an opera, as a musical, and as another film. It was adapted as a play by Edward Albee, though the play was panned by critics. The book has also been referenced by everything from academic articles to punk bands to stand-up comedians, and the name "Lolita" has come to be a slang term for a young girl who is sexually precocious. Although the book caused a severe reaction, it is still recognized as a significant (though controversial) work by a major author.

FURTHER READING

Diment, Galya. "Two 1955 Lolitas: Vladimir Nabokov's and Dorothy Parker's." *Modernism/Modernity*, April 2014, Vol. 21, Issue 2, pp. 487–505.

Shekhovtsova, O. "Spending the Night with Lolita: Vladimir Nabokov's Novel in the USSR." *Russian Studies in Literature*, Fall 2006, Vol. 42, Issue 4, pp. 52–72, 21p.

Wells, Ira. "Forgetting *Lolita*." *New Republic*, July/August 2015, Vol. 246, Issue 7/8, pp. 70–73, 4p.

Private Parts,
Howard Stern & Larry Sloman
(Simon & Schuster, 1993)

Private Parts is a memoir of the self-proclaimed "King of All Media" Howard Stern. The book's opening establishes its boundary-pushing nature by portraying an imagined male listener masturbating while listening to a guest talking about lesbian sex on Howard Stern's "shock jock" radio show. After this initial opening, the book focuses on Stern's childhood. In particular, he discusses the nature of growing up as a Caucasian Jew in a primarily African American area. These reflections dovetail with some of the prominent social issues of the time, including racial riots and popular culture movies examining race relations. He also discusses his early sexual desires and experiences in significant and frank detail. It also discusses his relationship with his wife and his early career experiences in radio. He looks at his efforts to establish a following in Detroit and then Washington DC before he made the move to New York, where he initially felt alienated, being snubbed by fellow radio personality Don Imus and belittled by one of the WNBC executives who Stern referred to as "Pig Vomit" both in the book and on the air. The book also discusses in frank detail Stern's views of the many celebrities that he interviewed over the years as well as the regular crew that Stern took on during his rise to fame. Although much of the book is autobiographical, Stern also devotes time to discussing his views on different ethnic categories as well as both male and female homosexuals. Stern also discusses celebrity feuds that he has had and his opinion of the stand-up comedians that he has interviewed. The book also looks at temptations that Stern experienced to cheat on his wife. The book concludes first with Stern discussing his response to his many critics and then with two psychologists evaluating Stern and his personality.

The book was an immediate commercial success despite some chains outright refusing to carry the book. In fact, Caldor department stores refused to sell the book and went as far as to remove the book from its listing of the *New York Times* bestseller books. The book was also made into a movie with Stern playing himself.

Critical reaction to the book was mixed. Some reviewers felt that the book's ability to bring more customers into bookstore made it a positive force, even if it had little literary merit. Other positive reviews compared Stern to Lenny Bruce, whose book *How to Talk Dirty and Influence People* was regarded by many as a significant and boundary-breaking text. Others felt that Stern's book was an attempt to follow Bruce's work but one that could not come out from under the shadow of Bruce's discussions of censorship and comedy. Other negative criticisms echoed those that Stern's radio show regularly received. In particular, the book was called juvenile, looking for easy laughs rather than legitimately pushing boundaries in comedy.

The book's challenges were so widespread and significant that it was listed at number 87 on the list of the American Library Association's list of one hundred banned books of the 1990s. Reasons for the book's banning varied. Some challenges cited the book's sexual content, others looked at the obscenity more generally. In addition, Stern's views on race, gender, and sexuality were offensive to a variety of readers. Although the book was seen as troubling to many, and although the book rarely receives defense for its literary merit, it is still a widely read text.

FURTHER READING

Gillette, Felix. "Howard's End." *Business Week*, March 16, 2015, Issue 4419, pp. 44–49, 6p.
Steinberg, Jacques. "Stern Likes His New Censor: Himself." *New York Times*, January 9, 2007, Vol. 156, Issue 53819, pp. E1–E7, 7p.
Strauss, Neil. "The Happiest Man Alive." *Rolling Stone*, March 31, 2011, Issue 1127, pp. 40–76, 37p.

Rabbit, Run, John Updike
(Alfred A. Knopf, 1960)

Rabbit, Run is a novel by major American author John Updike. The book follows Harry "Rabbit" Angstrom, a former high school basketball star who is now in his mid-twenties. Rabbit thinks of this time playing basketball with great nostalgia, because he is stuck selling kitchen gadgets and married to a woman, Janice, with whom he has a child. At the book's opening, Janice is also pregnant with their second child. Dissatisfied with his life, Rabbit decides that he is going to leave his family. After driving off and not finding his destination, Rabbit decides to visit his former coach, Marty Tothero. While having dinner with Tothero, Rabbit meets up with Ruth, a woman who sometimes engages in prostitution to make ends meet. Rabbit begins a relationship with Ruth. After dating for some time, Rabbit moves in with Ruth. Without Rabbit's financial contributions, Janice is forced to move in with her parents, but Rabbit is unmoved, and he remains with Ruth despite the efforts of a local priest to convince Rabbit to reconcile with his wife. Tensions raise, though, when Rabbit discovers that Ruth has had an affair with one of his rivals from high school. When Rabbit discovers this, he demands that Ruth perform oral sex on him. Shortly thereafter, Rabbit discovers that Janice has gone into labor, and he returns to her. Although Rabbit makes an attempt to reconcile with Janice, he quickly asks her to have sex with him, and she is upset, feeling like he is with her only out of a desire for sex. After their fight, Rabbit goes looking for Ruth, but she is not at her apartment. Knowing that he cannot return to

Janice, Rabbit checks into a hotel. Janice is so shaken by the recent turn of events that she takes to drinking and accidentally drowns her infant daughter. Rabbit learns of this only when he contacts the priest in order to ask for advice about returning to Janice. When he hears of his daughter's death, Rabbit does return, though he still has mixed feelings about Janice, and he absolves himself of any responsibility of the loss of their child. Around the time of the funeral, Rabbit hears from Ruth, and he discovers that she is pregnant. Despite this, and despite his continued lack of emotional connection to Janice, he refuses to ask for a divorce. The priest talks with Rabbit about his issues, suggesting that Rabbit is searching for something that he is not likely to find rather than finding fulfillment in what he has. While Rabbit ends up turning his back on Ruth, it is not entirely clear whether or not he intends to fully return to Janice.

The novel was fairly well received, earning praise from critics. Of particular note for many readers was Updike's use of present tense narration, which many found to give a greater feeling of urgency and immediacy. It also has been referenced a number of times in popular culture, perhaps most notably in the film *8 Mile*, starring rapper Eminem. The main character in the film is named Rabbit, and there are other references (including a song with the title "Run, Rabbit") to the book throughout the film. The book was adapted into a film in 1970, which was met with little acclaim. Updike revisited the character of Rabbit multiple times over the course of his career.

Even before the book was released, there was concern over the sexual content within it. Knopf, the publisher, had asked Updike to cut some of the most graphic sexual scenes. Updike made the requested cuts for the original edition, but those scenes were reinserted in later editions. Even the later, edited version of the book had met with challenges from various groups. In Ireland, the book was banned in 1962, though the ban has since been lifted. The complaints were not only about the portrayal of sex but also the promiscuity of the main character. Some readers found the lack of punishment or bad end for Rabbit to be a validation of adultery. In America, challenges came in both the 1970s and the 1980s, and these challenges were also rooted in complaints about the portrayal of sex, the portrayal of adultery, and discussions of prostitution. Although the challenges did not result in outright bans on the book, some of them did result in high school students needing parental permission to read it. Despite this, the Rabbit series, and *Run, Rabbit* in particular, remains widely read and discussed works of American literature.

FURTHER READING

Baker, Emmalee D., Julia M. Chavez, and Robert C. Hauhart. "Religious Naming in John Updike's *Rabbit, Run.*" *Explicator*, October–December 2015, Vol. 73, Issue 4, pp. 275–278, 4p.

Cooper, R. R. "Rabbit Loses the Race." *Commonwealth*, May 17, 1991, Vol. 118, Issue 10, pp. 315–321, 7p.

Purohit, Amulya Kishore. "Updike's *Rabbit, Run*." *Explicator*, Summer 2008, Vol. 66, Issue 4, pp. 229–233, 5p.

The Rainbow, D. H. Lawrence
(Thomas Seltzer, 1915)

The Rainbow is a novel written by British author D. H. Lawrence. It is a multigenerational story following the Brangwen family, who Lawrence would revisit in the book *Women in Love*. The family is a group of farmers and craftsmen who live in England in the second half of the 19th century and early part of the 20th century. Tom is the patriarch of the family. He has lived in the same relatively small area of England his whole life. While Tom is content with this, the women of the Brangwen family find it frustrating. Unlike the women, Tom is able to explore his sexuality, employing prostitutes and enjoying sex. The book then follows Tom as he falls in love with a Polish woman, Lydia, who immigrated to England to avoid persecution in her home country. The two get married, and Tom accepts her daughter, Anna, as though she were a daughter of his own, though Anna does not initially respond well to Tom. Lydia and Tom have children together, but they also have difficulties as they work through their cultural differences. Eventually, Anna becomes involved with one of Tom's nephews, Will. This upsets Tom, and it leads to significant friction after Anna tells Tom that he is not her father and, therefore, has no right to tell her how to live her life. Will and Anna have a daughter, but the two regularly bicker. Despite this, the pair have more children, which only worsens the situation. Eventually, Will dies in an accident, and Ursula, Will and Anna's child, finds herself having to pitch in to help the family. Still, Ursula is able to attend a university, bringing her away from the family land. While there, Ursula takes an interest in one of her female teachers. The pair become very close, but the teacher ends up marrying Ursula's uncle. Ursula returns home and takes a position teaching, though her experiences in teaching quickly become unsatisfying when she cannot relate to her coworkers. Ursula returns to the university for a short time, but she fails her exams. Despite Ursula's many troubles, the book takes its title from one of the closing images: a rainbow that Ursula sees that fills her with a sense of hope for the future.

The Rainbow met with some success. It was well received critically, but it also ran into significant trouble because of the legal challenges against it. In the United Kingdom, the book was tried for obscenity, and, after it was declared obscene, over one thousand copies were seized and burned. This significant resistance was not unusual for D. H. Lawrence. In fact, the negative reaction to the book led to significant hurdles and delays in the publication of its sequel, *Women in Love*. *The Rainbow* itself was not available in the United Kingdom for over ten years after the original trial. There were a variety of objections to the book, but the most significant and persistent was the questions about its open and direct discussion of human sexuality. In particular, the lesbian relationship and premarital sex were causes for scandal. Ironically, this content also is one of the things that became a hallmark of D. H. Lawrence's work and that have led many critics to appreciate Lawrence's work.

See Also: *Lady Chatterley's Lover* and *Sons and Lovers*.

FURTHER READING

Dervin, D. "Rainbow, Phoenix and Plumed Serpent: DH Lawrence's Great Composite Symbols and their Vicissitudes." *Psychoanalytic Review*, Winter 1980, Vol. 67, Issue 4, pp. 515–541.

Foley, Louis. "The Badness of Bad Words." *Reading Horizons*, Spring 1973, Vol. 13, Issue 3, pp. 115–119.

Manderson, Desmond. "Between the Nihilism of the Young and the Positivism of the Old: Justice and the Novel in DH Lawrence." *Law & Humanities*, Summer 2012, Vol. 6, Issue 1, pp. 1–23, 23p.

The Scarlet Letter, Nathaniel Hawthorne
(Ticknor, Reed and Fields, 1850)

The Scarlet Letter is a major work of American literature. The book follows a Puritan woman, Hester Prynne, who is accused of adultery. Because of this accusation, she is made to wear a scarlet letter "A," and she has to stand for three hours on a platform in the town square where the rest of the townspeople can watch and judge her. Despite this attempt to shame her, Hester stands with a type of dignity that angers the other Puritan women. The townspeople are further angered when Hester refuses to publically reveal the name of her child's father. As she is standing in front of the crowd, she sees her husband (who had long been presumed lost at sea) in the crowd. Hester is taken to the town jail. Her husband poses as a doctor to gain access to her. While he gives her a variety of herbs to help her health, the two talk about their marriage. Hester's husband admits that he had not been a good husband, and Hester admits that she had not always been a good wife. However, when the subject of her adultery comes up, she refuses to tell him who her child's father is. Her husband tells her not to reveal his identity, threatening to pursue her child's father to his doom if she does. Hester gives in to her husband's demands. Hester is forced to live on the outskirts of town, where she and her daughter, Pearl, get by on the small bit of money that Hester can make on her work sewing. As Pearl grows older, she becomes disrespectful and troublesome. Before long, members of the town suggest that Hester is a bad role model herself and that Pearl should be taken away from Hester. Fearing the loss of her child, Hester goes to the town's governor, and she pleads with the governor and two reverends (Reverend Dimmesdale in particular) not to let the town take her child from her. Dimmesdale and the other two are able to successfully ensure that Hester can keep her daughter. Not long after, Dimmesdale falls ill, and Hester's husband stays with him, treating him regularly. One night, while Dimmesdale is asleep, Hester's husband discovers that Dimmesdale himself wears a scarlet "A," indicating that he is Pearl's father. Not long after his, Dimmesdale does confess to Hester and her husband, but he does not build the courage to make a full, public confession. Hester tries to warn Dimmesdale that he is in peril, and she plans to help him escape. After this revelation, Dimmesdale's health improves, and his preaching takes on a new energy. After a particularly strong sermon, Dimmesdale goes to the platform where Hester was shamed, and he confesses his sin. Dimmesdale then dies, with Hester holding him as he perishes. Not long after this, Hester's husband also dies, apparently having lost his purpose after Dimmesdale's death. This results in Hester receiving an inheritance from her husband. Years later, Hester dies as well, and she is buried near Dimmesdale.

Upon its publication, *The Scarlet Letter* was a significant success, both financially and commercially. In fact, it was one of the very first books in American literature to be popular enough to experience mass production. It also was met with positive reviews from both American and European writers, who admired the symbolism and psychological depth found within the book. Despite this success and support, the book also immediately met with some backlash, particularly from religious leaders of the time. Many religious leaders of the time felt that handling adultery at all was problematic, and a story that portrayed someone who committed adultery in a sympathetic light was particularly troubling. Other readers were disturbed at the references to actual people that Hawthorne used as well as the negative portrayal of the Puritans as being judgmental and cruel.

Despite these objections, the book has maintained a consistent study and following since its original publication. It has been directly adapted into or used as the inspiration for well over a dozen films from around the globe. Some of these have been unsuccessful, like the 1995 adaptation starring Demi Moore and Gary Oldman, but other films, like the satirical adaptation *Easy A*, have been very well received. The book has also been the inspiration for dozens of songs and has been adapted for the stage multiple times. Beyond these references and adaptations, the book has been widely taught in schools across America.

While the book has been fully accepted as one of the major works of American literature, it still has been met with significant challenges. While the book only examines the aftermath of the affair (looking at the birth and raising of Pearl and of Hester's commitment to Dimmesdale), religious leaders and parent groups have challenged the book as recently as the late 1970s. Most of the challenges to the book root themselves in the same sorts of objections that the book saw at the time of its publication. The seemingly sympathetic portrayal of a woman who had committed adultery has led the book to face challenges that have been widespread and continuous.

FURTHER READING

Haviland, Beverly. "What It Betokened: Waiting for Hester in *The Scarlett Letter*." *Common Knowledge*, August 2015, Vol. 21, Issue 3, pp. 420–436.

Manheim, Daniel. "Pearl's Golden Necklace in *The Scarlett Letter*." *Explicator*, 2010, Vol. 68, Issue 3, pp. 177–180, 4p.

O'Malley, Maria. "Taking the Domestic View in Hawthorne's Fiction." *New England Quarterly*, December 2015, Vol. 88, Issue 4, pp. 657–680, 24p.

A Stolen Life, Jaycee Dugard
(Simon & Schuster, 2012)

A Stolen Life is an autobiographical book written by kidnapping victim Jaycee Dugard. Dugard was kidnapped in 1991, when she was eleven years old. Dugard was kidnapped by a couple, Phillip and Nancy Garrido. They kept Dugard captive for nearly eighteen years. Ironically, Dugard's parents had moved to the area, Arcadia, California, because they felt that it would be safer than Los Angeles, where they had been living. Dugard had approached the Garridos's car after they had stopped, assuming that the couple had simply wanted directions. Instead, Phillip used a stun gun to knock out Dugard and take her to their home. Dugard's stepfather had seen the abduction, but he was unable to stop it, making him a suspect. Dugard's biological father was also a suspect, though this was unknown to Dugard at the time. The couple who abducted Dugard took off her clothes before bringing her to their home. She was, though, able to hide a butterfly ring, something that she successfully hid for the entirety of her captivity, giving herself a feeling that she was able to hang onto some part of herself. She was told not to use her own name after her captivity began. Phillip began raping Dugard just days after she had been kidnapped. For much of her early captivity, Dugard was kept under close scrutiny, with her having to shower with Garrido and wear handcuffs most of the time. The Garridos kept Dugard cut off from not only social interaction but also information about the outside world. They also kept her completely dependent upon them, keeping themselves her only source of both food and socialization. In addition, they were very cruel and strict with her, only giving her a bucket for her toileting. During this time, Garrido also would go on drug binges forcing Dugard to listen to his rants about being chosen by God. He would also make her dress up for him. Partway through the captivity, Garrido's wife began to interact with Dugard, first apologizing to her and bringing her a stuffed animal in order to gain Dugard's trust. In the book, Dugard discusses the fact that, upon reflection, she recognized that this was a matter of manipulation, but, at the time, Dugard was impressionable and desperate enough to fall prey to it. Dugard eventually became pregnant as a result of the raping perpetrated by Garrido. Because of the captivity, Dugard was unable to receive proper medical care and preparation for childbirth. Instead, she had to prepare for the childbirth by watching television programs about giving birth. Dugard would have another child, also fathered by Phillip Garrido, three years later. During her captivity, there were a number of opportunities for Dugard to be rescued, but it was not until the FBI got involved out of concern for Garrido's behavior that Garrido was brought into custody and leaving Dugard finally free. Even after her freedom, Dugard was put under intense scrutiny because of the sensational nature of the crime. In addition to the proceedings against the Garridos, Dugard filed a suit against the federal government for failing to fully monitor Phillip Garrido, who was on probation at the time that he abducted Dugard. In addition to covering many of the facts of the case, Dugard gives a bit of background to her kidnappers as well as reflections upon how she was able to stay strong and survive during the captivity.

The book gained a significant readership, being part of the larger focus on Dugard and the case. Almost immediately, the book became a bestseller. It was praised by many for its unflinching discussion of the disturbing events, and Dugard was praised for opening a line of discussion about abduction, sexual abuse, and recovery from both of these heinous crimes. The book also was seen as a positive step for both Dugard and other victims of abuse, partially because it was written as part of her larger efforts with her therapist to move beyond the awful events during her captivity and to help Dugard reconnect with her family.

Despite the responses characterizing Dugard's book as uplifting or positive, there have been a number of challenges to *A Stolen Life*. It has been in the top ten of the American Library Association's "Most Challenged Books" list for a number of years. The core reasons for the challenges come from the book's frank portrayal of sexual abuse, the disturbing behavior of the Garridos, and for the open discussion of drug use. There has been significant backlash to the challenges that the book has faced, with defenders of the book arguing that a frank discussion is necessary both to destigmatize victims of sexual abuse and also to allow other victims to feel a sense of connection and validation. While some of the challenges have had success, many have had difficulty gaining traction, because defenders of the book stand firmly by the belief that banning the book would be silencing

Jaycee Dugard a second time, exacerbating the difficult treatment that she has already lived through. The book maintains a wide readership and has continued to be a commercial success.

FURTHER READING

Breuer, Howard. "Jaycee Dugard: Justice at Last." *People*, June 20, 2011, Vol. 75, Issue 24, p. 77.

Staff. "Why Didn't Jaycee Run Away?" *Newsweek*, September 14, 2009, Vol. 154, Issue 11, p. 68.

Tresniowski, Alex, Howard Breuer, Susan Young, Johnny Dodd, and Nicole Weisensee Egan. "Captive No More." *People*, September 14, 2009, Vol. 72, Issue 11, pp. 72–78, 7p.

Stranger in a Strange Land, Robert Heinlein
(Putnam, 1961)

Stranger in a Strange Land is a science fiction novel that follows a human who has been raised on Mars. In this world, the major religions of the world have significant influence over political and governmental matters. The government is comprised of a sort of League of Nations that is supported by a military power. Valentine Michael Smith, a small child at the book's opening, had been part of an Earth expedition to Mars, but he was the only member of the expedition to survive, and he was not able to return to Earth until twenty-five years after the mission, when a second expedition from Earth went to Mars. In the intervening years, Valentine has become acculturated to Martian ways. Still, the Martians who have helped him survive tell him to return to his home planet. Valentine does so, but, because he is unfamiliar with Earth's ways, the government confines him to a hospital room where he is only allowed to interact with male workers. This changes when nurse Gillian Boardman sneaks in to see Valentine. As they visit, the two share a glass of water, which Valentine takes to be an act of real significance because of his experiences on Mars. Nurse Gillian tells a reporter of this turn of events, and the reporter tells her that, because Valentine was the only person to survive the original expedition, he is considered the owner of all of Mars, making him extremely wealthy. The reporter then convinces Gillian to bug Valentine's room in hopes that they'll get enough information to convince the government to let Valentine go free, particularly because Valentine has become an object within a political struggle. When the government discovers the plan, they place the reporter in jail. Gillian tries to help Valentine escape.

When government workers come to take both of them back, Valentine sends them to the fourth dimension. Valentine is surprised to find that Gillian is greatly disturbed by his actions, and he becomes unresponsive. Not sure what else to do, Gillian takes Valentine to an author and physician that the reporter had told her about. Valentine and the author, Jubal Harshaw, discuss significant topics like war and religion, with Valentine often missing the core points or concepts of the topics. Harshaw helps Valentine to gain access to the large sums of money that the reporter had described, and he also helps Valentine to gain his freedom. Valentine becomes a type of celebrity, and he searches out different religions. He ends up spending time with high ranking members of the Forsterite Church of the New Revelation, a religion that promotes indulgence and uses nefarious means to dominate politicians. After interacting with these members, Valentine decides to start his own religion, the Church of All Worlds, which draws upon the teachings that Valentine received during his time on Mars. Before long, the new church is attacked by the Forsterites, who see the Church of All Worlds as both blasphemous and a rival. Although the main building is burned down by the Forsterites, Valentine is able to transport his followers to safety before they are injured. Still, the Forsterites put pressure on the police to have Valentine arrested. He escapes the police, telling Harshaw and his followers that he has left the Church of All Worlds a substantial amount of money, giving them the ability to pursue the works that he had set up. He also suggests that pursuing these projects and improvements is necessary to keeping Earth alive, as the Martians will eventually pose a threat to them. The Forsterites are eventually able to have Valentine killed, but he is able to communicate with Harshaw, comforting him. Harshaw eats from Valentine's body, as it is part of the Martian teachings and customs. Harshaw and Valentine's followers return to the church to help follow Valentine's ways. Meanwhile, Valentine begins operating in the afterlife, confounding the high ranking members of the Forsterites.

Upon its publication, the book was met with mixed reactions. Some critics panned the book, claiming that it was juvenile and relied too heavily upon sex and salacious content to generate interest. Others were a bit more charitable, admiring the book's ambition but taking issue with some of its execution. Despite these criticisms, the book was quite popular, winning the Hugo Award, a major prize for science fiction works. In addition to this recognition, it has been referenced in a variety of media, perhaps most notably by the bands The Police and Iron Maiden. The latter had a song with the title "Stranger in a Strange Land," though the lyrics were only obliquely related to the events of the book.

The book actually had two versions. In an early draft, Heinlein had a length of 220,000 words. The publisher had asked him to cut his book down dramatically. In response, Heinlein trimmed 60,000 words, much of it containing sections that were clearly critiques of American culture. This condensed version became the first edition of the book. In 1989, Heinlein's widow received full control of the manuscript, and she ended the publication of the condensed version, only allowing Heinlein's full original text to be published from then on. By 1989, some of the objections to the original material were less strong than they would have been at the time that the original version was published, and many readers tended to prefer Heinlein's preferred draft.

Despite these cuts and edits, the book did receive challenges. The book received challenges for its content because of speculation about its underlying themes. The book did contain discussions of sex and drug use, and this led to a challenge in Mercedes, Texas, in 2003. While the challenge did not result in a banning of the book, it did lead to restrictions on selections of what books could be taught and what books could be checked out without parental consent. Beyond that, the discussion of free love and drug use led to some sensationalist rumors that the book had ties to the Manson family, a group of criminals who were a demented offshoot of the hippie movement. They were responsible for brutal murders and a number of petty crimes. During the aftermath of the murders, there was a good deal of speculation over what drove Manson and his followers to commit these crimes, and Heinlein's book was one of the many texts that was cast under suspicion. Of course, no real tie was proven, and these rumors did not result in any long-term damage to its reputation. The rumors were fully debunked in 1981 when J. Neil Schulman asked Manson directly if the book had had any influence on him and Manson indicated that it had not. It remains a widely read text and has been included on Library of Congress list of books that helped to shape America.

FURTHER READING

Doherty, Brian. "Robert Heinlein at 100." *Reason*, August/September 2007, Vol. 39, Issue 4, pp. 48–54, 7p.

McGuirk, Carol. "God in a Yellow Bathrobe." *Science Fiction Studies*, March 2015, Vol. 42, Issue 1, pp. 151–157, 7p.

Price, Cynthia. "A Heinlein Child Pays Homage to the Master." *ETC: A Review of General Semantics*, October 2007, Vol. 64, Issue 4, pp. 349–353, 5p.

Tropic of Cancer, Henry Miller
(Obelisk Press, 1934)

Tropic of Cancer is a novel originally published in France but written by an American, expatriate writer. The book has autobiographical elements, though it is also told from a largely subjective perspective. The book does not have a conventional plot. Instead, it is a mix of both times and approaches to narrative, sometimes describing particular scenes and interactions between Miller and his friends and sometimes giving stream-of-consciousness narration from his perspective. The book generally examines Miller's efforts as a struggling writer, and it gives frank depictions of both his sexual desires (and escapades) and his view of society's deterioration. He gives a portrayal of his life in Paris that alternates between being tortured and being romantic, celebrating the sort of desire and unease that Miller claims is conducive to producing art.

The book's innovative style was hailed by many critics, who found this new approach to writing challenging in an interesting and inviting way. American literary figures like H. L. Mencken and European giants like George Orwell both gave praise to the book for its inventiveness and frankness. There were, however, other writers and critics who found fault with the book. In addition to their critiques of its "low" subject matter and style, many critics found the book to be demeaning toward women, as Miller treated female characters as sex objects. In the end, whatever the position writers or critics took, they recognized the noteworthy impact of the book.

It did not take long after the book's publication for it to start receiving significant challenges. The legal history of the book's sale in America is actually quite a complicated one. First, the book was banned in America in 1934, making it illegal for bookstores to import or sell copies. This led to some booksellers to be prosecuted for smuggling copies into the United States and other publishers to be faced with copyright infringement suits. In particular, Medusa Press published the novel in 1940 with an imprint claiming that the book was published in Mexico. After an investigation into the edition, the publisher was sent to jail for violating copyright law and publishing the book. In 1950, the American Civil Liberties Union became involved in the fight to import the book to the United States. The group's director was arrested for trying to import the book, and a court decision ruled that the book was too obscene for publication. In 1961, Grove Press (a house known for publishing challenging books) published the book and its sequel, *Tropic of Capricorn*, and after dozens of lawsuits across the United States with mixed findings, the U.S. Supreme Court ruled in 1964 that the book was not obscene. Around the same time, Canada ruled that the book was no longer obscene, though it had banned the book around the time of its first publication.

See Also: *Lady Chatterley's Lover*.

FURTHER READING

Decker, James M. "Literary Text, Cinematic 'Edition': Adaptation, Textual Authority, and the Filming of *Tropic of Cancer*." *College Literature*, Summer 2007, Vol. 34, Issue 3, pp. 140–160. 21p.

Nesbit, Thomas. "Death, Rebirth and the Self in *Tropic of Cancer*." *Nexus: The International Henry Miller Journal*, 2004, Vol. 1, Issue 1, pp. 149–162.

Turner, Frederick. *Renegade: Henry Miller and the Making of the Tropic of Cancer*. New Haven, CT: Yale University Press, 2012, p. 244.

Twilight Series, Stephenie Meyer
(Little, Brown and Company, 2005–2008)

Twilight is the title of the first book in the Twilight series, and it is also the title used to refer to the series as a whole. The first book follows Bella Swan as she moves from her mother's home to her father's, travelling from Arizona to a small town in Washington. Her father is a police officer in the town, and he is well known and generally well liked. Although Bella is shy, she begins to make friends, and she finds that she is fascinated by a group of siblings, the Cullens, who turn out to be a family of vampires. A romance kindles between Bella and Edward Cullen, though Edward is cautious, as he fears that he will hurt Bella. Still, things go well between the two of them until another vampire from outside the Cullen family discovers that the Cullens do not feed on most humans and that Edward has started a relationship with Bella. The Cullens try to save Bella, sending her to hide in Phoenix, near her mother, but the other vampire tricks and severely injures Bella. When she recovers, she returns to Washington with Edward, and they go to prom together. She continues to ask him to make her a vampire, and he continues to refuse.

The second book, *New Moon*, begins with Bella's eighteenth birthday. While she is unwrapping presents, she gets a paper cut. Unfortunately, one of Edward's brothers becomes overwhelmed when he smells Bella's blood, and he attacks her. After this, the Cullens decide to move away in order to keep Bella safe. Bella begins taking on dangerous activities, like cliff diving. Bella also finds solace in her friend Jacob, who turns out to be a werewolf. Jacob and his tribe of fellow werewolves protect Bella from vampires. During this time, Edward thinks that Bella has killed herself during one of her cliff-diving expeditions. Feeling lost, Edward goes to the Volturi, a group of vampire elite who make all major decisions among vampires. He asks them to destroy him, but they deny him this request. Bella intervenes, but that puts herself in danger from the Volturi, who tell Edward that he must either kill her or make her a vampire. Reluctantly, Edward agrees to make her a vampire. As Jacob discovers the plan to turn Bella into a vampire, he tells Edward that turning her would involve biting her, and Jacob's people and the Cullens have a truce based upon the Cullens not biting any humans. Bella tries to tell Jacob that she wants to be bitten to be turned into a vampire, but before she can fully argue her case, her father finds her and tells her that she needs to return to the house, because she is grounded for sneaking off to Italy.

In the third book, *Eclipse*, Edward is looking into a string of murders happening in Seattle. He believes that the murders are being committed by a newly made vampire who is not able to control his urges. Meanwhile, Bella also tells Edward that she wants to see Jacob. Things intensify even more when Edward proposes to Bella and she accepts. The happiness of this news is undercut by the discovery of a growing vampire army. The Cullens join forces with Jacob's werewolf family to defeat the malevolent vampires. After the battle, Bella tells Jacob that, while she does have feelings for him, she would prefer to be with Edward, and she tells her father that she and Edward intend to get married. The book ends with Jacob leaving the area.

In the final book of the series, *Breaking Dawn*, Edward and Bella get married. The book is divided into three parts, and the marriage and honeymoon make the first part of the book. After the wedding, Edward and Bella travel to a private island near Brazil. While there, Bella discovers that she is pregnant, and, because Edward is the father, the child his half human and half vampire. Bella feels that the baby is growing strangely quickly, and she and Edward return home, concerned. Most of the series is told from the perspective of Bella, but the second part of *Breaking Dawn* is told from Jacob's perspective. The second part begins with Bella's father telling Jacob's father that Bella is sick and needs to be quarantined. Not knowing about the pregnancy, Jacob interprets this as meaning that Bella has been turned into a vampire, which would mean that the Cullens had broken the agreement between themselves and Jacob's tribe. Jacob tries to get the tribe to fight the Cullens, but the leader refuses to make the first move without confirmation that the Cullens did, indeed, bite Bella. Not satisfied with that answer, Jacob tries to hunt down Bella so that he can prove that she is a vampire. When he finds out that it is the pregnancy that is weakening Bella, he tells her that she should not have the baby, because she will not be able to survive the pregnancy. Bella tells him that she will have the baby and that she will become a vampire. Enraged, Jacob turns into a wolf and runs off. Jacob's tribe discovers that Bella is pregnant, and they decide that they cannot allow her to give birth. The leader of the pack says that they need to kill both Bella and the fetus. When Jacob objects, the leader of the pack tries to overpower him, but Jacob evades him, assuming control over the pack. He then goes to the Cullens, warning them that they and Bella might be in danger. Jacob and his closest friends come to realize that the baby will not kill Bella; it simply needs to feed and, if she drinks blood, then the baby will be satiated. Although this works for some time, Bella is severely injured when she gives birth. While she is lying injured, Edward changes her into a vampire. While he is doing this, Jacob goes out after the newborn child, believing that she has killed Bella. Although he intends to stop her, he accidentally makes a psychic connection with her. For the book's third section, it shifts back to Bella's perspective. Her first bit of narration is describing the difficult transition from human to vampire. The narrative then shifts to the status of her daughter. Bella and Edward's daughter, Renesmee, is discovered by a vampire who believes her to be a child who was made into a vampire rather than a child who was born a half vampire. Because children turned to vampires are hard to control, they are generally destroyed. The vampire who discovered Renesmee goes to the Volturi, telling them about Renesmee. The Volturi initially judge the Cullen family as being guilty, and they order that the family and the child all must be destroyed. The Cullens reach out to other vampires, hoping to protect themselves, and Edward uses his psychic powers to let Jacob know that he has made a bond with Renesmee. With this in mind, Jacob and his pack come to the aid of the Cullens. As the various families of vampires come to the Cullens, they recognize that the Volturi have actually been trying to manipulate vampires across the world, trying to maintain their power rather than helping all vampires out. Bella discovers that she has the power to generate a kind of shield that will undercut the Volturi's powers, and other vampires reveal their powers as well. The Volturi travel to the Cullens, but things change when they realize that Renesmee is a child born a half vampire, not a child who was made into a vampire. Still, when they hear of the agreement that the Cullens made with Jacob's pack, they still accuse the Cullens of consorting with the enemies of vampires. However, Jacob's pack reveals that they are shape-shifters and not proper werewolves, leaving the Volturi uncertain of how to proceed. While they are trying to decide, another half human/half vampire is revealed, this one 150 years old. The hybrid human/vampire also tells the Volturi that his father intends to create an army of hybrids. The Volturi decide to leave the Cullens. Once they have left, Bella lets down her mental shield and shares with Edward her feelings and memories from both her human life and her vampire life.

The series was an immense commercial success, selling hundreds of millions of copies and being translated into over three dozen languages. It also was adapted into both graphic novel form and into a series of highly successful movies, which also spurred on significant sales of the books. The films broke a number of records for commercial success. The series also spawned a high number of parodies and references in a variety of media. Meyer, the series' author, had also intended to rewrite at least one of the books from Edward's point of view, but after a portion of the first rewrite was leaked on the Internet, she called off those plans. The books continue to have a steady readership, and there are even Twilight conventions as well as sections of larger conventions dedicated to science fiction or comic books in which the series is the core focus.

Critical reaction of the series was mixed. Many prominent critics and outlets praised the book for generating interest in reading for young adults. Interestingly, much of the positive reception for the book was based more upon its success as a trend than it was on the quality of the writing. Many writers, perhaps most notably Stephen King, have compared the Twilight series negatively to the Harry Potter series, indicating that J. K. Rowling is a much better writer than Stephenie Meyer. In particular, critics tend to cite the flatness of the characters and many plot conveniences of the series, arguing that Meyer lacks the polish and technical proficiency of most major writers. In addition, there was a significant backlash against the portrayal of gender and relationships in the book. In addition to the fact that Bella is often portrayed as a desperate, one-dimensional character who is emotionally dominated by Edward, a number of critics have argued that, according to the criteria set out by the National Domestic Violence Hotline, Edward and Bella's relationship could be deemed abusive. Even some psychologists have stated in the media that Bella could be an unhealthy model for young women to follow, because she is portrayed as being very dependent upon Edward and his family, making her fall into the cliché of the damsel in distress rather than being a strong female character. Meyer has dismissed such criticisms, claiming that Bella represents a new brand of feminism, but most feminist critics have distanced themselves from this claim.

There also was some criticism that the book preached an impractical message of abstinence, leading some critics to coin the term "abstinence porn." Interestingly, this claim is contrasted by the numerous challenges to the book for being too sexually explicit. In 2009, the series held the number 5 spot on the American Library Association's "Most Challenged Books" list. In addition to the complaints of being sexually explicit, the books were challenged for promoting a specific religious viewpoint, with some challengers focusing on Stephanie Meyer's Mormon beliefs. The final reason listed among the challenges was that it was "unsuitable for age group." This last category contained a number of (sometimes contradictory) motivations. In addition to concerns about Bella's behavior, sneaking off to see Edward and not telling her father some of her secrets, there were also some librarians who had concerns about Bella as a model for young female readers. In the end, most challenges remained challenges rather than successful bans, and the book has maintained a high level of visibility in part because of its many challenges and ongoing controversy.

FURTHER READING

Barbara, Stephen. "How Stephanie Meyer Cramps My Style." *Publishers Weekly*, December 7, 2009, Vol. 256, Issue 49, p. 54.

Merskin, Debra. "A Boyfriend to Die For: Edward Cullen as Compensated Psychopath in Stephanie Meyer's *Twilight*." *Journal of Communication Inquiry*, April 2011, Vol. 35, Issue 2, pp. 157–178, 22p.

Owens, Alexandra. "Limited by Stereotypes: Gender Bias in Stephanie Meyer's Twilight Series." *LOGOS: A Journal of Undergraduate Research*, Fall 2011, Vol. 4, pp. 124–137, 14p.

Ulysses, James Joyce
(Sylvia Beach, 1922)

Ulysses is a modernist novel by Irish writer James Joyce. The book is comprised of a number of episodes, all relating to the Greek epic, *The Odyssey*. The book is also partially a continuation of Joyce's book, *Portrait of the Artist as a Young Man*. The book opens with Stephen Dedalus and his roommate, Buck Mulligan, journeying to the roof of the building where they live. The two are not friendly, and things worsen when Buck tells Stephen that another person will be coming to live with them. The third person is English, which provides more friction with Stephen, who is Irish. Stephen says that he will no longer stay with Mulligan, because the third man has usurped his position, referring to the many suitors of Penelope in *The Odyssey*. The next episode sees Stephen teaching a history class focusing on Pyrrhus, who was known for achieving a military victory at such cost that it could be perceived as a victory in name only. Stephen then talks to the school headmaster, who espouses anti-Semitic views. The final episode of the first section is a mix of high and low events, with Stephen thinking about different philosophical ideas and also committing base acts, like picking his nose and urinating in public. The next section starts with episodes following Leopold Bloom, who is partially Jewish. Bloom and his wife Molly are both having affairs, which unsettles Bloom, though he continues to go through the motions of his marriage, and he does feel affection for Molly. After attending a funeral, Bloom goes to a newspaper office, looking to place an ad. By coincidence, Stephen also arrives at the office, though the two do not directly cross paths. Throughout these events, Joyce examines Irish and Catholic culture, examining the political and social dimensions. The book continues to follow Bloom and Stephen, taking various approaches to narrating their days and using different motifs, like food and music, all the while musing on different schools of philosophical and political thoughts. Bloom and Stephen finally meet in episode fourteen, where they end up going drinking together. In that chapter, Joyce uses pieces of English from various parts of the language's development, ending in an unusual delivery meant to imitate drunkenness. The following chapter is the close of the second section, and it is written in play format. It also is comprised largely of hallucinations from the perspective of Stephen and Bloom. The final section begins with Bloom and Stephen looking to sober themselves up, first at a cabman's shelter and then at Bloom's home. At Bloom's home, the two discuss the possibility of Bloom publishing some of Stephen's writing, though Stephen decides against it before leaving. After Stephen leaves, Bloom goes to bed with his wife, where the pair have a long and strange exchange of questions and answers. The final episode is an extensive inner monologue from the perspective of Molly Bloom.

Because of Joyce's unconventional style, every edition of the book has had numerous "mistakes," and editing the book has consistently proven to be problematic at best. In 1984, Hans Walter Gabler took on the task of providing a definitive, "correct" edition, though he received a significant and widespread backlash. Because of this backlash, in 1990, Gabler's edition was discontinued in favor of a previous version.

Critical reaction to the book differed wildly. Literary giants T. S. Eliot and Virginia Woolf took opposite stances, with Eliot proclaiming the book to be a work of literary genius, as it originated a number of literary innovations while still honoring a rich tradition of literature. Woolf, by contrast, noted the book's daring but proclaimed it a massive failure. Reaction to the book was not limited to writers and literary critics. Psychologist Carl Jung weighed in on the book as well, seeing the book as original and captivating.

The book has also been loosely adapted into other media. In 1958, an off-Broadway play based on one of the episodes from the book was produced, and it became a Broadway production in 1974. There have also been two film adaptations as well as a musical adaptation and a novel retelling of the story set in New York City. Scholarly study of the text has been sustained for decades.

Despite its status as a landmark text, the book has met challenges from a variety of sources. The book was originally published in serial form, and some sections of the book were banned upon publication, leading the United Kingdom to ban the book in its entirety. In 1920, one of the published sections was challenged in the United States because it contained a scene with a character masturbating. Defenders of the book claimed that the highly abstract language used in the scene would mean that many readers would fail to recognize what the content was, but, in the early 1920s, the book was put on trial, and it was declared obscene, leading the book to be banned in the United States. In 1933, American publisher Random House imported the book from France, leading to a second trial. This time, the book was deemed fit for publication and distribution in America. But the legal challenges were not the only challenges that the book faced. It also was burned in both Ireland and America. The book's challenges have generally subsided, and it has cemented its place in the literary canon.

FURTHER READING

Brown, Stephanie J. "The Great Criminal, the Exception and Bare Life in James Joyce's *Ulysses*." Criticism, Fall 2015, Vol. 56, Issue 4, pp. 781–805, 25p.

Haas, Robert. "A James Joyce Bestiary: Animal Symbols in *Ulysses*." ANQ, January 2014, Vol. 27, Issue 1, pp. 31–39, 9p.

Kikuchi, Shigeo. "The Two Walking Candles in James Joyce's *Ulysses*." Journal of Literary Semantics, April 2016, Vol. 45, Issue 1, pp. 77–89, 13p.

Whale Talk, Chris Crutcher
(Greenwillow Books, 2001)

Whale Talk is a novel by prominent young adult author Chris Crutcher. The book follows TJ, a young man of mixed descent (African American, Japanese, and white) who has been adopted by white parents. Although TJ is a gifted athlete, he refuses to take part in high school athletics, because he has a history of outbursts. Added to that is the anxiety that he sees his adoptive father deal with after he accidentally killed a child while driving and the background of his adoptive mother, who is a lawyer dealing with cases of child abuse. TJ's frustration builds as he sees a prominent athlete, Mike, belittling a cognitively disabled student. Mr. Simet, an English teacher at the high school who has befriended TJ, suggests to TJ that they start a swim team that will include students who feel like outcasts. TJ recruits an odd mix for the swim team, including the picked-on disabled student, a character who is overweight, another who is antisocial, and a variety of other outcasts. While TJ is assembling his team, a friend of the cruel athlete, Mike, is coming up against TJ's family. The man, Rich, has adopted the mixed-descent daughter (African American and white) of his new wife. TJ runs into the daughter, Heidi, and discovers that Rich is a racist alcoholic. Meanwhile, after almost all of the members of the swim team have earned letters, the rest of the school has grown suspicious of their success. TJ suggests that they prove their worth by a swimming race between Mike, the bully athlete, and Chris, the cognitively disabled swimmer that bears much of the brunt of Mike's taunting. After this success, TJ organizes a basketball team with the other members of the swim team and TJ's father. At a game, Heidi's father, Rich, pulls a gun on her, but TJ's father jumps in front of her, taking the bullet that was meant for Heidi. Before dying, TJ's father tells him the name of the woman whose child he accidentally ran over and with whom he had a one-night stand. TJ seeks out the woman that his father told him about, and he finds out that the woman had a child from the relationship with TJ's father. TJ finds the child (now a grown man) and connects with him, quickly becoming good friends.

The book quickly received a good deal of positive response, being referenced as a positive book for adolescents feeling like they were outcasts. It also received some rewards, like the Washington State Book Award and a "Best Books" honor from the American Library Association. The book was also translated into Japanese, with an interest in it partially because of the quarter-Japanese heritage of TJ.

Although some readers and reviewers saw the material as being generally helpful for adolescents, some objected to the material within the book. As early as 2001 (the year of the book's first publication), the book received a challenge in Missouri, with the objecting parent simply stating that the values shown in the book (presumably the violence and the father's one-night stand) were not what the parent wanted children reading. Despite the challenge, the book was retained by the school board. When the book was challenged in Portland, Chris Crutcher took part in an on-air debate with radio personality Lars Larson, marking one of several times when Crutcher has directly or publically weighed in on the issue of censorship of his books. The book has also been challenged a number of times for its use of obscene language. While these challenges rarely resulted in outright bans, it has resulted a number of times in having the book removed from class-reading lists. That said, there were instances when the book was banned outright, such as in the Limestone County School District in Alabama, where the book was banned districtwide for its profanity and use of the lord's name in vain. It has also been challenged for potentially being racially or socially offensive because of both material with mixed-heritage characters and the consistent challenges to authority figures within the book. All of this has made *Whale Talk* one of Crutcher's not only most challenged but also most talked about books.

See Also: *Athletic Shorts* and *The Sledding Hill*.

FURTHER READING

Krug, Julie. "Making Waves." *Writer (Madavor Media)*, May 2014, Vol. 127, Issue 5, pp. 22–26, 5p.

Lesesne, Teri S. "Banned in Berlin: An Interview with Chris Crutcher." *Emergency Librarian*, May/June 1996, Vol. 23, Issue 5, pp. 61–63, 3p.

Prince, Julie. "Teacher, Therapist, Free Speech Advocate: An Interview with Chris Crutcher." *Teacher Librarian*, December 2009, Vol. 37 Issue 2, p. 70–72. 3p.

Where's Waldo? Series, Martin Hanford
(Little Brown & Co., 1987)

Where's Waldo? is a popular series of children's books. The books lacked a narrative or writing. Instead, they were double-page images packed with characters. The goal of these books was to find the main character "Waldo," who was hidden among the characters. Waldo always looked the same in each picture, having glasses, a red-and-white-striped shirt, and a hat with a puffball on top. The series sold tremendously well, and its lack of narration allowed it to be published across the globe, because there was no need for translation. After the books' financial success, there were a number of attempts at adaptation. These ranged from a magazine to a television to a movie.

Although the books were generally seen as both pleasant and innocuous, the first book, *Where's Waldo?* received a significant number of challenges after readers noticed that there was a topless woman in one of the images, which many parents felt was inappropriate. The challenges came in so frequently that the book actually was in the top one hundred "Most Challenged Books" from 1990 to 2000 list compiled by the American Library Association. Despite these challenges, the books have remained a major force in children's publishing.

FURTHER READING

Fallon, Kevin. "Where's Waldo? Turns 25." *Newsweek*, September 24, 2012, Vol. 160, Issue 13, p. 52.
Peabody, Amanda. "Show Your Stripes! Where's Waldo? Celebrates 25 Years." *License! Global*, June 2012, Vol. 15, Issue 3, pp. 94–96, 3p.
"Where's Waldo? The Incredible Paper Chase." *Publishers Weekly*, October 19, 2009, Vol. 256, Issue 42, p. 54.

Women in Love, D. H. Lawrence
(Thomas Seltzer, 1920)

Women in Love is the sequel to D. H. Lawrence's book, *The Rainbow*. The book follows two sisters, Ursula and Gudrun Brangwen. The sisters meet two men, and they begin parallel relationships. Ursula, a school teacher, becomes involved with Rupert Birkin, a school inspector, and Gudrun, an artist, becomes involved with Gerald Crich, whose family became rich by owning coal mines. The four intermingle and discuss a variety of topics of the day, particularly politics and gender relations, giving Lawrence a chance to examine different ideas through the characters' conversations. Gerald's family experiences a series of tragedies, including the drowning death of his sister and the death of his father. As Gerald seeks comfort, he and Gudrun have sexual relations in Gudrun's parents' home while her parents are sleeping, something that would have been seen as scandalous at the time. Rupert and Ursula's relationship progresses as well, with Rupert asking for Ursula's hand in marriage and Ursula granting it. While the sisters and their love interests go on vacation, Gudrun's relationship with Gerald deteriorates as she becomes interested in another artist. Gerald attacks Gudrun, nearly killing her, but he relents and wanders off into the night, eventually freezing to death. Rupert is shaken by this, and he begins to withdraw from Ursula, telling her that, without Gerald, his interest in being part of her and her family's life has diminished.

Even before *Women in Love* came out, there were issues surrounding it. Lawrence had intended for the book to be part of its predecessor, but the manuscript was broken up into two books at the publisher's request. Lawrence also had to make a number of revisions to *Women in Love*, particularly after a series of legal difficulties with *The Rainbow*, including a ban in the United Kingdom that would last beyond the publication of *Women in Love* in other countries. In addition to the ban, Lawrence and the publisher had to deal with libel suits from people claiming to be the inspiration for the book. Reception to *Women in Love* was no less tumultuous. The book immediately received harsh criticism for its direct discussion and portrayal of sex. The book was seized in 1922 for its content, and it has been challenged repeatedly until recent years. In addition to its frank portrayal of sex, it also has come under fire when some readers have interpreted the concluding scenes as a subtle indication of homosexual desire between the two male characters, a charge that has led some critics to conclude that Lawrence himself was gay. Interestingly, more recent criticism has focused less on the sexual content or the possible homosexual desire and more on Lawrence's harsh portrayal of women. Many feminist critics have deplored Lawrence's work for marginalizing female characters, often treating them largely as objects of desire for the male characters.

Despite these challenges and criticisms, *Women in Love* has been a major object of study for scholars for decades. Lawrence is seen as a groundbreaking figure precisely for his frank discussion of human sexuality and desire. In addition to the critical attention that his work has received, the book has received attention in popular culture, having been adapted multiple times. Perhaps the most noteworthy adaptation was in 1969, when it was made into a film. The adaptation was noteworthy for two reasons. First, it earned Glenda Jackson an Academy Award, and, second, it was one of the first films to show male nudity. Like the book, the film was met with mixed reactions, but it was well received overall. The book, along with *The Rainbow*, was also adapted for television by the BBC, which is a bit ironic given that the United Kingdom had banned the books for an extended period of time. With the adaptations and critical study, the book remains a significant, though contested, work of British literature.

See Also: *Lady Chatterley's Lover, The Rainbow,* and *Sons and Lovers.*

FURTHER READING

Howe, Andrew. "Beastly Desires: Human/Animal Interactions in DH Lawrence's *Women in Love.*" *Papers on Language & Literature,* Fall 2002, Vol. 38, Issue 4, pp. 429–421, 13p.

Leone, Matthew. *"The Rainbow & Women in Love." English Literature in Transition, 1880–1920,* 2007, Vol. 50, Issue 4, pp. 487–490, 4p.

Tilghman, Carolyn. "Unruly Desire, Domestic Authority and Odd Coupling in DH Lawrence's *Women in Love." Women's Studies,* March 2008, Vol. 37, Issue 2, pp. 89–109, 21p.

Women on Top, Nancy Friday
(Simon & Schuster, 1991)

Women on Top is a follow-up to Nancy Friday's book, *My Secret Garden*, which was a collection of women's sexual fantasies. *Women on Top* looked in particular at female fantasies that were grounded in a sense of female figures in control, even having chapters on women in positions of physical dominance and women fantasizing about lesbian encounters. Friday used the emergence of these fantasies to form an argument that there had been another sexual revolution, one in which women felt a greater level of freedom and control in their sexual lives.

Not surprisingly, the book received significant challenges. In late 1996, the book was challenged in a library in Pennsylvania. While there was significant discussion within the community, the library board ultimately decided that parents would need to be in charge of determining what their children read rather than relying upon the library to screen books. However, they did adopt stronger selection criteria for what books made it on the shelves. In 1997, a library in Georgia did remove the book from shelves. The struggle over the book has continued, though the book has also been examined by a number of readers and feminist critics.

FURTHER READING

Stein, Joe. "Spicing It Up." *Time*, January 19, 2004, Vol. 163, Issue 3, pp. 117–118, 2p.

Walls, Jeannette. "Oh God, It's Friday!" *Esquire*, July 1996, Vol. 126, Issue 1, p. 16.

Wechsler, Pat, and Ruth G. Davis. "Nancy Friday's Secret Garden Gnome." *New York*, May 23, 1994, Vol. 27, Issue 21, p. 9.

4

SEXUAL ORIENTATION AND CENSORSHIP IN AMERICA

The role and portrayal of gay and lesbian characters in American culture is a long and complex one. Many of the discussions about potentially gay characters are less about overt portrayals of or commentary upon sexual orientation and more about the implication of homosexual relationships. In some cases, such as *Leaves of Grass*, the objections originated not because of portrayals of gay sex or homosexual desire but because of the sexual orientation of the writers themselves. Indeed, speculations over different authors' sexual lives have fueled some challenges. What this means is that speculation about either the sexual orientation of the authors or the characters can spark debate. These types of anxieties stretched from literary publishing to more commercial fare like *Batman*, which some critics claimed promoted homosexuality because it had three unmarried men living together without any women.

Although these anxieties were present for decades, the debate over portrayal of same-sex relationships intensified in the late 1970s and early 1980s. With books like *Annie on My Mind*, religious and parent groups felt concern over portrayals of underage characters who were gay. The general homophobia of the era exacerbated the anxieties over positive or even neutral portrayals of gay characters. As time went on, some of the homophobia diminished, but new issues sprang up in censorship battles. In addition to the portrayal of gay couples, books with adult characters who were gay and interacted with children drew major fire when they started being published in the 1990s. Books like *Arizona Kid* and *Daddy's Roommate* received harsh and widespread criticism when critics claimed that the pairing of gay adults and children of the same sex were upsetting or offensive. This debate was complicated by other events, like Ellen DeGeneres being the first star of a major network sitcom to come out both within the show and in her real life and a number of other actors, writers, and comedians coming out. Other events, like the brutal murder of Matthew Shepard and subsequent legislation advocating for stricter penalties for hate crimes, gave a real sense of urgency to the need for greater and more civilized discussion of sexual orientation.

Heterosexual writers began to include gay characters in major roles, like young adult novel writer Chris Crutcher who, in a number of his books, gave gay characters realistic conflicts and rich interior lives. Crutcher is also significant because he often directly related the debate about sexual orientation to religious movements and beliefs.

TIMELINE

1903—Gertrude Stein's QED published, giving a first-person account of a lesbian affair

1924—The Society for Human Rights was founded, establishing the first official group championing the rights of gays and lesbians

1948—*Sexual Behavior in the Human Male*, Alfred Kinsey, published, finding that homosexual activity is not limited to men who identify as primarily homosexual

1950—Mattachine Society founded, fighting for the rights of gays and lesbians; also "Employment of Homosexuals and Other Sex Perverts in Government" was distributed among congressmen, starting a massive firing of people believed to be homosexual

1952—Homosexuality is labeled a mental illness by the American Psychiatric Association (APA)

1955—Daughters of Bilitis founded, establishing the first group advocating for lesbian rights; also "Howl," Allen Ginsberg, published

1956—Evelyn Hooker study published, indicating that male homosexuality was not a mental illness, changing course from the 1952 pronouncement by the APA

1962—Illinois became the first state to decriminalize sodomy

1966—National Transsexual Counselling Unit established after a riot involving the police took place in San Francisco

1969—Raid on Stonewall Bar led to a riot between customers and the police, establishing what most come to see as the beginning of the modern lesbian, gay, bisexual, and transgender (LGBT) rights movement

1970—First gay pride parade

1972—Homosexuality taken off of the list of mental illnesses published by the APA

1977—Harvey Milk elected to office in San Francisco

1978—Harvey Milk assassinated

1979—LGBT groups participated in a march in Washington DC

1982—Wisconsin outlawed discrimination based upon sexual orientation, becoming the first state to do so; also *Annie on My Mind*, Nancy Garden, published

1987—ACT UP formed to deal with the perceived shortcomings of the government's treatment of the AIDS epidemic

1991—*Daddy's Roommate*, Michael Willhoite, published

1993—"Don't Ask Don't Tell" policy enacted for the military, forbidding questions about sexual orientation of applicants

1998—Matthew Shepard murdered for being gay, drawing attention to the severity of the problem of hate crimes

2000—Civil unions for same-sex couples legalized in Vermont

2005—*And Tango Makes Three*, Peter Parnell and Justin Richardson, published

2008—Same-sex marriages made legal in California

And Tango Makes Three, Peter Parnell and Justin Richardson

(Simon & Schuster's Children's Publishing, 2005)

This short children's book is loosely based upon a series of real events involving two male penguins at New York's Central Park Zoo. The zoo's keepers observed the two male penguins engaging in behaviors typically reserved for mates and, upon realizing the possible implication of these behaviors, gave the two male birds an egg to hatch and raise. The egg hatched, producing a female penguin who was named Tango. The book earned a number of honors for both storytelling and its portrayal of potentially charged subject matter, but it also received a good deal of scrutiny and opposition, receiving the designation of "Most Challenged Book of the Year" multiple times.

The authors of the book acknowledged that the book was written at least partially to give parents a way to discuss same-sex-parent families with children, but they also have indicated that it was not to explicitly promote a particular political or social agenda. Nevertheless, schools around the country received a good deal of pressure when the book was made available to the general student body. In Shiloh, Illinois, for instance, there was a strong push to put the book in a "restricted" section, which would require parental consent to access. While the district superintendent did not place the book in such a section, there was considerable public debate over this move. Across the country, much attention was paid to the placement of the book, with some critics claiming that *And Tango Makes Three* should be placed either in the nonfiction section, a special "alternative lifestyles" section, or even a section that could only be accessed by parents, not by students or children at all. In addition, there was much public debate about both the accuracy of the book (zookeepers acknowledged that, while the two male penguins exhibited behavior typically reserved for mates, they did not perform any homosexual acts) and the impact upon children that the book might have. In fact, while the book's focus on same-sex-parent families has rightly received significant discussion, the impact that it has had upon decisions about libraries and schools carrying books is seen by some as being even more significant than the content of the book, with the American Civil Liberties Union (ACLU) eventually taking a major role in the book's defense.

Currently, the book is still widely carried by schools and libraries, though with continued debate over issues like same-sex marriage and same-sex adoption, the challenges to the book are likely to continue, as is the defense of the book by a variety of groups.

FURTHER READING

Harvey, Jennifer. "And Tango Makes Three." *Children & Libraries: The Journal of the Association for Library Service to Children*, Winter 2013, Vol. 11, Issue 3, pp. 27–33, 7p.

Magnuson, Marta L. "Perceptions of the Self and the 'Other': An Analysis of Challenges to *And Tango Makes Three*." *School Library Media Research*, 2011, Vol. 14.

Young, Craig A. "Creating a Controversial Picturebook: Discussions with the Creators of *And Tango Makes Three*." *Journal of Children's Literature*, Fall 2011, Vol. 37, Issue 2, pp. 30–38.

Annie on My Mind, Nancy Garden
(Farrar, Straus & Giroux, 1982)

Annie on My Mind is a young adult novel that looks at two seventeen-year-old girls (Annie and Liza) from significantly different socioeconomic backgrounds, but who become friends and, eventually, enter into a romantic relationship. The book portrays the persecution of Liza for her sexual orientation. When she is "found out," the headmistress of Liza's private school tries to have her expelled, though the school's board supports Liza's right to stay at the school. The novel's positive portrayal of Annie and Liza and its negative characterization of their antagonists made the novel quite controversial for many readers. While there is some direct discussion of the physical acts between the two girls, the descriptions are not overly graphic or lurid, and much of the book discussed self-discovery or a feeling of connection rather than dwelling on physical desire.

Although the book was met with many positive reviews by critics, some schools and administrators were openly hostile to it. In 1993, a pro-LGBT group in Kansas distributed copies of *Annie on My Mind*, and there was a significant backlash, with some parents even burning the books. Nancy Garden, the book's author, reacted with shock, saying that burning books should have stopped in Nazi Germany. Rather than defending the book, the superintendent had the book pulled from the schools' library shelves. After the ACLU brought legal action against the district, the school had to return the book.

Despite (or perhaps partially because of) this controversy, *Annie on My Mind* has been very commercially successful. It has never been out of print since its first publication in 1982. In addition, the book and Nancy Garden have both received a number of honors for both the quality of the writing and the significance of the book as a cultural document.

FURTHER READING

Broz, William J. "Hope and Irony: *Annie on My Mind*." *English Journal*, July 2001, Vol. 90, Issue 6, pp. 47–53, 7p.

Meyer, Randy. "Annie's Day in Court." *School Library Journal*, April 1996, Vol. 42, Issue 4, pp. 22–25, 4p.

Sutton, Roger. "A Second Look: *Annie on My Mind*." *Horn Book Magazine*, September/October 2007, Vol. 83, Issue 5, pp. 543–546, 4p.

Arizona Kid, Ron Koertge
(Joy Street Books, 1988)

Arizona Kid is a young adult novel that follows a high school-aged boy, Billy, who feels uncertain and isolated. To gain some confidence, Billy travels to Arizona, where he spends the summer with his uncle, Wes, who is gay. Billy gets a job caring for horses at a racetrack. While with his uncle, Billy begins to gain a greater level of faith in himself, becomes physically stronger, and loses his virginity. Much of his increase in self-esteem comes from talking to his uncle about the struggles that he had in coming out as and being gay. Not surprisingly, both the open discussion of homosexuality and the frank discussions of sexual desire drew criticism and opposition at the time the book was published in the late 1980s. Although there was opposition, the book became quite popular, being listed as one of the "Best Books for Young Adults" by the American Library Association and eventually being republished by Little, Brown & Company.

Interestingly, Koertge is not known solely for his work as a young adult author. Although he has published other young adult works, such as *Coaltown Jesus* and *Stoner & Spaz*, Koertge has also published adult books, such as *The Ogre's Wife* and *Sex World*. He has also published poetry in respected literary venues. Perhaps because of his background in writing more complex works, Koertge engages in difficult material with *Arizona Kid* (as he does in *Stoner & Spaz* that features a teenaged boy with cerebral palsy becoming romantically interested in a drug-using teenaged girl). However, Koertge also has some of the typical features of young adult writing, such as fast-paced and humorous dialogue and a focus on young characters. Many critics find that these characteristics help to make Koertge's material more accessible to younger readers, but some feel that this accessibility is problematic, because it does not encourage these younger readers to examine material like coming out or sexual activity with the level of seriousness they deserve. Still, other readers were resistant to any real positive portrayal of gay characters at the time that the book first came out. In particular, the interactions between a teenaged male character and an adult, male homosexual character unsettled some parents. Not surprisingly, the book has been banned in many schools across the country. Over time, *Arizona Kid* has been vindicated, receiving praise from many readers and critics and being one of the major works of Koertge's career.

FURTHER READING

Blasingame, James. "Interview with Ron Koertge." *Journal of Adolescent & Adult Literacy*, March 2005, Vol. 48, Issue 6, pp. 526–527, 2p.

Koertge, Ron. "Legacy." *Horn Book Magazine*, July/August 2012, Vol. 88, Issue 4, p. 91.

Margolis, Rick. "Da Do Ron Ron." *School Library Journal*, October 2011, Vol. 57, Issue 10, p. 24.

Athletic Shorts, Chris Crutcher
(Greenwillow Books, 1991)

Athletic Shorts is a collection of short stories written for young adult readers. Each of the stories portrays a young athlete experiencing a major struggle. These struggles can run from pressure that the athletes feel from their parents to issues related to sports and gender to getting to know someone with AIDS. One of the most controversial stories involved a young boy with autism who repeats the racial slurs his father uses only within his home, never in public. The book received positive reviews, earning multiple awards. However, the book also was challenged by a small handful of parents for a number of reasons, including its use of obscene language, its portrayal of homosexuality, and its treatment of religion.

Although many of the themes might not seem particularly controversial today, at the time that the book came out, many parents and school officials felt that the material was too dark and too challenging for young adult readers. Interestingly, Crutcher's background as both a family therapist and a college athlete (Crutcher swam at Eastern Washington University) may well have given him the experience and perspective on these issues to portray them in a way that was interesting and helpful to teenaged readers struggling with issues arising from competition or the confusion of watching adults be close-minded or hurtful. Crutcher attempted to downplay some of the controversial material, even including a short preface to the story, "Telephone Man," clarifying that the story was meant to critique the use of racist terms rather than validate them. Nevertheless, the collection of stories was pulled off the shelves at an elementary school in South Carolina in 1995. At a middle school in Alaska in 2005, the book was challenged but ultimately remained on the shelves. Other small challenges occurred around the country, though the book (like many of Crutcher's) tended to receive sufficient support and interest to keep it available.

See Also: *The Sledding Hill* and *Whale Talk*.

FURTHER READING

Davis, Terry. *Presenting Chris Crutcher.* New York, NY: Twayne, 1997, pp. xxvi, 144.
Follos, Alison M. G. "Author Profile: The '3 C's' of Chris Crutcher." *Library Media Connection*, November/December 2006, Vol. 25, Issue 3, pp. 40–43, 4p.
Raymond, Allen. "Chris Crutcher: Helps Teachers Know Kids." *Teaching Pre K-8*, February 1990, Vol. 20, Issue 5, pp. 42–44, 3p.

Daddy's Roommate, **Michael Willhoite**
(Alyson Books, 1991)

Daddy's Roommate is a children's book written to open up discussions about gay parents. In the book, the main character's parents have divorced, and his father has found a life partner. The book describes the father and his partner doing relatively mundane tasks, such as taking care of their home, interacting with his son, and other regular activities. This treatment of the homosexual father as unremarkable actually angered some conservative commentators, because this neutral or positive treatment of a homosexual parent was new at the time of the book's writing.

Not surprisingly, the book received challenges from parents, though perhaps even more from conservative politicians. In 1995, Wasilla City Council member Sarah Palin worked to have the book removed from her hometown library. This led to scrutiny of both the book and of Palin. Michael Willhoite, author of *Daddy's Roommate*, made no secret of his disdain for Palin at the time. This disdain was only strengthened when Palin admitted to having lodged the challenge without having actually read the book. When Palin eventually became mayor of

Wasilla, she tried to get the town librarian to remove the book from the library, going so far as to fire the librarian after the librarian refused (although Palin did reinstate the librarian after sufficient public pressure had been applied). These sorts of acts made Palin a target for many liberal commentators as well as Willhoite, and this sort of very public discussion helped to keep *Daddy's Roommate* in the headlines, which, in turn, led groups to advocate for the book. During Palin's run for vice president, Willhoite stated that he saw her as unqualified for the office and very shortsighted on social issues.

One of the issues that many readers had with the book was likely the fact that a male child was with two gay men. While any text portraying gays or lesbians in a positive way during the 1990s would receive scrutiny and skepticism, texts that portrayed children and homosexual adults of the same gender often received an extra level of hostility from conservative critics. Antigay activists often made the claim that there was the potential for the children being molested as well as claimed that the books worked to indoctrinate young people into becoming gay. While this sort of accusation never was supported with legitimate evidence, it did not stop critics and parent groups from attacking books like *Daddy's Roommate* by Michael Willhoite and *Heather Has Two Mommies* by Leslea Newman. Still, this sort of attention and boundary breaking has helped to make the books in this category significant entries in both children's literature and the larger struggle for civil rights for the LGBT community.

See Also: *Heather Has Two Mommies*.

FURTHER READING

Newman, Leslea. "Heather and Her Critics." *Horn Book Magazine*, March/April 1997, Vol. 73, Issue 2, pp. 149–154, 6p.

Sadowski, Michael J. "In Biggest School Challenge, *Daddy's Roommate* Is Staying." *School Library Journal*, January 1994, Vol. 40, Issue 1, pp. 11–12, 2p.

Staff. "*Daddy's Roommate* Challenged in VT." *Library Journal*, July 1, 1995, Vol. 120, Issue 12, pp. 14–16, 3p.

Empress of the World, Sara Ryan
(Viking, 2001)

Empress of the World is a young adult novel that explores a girl's exploration of her sexuality. Nicola Lancaster is a bright girl but is still finding her way as the book starts. She is interested in archeology, and she attends a summer institute for gifted children to see if the field is what she truly wants to pursue. While there, Nicola befriends a variety of other gifted youths, such as Katrina, a computer-savvy young girl, Kevin, a composer who can express himself with music but not as well in social interactions, and Battle, a graceful dancer. As Nicola and her friends work through the intense summer programs, Nicola finds herself connecting most fully to Battle. Before long, the two develop romantic feelings for each other. This leads to a number of tensions, some from bullying that Nicola and Battle receive from other kids and also from the discord that develops between Battle and her father, whose religious views are at odds with a possible lesbian relationship. These tensions are also increased by jealousy and typical teenaged relationship problems. In the end, the various problems prove to be too much for the relationship, but Nicola has still gained a new perspective on her romantic interests.

Empress of the World gained a relatively small but very loyal following. Many readers (young readers especially) appreciated seeing struggles similar to their own being represented in commercial fiction. However, the book still faced challenges from administrators and parent groups. While there was some concern for different aspects of the book, the main focal point of the challenges was the heavy focus on a homosexual relationship between teenaged characters. In the same way that books like *Annie on My Mind* faced criticism from conservative quarters, *Empress of the World* was met with complaints and accusations about its portrayal of homosexuality. Unlike some texts (*Daddy's Roommate*, for instance), this book did not focus solely on the positive aspects of a homosexual relationship. Still, in 2002, the book faced challenges in Texas and other states.

FURTHER READING

Garden, Nancy. *"Empress of the World." Lambda Book Report*, November/December 2001, Vol. 10, Issue 4, pp. 29–31, 3p.

Jones, Trevelyn E., Luann Toth, Marlene Charnizon, Daryl Grabarek, Jeanne Larkins, and Francisca Goldsmith. *"Empress of the World* (Book Review)." *School Library Journal*, July 2001, Vol. 47, Issue 7, pp. 113–114, 2p.

Kneen, Bonnie. "Neither Very Bi nor Particularly Sexual: The Essence of the Bisexual in Young Adult Literature." *Children's Literature in Education: An International Quarterly*, December 2015, Vol. 46, Issue 4, pp. 359–377.

Howl and Other Poems, Allen Ginsberg
(City Lights Books, 1955)

Howl and Other Poems is a collection of poetry by Beat Generation writer Allen Ginsberg. The title poem, "Howl," was an attempt by Ginsberg to "write without restrictions," by which he meant to express himself in an open and raw way, trying not to let form or social barriers constrain his ideas and their artistic expression.

It is a lengthy poem with three sections. The first section is, in a sense, autobiographical, with Ginsberg describing a number of his friends, particularly focusing on their genius, their sense of freedom and experimentation, and the tragic ways in which they were dismissed or oppressed by the dominant culture. In the second section, Ginsberg turns his focus from the oppressed to the oppressor, embodied in the biblical "Moloch." Moloch becomes the embodiment of greed, competition, and selfishness as it appears in a capitalist culture. The second section is different from the first not only it its focus but also in its syntax and structure, a fact that many have cited when defending the precision and technique of the poem. The final full section returns to a sense of joy, dedicating itself to Carl Solomon (named "Rockland" in the poem), a fellow writer who Ginsberg had met in a mental institution. This final section gives the poem a sense of balance, returning to an excited state after the grim dip in the second section. Following the third section, there is a "footnote" in which Ginsberg declares a series of things holy. The list is broad and inclusive, referencing both things that many would agree are wonderful and also base things that shocked many readers.

The book in general and the poem in particular set off a sensation in a number of ways. It became a touchstone for the Beat writers and for the larger counterculture who identified with the celebration of experimenting with both love and drugs found in the poem. In addition, the bold, ambitious structure and approach of the poem earned it positive reviews from a number of readers and critics. Of course, not every critic immediately embraced the poem. Some objected to incorporation of base themes and images, though others saw this merely as a continuation of the sort of work done by Walt Whitman.

The poem has had a significant cultural impact beyond the world of publishing. It has been broadcast, adapted, and referenced in a variety of media. In an episode of *The Simpsons*, Lisa writes a piece borrowing from the opening of "Howl." In 1997, Boston-based radio station WFNX broadcast a reading of the poem, and they were met with some resistance, because it violated some regulations put forth from the Federal Communications Commission (FCC). In 2005, there was a string of linked celebrations ranging from San Francisco to Leeds, England, to honor the fiftieth anniversary of the poem's publication. It has also been referenced in a variety of films and writings that have been inspired by Allen Ginsberg and the rest of the Beat writers.

Not surprisingly, the poem has met with a variety of challenges. Upon its publication, the poem's publisher Lawrence Ferlinghetti was arrested for distributing obscene materials. This began a long legal battle that was settled in 1957, with the poem eventually being declared not obscene largely on the basis of its literary merit. Although the poem was deemed to not be obscene by legal standards, it did face additional challenges in the classroom and in libraries. In addition to the presence of obscene words and references to sex and drugs, the book has been challenged a number of times for its portrayal of homosexual desire and acts. In addition to these objections, the book's general countercultural emphasis and viewpoint have made them nervous. Still, it has come to be seen as one of the core texts in American literature of its time.

FURTHER READING

di Prima, Diane. "Knowing Allen Ginsberg." *Paterson Literary Review*, 2006, Vol. 25, Issue 35, pp. 13–19, 7p.
Pozen, David E. "Ginsberg's 'Howl.'" *Explicator*, Fall 2003, Vol. 62, Issue 1, pp. 54–57, 4p.
Tyell, John. "An Emotional Timebomb: Allen Ginsberg's 'Howl' at 60." *Antioch Review*, Fall 2015, Vol. 73, Issue 4, pp. 636–646, 11p.

It's Perfectly Normal/It's So Amazing, Robie Harris
(Candlewick Press, 1994/1999)

It's Perfectly Normal and *It's So Amazing* are both illustrated children's books dealing with sex and sexuality. The first book, *It's Perfectly Normal*, came about as a result of Robie Harris being asked by an editor to write a book about HIV and the AIDS virus. Robie agreed that the topic was important, but she also felt that it was better to deal with sex and sexuality in general rather than just these two diseases, partially because to focus only on sexually transmitted diseases would make sex seem dangerous and scary. The books are fully illustrated, showing naked bodies, sex acts, and biological processes like menstruation.

It's Perfectly Normal met predictably mixed reactions. It received some very positive reviews and reactions, earning "Best Book of the Year" honors from both *Publisher's Weekly* and *School Library Journal*. It also had received harsh criticism from some parents and even politicians, with some calling the book pornographic and suggesting that it was not appropriate for schools. Still, the book has consistently stayed in print, being translated into over twenty-five languages and going through a number of printings and editions. *It's So Amazing* also earned both praise and criticism for its dealing with taboo topics like homosexuality and masturbation, though it has been less frequently praised and criticized than *It's Perfectly Normal*.

The books faced both formal and informal challenges. In 2007, a woman in Maine began checking copies out of the local library, then refusing to return them, saying that they were inappropriate for young readers. More than a decade before that, *It's Perfectly Normal* was both challenged and banned, receiving a challenge in Utah for its discussions of masturbation and homosexuality and being banned in a school district in Washington after members of the school board decided that it promoted masturbation and fell into the category of child pornography. Across the country, the book has met with many challenges, with mixed results. Some of the challenges have been dismissed; some have resulted in the book's relocation from the children's section to the adult section of libraries. In some cases, the book has been banned outright. In addition to the reasons listed previously, the books were sometimes targeted for their discussions of abortion and other topics that were deemed as being against family values. Although these books continue to be controversial, they are in regular circulation in a number of libraries, and many teachers and parents appreciate using them as a starting point for talking to children and young adults about issues of sex and sexuality.

FURTHER READING

Heppermann, Christine M. "Laughing in the Face of Puberty." *Horn Book Magazine*, March/April 2000, Vol. 76, Issue 2, pp. 162–168, 7p.

Hersher, Rebecca. " 'It May Be 'Perfectly Normal,' but It's Also Frequently Banned.'" *Weekend All Things Considered*, NPR, September 21, 2014.

Willey, Paula. "*It's Perfectly Normal*: Changing Bodies, Growing Up, Sex and Sexual Health." *School Library Journal*, May 2016, Vol. 62, Issue 5, pp. 49–50, 2p.

Jack, A. M. Homes
(Vintage, 1990)

Jack is one of the first prominent young adult novels to explore a young person having a gay parent. The novel centers around Jack, a boy just under sixteen at the novel's opening. His parents get divorced, making Jack concerned about appearing normal and fitting in. Jack's mother begins a relationship with a man who drinks too much, making Jack feel alienated and frustrated. Things become even more complicated when his father takes him out fishing and tells Jack that he is gay. Jack is angered not only that his father did not tell him earlier, but that he did not realize that his father was gay even though some of Jack's schoolmates had realized it. Jack's family stands in stark contrast to his friend Max's, who seems to have the perfect or normal family that Jack yearns for. As the novel progresses, though, Jack discovers that Max's father is abusive after he sees Max's mother after she has been beaten. Although this unsettles Jack, he also starts to realize that every family has problems and challenges, and he begins to feel a greater level of comfort with his father and his family.

The novel had very mixed responses. Some readers were appreciative of Homes's work to provide a character who navigated the experience of learning that one of his parents was gay. It also received favorable reviews from prominent figures and publications, like the one completed by literary writer David Foster Wallace and published in the *New York Times Book Review*. The book not only earned favorable comparisons to J. D. Salinger's *Catcher in the Rye* for its examination of a young character not understanding how to navigate familial tensions and fitting in, but it also sometimes was referred to as being derivative of Holden Caulfield, not doing enough to distinguish Jack as a character. Still, the book has regularly been taught and read, earning it a steady stream of support.

Although many readers applauded the book for bringing focus to issues of homosexuality and acceptance, it did receive a number of challenges. In some cases, as in a school district in California, the book was voluntarily withdrawn from reading lists by teachers before the school board could make a determination about banning or keeping the book. In other places, such as North Carolina, the book was kept in the library but put in a restricted classification, requiring parental consent to check the book out. In both cases, the root of the challenge was listed as being a combination of discussion of sexuality and profanity used by the characters. Despite these challenges, the book is frequently used by educators to help initiate and direct discussions of acceptance, identity, and family dynamics.

FURTHER READING

Bittner, Robert. "Queering Sex Education: Young Adult Literature with LGBT Content as Complementary Sources of Sex and Sexuality Education." *Journal of LGBT Youth*, 2012, Vol. 9, Issue 4, pp. 357–372.

Giles, Jeff. "May We Be Forgiven." *Entertainment Weekly*, October 12, 2012, Vol. 22, Issue 1228/1229, p. 111.

Mann, Pamela. "May We Be Forgiven." *Library Journal*, August 1, 2012, Vol. 137, Issue 13, p. 84.

The Perks of Being a Wallflower, Stephen Chbosky
(Pocket Books, 1999)

The Perks of Being a Wallflower is a young adult, epistolary novel, with its teenaged protagonist, Charlie, writing to someone whose identity is unknown to the reader at the outset of the book. Charlie discusses some of his struggles in middle school and high school, most significantly deaths of two people close to him: his aunt and his friend, who committed suicide. Charlie befriends two high school seniors.

One of them, Patrick, is a closeted gay male who is dating one of the high school's football players. Charlie begins to develop feelings for Sam, the other senior. Though Sam does not share Charlie's feelings, she does open up to him about being the victim of sexual abuse. While Charlie is doing better socially, his sister is struggling, announcing to Charlie that she is pregnant with the baby of her abusive boyfriend. Charlie takes her to get an abortion. As the year comes to a close, Charlie begins to feel anxiety about losing touch with the graduating seniors, particularly with Sam, who will be attending college the following fall. Charlie and Sam begin to have physical relations, but he stops, suddenly remembering that his dead aunt had had inappropriate relations with him. The book closes with an epilogue in which Charlie's parents discover him seemingly dead to the world. After Charlie is admitted to a mental hospital, he comes out of his fugue and admits to his family what happened between him and his aunt. Charlie is then visited by his friends, and he seems to be in a good state.

Upon its publication, the book very quickly became a commercial success. Its publication through Pocket Books MTV imprint helped it to gain both prominence and interest among teen readers. Critical response to the book was not always as positive, with many reviewers saying that it was cliché or that it was derivative of other, richer texts like Salinger's *Catcher in the Rye*. That said, some reviews, like the one published by *The Onion*'s A. V. Club, did acknowledge that the book confronted material that other books for young readers generally avoided. In 2012, the book was adapted into a movie that was generally well received.

The book gained a cult following among many readers who, like Charlie, felt like outcasts or loners. Still, the book received some challenges, particularly where it was included on recommended or required reading lists by teachers. The book was challenged for a host of reasons, sometimes for its open discussion of sexuality, sometimes for its discussion of drugs and alcohol, and at other times for its portrayal of sexual abuse and the lingering aftereffects of this abuse. Ironically, the frank discussion of these topics is one of the things that some proponents of the book listed as a strength. In addition, because the book had developed a cult following, some parents raised concerns that a prominent homosexual figure in the book could influence young readers to become homosexual. The book received challenges in a number of places, including Wisconsin, Virginia, and Ohio. In fact, it was included among the top ten list for most frequently challenged books in 2009. The book was also among a group of books challenged by the group Parents against Bad Books in Schools, a conservative group advocating for the banning of books. Despite this, *The Perks of Being a Wallflower* was rarely banned outright in any school. Instead, there were sometimes restrictions on who could check the book out, such as requiring parental permission before a student could check out the book. Still, the book remains popular among young adult readers, as it gives them a realistic examination of high school-age characters that contrast with more science fiction or fantasy books such as The Hunger Games or the Harry Potter series.

FURTHER READING

Cart, Michael. "Best Books for New Adults." *Booklist*, May 1, 2013, Vol. 109, Issue 17, p. 65.
Stone, Phillip. "No Wallflower." *Bookseller*, June 29, 2012, Issue 5535, p. 22.
Zvirin, Stephanie. "Top Ten Gay and Lesbian Books for Youth." *Booklist*, June 1–June 15, 2001, Vol. 97, Issue 19/20, p. 1863.

A Separate Peace, John Knowles
(Secker & Warburg, 1959)

A Separate Peace is an American novel exploring the tensions and experiences of coming of age in its era. The book follows Gene Forrester as he returns to the preparatory school that he attended as a teenager. When he gets there, he first looks at a large, marble staircase, which fills him with unease. This unease increases when he also examines a tree. He recalls making his friend, Finny, fall out of the tree. After this introduction, the book follows Gene's recollections of his time at the school, where he had befriended Finny, his roommate at the time. Finny is the more outgoing of the two, and he is able to pull Gene into his schemes and his sense of enjoying life. One example of this comes when Finny wants to begin an informal club with an initiation rite of jumping from the tree that Gene looks at during the beginning of the novel and into the river that flows past it. While the two get along and, in some ways, egg each other on, Gene also finds himself confused by his feelings for Finny, alternating between deep affection and jealousy. Knowing that he cannot outperform Finny physically, he strives to become as successful as possible academically, though he also does try to compete with Finny physically from time to time. One example of this comes when both are in the tree. Angry with Finny, Gene shakes the branch that Finny is standing on, and Finny falls to the ground, breaking his leg so thoroughly that any career as an athlete that he may have had is ended. After the incident, Gene tries to be better as a person and to resolve some of the conflicts and confusions that he has felt at the preparatory school. While Gene is trying to repair his relationship with Finny and work on his personal issues, one of the other boys at the school begins trying to get the students to join the efforts to support the troops in World War II. The same person working to rally the students also hosts a debate where Gene is accused of intentionally trying to kill Finny, though it is not entirely clear whether or not the accuser thinks that Gene truly did it. Before the end of the debate, Finny leaves the room, and, in his rush, falls down the stairs that Gene is looking at during the book's opening. This only makes Finny's ability to compete in any form of athletics more and more impossible. Gene tries again to train, hoping to be the athlete that Finny cannot. World War II intrudes upon the boys lives' when a former classmate of theirs who has joined the military is reported as having gone AWOL. When Gene meets his friend, he finds out that the friend has become unhinged after seeing the horrors of war, though the friend has the clarity to recognize that Gene tried to push Finny out of the tree rather than having it happen on accident. Gene goes back to Finny, apologizing and trying to reconcile. The boys do reconcile with each other, but during a surgery to fix his leg, Finny gets an infection that kills him. The book then returns to the more recent time, with Gene looking at his former school and reflecting upon the nature of friendship, war, and life.

The book was a tremendous success, becoming a bestseller and being a finalist for the National Book Award as well as receiving other accolades and honors. In particular, the examination of war, friendship, and patriotism as well as the examination of a young man's search for identity very naturally tapped into the cultural anxieties and interests of America in the late 1950s and early 1960s. *A Separate Peace* was also adapted into films twice, once for release in theaters and once as aired on the television network Showtime. The films were both met with middling levels of success. The book also was often taught in schools, though the way that the themes were discussed varied a great deal from school to school and teacher to teacher.

Various readers have suggested that the nature of Gene and Finny's friendship was actually either homosexual or homoerotic, and this has led to a number of challenges. In 1980, in New York, the book was challenged in a school district. The group challenging the book argued that it contained too much sexual content despite the fact that no sexual acts are described in the book. The fact that there are no major female characters in the book (the school that Gene and Finny attend is a male-only school) suggests to many critics that the true reason for the challenge was the reading of the book as a portrayal of a homosexual interest on Gene's part. This led to two different defenses of the book. John Knowles, the book's author, issued a public statement indicating that he had no sense of a homosexual relationship between Gene and Finny, meaning that any challenge to the book based upon fears of promoting a homosexual agenda would be groundless. But there was also a less prominent defense of the book that suggested that any possible homosexual undertones were not grounds for challenging the book. In the end, the book continued to be available, and it has remained on reading lists and in libraries across the country.

FURTHER READING

Heinz, Linda, and Roy Huss. "A Separate Peace: Filming the War Within." *Literature Film Quarterly*, Spring 1975, Vol. 3, Issue 2, pp. 160–171, 12p.

Pitofsky, Alex. "Unseen Academy: John Knowles's *A Separate Peace*." *Papers on Language & Literature*, Fall 2013, Vol. 49, Issue 4, pp. 390–414, 25p.

Tribunella, Eric L. "Refusing the Queer Potential: John Knowles's *A Separate Peace*." *Children's Literature*, 2002, Vol. 30, pp. 81–95, 15p.

The Sledding Hill, Chris Crutcher
(Greenwillow Press, 2005)

The Sledding Hill is an experimental young adult novel, narrated from the perspective of Billy, a boy who died young. Billy's friend Eddie is working through the grief that he feels after having lost not only Billy but his own father as well. Even before this event, Eddie struggled, because he had attention deficit hyperactivity disorder (ADHD) and had difficulty keeping himself from stopping talking. After the death of his father and Billy, Eddie decides to stop talking all together. Eddie also begins to question God and the universe, asking what kind of God would allow his father to die. Eddie's mother takes the opposite approach, going to church more and speaking with Reverend Tarter, who is also teaching at the local high school. During the discussions between Eddie's mother and Reverend Tarter, Tarter says that Eddie's father's agnosticism was wrong, making Eddie dislike Tarter all the more. Tarter suggests that Eddie join a youth group in order to gain a greater sense of faith. Around this time, Eddie gets assigned a book by Chris Crutcher, *Warren Peece* (the novel does not exist in the real world, and it sets up a breaking of the fourth wall that makes the book postmodern and experimental). Eddie finds the book helpful in working through his grief, but Reverend Tarter speaks out against the novel, saying that the book has too much bad language and should not treat homosexual characters in a positive light. Tarter asks Eddie to help him in his quest to ban the book from the school. Eddie feels conflicted, liking the book but also feeling pressured to take part in the move against it. Eddie consults Billy's ghost, looking for guidance. Eddie realizes that he does not want to support Tarter, but he also does not want to lie or trick him; so, he takes part in the initial stages of fighting the book, but he does so knowing that he will end up provoking a question that will undo their efforts. Eddie eventually does announce that he supports teaching the book, and the members of the church accuse him of being insane, claiming that Eddie believes himself to be Jesus. During the hearing in front of the school board, Chris Crutcher, the author, shows up, arguing in favor of keeping the book. In the end, the book is banned from the school, but Eddie feels validated that he stood up for what was right and defended the book.

The book received very good reviews from prominent sources like *Kirkus* and *Publisher's Weekly*. It also received awards and honors. The book also received praise for its humor and energy. Like many of Crutcher's books, it also sold well, particularly because this book was seen as a kind of culmination of his work by many Crutcher fans. His work in bringing themes of sexual preference, religion, and disabilities had long been sources of anxiety for parent groups, and *The Sledding Hill* was seen as a direct commentary on these struggles by many long-time Crutcher fans. Crutcher had stated that he made a point of not using obscenity in any of the dialogue so that anyone wishing to challenge the book would have to point to issues of content rather than looking only at language issues.

Not surprisingly, the book did receive a number of challenges. Because of Crutcher's content and approach (including a debate about banning books), it is difficult to say what the real motivations for challenges to the book was. Some complaints referenced the portrayal of Christians within the book, particularly the groups in the book that worked to ban *Warren Peece*. Other challenges rested upon the notion that the material was unsuited for the age group. In most cases, the book was retained, although some records are inconclusive. Although many readers hold *The Sledding Hill* to be Crutcher's most sophisticated work, it received fewer challenges than some of his other books (*Whale Talk*, in particular), making it more significant for its discussion of censorship rather than for the censorship that it actually received.

See Also: *Athletic Shorts* and *Whale Talk*.

FURTHER READING

Blasingame, James, and Pam B. Cole. "The Sledding Hill." *Journal of Adolescent & Adult Literacy*, September 2005, Vol. 49, Issue 1, pp. 74–75, 2p.

Staff. "The Sledding Hill." *Publishers Weekly*, June 6, 2005, Vol. 252, Issue 23, pp. 65–66, 2p.

Sutton, Roger. "The Sledding Hill." *Horn Book Magazine*, July/August 2005, Vol. 81, Issue 4, pp. 468–469, 2p.

VIOLENCE

Violence has been part of storytelling from the very beginning. From Greek myths to the Bible to Beowulf, literary heroes have slain dragons, and villains have been brutally punished for thousands of years. From early on in American literature, violence has been a major theme. Stories covering the Revolutionary War, like *My Brother Sam Is Dead* by Christopher Collier, have shown the horrors of war and violence. Other periods of American history have likewise been examined in literature, such as Toni Morrison's *Beloved*'s portrayal of the violence in slavery.

In both of these cases, social and political influences complicate the nature of the violence, making it difficult to tell if the real source of the objection is the violence or the historical and political issues being examined. The simple depiction of two men fighting can set some parents on edge. Adding in the backdrop of slavery can make those same parents even more uncomfortable. And yet, other parties argue that that same backdrop makes an accurate depiction of the violence even more necessary so that readers understand the disturbing but true aspects of that period of history.

Of course, not all literary violence that is challenged comes from such politically charged contexts. Some of the criticism is predicated on the level of detail and the extremity of the violence. Books like *A Clockwork Orange* by Anthony Burgess and *In Cold Blood* by Truman Capote feature direct and clear portrayals of murder, and both books engage the perspective of the perpetrators, not demonizing them as most other texts looking at murder might. For this reason, many parents and other groups argue that these types of books set up negative behavior and troubling views for readers. Many critics make the claim that portrayals of violence in these books can actually lead readers to commit violent acts themselves. While these claims are difficult to prove (and many other critics claim that reading about these types of actions can be cathartic, letting readers work through feelings of aggression by imagining these acts), they have led many parent groups and other figures to call for the removal or censoring of these types of books.

A related but separate issue is the portrayal of violence within the context of war. For decades, there was a consistent effort to ensure that art portrayed military action in a positive light. Books like *Slaughterhouse V* by Kurt Vonnegut and *A Farewell to Arms* by Ernest Hemingway called into question the morality and utility of war and the impact of being a soldier. This made the true nature of objections to the portrayal of violence in books difficult to determine. *Slaughterhouse V* in particular angered people on several fronts, showing the devastation of American bombing efforts in World War II, calling into question various religious beliefs and practices, and portraying sex and sexuality in clear and direct ways. As American attitudes changed during the Vietnam War, these types of struggles became even more complex. With arguments about the nature and value of war and violence, portrayals of it in art and criticisms of those portrayals became even more multifaceted.

One of these facets was the level of realism of the violence. Books like *In Cold Blood*, which gave an account of actual murders, received markedly different criticism than some of Stephen King's works, like *It*, which featured unrealistic violence committed by and against a supernatural threat. Of course, King's book received criticism and challenges also based upon its portrayal of sex and its use of obscene language, but the clear contrast between these two works can show the difficulty of establishing clear and consistent expectations for the portrayal of violence in books.

Yet another consideration was who committed the violence. Books like *Killing Mr. Griffin* by Lois Duncan, in which a group of high school students kidnap and accidentally kill a teacher, were met with significant backlash from a number of parents, because they felt that it set a model for teenagers to engage in violent behavior against adults. Similarly, the use of children in *Lord of the Flies* by William Golding made the level and type of violence even more disturbing for many readers.

With the advent of film, television, and video games, the focus on the exposure of children to violence has increased, but the concern over the presence of violence in books may not have. While books still regularly receive challenges, other forms of media are generally the primary topic of discussion when it comes to children seeing violence. Still, with the rise of the young adult genre within the publishing industry, the discussion of censoring violence in literature continues to evolve.

TIMELINE

1907—The nation's first censorship board for films founded

1914—First effort for a national censorship of films established by the Women's Christian Temperance Union

1929—*A Farewell to Arms*, Ernest Hemingway, published

1947—Stephen King born; also NBC bans crime and horror programs from airing before 9:30 at night

1954—*Lord of the Flies*, William Golding, published; also hearings held by a Senate subcommittee on televised violence

1960—*Psycho* released

1962—*A Clockwork Orange*, Anthony Burgess, published

1966—*In Cold Blood*, Truman Capote, published

1967—*In Cold Blood* adapted into a film

1969—Manson Family brutally murdered Sharon Tate, Jay Sebring, Abigail Folger, Wojciech Frykowski, and Steven Parent, terrifying the nation

1971—*A Clockwork Orange* adapted into a film

1973—Director Stanley Kubrick cuts material from *A Clockwork Orange* to receive an R rating rather than an X rating

1976—*A Clockwork Orange* removed from a classroom in Colorado; also *Taxi Driver* released

1977—Ellis Rubin used a defense in court claiming that his client was addicted to television violence and was not responsible for committing murder

1978—*Killing Mr. Griffin*, Lois Duncan, published

1980—John Lennon assassinated

1981—*Cujo* by Stephen King banned

1984—First of Books of Blood series published, establishing Clive Barker as a major horror writer

1987—*It* published

1990—*It* adapted into television miniseries

1993—First-person shooter game *Doom* released; also the Ultimate Fighting Championship promotion founded

1994—*Pulp Fiction* released, establishing Quentin Tarantino as a major force in the film industry and bringing violent films into the mainstream

1996—*Fight Club* by Chuck Palahniuk published; also television parental guidance system first used

1997—*Grand Theft Auto* video game released, drawing significant backlash and reigniting debates about violence in video games

1999—School shooting at Columbine High School left twelve students and one teacher dead, along with many injured; also *Fight Club* adapted into a major motion picture

2004—*Saw* released, beginning a major horror film franchise

Drive-By, Lynne Ewing
(Harper Collins, 1997)

Drive-By is a young adult novel examining at-risk children dealing with significant social issues. The book opens with a family of siblings, Jimmy, Tito, and Mina, walking home from a birthday party. On the walk home, Jimmy is shot in front of his brother and sister. Prior to this, Jimmy had told Tito that being a member of a gang could only lead to death, and this leads Tito to wonder if Jimmy's death means that he was part of a gang. Unfortunately for him, Tito does not have to wonder about this for long, because members of a local gang approach him and tell him that he needs to take Jimmy's place in the gang or else he and his family will not be safe. This is confirmed when Tito and his mother try to collect Jimmy's last paycheck from a restaurant that they believe he worked at, only to find that he had not been employed there at all. There are other clues that confirm that Jimmy was likely in a gang, such as one of the family's friends describing to the police a different car than the one used in the drive-by shooting that Jimmy died in. Over the course of the book, Tito must negotiate the difficult territory between providing for his family and not meeting the same end as his brother.

Drive-By was Lynne Ewing's first book. Ewing began writing as a way to relieve stress from working at the Los Angeles County Department of Public Social Services, and much of her work was clearly informed by what she saw as part of her work. Ewing had been working on both *Drive-By* and *Party Girl*, another book, for years before seeing either published. Once they were published, Ewing saw her work met with both praise and controversy. The praise for *Drive-By* came for both its content and its style. Many readers were happy to see a segment of the population that was too often overlooked get some focus in young adult literature. The types of choices that Tito had to face dealt with a reality that had rarely been explored, so giving young readers a venue to discuss and learn about these conflicts was seen as significant by many critics. In addition, many critics praised Ewing for her narration style, which was spare and direct, mirroring the tension and bleak mind-set of Tito as he dealt with both his brother's death and also the impending conflicts with neighborhood gang members. In particular, Tito is frustrated by his brother, Jimmy, who seems hypocritical for advising Tito not to join a gang even though Jimmy himself is in a gang. In the end, Tito informs the police that his brother's murder was committed by gang members, and the gang members are arrested.

Of course, with the praise also came criticism. In particular, some parents and teachers felt that the book glamorized gang membership and drug use. Much of the work done by Jimmy was related to drugs, and the direct discussion of drugs and guns in a young adult work made some adults uncomfortable. In Houston, the book was challenged in a middle school for having disturbing violence. Despite this challenge, the book was generally well received in most schools and has maintained its positive reception.

FURTHER READING

Alpert, Mara. "Escape." *School Library Journal*, January 2005, Vol. 51, Issue 1, p. 128.

Anderson, Kristin. "The Summoning." *School Library Journal*, August 2007, Vol. 53, Issue 8, p. 114.

Evarts, Lynn, Trevelyn E. Jones, Luann Toth, Marlene Charnizon, Daryl Grabarek, and Dale Raben. "Outcasts." *School Library Journal*, June 2005, Vol. 51, Issue 6, p. 156.

A Farewell to Arms, Ernest Hemingway
(Scribner, 1929)

A Farewell to Arms is a novel about a love affair, set during World War I. The story is split into five books. In the first book, Fredric Henry is serving in the Italian military in Europe, where the war is coming to an end. While Fredric tours Italy, he meets Catherine Barkley, a nurse's aide who also served, and who is in a relationship with one of Fredric's friends. Despite this, Fredric pursues a physical relationship with Catherine. During this time, Fredric is injured, and many doctors recommend that he take an extensive leave in order to recover and undergo surgery. Instead of heeding this advice, Fredric decides to find a surgeon who will operate on him immediately, not waiting for him to get back to his original strength. While Fredric is recovering, Catherine is transferred to the hospital that Fredric is staying in. As she helps him to recover, the two begin to develop a genuine and meaningful affection for each other. Once Fredric has mostly recovered, he finds that he has a short time before he will need to return to the front lines of the war; so he plans to take a trip with Catherine. The two do well together, but before Fredric returns to the war, he finds out that Catherine is pregnant. Back in the war, Fredric witnesses and participates in some of the intense violence that is part of war. After a particularly difficult conflict, Fredric dives into a river to save himself, and he decides that he will no longer fight. Fredric successfully finds Catherine, and the two leave the military completely. While they are enjoying each other's company, Fredric finds out that the police are looking to arrest him for deserting his military duty. He and Catherine escape to Switzerland, posing as tourists. While the two are happy for a time, when Catherine goes into labor, things fall apart. Catherine dies while giving birth, and the child is stillborn. The novel ends with Fredric leaving the hospital, stunned by the turn of events.

Like much of Hemingway's work, *A Farewell to Arms* was influenced by his life. He did, in fact, become infatuated with a nurse, but the relationship between Hemingway and the nurse was much less extensive than the one portrayed in the novel, though many readers assumed that the book was autobiographical. The book was originally published serially in *Scribner's Magazine*, and the editors cut out much of the profanity found in the novel, replacing the obscene words with dashes. Despite the original censoring of certain curse words, the issues of *Scribner's* containing excerpts of the book were banned in Boston, where they were deemed indecent. In addition to these concerns over impropriety, the portrayal of army life was of concern to some readers. In particular, the book was banned in Italy for its portrayal of the Italian military. Despite these challenges, the book has been taught and studied in schools at a variety of levels, becoming one of Hemingway's most respected books. It has been adapted into film and referenced in a variety of media, helping to maintain its sense of significance in American literature and culture.

FURTHER READING

Armstrong, Joel. " 'A Powerful Beacon': Love Illuminating Human Attachment in Hemingway's *A Farewell to Arms*." *Hemingway Review*, Fall 2015, Vol. 35, Issue 1, pp. 5, 78–96.

Cain, William E. "The Death of Love in *A Farewell to Arms*." *Sewanee Review*, Summer 2013, Vol. 121, Issue 3, pp. 376–392, 17p.

Kim, Wook-Dong. " 'Cheerful Rain' in *A Farewell to Arms*." *Explicator*, April–June 2015, Vol. 73, Issue 2), pp. 150–152.

Fight Club, Chuck Palahniuk
(W. W. Norton, 1996)

Fight Club is a satirical novel following an anonymous and unreliable narrator as he seeks an outlet for his frustration. Although the novel has some jumps in chronology, the core narrative begins with the narrator relating his insomnia and ennui brought on by his soul-crushing job working for a car company and the detached feeling that he experiences from his many trips across the country for work. The narrator is told to seek out a cancer group to get a sense of purpose in his life. While attending these groups, the narrator begins to find a degree of peace. This release is cut off from the narrator, though, when a woman named Marla begins coming to the same groups that he attends. The narrator realizes that Marla is also just pretending to be ill, and he feels that he cannot experience the same type of release that he did prior to Marla coming to the meetings. Feeling frustrated again, the narrator leaves on a vacation, where he meets Tyler Durden. When they return from the vacation, the two meet up again, and Tyler asks the narrator to fight him. The two fight, though they both end up enjoying the fighting, bonding over their shared violence. After fighting with each other for a while, the narrator and Tyler begin a "fight club," where men can come and fight each other in secret. This new form of release works again for the narrator until Marla comes back into the narrator's life, starting a relationship with Tyler. Meanwhile, the members of the narrator and Tyler's fight club begin to stage elaborate and dangerous pranks under Tyler's direction. These pranks generally put forward an anticorporate and anticonsumerist agenda, taking on big companies or forms of corporate greed. These pranks (known as "Project Mayhem") escalate until one of the members dies. As the narrator seeks out Tyler to confront him about the problems with Project Mayhem, the narrator becomes aware that he and Tyler are actually the same person; they are different personalities sharing the same body, and he decides that he must stop Tyler. Things continue to escalate until Tyler disappears and the narrator tries to kill himself. Afterward, the narrator awakens in a mental hospital, where workers tell him that they are loyal members of Project Mayhem, and they will be ready when Tyler returns.

The book was met with mild enthusiasm until it was adapted into a feature film directed by David Fincher and starring Brad Pitt and Edward Norton. The film did not meet with significant commercial success, but it did meet with critical success, and it became a cult favorite. This led to renewed interest in the book. Palahniuk has regularly noted that, while he was somewhat involved in the writing of the screenplay for the movie, most of the time that he was supposed to be devoting to giving input into the screenplay, he was working on subsequent novels. *Fight Club* became a breakthrough novel for Palahniuk, who would continue writing controversial novels, even having some works that made audiences pass out while he was giving readings. *Fight Club* set the mode for many of these works, looking at subcultures, violence, and deviant sexuality. The book also had a degree of autobiographical material. In particular, the sort of anticorporate acts committed by Project Mayhem are in line with the Cacophony Society, a group of "free spirits" who were strongly influenced by the Merry Pranksters in their vision and execution. Palahniuk has detailed some of the acts that he engaged in as part of the society in his nonfiction work, but it is clear from a number of interviews with him that he has incorporated the sorts of views and values that were part of his recreational exploits into his writing.

Fight Club was banned in a number of places and for various reasons. In China, it was banned because officials felt that the book gave too much detail in its description of how to make explosives. Of course, while the official reason would make a logical case for banning the book, the antiauthority message of the book no doubt did not help matters. In addition to the banning in China, *Fight Club* was banned in a town in Texas, where parents complained about its portrayal of violence and explicit themes. Like many other authors whose works have been banned, Palahniuk was left largely undisturbed by these moves to ban his work. The book's cult following actually helped to launch and establish Palahniuk's career. If anything, Palahniuk has seemed to become bolder with subsequent works, taking on themes of religion, politics, drugs, and many other taboo topics. While some of his other works have also been adapted into films, *Fight Club* has clearly gained the largest critical acclaim and cult following. In addition, Palahniuk is often asked about the existence of "real" fight clubs. He has indicated that he has no association with any existing fight club, if any actually exist, though he has sometimes reported that he is aware of one being organized in England. Palahniuk has actually even published a prequel story and has announced plans to publish a graphic novel sequel to the book, with the sequel following the narrator after he has married and had a son, only to have Tyler reemerge, kidnapping the narrator's son. While the prequel and the sequel have not achieved the notoriety of the original, they do demonstrate both the book's lasting impact and Palahniuk's investment in the characters, themes, and ideas found in the novel.

FURTHER READING

Burgess, Olivia. "Revolutionary Bodies in Chuck Palahniuk's *Fight Club*." *Utopian Studies: Journal of the Society for Utopian Studies*, 2012, Vol. 23, Issue 1, pp. 263–280.

Garrison, Justin. " 'God's Middle Children' Metaphysical Rebellion in Chuck Palahniuk's *Fight Club*." *Humanitas* (10667210), 2012, Vol. 25 Issue 1/2, pp. 79–106, 28p.

Valby, Karen, and Noah Robischon. "Chuck Palahniuk Does Not Attend Night Club." *Entertainment Weekly*, September 26, 2003, Issue 730, pp. 62–66, 5p.

The Goats, Brock Cole
(Farrar, Straus and Giroux, 1987)

The Goats is a young adult novel looking at hazing and trickery. The book is set in a summer camp, and it follows a girl, Laura, and a boy, Howie, neither of whom is popular. Because they are not popular, the majority of the children at the camp decide that they will play a cruel trick on them. They take both of their clothes and leave them stranded in the woods on an island. Before the children leave Howie and Laura, they refer to them as goats, laughing as the pair are left to fend for themselves. The stranded children decide to swim from the mainland, trying to get back to the camp area before the campers who left them stranded can return. When they do return, they try to get away, but they quickly come to realize that they will not be able to leave camp, because Howie's parents are out of the area, and Laura's mother will not pick her up early. So, Howie and Laura (often referred to as "the boy" and "the girl" instead of by their proper names for much of the text) spend the rest of the time learning to survive out in the woods. This involves a number of problematic actions, including stealing clothes and money to help get by. They also find a deserted room to stay in, keeping themselves safe from the cruel campers. Howie and Laura learn to help each other out, as when Laura is being interrogated by two adults and Howie pulls a fire alarm to let everyone evacuate the building, freeing Laura from the adults' attention. During this time, Laura and Howie also become very close. While they stop short of genuine physical intimacy, they clearly have feelings of affection for each other, and they also have a good deal of physical contact, and they see each other naked. Although the children go on a number of adventures and develop a genuine closeness with each other, the ending and the nature of the relationship between the two are left a bit ambiguous in the end, though, after Howie originally believed that he wanted to remain in the wood indefinitely, living as they did for most of the book, they do realize that they cannot really survive in the woods for the rest of their lives.

The book was one of a number of books written by Brock Cole. The book sold well and also was made into a movie, *Standing Up*, in 2013. The film was a moderate success. *The Goats* had received a number of rewards and nominations as well.

The book has been challenged a number of times. In particular, the combination of sexual content (the nudity of the children as well as a few passages that deal with the children having curiosity about each other's bodies) and the breaking of rules by the children raised concerns for a number of parents. Some of the challenges were dismissed, but, in a number of places, the challenge resulted in students needing signed permission slips in order to read the book, even if it was part of a class-reading list. Still, the book is regularly read as part of class projects looking at bullying, freedom, and self-reliance.

FURTHER READING

Alderdice, Kit. "Brock Cole: Children Braving an Adult World." *Publishers Weekly*, February 17, 1997, Vol. 244, Issue 7, pp. 197–198.

Glenn, Wendy J. "Brock Cole: The Good, The Bad, and the Humorously Ironic." *ALAN Review*, Winter 1999, Vol. 26, Issue 2, pp. 26–29.

Scales, Pat. "Brock Cole's *The Goats*." *Book Links*, September 1997, Vol. 7, Issue 1, pp. 56–59.

The Hunger Games Series, Suzanne Collins
(Scholastic, 2008–2010)

The Hunger Games is a major young adult novel trilogy. The books are set after a major revolution in America. After the revolution, the people of the world, now called Panem, are split into thirteen districts, though the thirteenth district is believed to have been destroyed. Every year, the districts must send two tributes (one boy and one girl) to compete in a battle to the death, with the winning tribute earning extra rations for his or her district. Generally, the wealthy districts are able to field the most competitive tributes. In the first book, *The Hunger Games*, Katniss Everdeen, a girl from District 12, a poor area, volunteers to become tribute after her younger sister is chosen as tribute for the district. Katniss and the male tribute, Peeta, begin their training for the Hunger Games under the watch of the only living tribute to have come from District 12, Haymitch Abernathy. Although Haymitch is intelligent, he spends most of his day drunk, which angers Katniss. Eventually, Haymitch does take the training seriously. Leading up to the games, Peeta admits to having feelings for Katniss in a television interview, garnering support and sympathy from viewers who are able to send food, medicine, or other items to the tributes while they compete in the games. Katniss finds herself having feelings for Peeta but also wanting to stay loyal to Gale Hawthorne, a boy that she hunts with and knows well back in her home district. Nevertheless, Haymitch encourages the public sense of love between Peeta and Katniss. At the games themselves, Katniss is forced to kill a number of other tributes, and her life is often in danger. Eventually, she and Peeta are the final tributes. Katniss tells Peeta to take a handful of poison berries, making sure that the cameras giving a live feed of the Hunger Games to the people of Panem catch the fact that both remaining tributes have the berries. This way, everyone will see that Katniss and Peeta have decided that, if both cannot survive, then neither will. Peeta is uncertain, but Katniss tells him to trust her. Before the two can consume the berries, the Capitol makes a third announcement, this time saying that both Peeta and Katniss are winners. The two work through the post–Hunger Games interviews, maintaining the image of two people infatuated with each other. When they return to District 12, they are both received well by the people there, but things have become awkward between Katniss and Gale because of the connection between her and Peeta.

The second book, *Catching Fire*, sees Katniss and Peeta preparing to take their victory tour of the districts. The president of Panem makes a surprise visit, talking to Katniss alone about how her actions have encouraged rebellion. There are, indeed, a number of rebellions coming after Katniss's win. It is announced that this year's Hunger Games will not use new tributes, instead pulling them from the surviving tributes of each district. Katniss and Haymitch decide that Peeta has to be the victor that year. The tributes find that the Hunger Games are being held in a jungle. Katniss and Peeta stick closely together, and they soon find themselves joined by two other tributes, both from District 4, one of whom is eighty years old. The party tries to cooperate, but some of them die off during the games. Katniss finds out that one member of their group is planning to catch lightning that will be coming as one of the scheduled attacks so that he can kill some of the remaining competitors. Katniss, instead, uses the lightning to disrupt the force field that marks the edge of the Hunger Games's field of play. The resulting explosion does destroy the field, but it also knocks Katniss unconscious. When she wakes up, she discovers that she and other members of the group are being transported to District 13, which is, indeed, still populated. When the group arrives at District 13, Katniss's friend Gale is there, and he tells her both that her family is safe and that the rest of District 12 has been destroyed by the Capitol in retaliation for Katniss's actions.

The third book, *Mockingjay*, finds Katniss, her family, and the other escaped tributes living in District 13, which has its own restrictive rules and regulations and is looking to overthrow the Capitol. While Katniss supports their desire for revolution, she also feels used by the leaders of the district, and she agrees to help them only if they agree to not persecute any of the surviving tributes from the games and if she is the one allowed to kill the president of Panem once he is captured. Peeta is brought to District 13, but the rebels discover that Peeta has been brainwashed to be loyal to the Capitol and antagonistic to Katniss. Katniss and the other rebels continue to fight the Capitol. While Katniss and her crew are in the Capitol, they are attacked by a number of threats that seem to be taken from the Hunger Games themselves. Many of the group members are killed, and Katniss witnesses the death of her own sister. While Katniss herself is injured, she survives, and District 13 is able to take over the Capitol. While Katniss is recovering from her injuries, she visits the former president of Panem, who is now held as a captive. After the meeting, Katniss becomes suspicious that the leader of District 13 will have the same sort of cruel, authoritarian regime that the Capitol had always had. This suspicion is confirmed when the leader of District 13 suggests that the former leaders of the Capitol are punished by having to watch their own children fight to the death, essentially recreating the Hunger Games. Katniss is sent to be the former president's executioner as per her agreement with the leader of District 13. When the time comes, instead of shooting the former president, though, Katniss shoots and kills the leader of District 13. Katniss tries to kill herself before the new government can punish her, but Peeta stops her. A riot ensues, but Peeta and Katniss are able to escape. Katniss is sent to the decimated District 12, where she slowly recovers. After a time, Peeta returns to District 12 as well, along with a few others. The series ends with an epilogue set twenty years after the rebellion. Katniss and Peeta are together, having had children.

The book was a tremendous commercial success, topping the *New York Times* best-seller list and appearing on it for more than one hundred weeks in a row. It met with mixed critical reception. Still, many young readers were very loyal to the series, and the books won a number of awards for young adult and science fiction writing, including the California Young Reader Medal and the Golden Duck Award. Many critics also appreciated the direct and bold discussion of social class, with the rivalries between districts and tributes showing an oppressive class system.

After the success of the books, the story was adapted as a series of four films, with the third book being split into two movies. The films, like the books, were tremendously commercially successful. In fact, the films set box office records. The films also received generally positive reviews.

The book also received some criticism for its similarity to a Japanese novel, *Battle Royal*, which also featured a government forcing people to fight to the death. Suzanne Collins, the series author, has consistently indicated that she was unfamiliar with the book prior to writing it. She has also indicated that her inspiration was from Greek mythology, with the story of Theseus and the Minotaur being her primary source of inspiration.

Despite these complaints and issues, the book had a tremendous cultural impact. In Thailand, protestors had used a three-finger salute like the one that Katniss had used to honor Rue. They were meant to symbolize a grassroots rebellion against the oppressive government, much like the one that ruled over Panem. After the gesture became popularized in Thailand, some theaters there stopped showing the movie, exhibiting the same type of censorship and oppression that the Capitol used to keep the residents of Panem from rising up. This was one of the multiple times that the story was challenged, in this case for its subversive political views and material.

Beyond the comparisons to other works and governmental censorships, the series was met with challenges because of its content. The book was in the top ten in the American Library Association's "Most Challenged Books" list for much of the 2000–2009 decade. In fact, in 2011, the three books in the series occupied the top three positions on the list. The reasons for these challenges have varied. Most of them have dealt with the level of violence in the books. Because the books were marketed as young adult novels, the complaints were often that the material was not well suited to the age group. There were also questions regarding the possible religious content or viewpoint of the book. Some of the traps set in the games and the different animal breeds and knowledge of plants were associated with the occult, according to some groups. Finally, some questioned whether or not the sexual content was too prominent for young readers. The challenges to the books did not lead to the defeat of the book. It still has become and stayed a major pop cultural phenomenon, inspiring toylines, memes, and a host of imitations.

FURTHER READING

Aitchison, David. "The *Hunger Games*, *Spartacus*, and Other Family Stories: Sentimental Revolution in Contemporary Young-Adult Fiction." *Lion & the Unicorn*, September 2015, Vol. 39, Issue 3, pp. 254–274, 21p.

Hubler, Angela E. "Lois Lowry's and Suzanne Collins' Dystopian Fiction Utopia and Anti-Utopia." *Against the Current*, July/August 2014, Vol. 29, Issue 3, pp. 23–27, 5p.

Seltzer, Sarah. "Hunger Pangs." *Bitch Magazine: Feminist Response to Pop Culture*, Summer 2011, Vol. 15, Issue 51, pp. 38–42, 5p.

In Cold Blood, Truman Capote
(Random House, 1966)

In Cold Blood is a true-crime book originally published serially in the *New Yorker* magazine and then collected into a full book. The book examines the lives and crimes of Dick Hickock and Perry Smith, two ex-convicts who robbed and murdered Herbert Clutter and his family after being paroled from prison. The family was very well respected by the people in town, and Herbert Clutter had given jobs to a number of men working on the family farm. The two criminals had heard from another prisoner that the family had a safe with money in it, so they had targeted the Clutters. When the criminals broke into the Clutter's house and realized that there was no safe, they tied up the family, ransacking the home in hopes that they could find something of value. When their search failed to turn up anything, they killed the family. The men then fled the state, though they were eventually caught and brought back to Kansas, where they had committed the crimes. After being brought in for questioning, both Hickock and Smith admitted to their involvement with the murders, though there was some disagreement about which of them killed which members of the family. Both men attempted to plead not guilty by reason of insanity, but they were found to be competent to stand trial, and the jury quickly found them guilty. The men were put on death row, where they lived for five years before being hanged.

Capote's book caused a sensation for a number of reasons. Of course, the violent nature of the crime and the seeming innocence and goodness of the victims brought a great deal of shock. Beyond that, the level of research that Capote undertook was seen by many as remarkable. Capote spoke with the townspeople where the crime took place, and he also had extensive interviews with both Hickock and Smith while they were on death row. This led many readers and critics to complain that Capote had become too sympathetic to the men, and, indeed, the childhood background that he included and the portrayal of them were often surprisingly sympathetic for a true-crime book. This led to a number of rumors and complaints about the book. Some speculated that Capote, who was gay, had developed feelings for or a relationship with Smith. Others did follow-up research, checking Capote's facts against the recollections of townspeople, and they claimed to be able to contradict Capote's account. Other critics simply said that it seemed more like a work of art than of true journalism. In fact, Capote, along with Tom Wolfe and Hunter S. Thompson, was often associated with a school of New Journalism where the writer did not pretend to be objective, instead commenting directly upon the story. The book also drew criticism for relying upon gore and violence to build interest within the reader.

Despite these objections, many readers and critics responded positively to Capote's work, finding the book to be compelling and the level of personal involvement from Capote to be impressive. The book was also a major commercial success, and it inspired a number of adaptations. In 1967, the book was first adapted into a film, which earned four Academy Award nominations. In 2005, the film *Capote* was released. It focused less on the narrative of *In Cold Blood* and more of the process of researching the book that Capote undertook. Philip Seymour Hoffman, who portrayed Capote, won the Academy Award for Best Actor. Just a year later, Capote's life again served for the inspiration for a film, this time under the name *Infamous*. The fact that the writing of the book and the author's life have received so much interest and scrutiny is an indication of the rare position that the book occupies. The book itself has also inspired television and graphic novel adaptations.

Not surprisingly, the book has been challenged multiple times. The most notable challenge began in 1999 and ran through 2000, when a group in Savannah, Georgia, demanded that the book be banned. It was, for a time, removed from schools, because it was found to have graphic violence, references to sex, and obscenity, but after supporters rallied to the cause, the book returned to schools. Because the book helped to shift the genres of journalism and true-crime novels, it continues to be read, taught, and studied.

See Also: *To Kill a Mockingbird*.

FURTHER READING

Garrett, George. "Then and Now: *In Cold Blood* Revisited." *Virginia Quarterly Review*, Summer 1996, Vol. 72, Issue 3, pp. 467–474, 8p.

Murray, Edward. "Truman Capote Reports on the Filming of *In Cold Blood*." *Saturday Evening Post*, January 13, 1968, Vol. 241, Issue 1, pp. 62–65, 4p.

Voss, Ralph F. *Truman Capote and the Legacy of In Cold Blood*. Tuscaloosa, AL: University of Alabama Press, 2011, pp. xii, 246.

Killing Mr. Griffin, Lois Duncan
(Little Brown, 1978)

Killing Mr. Griffin is a young adult novel that has been the inspiration for a number of films and the subject of a good deal of debate. The book looks at an English teacher, Brian Griffin, who is seen by the students in his school as being overly strict. After he gives Fs to group of popular students, they decide that they will get revenge upon him by playing a trick. The group of popular students (David, president of the senior class, Jeff, a basketball player, and Betsy, a cheerleader) also enlist Susan, a girl who is seen as nerdy and is not usually included in activities with the popular students. The boys kidnap Mr. Griffin, taking him to a spot in the woods where they believe that they will not be found. As the boys are harassing Mr. Griffin, they find that he has medicine, though they do not immediately know what it is for. When they see that the medicine is labeled as being nitroglycerine, they smash it, hoping to see it explode. When it does not, they return to taunting Mr. Griffin, eventually leaving him alone overnight. When David checks on Mr. Griffin, he finds Mr. Griffin dead, burying the body. The next day, Mr. Griffin's wife reports him as missing, and an investigation into his whereabouts begins. The kids panic as the investigation proceeds, and some of them begin to turn on each other. The kids continue to try to cover their tracks, even plotting to kill again in order to protect their secret. Instead, the entire plot is revealed, and all of the students (other than Susan) end up in jail. Susan avoids jail time because of her willingness to testify, and Mark is diagnosed as being a psychopathic killer.

The book has generated a good deal of attention over the years. It has sometimes been used in schools for teaching young adults about the dangers of peer pressure. It also earned some critical success, being acknowledged as a "best book" by the American Library Association in 1978, and it also won a number of state-level honors across the country. The book also inspired a made-for-television movie in 1997, though the film was less well received than the book.

Although the book has been taught and read widely, it has also met with significant challenges, being in the top one hundred "Most Challenged Books" from

1999 to 2000 as listed by the American Library Association. It has been both challenged and banned. In South Carolina, for instance, the book was removed from class-reading lists, but it was allowed to stay on the shelves in school libraries. By contrast, in Florida, the book had been challenged, but it was retained on the class list. The reasons for these challenges typically fell into three categories. The first was violence, with references to the brutality shown to Susan, the harshness of the boys toward Mr. Griffin, and the murder of the grandmother. The second was obscene language used by some of the young adult characters, particularly the language directed toward Mr. Griffin. Finally, many parents objected to the bad behavior of the characters, finding Mark's actions in particular to be disturbing. While the book has always been controversial, coming in at the fourth most challenged book in the year of its first publication, it has consistently had a sustained readership, and it helped to cement Lois Duncan's reputation as a commercially successful writer.

FURTHER READING

Campbell, Patty. "The Sand and the Oyster, YA and OP." *Horn Book Magazine*, September/ October 1997, Vol. 73, Issue 5, pp. 543–549, 7p.

Lesesne, Teri S., and G. Kylene Beers. "Books for Adolescents." *Journal of Adolescent & Adult Literacy*, December 1996/January 1997, Vol. 40, Issue 4, pp. 316–317, 2p.

Staff. "Killer Reviews." *Teacher Magazine*, April 1999, Vol. 10, Issue 7, p. 47.

Lord of the Flies, **William Golding**
(Faber and Faber, 1954)

Lord of the Flies is a British novel by author William Golding. It is an allegorical novel that examines a group of young boys alone on an island, spiraling out of control. At the book's beginning, a British plane has crash-landed on a deserted island, and the only survivors are the young boys. Two of the boys, Ralph and "Piggy" (an overweight boy with glasses), find a conch shell, which they blow into in order to call any other survivors. When the other survivors make it to the area with Ralph and Piggy, they decide that everyone should vote to determine who the leader is. Largely because of Ralph's use of the conch shell, most of the boys vote for him. After some discussion, it is determined that, to keep order, only the person holding the conch shell shall be allowed to speak. As the boys begin to delegate responsibilities, another boy, Simon, emerges as another leader. Yet another boy, Jack, organizes a hunting party, and Simon begins to construct shelters. Soon, rumors start that the island has a dark, predatory force that they refer to as "the beast." Ralph tries to cut these rumors short, but Jack tries to increase his influence over the other boys by claiming that he will be able to find and kill the beast. As tensions rise, Ralph says that he wants to step down as leader, but Piggy tells him to keep his post. Not long after this, there is a jet fight above the island, and one of the pilots ejects from his jet, but he is dead by the time that he reaches the island. The incident increases tensions between Ralph and Jack, and Jack says that he will go to the other side of the island to track down the beast at an area of stones. The journey does not succeed, and things deteriorate after this, with Jack and his followers deciding that they should take control of Piggy's glasses, as it is the best means of starting fires. They kill Piggy and destroy the conch. After this, Jack instructs his followers to find and kill Ralph. In their pursuit, they set fire to the forest, and most of the island burns. Just as his situation seems hopeless, Ralph finds that a group of British adults have found the island. Ralph bursts into tears and recounts all of the events. In the presence of one of the adults, Jack and his followers likewise burst into tears. The adult is left revolted by the actions of the children, and he leaves them momentarily to gather themselves.

Although it contains a good deal of disturbing material, the book has had consistent success and attention. It was cited as a reason for Golding winning the Nobel Prize for Literature, and it has been taught and studied on multiple levels for decades. Although it was not an immediate success in America, it has come to achieve a significant place of regard, and it has had a strong presence in popular culture, with four film adaptations, a major adaptation for the stage, and references in a variety of media, including a *Simpsons'* episode in which the children end up alone on an island.

Although the book has received significant critical and commercial success, it has been met with a number of challenges. Obviously, the presence of violence has been a principal objection for many parents, but, as with many books, whether this is the root cause of the objections is difficult to say.

The first challenge to *Lord of the Flies* in America came in 1974, when a group in Dallas, Texas, found the book too violent and negative. Although the book was not outright banned from the challenge, it did impact some parents' view of the book. In 1981, the book was once again challenged in the United States when parents claimed that the book portrayed the boys as little more than animals (citing both the portrayal and the murder of Piggy). In the following years, the book was met with resistance for its direct and clear discussion of both violence and sexual thoughts among the boys. During these debates, there were consistently two sides within the argument, one arguing that the material was too troubling for children and the other arguing that that unsettling quality was part of the book's strength. Although the challenges to the book are unlikely to end, the book also has not faltered in the focus and dedication with which it has received attention. For these reasons, even the challenges to the book are likely to not have a major impact upon its literary stature.

FURTHER READING

O'Rourke, P. J. "Lord of the Flies." *National Review*, November 19, 2015, Vol. 67, Issue 21, p. 83.

Rahman, Mohammad. "Thematic Evaluation of William Golding's *Lord of the Flies*." *Language in India*, April 2014, Vol. 14, Issue 4, pp. 225–240, 16p.

Watt, Gary. "The Law of Dress in *Lord of the Flies*." *Law & Humanities*, 2014, Vol. 8, Issue 2, pp. 174–191, 18p.

Summer of My German Soldier, Bette Greene
(Bantam, Doubleday, Dell, 1973)

Summer of My German Soldier is a novel set in a small town in Arkansas at the end of World War II. The book begins with the protagonist, Patty Bergen (a Jewish girl), watching German prisoners of war arriving in their town. She and many of the other townspeople watch them being led off to a prison, and Patty is disturbed by the general lack of reaction. Patty struggles to fit in with her family, feeling alienated. As she works in her parents' store, she sees some of the prisoners of war come in. One of them, Anton Reiker, can speak English, but the others cannot. Patty interacts with Reiker, helping him to pick out some things, and she becomes enamored with him. Not long after, Anton escapes. Patty finds and offers to help hide him. She visits him regularly, bringing him food and talking to him as often as she can. Patty is questioned about Anton, but she lies to the authorities. Patty continues bringing food and even clothes to Anton. Still, Patty becomes frustrated with Anton, feeling that their relationship is one-sided, with her taking all of the risk and providing everything while Anton simply uses her. As Patty's father continues to mistreat her, she decides that she will help Anton to escape. Patty asks Anton to let her come with him, but he tells her that it would be impossible. Patty confesses her love to Anton, and he returns the declaration, but he does leave without her. After some time passed, the Federal Bureau of Investigation (FBI) returns to Patty's family's store, looking to question her. The questioning agent tells her that Anton had been found and shot. When Patty's role in protecting Anton becomes clear, she is told that she will need to stand trial. In the end, Patty is only sent to a reform school. Patty's grandmother comes to visit her in the reform school. Patty asks her grandmother why her parents do not love her, and her grandmother says that the problem is her parents, not Patty.

The book was very well received after its publication, earning honors from both the *New York Times* and the American Library Association. Many critics and readers acknowledged the complex storytelling that examined the interactions between a Jewish American and a soldier who would have been fighting for the Nazi regime. Because of the book's success, it has been twice adapted, once in 1978, when it was made into a made-for-television movie. The movie was also well received, earning an Emmy. The story was also adapted as a musical in 2002. For its deep sense of emotion and handling of charged subject matter, the book has continued to have a positive reputation, often being used in schools to help teach American history.

Perhaps because of the book's inclusion on reading lists, it has received significant scrutiny from different parent groups. Complaints against the book covered a wide range of territory, including the portrayal of child abuse (there are many incidents of the father beating Patty, and both of the parents seem generally neglectful). There were also complaints about some of the racial and cultural issues, particularly with the backdrop of the Nazis and the Holocaust. In addition, there were some racial slurs used throughout the book. There were also complaints about some of the portrayal of sexual desire. In particular, the idea of a young woman hiding a man and having a romantic interest troubled many of the parents of young readers. While the book was not outright banned, it was removed from some classroom-reading lists.

FURTHER READING

Ban, Charlie. "Holocaust Book Spurs Study of Jewish Culture, Customs." *Valley News Dispatch*, Tarentum, PA, November 10, 2007.

Greene, B. "Summer of My German Soldier (Book)." *Journal of Adolescent & Adult Literacy*, September 2004, Vol. 48 Issue 1, pp. 57–58, 2p.

Rossi, Jessica. "*Summer of My German Soldier* (Review)". 21st Century; Sep91, Vol. 3 Issue 1, p28.

5

DRUGS AND ALCOHOL AND CENSORSHIP IN AMERICA

There is a rich tradition of presenting intoxication in written texts. Even the Bible has references to drunkenness. However, many of the challenges to books that contain discussions of drugs and alcohol come not just because the texts present any portrayal of drug and alcohol use, but because of claims that the portrayal of these activities are positive in nature. While this can hold true for some books, such as Hunter S. Thompson's *Fear and Loathing in Las Vegas*, it can sometimes be hard to separate the political or social views contained in the books from the portrayal of drugs. *Fear and Loathing in Las Vegas* also had been challenged partially for its level of detail in its discussion of drugs. Author Hunter S. Thompson (who often claimed to use drugs and, in fact, sometimes took drugs on camera) would give detailed discussions of the effects of drugs and the practices of drug culture, leading some groups to have concerns over the information that young readers might find. Likewise, some editions of William S. Burroughs's *Naked Lunch* contained an appendix frankly discussing the addictive nature of various drugs. While some critics claimed that Burroughs's description of some drugs (marijuana, for instance) as not being addictive was irresponsible, his discussion of heroin (a drug to which he was addicted for much of his life) was very clear about how difficult overcoming addiction was, both psychologically and physically. This kind of frank discussion made some readers claim that the suggestion that Burroughs glorified drugs was unfounded. Like *Fear and Loathing*, *Naked Lunch* was also challenged for reasons other than the portrayal of drug use, most clearly because of the obscenity contained within the book.

While Burroughs and Thompson gave honest discussions of their experiences with drugs, other texts were more sensational in their portrayal. *Go Ask Alice* by Beatrice Sparks, for instance, was originally described as a real account of a young person who succumbed to drugs. However, subsequent investigations of the book found many of the claims to authenticity to be dubious at best. It came to be seen by many as part of a larger hysteria about drug use among young people, like the film *Reefer Madness* (originally released in 1936), which came to be seen as a campy film worthy of laughter rather than a genuine or accurate examination of the drug culture.

Many of the texts that included drug use ended up being challenged for either violence or sexual content. Books like *American Psycho* and *The Great Gatsby* had a good deal of drug and alcohol use, but the use of intoxicants was overshadowed by other elements in the stories—infidelity, murder, or other disturbing acts. In some cases, like *Family Secrets*, the book by Norma Klein, the intoxicants were often used as plot devices, in which the drugs and alcohol lowered the inhibitions of the characters, leading to the problematic behavior that they would later engage in. This also made it difficult to determine whether the conflicts came from the portrayal of drugs or the portrayal of other activities.

Another context that often influenced the way that drugs and alcohol were presented within the narrative was the genre of the piece. In dystopian science fiction novels like *1984* and *A Brave New World*, the drugs and alcohol were not presented in a philosophically positive light. Instead, they were presented as part of a larger method employed to keep the population docile under the control of the authoritarian governments portrayed in the novels. Like in some of the other books with heavy drug and alcohol use, these texts also characterized the use of intoxicants as part of a larger lifestyle of decadence.

Of course, the concerns about drugs and alcohol in literature have been influenced by changing attitudes toward drugs and alcohol in the larger culture. In the first quarter of the 19th century, the temperance movement in America began to demonize drinking. The members of the movement viewed their work as a way to fight the domestic violence that could occur when husbands drank too much. They eventually succeeded in getting the Eighteenth Amendment passed, resulting in prohibition of the sale and consumption of alcoholic beverages in America, though the amendment was later repealed. In more recent times, alcoholism has come to be recognized as a disease rather than a moral weakness of character, leading readers to come to see tales of drinking as tragic.

Public attitudes toward other drugs have also shifted significantly over the years. As early as the 16th century, opiates were used as painkillers. In many ways, the effects of this lack of understanding are still being felt today, with addictions to prescription painkillers based in opiates and with a variety of recreational opiates being abused. Marijuana, on the other hand, was often characterized harshly by governmental agencies. In particular, when marijuana and other drugs like peyote became associated with the countercultural movement seeking to expand their consciousness, the mainstream media demonized marijuana, claiming that it would turn users into dangerous drug addicts. While these characterizations did scare some potential users away from pot, the exaggerated portrayal of drugs eroded the credibility of the government for many audience members.

In the 1980s, cocaine would come to symbolize, for many, the decadence of the upper class looking for good times while many members of the lower and working class struggled. In books like Bret Easton Ellis's novel *American Psycho*, the use of cocaine portrayed not only the fevered desire for pleasure but also the fact that the desire for constant physical gratification could not last, that the upper class would eventually burn itself out.

While alcohol was often part of the mix of drugs in controversial texts, its unique status as a legal intoxicant gave it a special place in debates over what was appropriate for younger readers. While no text seemed to set out to glamorize drinking for younger people, different groups had widely different reactions to portrayals of alcoholics, particularly when the alcoholics were also parents and the books were geared toward younger readers. Certainly, in more contemporary young adult literature, such as *The Perks of Being a Wallflower* by Stephen Chbosky, the portrayal of recreational drug use has been a point of discussion, but it has not been the focus or lightning rod that it would have been in earlier generations.

TIMELINE

1804—Morphine discovered

1861—Morphine used widely in the Civil War, leading to rampant addiction

1873—First temperance movement formed in New York, fueled by feminists looking to reduce domestic violence coming from alcohol abuse

1914—William S. Burroughs born

1915—Marijuana banned in California

1920—Eighteenth Amendment passed, banning alcohol in America

1925—*The Great Gatsby*, F. Scott Fitzgerald, published

1933—Eighteenth Amendment repealed, making alcohol legal once more

1935—Alcoholics Anonymous founded

1936—*Reefer Madness* released in an effort to scare young people away from use of marijuana

1937—Hunter S. Thompson born

1953—Narcotics Anonymous established; *Junkie*, William S. Burroughs, published

1957—*On the Road*, Jack Kerouac, published

1959—*Naked Lunch*, William S. Burroughs, published

1966—Bob Dylan released "Rainy Day Women 12 & 35," featuring the lyric "Everybody must get stoned"

1967—Song "Heroin" released by the Velvet Underground; also "Lucy in the Sky with Diamonds" released by the Beatles

1969—Operation Intercept launched by Nixon administration in an attempt to stop import-
    ing of illegal drugs; also "Sister Morphine" released by the Rolling Stones

1971—Phrase "War on Drugs" coined by Nixon; also Cheech and Chong begin their com-
    edy partnership

1972—*Fear and Loathing in Las Vegas*, Hunter S. Thompson, published

1973—Drug Enforcement Agency created

1977—Eric Clapton released the song "Cocaine"

1980—Mothers against Drunk Driving founded

1986—"Just Say No" campaign launched by Nancy Reagan

1991—*American Psycho*, Bret Easton Ellis, published

1992—*The Chronic* released by Dr. Dre

2000—*Requiem for a Dream* by Darren Aronofsky released

2004—*Marijuana-Logues* first performed by Doug Benson, Arj Barker, and Tony Camin

2005—*Weeds* by Jenji Kohan premieres

2008—*Breaking Bad* by Vince Gilligan premieres

American Psycho, Bret Easton Ellis
(Vintage Books, 1991)

American Psycho follows Patrick Bateman, a wealthy, young professional living in New York in the 1980s. The book does not have a typical, linear plot. Instead, it revolves around a number of scenes combining Bateman's work life, his drug-and-alcohol-fueled partying, his casual sex life, and a number of murders that he commits, generally choosing homeless people, though sometimes against other members of his social circle. Partway through the book, the reader is led to question how many of these events truly happened and how many existed only as delusions on his part. Part of this questioning comes from an ongoing investigation into murders where Bateman is targeted, and part of the question comes from the extreme, over-the-top nature of many of the crimes that he claims to have committed. Interspersed among these scenes are strange monologues in which Bateman considers various aspects of the country and pop culture in particular. Long ruminations about popular 1980s musicians like Huey Lewis and Genesis disrupt the flow of the book's narrative, adding to the general questioning on the part of the reader. During all of this time, Bateman occasionally tries to confess his crimes and his general madness to his friends, but they continually dismiss his claims, suggesting that Patrick Bateman being a real threat is ludicrous.

American Psycho was controversial before it was even officially published, and it has continued to be a lightning rod for decades. Bret Easton Ellis had reached a level of prominence at the age of twenty-one, in 1985, with his novel *Less than*

Zero, which looked at decadent, rich young characters in California. His examination of drug use, casual sex, and betrayal was received as a work of genuine daring and vision to some, but a work of questionable craft and character to others.

Originally intended to be published by Simon & Schuster, *American Psycho* was pulled by the company before it hit shelves. Although the official reason given was "aesthetic differences," critics immediately speculated that the reason for pulling the book was its graphic content and disturbing nature. Vintage Books bought the rights, and the book came out to a mixture of acclaim, dismissal, and harsh criticism. Not long after its release, the book brought about such negative reactions that Easton Ellis began to receive death threats. One of the core reasons for this level of negative reaction was the treatment of women in the book. Not only did the protagonist hire prostitutes and objectify women, he also committed murder and torture. The treatment of drugs, sexuality, and violence also made many readers take offense to the book in the same way that earlier generations of critics took issue with William S. Burroughs's controversial novel, *Naked Lunch*, published in 1959, which also used dark and extreme events and characters to make daring social critiques. While some readers find the book to be a critique of the selfishness of the 1980s, others find the relationships in the book to recreate the problematic views of the 1980s rather than truly critique them. Easton Ellis himself has regularly indicated that he meant the book to ridicule the culture that he saw among the rich while he was growing up. Prominent feminist activist and author Gloria Steinem strongly opposed the publication and sale of the book. Although Easton Ellis has continued to publish books, many of them with disturbing depictions of sex and drug use, none of them met with the resistance that *American Psycho* did.

The book was made into a film, which premiered at the Sundance Film Festival in 2000. Like the book, the film was also met with a variety of obstacles and objections. These ranged from a struggle over who would direct and who would star in the film to a struggle over whether or not the film would receive an NC-17 rating, which would severely restrict its distribution. Eventually, the film received an R rating after the director made some strategic cuts, though it still met with protests and objections for its graphic content and treatment of women. Interestingly, many film critics actually treated the film quite well, noting some of the same features that proponents of the book did in its quality. Roger Ebert praised the bravery of Christian Bale (who eventually landed the lead role), while other critics cited the dark humor of the film and its critique of the greed and self-serving nature of American culture in the 1980s as key features marking the film's quality. After the success of the film, the text was adapted as a musical in 2013. The book remains the most prominent text of Easton Ellis's career.

See Also: *Naked Lunch*.

FURTHER READING

Gordon, Amanda. "Crazy for Psycho." *Bloomberg Businessweek*, May 9, 2016, Vol. 87, Issue 4474, p. 78.

Serpell, C. Namwali. "Repetition and the Ethics of Suspended Reading in *American Psycho.*" *Critique*, Fall 2009, Vol. 51, Issue 1, pp. 47–73, 27p.

Szetela, Adam. "Consumer Ideology and the Violent Subject: The Murderous Consequences of 1980s Advertising in Bret Easton Ellis's *American Psycho.*" *Ethos: A Digital Review of Arts, Humanities and Public Ethics*, April 2014, Vol. 1, Issue 1, pp. 36–45.

Fear and Loathing in Las Vegas,
Hunter S. Thompson
(Random House, 1972)

Fear and Loathing in Las Vegas is a piece of "gonzo" journalism that originally appeared in serial form in *Rolling Stone* magazine. It is difficult to give an exact plot due to the book's unconventional structure, bizarre narrative style, and dubious blend of journalism and exaggeration. The book begins with Thompson and his attorney driving to Las Vegas to cover an off-road motorcycle race, with their trunk filled with a number of illegal drugs as well as a good deal of alcohol. At Las Vegas, Thompson and his attorney make a scene at their hotel, being too intoxicated to function normally. Eventually, Thompson does attend a part of the race that he was sent to cover, but he grows bored and returns to his hotel, where he find that his attorney is too high on drugs to be managed. When Thompson wakes up the next morning, he finds that his attorney has fled, and Thompson decides that he should also leave, because he cannot pay the massive hotel bill that he and his attorney have accumulated. Partway back to California, Thompson is pulled over by a highway patrolman, who seems not to know what to make of Thompson, but who lets him go. Thompson calls his attorney, who seems surprised that Thompson left Las Vegas in the first place, as he had sent Thompson a telegram telling him that he had been hired to cover a national district attorney's convention focusing on drug use. Thompson returns, and he finds that his attorney has returned to Las Vegas as well. The duo attend the convention for a bit, but they also cause a number of problems around the city of Las Vegas, eventually leaving before they can get caught.

The book's serialized sections were met with positive responses, but the book as a whole did not initially receive positive reviews from critics. However, even the people who dismissed the book because of its portrayal of drug use recognized both its innovative writing style and its meaningful cultural observations. As the book began to achieve popular success, critics began to give it more attention and positive feedback. In particular, Thompson was recognized for his innovative use of what he called gonzo journalism, which was a blend of astute observation and personal invention that was meant to give a description of the country's state that could not be described by objective journalism. Later in his career, Thompson referred to the book as a failure, saying that it did not achieve the sort of real-time coverage of the experience that he had hoped for. He also had hoped that the book would be a bigger commercial success than it had been, though it had achieved a large readership and had partially inspired a film adaptation, *Where the Buffalo Roam*, in 1980, starring Bill Murray as Hunter S. Thompson. In 1995, the book was adapted again by director Terry Gilliam, with Johnny Depp starring as Thompson. The movie was not a major commercial success, but it has achieved a significant cult following over the years. Surprisingly, even with the book's explicit portrayal of drug use, it was not outright banned anywhere. One likely reason for this is that the reputation and content of the book gave it a relatively narrow readership. In addition, the book's unconventional nature makes it difficult to categorize and, therefore, study. The heavy emphasis on drug use and political reporting make it unusual as a piece of literature, and the stylistic innovations and liberal use of exaggeration make it unusual as a piece of journalism. Together, these traits make it an unlikely text to be adopted for the classroom, which makes it less of a target for challenges. Still, the book has met its share of challenges, though it is difficult to say if the challenges are primarily because of the portrayal of drug use or the outrageous political and social views, which range from accusing major political and social figures of being Nazi sympathizers to the conspiracy of Thompson and his attorney mistreating a minor. In 1979, the book was banned in an Ohio high school with the stated reason being a combination of obscene language and detailed discussion of drug use. Although the small number of challenges and complaints against the book have not had a significant impact upon the long-term reputation of the book.

See Also: *Fear and Loathing on the Campaign Trail '72.*

FURTHER READING

Alexander, Robert. " 'The Right Kind of Eyes': *Fear and Loathing in Las Vegas* as a Novel of Journalistic Development." *Literary Journalism Studies*, Spring 2012, Vol. 4, Issue 1, pp. 19–36, 18p.

Lidz, Gogo. "Warning Jello Shots." *Newsweek Global*, August 14, 2015, Vol. 165, Issue 6, pp. 56–59, 4p.

Staff. "Hunter S. Thompson's *Fear and Loathing in Las* Vegas." *Publishers Weekly*, November 9, 2015, Vol. 262, Issue 45, p. 46.

Fear and Loathing on the Campaign Trail '72, Hunter S. Thompson
(Straight Arrow Books, 1973)

Like Thompson's other works, *Fear and Loathing on the Campaign Trail '72* is a mixture of reporting, political analysis, and personal essay that originally appeared as serial entries in *Rolling Stone* magazine. It is difficult to pinpoint a single, central narrative to the book, but Thompson follows candidate George McGovern as he makes the surprising transition from unlikely candidate for the Democratic Party presidential nominee to presidential candidate in 1972. Thompson is both reporter and participant in this contest, as he not only discusses what he observes in McGovern's campaign but also influences the campaign, as he does in spreading rumors about Democratic presidential hopeful Ed Muskie, who Thompson secretly accused of having a drug addiction. After the book's publication, when pressed about his role in the spreading of these rumors, Thompson claimed that he had upheld his journalistic duties, because there were rumors that Muskie was addicted to a drug; it was simply the case that Thompson himself was the source of these rumors. Thompson also made other wild accusations, like the claim that a hotel in Milwaukee was run by former Nazis and had a sadomasochistic dungeon in its basement and that he had told members of a Nixon youth rally that prominent journalist Walter Cronkite was a participant in white slavery. These sorts of bizarre accusations and observations dominate much of the narrative. Still, there are genuine moments of incisive social critique that recognize both the paranoia of Richard Nixon and the larger problems in American politics. Like Thompson's other works, most notably *Fear and Loathing in Las Vegas*, this book is a mixture of incisive reporting and outright ranting. A number of Thompson's observations serve to critique the mainstream press, such as his claim that the mainstream press drank so heavily that they were fundamentally incapable of covering the presidential race. Of course, given Thompson's frank discussion of his own use of drugs and alcohol, this sort of accusation is particularly ironic.

In addition to his harsh critique of journalists, Thompson gave direct (if satirical) portrayals of key political figures such as Gary Hart, who aided McGovern and would go on to run for president himself. As with many of the key political and social figures within the book, it is difficult to see where Thompson's genuine views leave off and where his "real" views begin. Of course, it is even more difficult to recognize whether Thompson himself was able to make these distinctions. In some instances, Thompson was genuine and unfiltered in his support, as he was in his discussions of McGovern; but in other discussions, Thompson's flare for humor and exaggeration took over.

As with most of Thompson's other works, *Fear and Loathing on the Campaign Trail* was met with resistance. In particular, this work had a much clearer political bent than Thompson's more purely rebellious *Fear and Loathing in Las Vegas*. Thompson's strange celebrity also added to some of the challenges that the book faced, with his frank and animated appearances on talk shows adding to the *Fear and Loathing* image. There were challenges to the book, such as in Texas in 1976, but it did not receive either the harsh criticism or the larger commercial and critical success that *Las Vegas* did.

See Also: *Fear and Loathing in Las Vegas*.

FURTHER READING

McDonell, Terry. "High Balls." *Esquire*, June/July 2016, Vol. 165, Issue 5/6, pp. 23–26, 4p.
Nuttall, Nick. " 'Apocalypse and Hell': Hunter S. Thompson's American Dream." *Literary Journalism Studies*, Spring 2012, Vol. 4, Issue 1, pp. 103–116, 14p.
Worden, Daniel. "Neo-Liberal Style: Alex Haley, Hunter S. Thompson and Countercultures." *American Literature: A Journal of Literary History, Criticism, and Bibliography*, December 2015, Vol. 87, Issue 4, pp. 799–823.

Go Ask Alice, **Beatrice Sparks**
(Prentice Hall, 1971)

Go Ask Alice is a book that caused a significant sensation. Originally published anonymously, the book presented itself as a diary that has been kept by a teen-aged girl. The girl has her life uprooted when her father, a college professor, takes a new job in a new city. Although the narrator is, initially, hopeful that she will fit in at her new location, she finds herself to largely feel like an outcast when she begins school. She does make one friend, Beth, but at the end of the narrator's first year in her new school, Beth is sent off to summer camp. The narrator, not wanting to stay in her current city, goes to her hometown, spending the summer with her grandparents. At that time, the narrator begins to experiment with drugs and sex. She also loses her friendship with Beth, and she replaces Beth with a trendier girl, Chris. Chris and the narrator find boyfriends who are in college, and they continue to do drugs and push boundaries, helping their new boyfriends to sell drugs. After the pair leave their boyfriends, they head to San Francisco, where their drug use gets harder. After a string of bad experiences, Chris and the narrator return to their hometown. Eventually, the narrator parts ways with her friends, and she becomes homeless, staying in shelters. The narrator has a bad trip and ends up in a mental hospital. When she does get released and goes home, the narrator begins to dread returning to school, but she does find a new boyfriend, and she stays clean for some time. The book ends with an epilogue that states that the narrator died of an overdose.

The authorship of *Go Ask Alice* has been the matter of significant discussion. Originally published as "anonymous" but edited by Beatrice Sparks, a psychologist, the book was presented as a real, cautionary tale. Quickly, though, Sparks was identified as the author after skeptical journalists and critics tried to find out more information about the narrator. When this revelation came to light, many critics and reviewers assumed that Sparks had taken many of the details from a diary of one of her patients, though with some embellishments. Because there was no single figure to research, the reality of the narrative was a major source of debate. In particular, many people began to think that Sparks wrote sensationalist portions of the book exploiting her access to young people's issues for her writing career and financial interests. These types of concerns only deepened when Sparks wrote a follow-up, *Jay's Journal*, which followed the descent of a young man into madness as he got involved with the occult and eventually committed suicide. This second book, along with a lack of any evidence that Alice actually existed, made many become skeptical about Sparks's work. Her reputation only worsened when she put out a string of further diaries.

Despite all of these questions and controversy, the book sold well and was adapted into an ABC movie of the week in 1973.

The book was the focus of a number of challenges for a variety of reasons. The principal reason for the challenges was typically for the use of drugs and the sexual content of the book. It has consistently been in the top ten "Most Challenged Books" put out by the American Library Association. The challenges began in the first half of the 1970s and have spanned the country, from Michigan to Texas to Rhode Island. The book was removed a number of times, though many of the places also simply put it in a restricted category, requiring parental permission before checking it out. These challenges came to fruition during the *Island Trees School District v. Pico* case. The Supreme Court found that the books discussed in the case were generally challenged on the basis of their conceptual content rather than their level of obscenity, meaning that banning them from school libraries would interfere with the authors' rights to free speech. Of course, *Go Ask Alice* was one of the few exceptions, where the content was obscene. Still, the Supreme Court found in favor of keeping the books available. Despite this ruling, multiple dissenting opinions were issued by some of the justices who felt that the school board should have local authority to ban or allow books or that the school is an educating agent, not a governing agent, so the banning of books from school libraries is fundamentally different from banning them in stores. *Go Ask Alice* is a unique text in that it has a significant impact upon the American cultural landscape despite the fact that it has limited literary merit. Unlike other books that have been challenged, *Go Ask Alice* might be more interesting for its role in discussions of freedom of speech than it is for its actual content.

FURTHER READING

Adams, Lauren. "Go Ask Alice." *Horn Book Magazine*, September/October 1998, Vol. 74, Issue 5, pp. 587–592, 6p.

Jones, Elona. "Go Ask Alice." *Bitch Magazine: Feminist Response to Pop Culture*, Summer 2012, Vol. 16, Issue 55, pp. 38–41, 4p.

Nilsen, Alleen Pace. "The House That Alice Built." *School Library Journal*, October 1979, Vol. 26, Issue 2, pp. 109–112, 4p.

The Great Gatsby, F. Scott Fitzgerald
(Scribner's, 1925)

The Great Gatsby is F. Scott Fitzgerald's most famous work and is widely regarded as the "Great American Novel." The book is told by Nick Carraway, though Nick is not the central protagonist of the novel. Instead, the most active character is Jay Gatsby. Nick has come to New York from the Midwest after serving in the military and graduating from Yale University. He takes a job in finance and rents a home near Gatsby's enormous mansion. Nick sees large, boisterous parties happening at Gatsby's home, but Gatsby rarely seems to be present among most of the party-goers. Looking for friends, Nick goes to have lunch with his cousin, Daisy, and Tom, who is both Daisy's husband and a former schoolmate of Nick. The pair introduce Nick to Jordan, a young woman, and Jordan and Nick begin a relationship. After Jordan reveals to Nick that Tom has a mistress, Tom takes Nick to a party where the mistress is present. Nick sees Tom lose his temper and assault his mistress, showing that the party lifestyle is not as purely pleasurable as it first may have seemed. Nick continues to work in finance and make the rounds socially, eventually being invited to a party at Gatsby's mansion. There, Nick and Jordan get to meet Gatsby in person, a rare event. Gatsby recognizes Nick from their time in the military. Afterward, Jordan tells Nick of Gatsby's history with Nick's cousin Daisy, letting him know that much of Gatsby's lavish lifestyle is an attempt to impress and win back Daisy. Nick is impressed by Gatsby, and he invites Daisy to his house, surprising her when Gatsby is also there. While Daisy is initially standoffish, she and Gatsby quickly rekindle their romance. Tom becomes suspicious of Daisy and Gatsby, and he is jealous, despite the fact that Tom himself is having an affair. Tom confronts Gatsby in front of Daisy, Nick, and Jordan, claiming that his marriage to Daisy is stronger than anything that Gatsby could hope to have with her. In addition, he accuses Gatsby of being a criminal who is rich only because he was behind bootlegging (the illegal selling of alcohol). After this, Daisy indicates that she will stay with Tom rather than leaving him for Gatsby. As Tom, Nick, and Jordan drive home from this event, they find out that Gatsby's car was involved in an accident that has killed Tom's mistress. Nick further learns that Daisy was driving the car at the time, but Gatsby has said that he will take the blame. After Gatsby has been blamed for the accident, Tom's mistress's husband tracks down and kills Gatsby, then commits suicide. Nick is left to host a funeral for Gatsby, though it is a surprisingly modest one. Afterward, Nick returns to the Midwest, disillusioned with the East Coast and the lifestyle of the rich.

The book was very quickly a significant critical success, though the sales figures had disappointed Fitzgerald, who was hoping to make significant money off of the book. Many critics enjoyed the novel's lively story and found the characters engaging. Even critics who generally were unimpressed with the book recognized individual passages that showed sound writing. Significant writers like T. S. Eliot, Willa Cather, and Edith Wharton also were very supportive of the book, helping it to achieve and maintain a significant reputation. As time has gone by, the reputation of the book has only grown. For decades, the novel has been adapted into a variety of media, including ballets, radio shows, plays, and more than a half dozen film adaptations, often starring or being directed by major figures of the day.

While the book has generally been established as a masterpiece, it did face some challenges. Most of the challenges to the book are rooted in the book's references to sex, in particular the extramarital affairs of both Tom and Daisy. There have also been complaints about the language and the relatively lighthearted portrayal of both drinking and bootlegging. In 1987, a group did succeed in banning the book at Baptist College in South Carolina, though other complaints have not often led to outright banning. Groups objecting to the challenges of the book have pointed out that the discussions of sex are relatively oblique, with phrases like "he took her" being much less graphic than discussions of sex in other texts. These points, the modifications, and the general reputation of the book have kept many of the challenges from being successful.

FURTHER READING

Bunce, Selvi. "Love and Money: An Analysis of The Great Gatsby." Language in India, June 2015, Vol. 15, Issue 6, pp. 164–168, 5p.

Hauhart, Robert C. "Religious Language and Symbolism in The Great Gatsby's Valley of Ashes." ANQ, September 2013, Vol. 26, Issue 3, pp. 200–204, 5p.

Meehan, Adam. "Repetition, Race and Desire in The Great Gatsby." Journal of Modern Literature, Winter 2014, Vol. 37, Issue 2, pp. 76–91.

Naked Lunch, **William S. Burroughs**
(Olympia Press, 1959)

Naked Lunch is the most famous of William S. Burroughs's books, and it was the center point of a major debate over obscenity and American literature. A clear summary of the book's plot is difficult, because it is told in a nonlinear fashion, which was part of the stylistic innovation that Burroughs became famous for. The book follows William Lee, a fictionalized version of Burroughs himself. Like Burroughs, Lee is an addict, and, also like Burroughs, Lee works to evade capture by the police. To keep from being brought in, Lee travels from America to Mexico. In Mexico, he finds Dr. Benway, who tells him of the various strategies that he employed on behalf of governments to demoralize their citizens. Lee also learns of "the Black Meat," a fictional substance that most critics understand to be heroin. The book then shifts to Annexia, an area kept under harsh, authoritarian rule. This area allows Burroughs to explore themes of domination and fear as methods of governing people. Toward the end of the book, Lee kills two police officers in an attempt to evade capture.

The book was a sensation in many different ways. On a technical level, Burroughs was lauded for his use of the "cut-up technique," in which he assembled a disjointed narrative that jumped from scene to scene with no clear sense of coherence. This sort of seemingly random order came out of the surrealist tradition, and it was admired by the Beat Generation of writers for its wildness and its representation of the effects of serious narcotics. In fact, one of the reasons that many readers admired the book was for Burroughs's frank portrayal of the negative effects of both hard drugs and strict governmental manipulation and control. Sections of the book were published in both national literary magazines and also in a student-run literary magazine, *Chicago Review*, though the fallout from its inclusion in the *Chicago Review* led to stricter administrative control over the magazine's future issues.

The book developed a cult following and has been the subject of regular critical and scholarly examination. Director David Cronenberg successfully adapted the novel into a film in 1991. Like the book, reviews of the film were mixed, with many Burroughs fans admiring Cronenberg's ability to weave together pieces of the book and pieces of Burroughs's biography to produce a coherent story. Others, though, found the movie to have much of the book's dark and disturbing material as well as the negative portrayal of women. Still, the book won a number of awards, though it was not one of Cronenberg's most prominent films.

The book itself, though, has been consistently remembered as one of the most controversial in the history of American literature. At first, the book was banned on both costs. In Boston, the book was banned for its portrayal of violence against children as well as its copious use of profanity. At the trial testing the legality of the book's banning, many prominent writers of the day, most notably Norman Mailer and Allen Ginsberg, testified to the book's social merit, describing it as a work of genuine artistic expression rather than true obscenity. The book's defenders were also able to point to the fact that the book had been published successfully in France by Olympia, though there had been some minor challenges to the book there as well. In later editions of the book, transcripts of the obscenity trial were included. The book continues to be the subject of significant debate, with many appreciating its honest appraisal of drugs and its stylistic innovations and others finding the book to be crass, homophobic, and misogynistic. In the end, the book may be one of the few that genuinely deserves both the adulation and the concern about its potentially offensive content.

See Also: *Howl and Other Poems*

FURTHER READING

Murphy, Timothy S. "Intersection Points: Teaching William Burroughs's *Naked Lunch*." *College Literature*, Winter 2000 Special Issue, Vol. 27, Issue 1, pp. 84–102, 19p.

Walker, Jesse. "The Sultan of Sewers." *Reason*, July 2014, Vol. 46, Issue 3, pp. 54–60, 6p.

Wilson, Meagan. " 'Your Reputation Precedes You': A Reception Study of *Naked Lunch*." *Journal of Modern Literature*, Winter 2012, Vol. 35, Issue 2, pp. 98–125, 28p.

The Outsiders, S. E. Hinton
(Viking Press, 1967)

The Outsiders is the most well-known of S. E. Hinton's books, though it was written largely while she was under the age of eighteen. The book follows a young man who goes by the name of Pony Boy. Pony Boy is part of a group of working-class young men known as "the Greasers," because many of them use a type of hair gel to slick back their hair, making it appear greasy. Their main rivals are known as "the Socs," a term short for "the socials," partially because they are part of a higher social class than the Greasers. The book opens with Pony Boy being attacked by a group of Socs. After this conflict, tensions escalate when Socs see Pony Boy walking with Cherry Valance, a Soc girl who is friendly with the Greasers. Pony Boy comes home late, and his oldest brother, Darry, yells at him for not checking in to show that he was okay. The two argue and Darry hits Pony Boy. After that, Pony Boy leaves, meeting up with another Greaser, Johnny, to run away. The Socs find the pair, and, after some scuffling, Pony Boy stabs a Soc, killing him. Darry helps Pony Boy to go into hiding. Pony Boy and Johnny hide in an abandoned church, where Pony Boy reads *Gone with the Wind* to Johnny. Eventually Johnny decides that he would rather turn himself in than continue to live in hiding, but, as the pair are leaving, they see that the building has caught fire. Realizing that there are still children inside the building, Pony Boy, Johnny, and Darry all go back in. Pony Boy passes out, and, when he wakes up, he finds that Johnny's back was broken. Darry goes to Pony Boy, and the two reconcile. The town newspaper declares Pony Boy and Johnny heroes for their efforts to save the children. Despite this reception, the Socs still want revenge upon Pony Boy, and the groups continue to fight. Eventually, Pony Boy stands trial, and the judge declares that Pony Boy should not be held responsible. As Pony Boy returns to school, he struggles, suffering from guilt. Eventually, an English teacher helps him to work through it by writing an essay. The last lines of the book are from Pony Boy's writing, and they are the same words as the first line of the book, implying that Pony Boy is the author.

The book was not a commercial success at the time of its publication, though it was recognized with multiple awards both at the time of its publication and in the following years. Some of the themes and struggles represented in the book were not familiar territory in mainstream writing. However, as the years went on, it built a steady and loyal readership, and it gained prominence in 1983, when the book was adapted into a film by director Francis Ford Coppola. The book's reputation also grew after the young adult genre gained greater critical and popular attention. In fact, some critics cite *The Outsiders* as one of the first major works in young adult literature in America. It also gained a loyal readership partially because it gave representation to groups who had largely been shut out of popular literature, namely, young men from lower-class backgrounds.

Interestingly, the thing that drew many readers to the book was also one of the sources of the book's challenges. In 1986, a group in South Milwaukee, Wisconsin, requested that the book be taken off of an eighth-grade reading list. Their two principal complaints were that the book featured too much drug and alcohol use and that the main characters in the book came from "broken homes." Pony Boy, for instance, was raised by his oldest brother rather than by his parents. Although the challenges based upon the issue of drug and alcohol use have generally subsided (though not before putting the book in the top fifty "Most Challenged Books" of the 1990s), a new set of objections to the book have emerged. At a middle school in Virginia in 2001, the book received a challenge because some parents felt that the book glorified gang rivalries. Although the book has sometimes been removed from reading lists, it has not been outright banned, and interest in the book has not died down.

FURTHER READING

Hunt, Lisa. "SE Hinton: Still Connecting after All These Years." *Library Media Connection*, May/June 2011, Vol. 29, Issue 6, pp. 42–43, 2p.

Mills, Randall K. "The Novels of SE Hilton: Springboard to Personal Growth for Adolescents." *Adolescence*, Fall 1987, Vol. 22, Issue 87, pp. 641–646. (EJ365687)

Olson, Christina L. "Presenting SE Hinton". *School Library Journal*. December 1987, Vol. 34, Issue 4, p. 107.

6

Bad Behavior and Censorship in America

While some of the texts discussed under this section do include very specific acts of disrespect (such as Louis Sachar's novel *The Boy Who Lost His Face*, in which characters are portrayed making an obscene gesture), others are less easy to pinpoint a specific and easily described set of behaviors. In the Junie B. Jones series, for instance, the title character is rude to adults like her parents, grandparents, and teachers. It also is the case that the definition of what constitutes "bad behavior" or "rudeness" has changed significantly from generation to generation. Certain forms of behavior that were considered unthinkable in the 1950s would become relatively commonplace just a few decades later. For this reason, it is essential to examine the historical context surrounding various texts in order to appreciate why any text might serve as a particularly contested cultural object.

Popular culture has long been a driving force in societal norms of what is or is not proper. Looking at television programs like *The Simpsons*, where the children would outsmart adults and ridicule or disrespect them, often can have a deep impact upon the generation that watches these figures as they come of age. In fact, some pop cultural figures have become the center of major political debates, with then vice president Dan Quayle criticizing television character Murphy Brown for having a child as a single mother in 1992 during the reelection campaign for the president George H. W. Bush. This sort of debate actually helped to boost the value placed upon popular culture, because it made popular culture part of the larger academic and political conversations.

That said, it was not only pop culture texts like television shows and movies that received negative attention for bad behavior. Some books that have come to be seen as important works of literature also have been challenged for the behavior that they have shown, perhaps none more so than Mark Twain's *The Adventures of Tom Sawyer*. *Tom Sawyer* is a particularly apt example in that it addresses the behavior of children rather than the behavior of adults. For characters like Tom Sawyer, criticism could sometimes come for as small of actions as selfishness or disrespect toward adults. Beyond simple rudeness, the complaints were often related to children saying obscene words or using drugs or alcohol. In other words, while many of the complaints were related to behaviors that children could easily imitate, only a subset of these were genuinely and clearly damaging to the child or the culture at large.

The books in this category are also interesting, because the challenges and defenses that the books experience are often along different lines than books in other categories. In the challenges related to racial content, for instance, there are often clear alliances that form to promote intercultural awareness and the defense of oppressed or marginalized groups. In the category of bad behavior, however, the specific details and actions triggered a challenge. This can make the challenges harder to sustain, because complaints about issues like spelling errors or minor rudeness to adults can seem tame to subsequent generations. Still, the malleable nature of the complaint makes it a continued source of challenges to books.

TIMELINE

1876—*The Adventures of Tom Sawyer*, Mark Twain, published

1884—*The Adventures of Huckleberry Finn*, Mark Twain, published

1905—Marx Brothers film career begins

1934—Original Three Stooges of Moe, Larry, and Curly begin their careers together

1947—Lenny Bruce's career begins

1951—*Dennis the Menace* has first appearance in U.S. newspapers; also *Catcher in the Rye* published

1959—*Dennis the Menace* premiered as television show

1964—*Harriet the Spy* published

1966—Lenny Bruce died

1967—*Cool Hand Luke* released; *The Outsiders* published

1971—*Dirty Harry* released, portraying a brutal police officer and antihero as a central, sympathetic character

1972—*The Godfather* released

1974—The Ramones formed, helping to create the punk rock genre; also President Richard Nixon resigns after the Watergate scandal

1975—Sex Pistols formed, further establishing the genre of punk rock; also *One Flew over the Cuckoo's Nest* released to significant acclaim

1976—*Taxi Driver* released, giving a disturbed and alienated character a central role

1979—Original *Mad Max* film released

1982—Comedian and performance artist Andy Kaufman begins his career as a wrestling villain

1987—*Married with Children* premiered

1989—*The Simpsons* premiered; also *Seinfeld* premiered; also Andrew Dice Clay banned from MTV for cursing on the air

1992—President George H. W. Bush gave speech criticizing *The Simpsons*; also Junie B. Jones series first published

1996—Stone Cold Steve Austin rises to prominence in wrestling, making him an early anti-hero character attaining popularity despite breaking rules and challenging authority; also *Harriet the Spy* adapted into a film

1997—Captain Underpants first published

1998—President Bill Clinton impeached

1999—*The Sopranos* premiered

2006—*Dexter* premiered

2011—*Game of Thrones* premiered

The Adventures of Tom Sawyer, Mark Twain
(American Publishing Company, 1876)

The Adventures of Tom Sawyer follows two boys, Tom Sawyer and Huck Finn, as they look for fun and adventure. Sawyer lives in a respectable home while Finn lives with his alcoholic father, who does not give Huck any exposure to culture or education. After a variety of hijinks (tricking someone else into painting a fence for him, swindling children out of Sunday School tickets, and more), Tom Sawyer turns his attentions to a new girl in town, Becky Thatcher. After having some success in courting her, Sawyer is given the cold shoulder when Becky realizes that he had pursued another girl in the same way that he pursued her. Seeking out more fun and intrigue, Sawyer talks Finn into visiting a graveyard at night, where the pair stumble across grave robbers, one of whom is "Injun Joe." Injun Joe kills one of the other grave robbers after an argument about gold that they found. At this point, Sawyer and Finn leave town, not coming back until after they realize that their families assume that they are dead. Sawyer finds it comical that he should be able to observe his own funeral, but eventually the pair feel badly enough to announce that they are still alive. Sawyer even testifies in a trial, helping to keep someone from being erroneously jailed for the murder Injun Joe committed. After the pair's return, Sawyer returns his attentions to winning over Becky Thatcher. He experiences some success on this front, but this leads him to become bold, and he and Becky become lost as part of a picnic. Finn ends up coming to the rescue, not only making sure that Becky and Sawyer are saved but also aiding in the capture of Injun Joe, which results in Sawyer and Finn receiving significant financial rewards.

Prior to *The Adventures of Tom Sawyer*, Mark Twain had had a small number of successful publications. He had published sketches and some semiautobiographical travel writings, such as *Innocents Abroad* and *Roughing It*. *Tom Sawyer* was based at least partially on Twain's own life, with the title figure being loosely based on Twain himself as a child. The book was fairly well received, though there were some critics who found some of the treatments in the book a bit flat, and some who complained about the book's abrupt ending. The major difficulty that the book faced was some libraries refusing to carry it starting shortly after its publication because of the immoral or disrespectful behavior of Tom Sawyer and Huckleberry Finn. However, the book sold very well, and it became one of Twain's most memorable works. The reputation of the work has varied over the years, with some generations finding the characters to be overly simplified. However, major critics have generally appreciated both Twain's representations of American culture and his skewering of a variety of hypocrisies. Although the book has met with resistance from some readerships, it has been carefully studied, taught in schools, and honored in a variety of ways, making it an important work of American literature.

The Adventures of Tom Sawyer is seen by many as a model for American literary humor. Its mix of high and low humor has made it popular with a variety of audiences. Some readers have said that it is a book that can be read at every stage of a person's life, because it is such a rich and complex text that studies the worldviews of both children and adults. Unlike *The Adventures of Huckleberry Finn*, *The Adventures of Tom Sawyer* does not put a primary focus on issues related to slavery. There are still portrayals and bits of language that would be offensive to modern-day readers (the main villain of the book is Injun Joe, a half-Native American character), but these are more simply typical reflections of the thinking of Twain's era than they are troubling for their surprising or unusual use of racial prejudice for humor. Like *Huckleberry Finn*, *Tom Sawyer* has been adapted to a variety of media over the years. Beginning in1917, the book has been adapted for the screen over a dozen times around the world.

See Also: *The Adventures of Huckleberry Finn*.

FURTHER READING

Batzer, Benjamin David. "The Antics of Pretend Play: Tom Sawyer's Narrative(s) of Empowerment." *Midwest Quarterly*, Autumn 2015, Vol. 57, Issue 1, pp. 83–96, 14p.

Jones, Malcolm. "Our Mysterious Stranger." *Newsweek*, August 9, 2010, Vol. 156, Issue 6, pp. 36–41, 6p.

Staff. *"The Adventures of Tom Sawyer."* *Scholastic Scope*, September 2, 2013, Vol. 62, Issue 1, pp. 10–15, 6p.

The Anarchist Cookbook, William Powell
(Lyle Stuart, 1971)

Originally published as part of the larger countercultural movements coming out of the Vietnam era, the book was simultaneously dismissed and reviled by authorities. The book contained "recipes" and recommendations for producing explosives, drugs, and other illegal substances and activities. Although the instances of actual cases of terrorism or illegal activity inspired directly from the reading of this book are relatively few (and difficult to document in any definitive way), *The Anarchist Cookbook* has maintained a consistent cultural interest, much in the same way that films like *Reefer Madness* have, as a sort of quasi-historical document, marking the spirit of the times.

Still, the sheer potential for damage makes *The Anarchist Cookbook* an understandable source for controversy. Almost from its first publication, the book was a lightning rod. The Federal Bureau of Investigation (FBI) publically challenged it in late 1971, and many school libraries refused to carry it. This became even more significant when copies of the book were stolen from libraries. In these cases, the book was not necessarily banned, but it was simply not replaced. When the publisher, Lyle Stuart, was bought out in 1991, *The Anarchist Cookbook* was the only book of Stuart's that was not put into the new publisher Steven Schraggis's catalog. After the events of September 11 in particular, the book was heavily criticized for its potential to enable aspiring terrorists. In fact, the author himself said that he did not support the continued publication of the book. Still, with the rise of the Internet, some of the recipes and advice found in the book were readily available elsewhere, and with the rise of security measures and advances in technology, much of the book's material was rendered irrelevant. In the end, the book has been seen to function more as a sign of the old counterculture than a truly dangerous text.

FURTHER READING

Dokoupil, Tony. "Sorry about All the Bombs." *Newsweek*, February 28, 2011, Vol. 157, Issue 9, pp. 46–48, 3p.

Honan, Mathew. "The Anarchist Legacy." *Wired*, February 2011, Vol. 19, Issue 2, p. 68.

Mosher, Mike. "Anarchy Doesn't Rule." *Fast Company*, September 2004, Vol. 9, Issue 86, p. 25.

Captain Underpants Series, Dav Pilkey
(Blue Sky, 1997)

Captain Underpants is a series of illustrated children's books that follow the adventures of students George Beard and Harold Hutchins and their school principal, Mr. Krupp, who transforms into Captain Underpants any time that he hears fingers snapping. Captain Underpants is so named because he wears only a cape and his underpants when he fights crime. The books all focus on silly villains that are often defeated more by luck or random turns of events than effective crime fighting from either the boys or Captain Underpants himself. The villains are also often based on bodily functions or low humor, like Dr. Diaper or the Talking Toilets. In addition, the books often show adults (teachers and the principal in particular) as overly harsh and often incompetent. The initial book was quite successful, spawning well over a dozen books between the main series and its spin-offs.

While the books are very popular with young readers, they have met with a number of challenges, ranking number one on the American Library Association's list of "Most Challenged Books" in 2012. The complaints against the books are largely rooted in the notion that they contain too much material that is not appropriate for young readers. The jokes rooted in bodily functions and the appearance of a grown man in his underwear upset many parents, teachers, and school librarians. In addition, the bad behavior of George and Harold has been seen by many authority figures as encouraging children to be rude and disrespectful to adults. Defenders of the series argue that the books actually show the world from a child's perspective, which can bring in many children who might not otherwise read. In response to the complaints, Pilkey actually began to include figures in the books that were clearly stand-ins for his critics. The librarian at George and Harold's school (Miss Singerbrains, or "missing her brains"), for instance, banned all but one of the books in the library and often kept children out of the library all together. This sort of characterization of his critics not only delighted his fans but also served to anger his critics further. Still, as many challenges as the books have faced, their popularity has remained strong, and they even has been slated to be adapted as a film.

FURTHER READING

News Limited Australia Staff. "Captain Underpants Leads Banned Works." *The Australian*, April 16, 2013, p. 9.

Reid, Rob. "Talking with Dav Pilkey." *Book Links*, June 2011, Vol. 20, Issue 4, pp. 18–22, 5p.

Stallcup, Jackie E. " 'The Feast of Misrule': Captain Underpants, Satire and the Literary Establishment." *Genre: Forms of Discourse and Culture*, Spring–Summer 2008, Vol. 41, Issue 1–2, pp. 171–202.

Catcher in the Rye, J. D. Salinger
(Little, Brown and Co., 1951)

Catcher in the Rye is a novel centering around the experiences and musings of Holden Caulfield, a frustrated and alienated young man. Holden is a student at an exclusive, private prep school in New York, though he is not particularly successful. In addition to struggling academically, he also does not fit in socially. When he tries to be the manager for the school's fencing team, he ends up losing the team's equipment on the subway. In addition, at the book's opening, Holden has been kicked out of school. Despite this, Holden returns to his dorm room where he tries to read. He's disturbed first by a fellow student and then by his roommate, who has just returned from a date with Holden's former girlfriend. This bothers Holden, because he knows that his roommate is a womanizer, and his roommate did not even use the girl's correct name as he tells Holden about the date. Holden starts a physical confrontation with his roommate, but Holden quickly loses. After this, Holden leaves the campus, checking into a second-rate motel, where he plans to wait until he returns to his parents' home for the Christmas break. Before going out for the evening, Holden thinks about his frustrating romantic life and about his virginity. After these reflections, Holden goes out dancing with three older women. Holden ends up paying for everyone's drinks, but he finds that he cannot connect to the women. Frustrated, Holden seeks out a prostitute, who follows him back to his hotel room. Once she shows up, Holden decides that he would rather talk to her than have sex with her, partially because he recognizes that she is his age, and he finds it troubling that a girl his age would be a prostitute. Although Holden pays her when she leaves, the girl returns to his room with her pimp, who punches Holden in the stomach while the girl takes money from his wallet. Exhausted, Holden sleeps for a brief time. When he wakes up, Holden is depressed and lonely, so he seeks out Sally Hayes, whom he had previously dated. She agrees to see a play with him. On the way to the play, Holden tries to find an album to buy as a present for his younger sister. While looking at records, he hears a boy singing the song from which Salinger took the title for his book, and this leaves Holden, once again, depressed. After seeing the play, Sally and Holden go skating. While the beginning of the date goes well, Holden asks Sally to go off with him and live in the wilderness. When she tells him that she is not interested, Holden snaps at her, then tries to apologize, but she leaves him. Holden drinks heavily to drown his sorrows and decides that he wants to find the ducks in the Central Park lagoon. Unfortunately, as he searches for them, he breaks the record that he bought as a present for his younger sister, which saddens him and makes him feel worthless. Holden decides that he has to return home to see his sister, who is the one person that he feels he can actually communicate with and connect to. As he makes his way back to his house, he thinks about how much that he's changed in his life, and how everything that he's known has changed. He also fantasizes about being a protector of children. This fantasy is rooted in a misunderstanding of the lyrics of the song, "Coming through the rye." Holden sees that his parents are not home, and he stays the night at the home of one of his high school English teachers. The teacher has drinks and gives Holden advice about life, but Holden does not trust the advice. In addition, after Holden falls asleep, he is woken when his teacher is patting his head. Holden suspects that his teacher is making sexual advances on him, and he leaves. The next day, Holden finally sees his sister. He tells her that he wants to move out west, but he decides not to after she says that she wants to go with him. So Holden takes her to the zoo, where he sees her on the carousel. He feels a rare moment of happiness as he sees her enjoying the ride. The book ends with Holden not only briefly and obliquely referring to spending some time in an institution but also saying that he will return to school in the fall, hoping that he will have an easier time applying himself and finding a place and a group of people where he might fit in a bit more than he has up to that point.

Catcher in the Rye was very well received from its first publication, and it has maintained its positive literary reputation. It was on a number of "best books of the 20th-century" lists. Interestingly, its supporters have spanned a variety of backgrounds and political viewpoints, from literary scholars to George H. W. Bush. Critics who have appreciated the book point to Salinger's distinctive but natural voice, which helps to characterize Holden and establish a clear and well-rendered worldview. They also appreciate his frank and striking discussion of alienated, disaffected adolescents, particularly of Salinger's generation. That said, some critics and readers have found the book a bit flat, tapping more into teenage feelings of angst rather than genuinely new or meaningful critiques of society. Despite these complaints, the book's reception has been overwhelmingly positive.

In addition to its noteworthy critical reception, the book has been famous for its challenges and its controversies. In 1960, a teacher in Tulsa, Oklahoma, had assigned the book for his course, and the reactions were negative enough that the teacher lost his job. He was reinstated shortly after, due to support for both the teacher and the novel. For nearly two decades, the novel was the most challenged book in America. The reasons for the challenges were varied. Some complaints from the 1970s and 1980s, one in Washington in particular, were that the book was part of a Communist plot to encourage bad behavior among American youth. Other, more specific complaints have come in through the years. Holden's language, which may not seem particularly transgressive to the eyes of readers a few generations later, was controversial at the time. Words like "ass" and even "lousy" were seen as problematic to readers of Salinger's time. Salinger's work also was met with accusations that the novel undermined family values and a belief in religion. Other challengers of the book indicated that they believed that the book promoted drinking, smoking, and other bad behaviors. In addition to citing the importance of freedom of speech, proponents of the book have also pointed out that, despite the portrayal of bad behavior within the book, Holden is neither happy nor successful, making it difficult to argue that Salinger's portrayal actually encourages the behaviors that he portrays in the book.

Beyond the challenges based upon these objections, the book has gained another, very distinctive notoriety. In particular, major shootings have been related to the book. In the cases of both President Reagan's shooting and John Lennon's assassination, the shooters have either had a copy of the book or have referenced the book as part of their inspiration. This is likely because the alienated and frustrated existence of Holden Caulfield strikes a chord with readers who feel like outsiders and misfits. This odd fact has given the book a cult popularity that has been referenced by a variety of comedians and pop culture texts and figures. Interestingly, Salinger, who was known as a recluse, has been resistant to having the book adapted as either a play or a film despite many prominent actors and filmmakers expressing interest in adapting the novel. This is likely because the 1949 film *My Foolish Heart* deviated from the plot of Salinger's story "Uncle Wiggly in Connecticut," and the film was also very poorly received by both critics and audiences. The failure of *My Foolish Heart* soured Salinger on Hollywood. This sort of tight control also added to the book's mystique, helping to cement it as a talked-about book that had a tremendous cultural impact, despite the attempts to keep it out of young readers' hands.

FURTHER READING

Dashti, Sorour Karampour, and Isa Baizura Binti Bahar. "Resistance as Madness in *The Catcher in the Rye.*" *Theory and Practice in Language Studies*, 2015, Vol. 5, Issue 3, pp. 457–462.

Privitera, Lisa. "Holden's Irony in Salinger's *The Catcher in the Rye.*" *Explicator*, Summer 2008, Vol. 66, Issue 4, pp. 203–206, 4p.

Yahya, Wan Roselezam Wan, and Ruzbeh Babaee. "Salinger's Depiction of Trauma in *The Catcher in the Rye.*" *Theory and Practice in Language Studies*, 2014, Vol. 4, Issue 9, pp. 1825–1828.

Catch-22, Joseph Heller
(Simon & Schuster, 1961)

Catch-22 is a satirical novel set in World War II. It centers around the 256th Squadron, a group that flies over Italy but works hard to avoid overly dangerous missions. The group is captained by John Yossarian. In an effort to avoid a particularly dangerous mission, one of the members of the squadron manipulates information to avoid going on a mission. When their superior finds out, he decides to send them on a particularly dangerous mission. When the members of the squadron realize the level of danger that they will likely face, they decide that they should try to be designated as insane in order to avoid active participation in the war. Yossarian himself enjoys time resting in the hospital. Unfortunately for Yossarian and the other men, the U.S. Air Force has created a mechanism known as "Catch-22" to make the designation of insanity virtually impossible. Any pilot looking to avoid dangerous missions by claiming insanity would, by the desire to leave danger behind, prove himself sane. Although the book does follow a specific narrative, the narration comes from multiple perspectives, often repeating the same events, just being told from a different perspective. Because of this splintered point of view, the book jumps around in time, not following a single, linear narrative.

The novel had a wide variety of reactions when it first came out. Many readers appreciated that it satirized bureaucracy, showing the significant gap between the rules within a system and the people most affected by those rules. Critics of the book found the splintered point of view too confusing and unnecessary. Some critics also said that the book seemed like a series of repetitive jokes more than a coherent and socially significant novel. Despite some of its critics, the book became very popular among college-aged readers who were disenchanted with mainstream culture and large systems of power. Interestingly, Heller himself stated that the book was meant to critique the witch hunts and paranoia of McCarthyism as well as the Korean War rather than World War II. In 1970, the novel was adapted into a film starring such significant actors as Alan Arkin, Bob Newhart, Martin Sheen, Jon Voight, and Orson Welles. The film was adapted by Buck Henry and directed by Mike Nichols, the team who also had adapted *The Graduate*. Unlike *The Graduate*, *Catch-22* received a lukewarm reception from viewers and critics alike.

Although the book was popular with some groups, it did face some significant challenges. In 1972, the book was challenged in Ohio for containing vulgar language. In particular, members of the squadron referred to some women as "whores." Whether this was the actual reason for the book's challenge or not is debatable. Certainly, the disturbing material in the book (the members of the squadron dying and the rape of one of the female characters) made some readers and parents uncomfortable. In addition, the taking on of McCarthy was a very bold move, even if it was veiled. The book was, if not a clear attack on McCarthy, at the very least a clear critique of bureaucracy and, beyond that, war and the military. Because of this, there were a number of objections to the book based upon the notion that it was not patriotic. Although the book was challenged, it did not necessarily receive the wide-ranging challenges that other books were met with. The most frequently noted challenges came in Ohio, Texas, and Washington.

FURTHER READING

Doloff, Steven J. "Heller's *Catch-22*." *Explicator*, Spring 2007, Vol. 65, Issue 3, pp. 180–182, 3p.

Garrett, Leah. "Joseph Heller's Jewish War Novel *Catch-22*." *Journal of Modern Jewish Studies*, November 2015, Vol. 14, Issue 3, pp. 391–408, 18p.

Podhoretz, Norman. "Looking Back at *Catch-22*." *Commentary*, February 2000, Vol. 109, Issue 2, pp. 32–37, 6p.

A Clockwork Orange, **Anthony Burgess**
(William Heinemann, 1962)

A Clockwork Orange is a dystopian novel that examines issues of justice, morality, and individual freedom. The book is set in England in the near future. In the beginning, the main character, Alex reflects upon his violent and rebellious life with his gang. Alex and his gang commit various crimes, including breaking into a couple's house, beating the husband, and raping the wife. The group continues making trouble. After a night of drugs and violence, Alex decides to take a day off of school. Early in the day, Alex is visited by what is essentially his parole officer. Although the officer tells Alex that he's putting himself in danger, Alex does not seem to be concerned. That night, Alex returns to his group, where he finds himself challenged. There is a demand that the group begins to take on more serious crime. Alex beats two of his group's members but then agrees to take on harsher acts. However, after breaking into a home, the group turns on Alex, beating him and leaving him to be picked up by the police. At this point, the book takes a shift, following Alex through his rehabilitation. While Alex is in jail, he gains favor from the prison chaplain, leading him to be selected for an experimental treatment known as the Ludovico technique. The technique plays upon the understanding of Pavlovian responses coming from building associations. Alex is forced to watch films containing violent and sadistic sexual acts. While Alex watches these films, the doctors watching him pump him with chemicals that make him feel ill and uncomfortable. While Alex is fine with having these desires removed from him, he is disturbed by the fact that they play Beethoven's music while he watches the films, making him associate Beethoven with discomfort and illness as well. This leads to Alex's release, but not everyone supports the technique. The prison chaplain refers to Alex as "a clockwork orange," meaning that he has lost the ability to decide whether he behaves in a moral or immoral way, and this is fundamentally wrong, because it removes free will in a way that only God should be able to do. Still, Alex is released from prison. When he returns to his parents' home, he finds that they have rented out his room to help earn money. Alex receives harsh treatment from a variety of his former victims until he's left outside of a cottage. The cottage turns out to be the same one that Alex and his gang broke into at the beginning of the book. Alex is taken in by the very person whom he and his friends assaulted. While talking to the man, Alex finds out that the wife of the man had died from injuries that came from the rape Alex and his friends perpetrated upon her. After this discussion, Alex tries to kill himself. When Alex regains consciousness, he finds himself in a mental hospital, where government officials offer him a good job in order to help him back on his feet. While listening to them, Alex dreams of committing more violent and sexual acts, helping him to realize that the Ludovico technique had been undone, and he could once again engage in the antisocial activities that had landed him in trouble in the first place. As the book closes, Alex finds himself going through the motions of committing some crimes with a new group of followers. Interestingly, the final chapter where Alex begins to lose interest in criminal activities was omitted from the first publication of the book in America.

A Clockwork Orange is noteworthy for a number of reasons beyond the controversy surrounding it. The author, Anthony Burgess, was both a writer and a scholar. His studies of James Joyce helped him to create the system of slang known as Nadsat. Nadsat, the primary mode of speaking for Alex and his friends ("droogs" in Nadsat), is a combination of English, Russian, and other terms and systems. This innovative treatment of language helped to establish the underworld of the book while also masking some of the more violent or disturbing acts in the book. It also gave a sense of the criminal class of the book, with one of the government officials referring to it as partially being a "gypsy" language, putting emphasis on the marking of the lower class as deviant. In addition to the language of the book, it is noteworthy for Burgess's own discussion of it. Years after it was written, Burgess claimed to dislike the book, saying that he had written it quickly and primarily to make money rather than give any sense of artistry. How seriously to take these claims has been debated by some, but most agree that Burgess did not view the book as an artistic success. The book has also had a significant impact upon popular culture, having been adapted into a film by Stanley Kubrick in 1971 (not surprisingly, the film was, like the book, met with a number of challenges). The film and book have been referenced by major cultural touchstones from Andy Warhol to The Simpsons. The book has also been at the center of a number of discussions of "the aesthetics of violence," that is to say, the stylization and appearance or artistry of violence. This comes partially from Alex's interest in and appreciation of high culture, like Beethoven's music along with his thirst for an outlet for his darker desires.

The book did not come into full popular prominence until after the release of Kubrick's film adaptation. This is also when the challenges to the books began to come in America. In 1976 and 1977, the book began to be removed from schools. The stated reason was that the book contained "objectionable language," but the book's proponents speculated that the primary reasons for the book's removal were because of the acts performed by Alex and his droogs and also the challenging of authority found in the book, particularly the way that it portrayed authority figures that were proponents of the rehabilitation technique that left Alex helpless. This speculation was fueled by the use of Nadsat, which cloaked many of the most severe acts in the book's slang.

FURTHER READING

Krämer, Peter Basingstoke. *A Clockwork Orange*. England: Palgrave Macmillan, 2011.

McQueen, Sean. "Adapting to Language: Anthony Burgess's and Stanley Kubrick's *A Clockwork Orange*." *Science Fiction Film and Television*, Autumn 2012, Vol. 5, Issue 2, pp. 221–241.

Stewart, David. "The Pulp of a Clockwork Orange." *Human Communication*, Spring 2011, Vol. 14, Issue 1, pp. 17–29, 13p.

Crazy Lady, Jane Leslie Conly
(HarperCollins, 1993)

Crazy Lady is a children's novel set in Baltimore, Maryland, in the 1980s. The novel is told in flashback from the point of view of a teenage boy, Vernon Dibbs. Vernon tells of his life as a seventh grader. He faced a number of difficulties as one of five children to an undereducated factory worker. This situation was worsened when Vernon's mother died, an event that comes shortly before where Vernon starts his story, though the event looms large in the minds of the Dibbs children. Because their father works second shift, the Dibbs children are responsible for much of the housekeeping and caretaking for the younger children. Partially because of these responsibilities, Vernon struggles in school, having been held back one year and waiting to hear if he will be held back again. As a result of the pressures that he feels, Vernon seeks negative outlets for his tension. In particular, he and his friends often tease Maxine Flooter, an alcoholic woman that the group refers to as "the crazy lady." Flooter is teased not only for her behavior but also for the constant presence of her son, Ronald, who is cognitively delayed. The teasing about her son particularly frustrates Flooter. Vernon's perspective on Flooter begins to change when the two of them both argue with a local shopkeeper over the prices of some of his goods. Flooter compliments Vernon on his handling of matters even though Vernon was kicked out of the store. As the two talk, Flooter tells Vernon that her neighbor can help Vernon with his schoolwork. When Vernon tells Flooter's neighbor, Miss Annie, that he cannot pay her for her help, Miss Annie tells him that she will continue to help him if he, in turn, helps out

Flooter. Vernon grudgingly agrees, and he begins to form a friendship with Ronald. His sympathies come largely from seeing the nature of Ronald's life, as Maxine Flooter is often intoxicated and, sometimes, in jail as the result of her alcoholism. Although this change is largely positive for Vernon, the time that he spends with Ronald and working on his homework has led him to stray a bit from his own family. The siblings resent his absence, but Vernon's staying out or up late leads him, ironically, to forge a deeper friendship with his father, who stays up late listening to the radio. When Vernon meets Ronald's teacher, he finds out that the teacher would like to see Ronald participate in the Special Olympics. Vernon agrees to help, and he enlists the help of his old friends to make this happen. To Vernon's surprise, he finds out that one of the friends who used to make fun of the Flooters has a cognitively disabled brother that he kept secret. As part of his efforts to help Ronald take part in the Special Olympics, Vernon organizes a block party to help raise money. Unfortunately, Maxine shows up to the event intoxicated, and, after she makes a scene, the party unravels. This event and a scene at church where Maxine berates a number of people, including Vernon, lead Vernon to stop speaking to Maxine. Vernon continues to check in on Ronald, but he refuses to discuss anything with Maxine, despite her efforts to speak to him. Ronald successfully competes in the Special Olympics with the help of Vernon. When Ronald's teacher gives the two of them a ride home, Vernon discovers that Maxine is planning to send Ronald to live with a family in North Carolina. Vernon is irate, and he immediately confronts Maxine, who tells Vernon that she recognizes that she is not able to give Ronald the care that he needs and that she knows North Carolina will be a better environment for Ronald. On the day of Ronald's departure for North Carolina, Maxine is absent. As Ronald's new family drives him off, Vernon runs after the car until he trips on a curb. As Vernon is on the ground, crying, his father approaches Vernon, letting him know that he is there for Vernon, a clear contrast to Ronald's mother.

The book was critically well received, earning a Newbery Honor in 1994. In particular, the strong emotional core of the book, its frank examination of poverty and the effects of poverty, and its positive portrayal of the disabled made it a favorite of many readers. Also, the complex character of Vernon, who changes significantly over the course of the book, was seen by many as a rich and interesting part of the story. Unlike some stories for younger readers, the sorts of conflicts and troubles that Vernon faces have no purely right or wrong solutions, and this type of complexity is one of the traits that sets the book apart.

Still, the book did receive some challenges. Like many of the books that portray bad behavior by young characters, *Crazy Lady* received criticism for its inclusion of vulgar language from the young characters. Although it was typically not part of the official criticism, it is likely that some of the negative reactions came from the honest portrayal of an alcoholic parent as well. In addition, the book's examination of dark themes, like the loss of a parent and the anxieties and tensions that arise from that loss, may well have played into the discomfort that some parents and teachers may have felt toward the book. There is some minor speculation that the portrayal of Vernon's father may also have played into some of the challenges. As Vernon worked to increase his own education, he also ended up helping his father to learn to read. While this was regarded by many readers as a touching storyline, the portrayal of a parent as dependent upon a child (particularly coupled with the portrayal of Maxine as being unable to care for her son) may have led some teachers and parents to feel that the book raised issues that not every child could handle. Still, the book is beloved by many readers who find it to be an uplifting story of personal progress despite the struggles initially faced by both Vernon and Ronald.

FURTHER READING

Goldsmith, Francisca. "Impetuous R, Secret Agent." *Booklist*, September 1, 2008, Vol. 105, Issue 1, pp. 95–100, 6p.

Vasilakis, Nancy. "Crazy Lady!" *Horn Book Magazine*, July/August 1993, Vol. 69, Issue 4, p. 465.

Vasilakis, Nancy. "While No One Was Watching." *Horn Book Magazine*, July/August 1998, Vol. 74, Issue 4, pp. 484–485, 2p.

Cut, **Patricia McCormick**
(Scholastic, 2000)

Cut is a young adult book dealing with self-mutilation and psychological issues. The book follows Callie McPherson as she works through therapy at Sea Pines, a treatment facility that has received the nickname "Sick Minds." Callie is in the facility to deal with various psychological issues, most notably her self-mutilation or "cutting." Still, during most of her initial stay, Callie refuses to speak to anyone, most notably her therapist. Eventually, Callie's therapist draws Callie out, getting her to discuss her motivations for cutting and helping her to understand why she engages in these practices. After this breakthrough, Callie grudgingly begins to strike up friendships with the other people receiving treatment at Sea Pines. The discussions that Callie has with a new resident, Amanda, and her therapist help Callie to recognize the source of the frustration that leads her to cut herself. Amanda, a fellow cutter who proudly displays her scars, is particularly helpful to give Callie perspective on her issues. The motive for Callie to resort to self-mutilation stemmed from issues with her family. Her brother's chronic illness led Callie's mother to quit work and take care of him. Given her mother's quitting work, Callie's father was often gone at work, trying to earn extra income. All of this left Callie feeling abandoned and powerless, which led to her seeking an outlet for her rage. After gaining a clearer sense of the reasons for her motivation, Callie begins to have a more normal life.

The critical response to *Cut* was overwhelmingly positive. Both *Kirkus Reviews* and *Publishers Weekly* gave very positive responses to the book, noting that it gave a positive portrayal of adolescents struggling with issues of mental illness. In particular, the fact that Callie struggled in the early going and that it took a combination of both peers and experts in helping her to overcome her struggles was cited as evidence that the book's narrative was both realistic and meaningful. Despite these sorts of accolades, the book did receive challenges from parent groups. The book contained some scenes that were seen as too graphic for young readers. While there are indeed scenes that describe the act of cutting in clear detail, it is hard to say whether the core of the objections came from the graphic nature of the descriptions of a young person cutting herself or whether the concern was that the book glorified cutting or gave young people a model to follow if young people had a desire to act out in some way. Although there were some concerns for how the book presented issues of mental illness, the concerns were part of a larger discussion of mental illness that come out of the early 2000s era, including *Girl Interrupted*, which also looked at a young female who was working through psychological issues.

FURTHER READING

Hill, Rebecca A. "Talking with Patricia McCormick." *Book Links*, October 2010, Vol. 20, Issue 1, pp. 21–22, 2p.
Staff. "Never Fall Down." *Publishers Weekly*, March 26, 2012, Vol. 259, Issue 13, p. 83.

Fahrenheit 451, Ray Bradbury
(Ballantine Books, 1953)

Fahrenheit 451 is a major American science fiction novel. It's structured in three sections, and it follows Guy Montag. The first section establishes Montag as a "fireman," someone who burns books that the government has banned. Montag's world is shaken first when he meets a young girl who is his new neighbor and is also a nonconformist, something very dangerous to be in the world of the book. Things worsen when Montag finds that his wife has tried to commit suicide by overdosing on drugs. At work, Montag steals a book from a house that he and his coworkers have been sent to take the books from. Montag then begins to have doubts about his work. He brings up the fact that he would like to quit his job, but his wife reacts badly, telling him that it would ruin them financially. While Montag is home, his boss, Captain Beatty, visits him, warning Montag not to get sucked into the allure of the books. This further divides Montag and his wife.

The second section leads to Montag seeking out an English teacher named Faber. Montag and Faber team up, and Montag tries to interest his wife and neighbor in some of the books he has. After a warning from Faber, Montag buries most of the books that he has stolen in his yard, but he does bring the Bible back to the station, where he presents it to Beatty, his boss, who tosses it out. They then are called out. To Montag's shock, the call leads to his own house.

The third section opens with Beatty telling Montag that he has to burn down his own house, letting him know that Montag's wife and her friends are the ones who had reported him for stealing books. Montag sees his wife leaving the house, and he tries to talk to her, but she does not acknowledge him. Montag burns down his own house. While he does so, Beatty realizes that Montag is being instructed by the earpiece. He threatens to find and punish Faber for his involvement, but Montag sets Beatty on fire, then escapes. Montag goes to Faber, asking him for guidance. Faber tells him about an area with book readers where he might find support. Montag finds this group, and he connects to them, appreciating their commitment to reading and knowledge. While he enjoys this connection, the whole group sees bombers fly overhead, destroying much of the city that Montag came from. He hopes that Faber has safely escaped, but he knows that his wife and her friends have been killed in the attack. The book closes with one of the readers telling Montag that mankind is like a phoenix, deteriorating, burning down, but always rising from the ashes.

Fahrenheit 451 was the culmination of a series of related works by Bradbury. He had previously written short stories about totalitarian governments, and he had written a novella about book burning. After the success of these works, Ballantine encouraged Bradbury to expand these works into a larger book. The book was very well received by most critics, with many praising its astute observations about American culture and the lack of engagement many citizens have with their government and their literature. Not all reviews were fully positive, though. Even prominent sources like the *New York Times* gave it lukewarm reviews, claiming that it was more of a hysterical complaint about modern culture than a careful criticism. Commercially, the book was a success, and it led to a number of adaptations. The book has appeared in play, television, and film formats both in America and in Europe, though most of the adaptations have not received the acclaim that the book itself has. It also continues to be taught in high schools around America.

Given the level of attention that the book has received, it is not surprising that it also has met with challenges. Even Bradbury's publisher had taken steps to manipulate the content. In 1967, they began publishing censored versions of the text, removing some of the obscene words and changing a drunken man into a man who was merely sick. Ballantine Books did this in hopes of preventing challenges when the book was taught in high schools. This version existed for over a decade before Bradbury was made aware of these changes. Once he saw the edited version, Bradbury demanded that his original version be the only one published. In addition to having the original text restored, all editions published after 1980 include an afterword by Bradbury discussing the importance of preserving the original content, particularly in a book focused on censorship. After the original text was restored, the book began to receive challenges. In 1987, a school board in Panama City, Florida, placed the book in a classification of texts that were not suitable for classroom use. There was considerable backlash to this move, including a class-action lawsuit and student protests. After significant media focus, the school board removed their classification system, meaning that *Fahrenheit 451* often was banned by default. In 1992, the editing done by the publisher was essentially reenacted as a school in Irvine, California, distributed copies of the book with all of the obscenities blacked out. Again, student and community protests led to the book's original version being restored. In 2006, the book was challenged in Texas, where a parent demanded that the book be banned after the parent's daughter reported obscenities and depictions of the Bible being burned in the book. Neither the parent nor the student recognized that the burning of the Bible was portrayed in a negative way, and much of the focus of the parent's complaint revolved around obscenity and references to drunkenness. While the student got out of finishing the book (she was allowed to read an alternative text), it did not receive an outright ban. Ironically, the book had been assigned to the class as part of a "Banned Books Week" project. Despite these challenges, the book continues to be widely read and taught in schools.

FURTHER READING

Bradbury, Ray. "Fahrenheit 451." *Literary Cavalcade*, January 2001, Vol. 53, Issue 4, pp. 6–13, 8p.

Hollier, Denis. "Fahrenheit 451 Below." *Raritan*, Summer 1996, Vol. 16, Issue 1, pp. 93–102, 10p.

Lee, Sunjoo. "To Be Shocked to Life Again: Ray Bradbury's *Fahrenheit 451*." *Explicator*, April–June 2014, Vol. 72, Issue 2, pp. 142–145, 4p.

Family Secrets, Norma Klein
(Dutton Books, 1985)

Family Secrets is a young adult novel. The book looks at two childhood friends who see each other every summer as their families stay at beach houses. The two, Peter and Leslie, begin an intimate relationship the summer before their final year of high school. While Peter and Leslie make their connection, Leslie discovers that they are not the only members of the family who have connected. In particular, Peter and Leslie discover that Leslie's mother and Peter's father are having an affair with each other. This is confirmed when both sets of parents announce that they will be filing for divorce, leaving Peter and Leslie to contemplate the fact that they will soon be stepsiblings instead of just friends and lovers. The pair also have the pressures of the upcoming school year to deal with. In particular, Peter is looking to gain acceptance to Harvard, and Leslie is rehearsing for a high school play that will help her to prepare for her studies of drama when she attends college. As the families separate at the end of the summer, Peter moves in with his mother. The living arrangements eventually leave Peter and Leslie living together, with Leslie's mother and Peter's father marrying each other shortly after they end their respective marriages. After living under the same roof for a brief time, Leslie and Peter decide to call off their physical relationship, finding it too awkward to continue things under the new living and family arrangements. However, it is not long before the newlyweds begin to see their marriage deteriorate. After Leslie's mother and Peter's father break up, Leslie and Peter decide that, the summer before they part ways and go to college, they will take a road trip together, enjoying their last bit of time as lovers.

The book received some commercial success, selling well as a romance novel for young adults. Critical reviews were mixed, with many reviewers find the plot contrived and the characterization inconsistent. Still, a number of young readers enjoyed the book, finding it exciting and an original portrayal of adolescent desire and tension.

The book has been challenged many times, not surprisingly. It was in the top one hundred "Most Challenged Books" from 1990 to 1999 according to the American Library Association. There have been a wide variety of reasons listed for the challenges. A common reason is that the book portrays sexual encounters between young people in a positive light. There also is a reference to birth control, which left some parents concerned. In addition, the first sexual encounter between Peter and Leslie happened in part due to their partaking of marijuana. The pair also regularly drink alcohol together during their times together. In addition, some parents were uncomfortable with the divorce and remarrying of Peter's father and Leslie's mother. Also, although Peter and Leslie are technically not related by blood, some challenging parties claimed that the book promoted incest. While the book did receive some limitations because of these challenges, the book often remained on shelves, partially because the challenging bodies sometimes made larger claims about the book's transgressive or offensive nature, going beyond what they could reasonably prove. Another mitigating factor was the fact that the book was perceived more as a piece of popular, commercial fiction, simply being in libraries and read for pleasure rather than being a book seen as having legitimate social merit and included on many class-reading lists.

FURTHER READING

Noah, Carolyn. "Presenting Norma Klein (Book Review)." *School Library Journal*, October 1988, Vol. 35, Issue 2, p. 169.

Staff. "Milestones." *Time*, May 8, 1989, Vol. 133, Issue 19, p. 65.

Zeisler, Andi. "A Norma Life." *Bitch Magazine: Feminist Response to Pop Culture*, Fall 2006, Vol. 10, Issue 33, p. 70.

The Great Gilly Hopkins, Katherine Paterson
(T. Y. Crowell, 1978)

The Great Gilly Hopkins is one of the first young adult novels to directly address the issue of foster homes from the perspective of a child. The book follows Gilly Hopkins, a seemingly confident and often aggressive young girl who has grown up in foster care. At the book's beginning, she is preparing to enter a new home, something that she dreads, because she dislikes the upheaval that it represents. Instead, she wants to be able to settle down and stay with her mother, and she keeps a picture of her mother nearby to maintain a sense of hope. In the new home, Gilly immediately takes a negative attitude, deciding that she will dislike the "fat hippo," which is how she refers to her new foster mother, Mrs. Trotter. She also quickly comes to dislike William, a seven-year-old boy with mental challenges, and Mr. Randolph, and elderly African American man who is blind. Both William and Mr. Randolph receive some care and support from Mrs. Trotter. Gilly decides that she will steal money so that she can escape from her new foster home and try to find her mother. Gilly tries sending her mother a letter, telling her that she is coming, and she tries to escape, but she is found by the police. A short time after Gilly's attempt to escape, she and Mrs. Trotter are visited by Gilly's grandmother, who had just recently discovered that Gilly was her granddaughter. As Gilly's grandmother takes her from Mrs. Trotter, Gilly begins to realize how kind Mrs. Trotter was and that she actually was beginning to enjoy being with Mrs. Trotter. Still, Gilly is able to connect with her grandmother, and she is glad to learn about her family and her history a bit more. While staying with her grandmother, Gilly is visited by her mother. Although Gilly is excited at first, when she sees her mother, she sees that her mother looks nothing like the picture that Gilly has been holding onto. She also discovers that her mother came to get money from Gilly's grandmother, not truly to see Gilly. This all impacts Gilly greatly, and she calls Mrs. Trotter, pleading with her to take her back. However, Mrs. Trotter convinces Gilly that she should stay with her grandmother, because they are true family, and Gilly comes to accept this.

The book was very well received, earning such accolades as a National Book Award in the children's literature category and a Newberry Honor, among several others. It has also inspired a film that was released in early 2016. The book was also notable for a number of events that happened over the course of the challenge that was leveled against it. In a school district in Virginia, a parent brought a challenge against the book, listing the obscene words said by Gilly Hopkins and also complaining that the protagonist often took the lord's name in vain. The school district created a panel to judge the book's merit, and the panel twice determined that the book was appropriate to remain on the district's library shelves. Part of this decision came from the revelation that the parent lodging the complaint had never actually read the book; she had only had the obscenities reported to her out of context. Despite this determination by the panel, the district's superintendent had the book removed. After the removal, the author of the book, Katherine Paterson, wrote an open letter defending her use of obscene words, claiming that Gilly would have seemed less real if she had been a more tame and innocent character. The media also picked up on a fifth-grade boy who wrote a book report that referred to the book as "a miracle," because seeing a character in print who misbehaved but was then redeemed helped to give him hope. With all of the attention and accolades garnered for *The Great Gilly Hopkins*, the challenges to the book may have ironically helped the book's status and sales rather than hurt them, and they have helped to make the book a widely read and well-defended one.

FURTHER READING

Cairns, Sue. "Power, Language and Literacy in *The Great Gilly Hopkins*." *Children's Literature in Education*, March 2008, Vol. 39, Issue 1, pp. 9–19, 11p.

Hagan, Carey E. "One Tough Cookie." *Horn Book Magazine*, September/October 2011, Vol. 87, Issue 5, pp. 47–50, 4p.

Stokes, Phyllis. "A Look at Foster Care in *The Great Gilly Hopkins*." *Virginia English Bulletin*, Winter 1986, Vol. 36, Issue 2, pp. 30–35.

Harriet the Spy, Louise Fitzhugh
(Harper & Row, 1964)

Harriet the Spy is a children's novel that has achieved significant and lasting acclaim. It follows Harriet Welsch, an eleven-year-old girl who lives in New York and dreams of becoming a writer. Harriet's nanny, Ole Golly, discovers Harriet's aspiration, and she encourages her to keep a journal to begin the practice of writing. Harriet takes this suggestion seriously, following people and taking notes about their behaviors. Harriet is typical of precocious children in that she often takes things seriously and can be unconventional, insisting that tomato sandwiches are the only sandwiches that she can eat and maintaining that she must regularly pursue her craft. Despite these minor oddities, Harriet has some close friends, such as Sport, a young boy who is gifted in athletics, and Janie, who wants to become a scientist. Harriet is also very close to her nanny, and she is devastated when her nanny announces that she will soon be getting married and leaving the family. Harriet's parents are likewise disappointed, because they have come to rely upon Ole Golly, not being very hands on with Harriet. Harriet's problems continue when, during a game of tag, she loses her notebook to a classmate who reads through it and reports that Harriet has been keeping unflattering notes on the whole class. Even her close friends are the subject of derisive observations, like when she compares Sport to an old woman, because he spends too much time worrying about his father. The students then gang up on Harriet, forming a "Spy Catcher Club" to harass her and exclude her from social interactions. This only serves to further alienate Harriet from her classmates, and she spies on them all the more, beginning to plot her revenge. Things only deteriorate, with Harriet feeling guilty for what she's written and getting in trouble for getting petty revenges on members of the Spy Catcher Club. Things come to a head when she fails to turn in homework and stays in bed, feeling too depressed to go to school. All of this leads her grades to suffer, at which point Harriet's parents take her to see a psychiatrist. The psychiatrist encourages Harriet to reestablish contact with Ole Golly. When Harriet does, telling Ole Golly of the problems stemming from her notebook, Ole Golly tells Harriet that her only two choices are trying to lie her way out of what she has written in her notebook or simply to apologize. She also notes that she recognizes that Harriet will not like either option. Around the same time, many of the children tin the Spy Catcher Club leave it behind, growing tired of the central figure's bossiness. Harriet's parents talk to Harriet's teacher, and they decide that Harriet could benefit from being involved with the school newspaper. When Harriet begins to run the paper, people come back to her side, and she is able to write positive stories instead of negative secrets, and she is able to offer a public apology. In addition to a general acceptance, Harriet's new course lets her reconcile with Sport and Janie.

The book quickly became a major success, selling well and earning high praise for its entertaining and realistic portrayal of the petty conflicts that can arise among children. In 2012, the book was in the top twenty children's novels according to *School Library Journal*. It has also been adapted into other media a number of times, once as a film in 1996 (the first to be produced by Nickelodeon's feature films production company) and twice for television. Both Fitzhugh and others have written sequels to the book, but none of them have garnered either the critical or commercial success of the original. Still, *Harriet the Spy* has sold continuously and quite well for decades, and it has been translated into a half dozen languages.

Despite this long-standing success, the book has been met with challenges. In 1983, it was put into a group with *Are You There, God?* and *Blubber* by Judy Blume, along with other books. This challenge came at a school district in Ohio, where some parents claimed that these books encouraged bad behavior from children. Despite these objections, the school board decided to keep all of the children's books available to students. In *Harriet* in particular, the suffering of Harriet and the lessons learned by the book's end helped to validate the book's awareness of moral and ethical concerns for children.

FURTHER READING

Busis, Hillary. "Harriet the Spy and Me." *Entertainment Weekly*, February 28, 2014, Issue 1300, p. 76.

Gantos, Jack. "I Spy, Harriet and I." *Horn Book Magazine*, May/June 2014, Vol. 90, Issue 3, pp. 31–33.

Mercier, Cathryn M. "Becoming a Book Detective." *Horn Book Magazine*, May/June 2014, Vol. 90, Issue 3, pp. 41–42.

How to Eat Fried Worms, Thomas Rockwell
(Franklin Watts, 1973)

How to Eat Fried Worms is a children's novel following a boy, Billy. Billy, Alan, and Joe visit Tom at his house. As they talk to Tom, they find out that he got in trouble for not eating his dinner, and the boys discuss what they would eat and what they would not. After going through a list, someone asks Billy if he would eat mud, and he says that he would, which leads someone to ask if he would eat worms. When Billy says that he would eat worms, someone dares him to eat fifteen worms in fifteen days. Alan and Joe tell Billy that they will give him money to buy a minibike if he can eat them, but that he will have to pay them money if he does not follow through. Billy takes the bet, and he begins eating worms, trying different ways, like putting mustard and ketchup on them. Alan and Joe consistently try to trick Billy into not eating his daily worm, trying to get him to forget, gluing worms together, and even locking him in a closet. But, with the help of his friends and parents, Billy does succeed at eating his fifteen worms, and he gets the money to buy the minibike that he had wanted.

The book was Rockwell's third, and it was fairly well received, selling over three million copies and winning a number of awards. It has been adapted both for television and film, both of which had generally positive receptions. Still, the book did face challenges. In the 1990s, it had multiple challenges on the basis of showing irresponsible or undesirable behavior. The specific objections generally fell into one of two categories. The first was the eating of the worms, which some parents found to be disturbing. The second was the betting and daring that took place among the boys. Again, some parents expressed concerns about the possible negative consequences of this sort of behavior. None of these challenges had a major impact upon the book's long-term success, and many readers have expressed surprise that the book was challenged at all.

FURTHER READING

Hill, Rebecca A. "The Gross and Gory: Making a Reading Connection with Boys." *Book Links*, May 2009, Vol. 18, Issue 5, pp. 6–10.

Maya, S. "How to Eat Fried Worms." *Scholastic News*—Edition 4, January 27, 2014, Vol. 76, Issue 13, p. 7.

Zingher, Gary. "Wild Moments and Wacky Situations." *School Library Media Activities Monthly*, April 2002, Vol. 18, Issue 8, p. 41.

James and the Giant Peach, Roald Dahl
(Alfred A. Knopf, 1963)

James and the Giant Peach is one of Roald Dahl's many children's books. In it, four-year-old James Trotter is forced to live with his aunts after his parents are killed by rhinoceroses. His aunts are cruel to him, leaving him to sleep in their attic. They also beat him and leave him malnourished. James wanders when he can, and, during one of his wanderings, he finds an old man who tells him how to brew a potion that will give him happiness. As James tries to bring the ingredients for the potion to his home, he accidentally spills many of them on a peach tree near his aunts' house. The tree soon grows a huge peach. The aunts react by charging people money to see the giant peach. When the aunts send James to clean up all of the garbage that the crowds have left around the peach, James finds out that there is a group of insects and worms living inside of the peach. The magical ingredients have also made the animals large, and it has also given them the ability to speak. The group, along with James, decide that they will take an adventure in the peach. One of the insects, a centipede, bites the peach's stem. When it drops from the tree, the peach falls and crushes both of his aunts. The peach then rolls into the sea, where it is surrounded by sharks. Needing to escape, the group tricks a group of seagulls, then harnesses hundreds of them to fly the peach around, making it look much like a hot air balloon, and they decide to cross the Atlantic. The group has a number of adventures, including one of them falling into the ocean and running into "Cloud Men" who control the weather. The Cloud Men become a regular source of antagonism for the group, with one of them trying to board the peach after the group smashes a rainbow made by the Cloud Men. The trip ends when a plane goes by and cuts the strings that attach the birds to the peach. The peach falls onto the Empire State Building in New York, which punctures the peach. People in the building first see James and his crew as monsters, but, after he tells the people his story and lets the children below eat the peach, they are all seen as heroes. In the end, the peach's pit is rolled to Central Park, where James and his new friends use it as a home.

The book quickly became one of Dahl's beloved works. It sold well and was received well by fans. In fact, the book referenced some of Dahl's other works, including *Charlie and the Chocolate Factory* and *The BFG*. It also was adapted multiple times. Although Dahl consistently refused to sell the rights during his life, his widow allowed it to be adapted into a film in 1996, and it was also adapted into a musical in 2010. The movie was not quite as popular and commercially successful as the book, but it received some positive reviews.

While the book was not one of the most disturbing or dark of Dahl's works, there were a variety of challenges to it. In Florida, the book was challenged for its use of the occult, citing the ingredients that initially led to the giant peach's growth. There were two challenges in Wisconsin, one claiming that there were subtle sexual overtones in the book and another saying that the language was too vulgar for young readers (the word "ass" was the particular point of objection). There were other challenges that came out of the tobacco and alcohol use of the characters and some of the violence that some of the characters face. Although these objections were raised, teachers and librarians generally supported the book, and little actual damage was done to its reputation.

FURTHER READING

Ansen, David. "Aboard a Magic Peach." *Newsweek*, 4/15/1996, Vol. 127 Issue 16, p. 77.

Curtis, James M. "In Absentia Parentis: Confronting the Uncanny Orphan in Roald Dahl's *James and the Giant Peach*." *Children's Literature Association Quarterly*, Winter 2015, Vol. 40, Issue 4, pp. 355–370.

Tisdale, Sallie. "The Real Happy Ending." *Utne Reader* (87500256), January/February 1988, Issue 25, p. 114.

Junie B. Jones Series, Barbara Park
(Random House, 1992–2013)

The Junie B. Jones books are a popular children's series told from the perspective of a young girl. The books take on a variety of topics that are familiar to children, including losing teeth, having anxiety about riding the school bus, and dealing with difficult children at school. Junie B. Jones, the title character, narrates the books with a mixture of journal entry and straight narration, and her writing is filled with spelling errors and misunderstandings that are both typical of children and also humorous. She lives with her mother and father and her infant brother Olly. In addition, she regularly incorporates her stuffed elephant, Philip Johnny Bob, who serves as a sort of imaginary friend as well into her adventures. Other characters include Junie's grandparents, children at school that she gets along with, like Lucille and Herbert, and children that she sees as rivals or antagonists, like Paulie Allen Puffer and May. May in particular often looks for reasons to tattle on Junie B. Jones, and she refuses to say the "B" in Junie B. Jones's name, leading to a natural rivalry. Junie B. Jones also often writes about her teachers in ways that are not necessarily outright cruel but do not show the level of respect that characters in previous children's books have shown. In particular, she often tries to argue her way out of tasks and punishments, and she simple refers to her kindergarten teacher as "Mrs.," not bothering to use her full name. In first grade, Junie B. Jones has Mr. Scary for a teacher, whom she unintentionally antagonizes throughout the books. Most of the books involve Junie B. Jones overcoming a basic problem or fear (being afraid of the tooth fairy or clowns, for instance) in a comical way, with many side stories incorporated into the narrative.

The books gained a consistent and very loyal readership, keeping the series going for over two dozen books. The first entry in the series, *Junie B. Jones and the Stupid, Smelly Bus*, sold very well and received high praise from publications like *Publisher's Weekly*. Subsequent entries continued this pattern of pleasing audiences and critics. Many readers appreciated the realistic portrayal of a young character, a child who acted on impulse and misunderstood many of the more subtle or complicated discussions that adults would have. Barbara Park continued writing the books until her death in 2013.

Despite this loyal following, the series did receive a number of challenges. There have been two different, but related, sources of these objections. The first is that Junie B. Jones tends to talk back to adults, and this is portrayed in a humorous way rather than in a way that discourages imitation of the behavior. Defenders of the series have pointed out that Junie B. Jones does, indeed, get in trouble for her disrespectful ways, earning poor grades at times and being punished at other times. The other principal objection was that the spelling and writing errors found in Junie B. Jones's speech and diary entries could encourage poor performance by her readers. While these challenges did not frequently result in actual bans, they did bring about a significant backlash to the series. The author, Barbara Park, gave two reactions. First, she indicated that her inclusion on the one hundred "Most Challenged Books" from 2000 to 2009 list put out by the American Library Association put her in very good company, including some of Park's favorite authors like Maya Angelou and Toni Morrison. However, as the challenges continued to come, Park seemed to lose this enthusiasm, indicating that she found some of the comments made in association with these challenges to be hurtful. After the death of Park, the challenges to the books have subsided a bit, and the series has retained a significant following of both readers and critics who are drawn to the engaging character of Junie B. Jones and the innovative storytelling from Barbara Park.

FURTHER READING

Ratzan, Jill S. "You Are Not the Boss of My Words: Junie B. Jones, Language and Linguistics." *Children & Libraries: The Journal of the Association for Library Service to Children*, Winter 2005, Vol. 3, Issue 3, pp. 31–38.

Staff. "Children's-Lit Girls Gone Wild." *Time*, August 13, 2007, Vol. 170, Issue 7, pp. 18–19.

Wickstrom, Carol D., Joan Scott Curtis, and Kayla Daniel. "Ashley and Junie B. Jones: A Struggling Reader Makes a Connection to Literacy." *Language Arts*, September 2005, Vol. 83, Issue 1, pp. 16–21.

A Light in the Attic, Shel Silverstein
(Harper & Row, 1981)

A Light in the Attic is a collection of humorous poems and illustrations for children, written by Shel Silverstein. It came after Silverstein's book *Where the Sidewalk Ends* and prior to his *Falling Up*, both of which were similar in genre and style to *A Light in the Attic*. The poems often center on absurd conflicts and light approaches to serious subject matter like death and physical pain.

While many readers appreciated the humorous nature of these pieces, there were some objections. There were two principle sources of objection. The first was that it portrayed bad behavior in children, with poems like "How Not to Have to Dry the Dishes," encouraging children to not follow through on doing chores, and "Little Abigail and the Beautiful Pony," encouraging children to make unreasonable requests. This was the core reason for a request from parents in Lake County, Florida, to have the book banned. The ban did take effect for a short time before other parents and teachers were able to get it overturned. Elsewhere, the book was challenged (though not successfully banned) because of its references to ghosts and demons. Despite these challenges, the book has established and maintained a consistent readership, earning awards and achieving considerable and lasting commercial success.

FURTHER READING

MacDonald, Ruth K. *Shel Silverstein*. New York, NY: Twayne, 1997.
Radomski, Kassandra. "Masters of Verse." *Appleseeds*, March 2010, Vol. 12, Issue 6, pp. 16–18.
Thomas, Joseph T., Jr. "Reappraising Uncle Shelby." *Horn Book Magazine*, May/June 2005, Vol. 81, Issue 3, pp. 283–293.

My Brother Sam Is Dead, James Lincoln Collier and Christopher Collier
(Scholastic, 2001)

My Brother Sam Is Dead is a piece of historical fiction written for children. It is set around the time of the American Revolution, and it follows Tim Meeker, a boy living in Connecticut. Tim's family is loyal to Britain, unlike many of the colonists. Their beliefs are challenged after Tim's older brother, Sam, returns from Yale and announces that not only is he sympathetic to the rebel cause, but he also has enlisted in the Continental army and will be fighting against the British. Tim's parents kick Sam out, but Sam steals his father's rifle before leaving, intending to use it in the war. The family becomes divided over how to react to Sam's actions, and when Sam comes back to talk to the family, Tim is the only one who will speak to him. Tim finds out that Sam is sending messages back to his girlfriend and also to a neighbor who is receiving intelligence about the British army. In the meantime, the family continues their work in the tavern that they own and run. However, on one business trip, Tim's father is abducted by roaming criminals. Tim's own loyalties and opinions begin to shift as he sees the British soldiers in action, with one of his friends being killed by them and another being taken prisoner. Tim also discovers that his father and friend both died after falling ill on a prison ship. In response, his mother begins to slide into alcoholism. Worsening matters is the continued presence of the British soldiers, who take weapons from the families and treat the patriots poorly. As food becomes scarce, tensions continue to flare, and Sam is framed for trying to steal cattle to feed himself. The Continental army ends up executing Sam publically. The book ends with Tim reflecting upon the war as an old man and saying that he wants to make sure that modern readers know what life was like during the war.

The book was generally well received, and it was a commercial success, selling well within the Scholastic catalog. Some critics praised it for its realism and careful research. It also was well received for its focus on issues of social relevance and political debate, examining both sides of the war as well as thinking about the individual and familial impact of wars and political debates.

The book did face some challenges, generally falling into two categories. The first was some of the profanity used as the family argued and soldiers spoke to each other. The other complaints were related to the drinking of the mother as well as some instances of minors drinking in the book. Most of the complaints against the book were dismissed. The Muscogee County School District board in Columbus, Georgia, for instance, voted unanimously to keep the book after it was challenged. In other places, challenges attained a bit greater sense of success, but, by and large, the book was supported rather than banned.

FURTHER READING

Freeman, Judy. "Books about All Kinds of Heroes." *Instructor-Intermediate*, April 1998, Vol. 107, Issue 7, p. 28.

Hurst, Carol O. "Books on the Line." *Teaching Pre K-8*, November/December 1991, Vol. 22, Issue 3, pp. 112–114.

Rogow, Roberta. "*My Brother Sam Is Dead* (Book Review)." *School Library Journal*, December 1974, Vol. 21, Issue 4, p. 45.

One Flew over the Cuckoo's Nest, Ken Kesey
(Viking Press, 1962)

One Flew over the Cuckoo's Nest is a major American novel and is seen as a major touchstone of the counterculture of the 1960s. The book is told from the perspective of an unreliable narrator, a Native American mental patient who goes by the name of Chief Bromden. The central narrative of the book follows a new inmate to the institution, Randle McMurphy. McMurphy ended up in the institution because he pretended to be insane in order to avoid jail after being caught for committing battery. From the beginning of his time in the institution, McMurphy represents a discipline problem, consistently butting heads with the head nurse, Nurse Ratched. Although McMurphy demonstrates antisocial and aggressive behavior, Ratched is generally portrayed as the villain, because she uses her authority more to dominate the patients than to help them actually leave behind their psychological issues. In addition, she uses the orderly staff to physically intimidate unruly patients. McMurphy sets up gambling, he makes lewd comments to Nurse Ratched, and he organizes and leads the ward's basketball team. McMurphy also makes an effort to pull up a tub and throw it through a window to escape. Although he is not able to, McMurphy tells the other patients that his attempt to escape makes him more active than many of them, who simply accept their fate.

In particular, he is angry that some of the patients are in the ward voluntarily, and they could leave at any time. In order to make the patients appreciate the outside world, McMurphy sneaks several of the other patients out of the ward to go on a fishing trip. After some trouble that came from the trip, Ratched uses electroshock therapy to punish McMurphy and Chief Bromden. After this, McMurphy's desire to upset Ratched only deepens. He bribes the watchmen to let him bring in prostitutes and alcohol, and he also breaks into the pharmacy on the ward, taking out some of the drugs. McMurphy convinces one of the prostitutes to sleep with Billy Bibbit, a young man who has not yet lost his virginity. When Ratched returns to the ward in the morning, she finds McMurphy, Billy, and the prostitutes. Rather than confront McMurphy directly, Ratched goes after Billy, who she knows is weaker. She tells Billy that she will tell his mother that he has slept with a prostitute. Billy is terrified, and he commits suicide. Enraged, McMurphy attacks Ratched. The orderlies pull him off of Ratched before McMurphy can actually kill her, and he is moved into the "Disturbed" ward and then given a lobotomy. While both McMurphy and Ratched are gone, several of the patients, who are there voluntarily, leave, and others find ways to transfer into other wards. When McMurphy returns, he is functionally brain dead, and when Ratched returns, she is not able to speak, weakening her position. Rather than watching McMurphy remain technically alive but not genuinely active, Bromden smothers McMurphy, killing him. Bromden then uses the same tub that McMurphy had tried to lift, this time successfully taking the tub off and throwing it out a window so that he can leave the hospital.

The book tapped into the spirit of the times, finding a loyal and immediate readership among members of the counterculture, who admired its harsh portrayal of authority figures and mainstream culture. It also helped to contribute to Kesey's reputation, which he had developed as part of the Merry Pranksters, a group of writers and artists who were known for doing recreational drugs and committing mild acts of rebellion to upset established power structures and systems. The book was also adapted multiple times, once in 1963, when it was adapted into a play, and once in 1975, when it was adapted into a major motion picture starring Jack Nicholson as McMurphy. The film was a major success, winning all five of the major Academy Awards (Best Picture, Best Director, Best Screenplay, Best Actor, and Best Actress) for the year. The success of the film renewed interest in the book.

Not surprisingly, the book was challenged multiple times. As with many challenged books, the true reason for the challenges can be hard to determine. Given its antiauthority viewpoint, it was an immediate target for a variety of groups. In 1974, a group of parents in Ohio demanded that the book be removed because of the sexual content and what they saw as the glorification of criminal and antisocial behavior. It was banned in New York, Maine, and Idaho, and the teacher who had assigned the book in Idaho actually lost his job for including it on the reading list. Unsuccessful bans occurred in New Hampshire, California, and other places. Despite the book's challenges, the novel and the film inspired by it have maintained their places both as beloved texts and as significant works of American art.

FURTHER READING

Nastu, Paul. "Kesey's *One Flew over the Cuckoo's Nest*." *Explicator*, Fall 1997, Vol. 56, Issue 1, p. 48.

Waserman, Dale. "*One Flew over the Cuckoo's Nest*." *Literary Cavalcade*, May2001, Vol. 53, Issue 8, p. 4.

Wolcott, James. "Still Cuckoo after All of These Years." *Vanity Fair*, December 2011, Issue 616, pp. 134–137.

Staying Fat for Sarah Byrnes, Chris Crutcher
(Greenwillow Books, 1993)

Staying Fat for Sarah Byrnes is a young adult novel by well-known author Chris Crutcher. The book follows a pair of young friends, Eric and Sarah Byrnes. The pair originally became close because they were both outcasts, Eric because he was overweight and Sarah because she had burn scars over much of her body. As part of Sarah and Eric's closeness, they had written a secret school newspaper, and they had one article about a bully, Dale Thornton, who eventually became friends with Eric and Sarah, looking out for them. After Sarah becomes catatonic and is transferred to a mental hospital, Eric looks for ways to break through her fugue to connect with her. Eric is also faced with pressure as he joins the school swim team. While he does well in his time on the swim team, he also recognizes that the exercise is leading to him losing weight, and he is concerned that if he becomes too lean, then he will no longer be an outcast, and he will lose his natural connection to Sarah Byrnes. During Eric's efforts to find a way to get Sarah talking again, Dale helps Eric to find out that Sarah's father is abusive and that he intentionally burned her when she was a child. Shortly after Eric discovers this, Sarah Byrnes begins to talk again, admitting that she had been faking her disorder so that she could be away from her father. Sarah has come to believe that her abusive father is going to kill her soon. Eric tells the swim coach, Ms. Lemry, that he is concerned about Sarah, and Ms. Lemry says that she can help to hide Sarah. In addition to being the swim coach, Ms. Lemry teaches a class on civics and contemporary American life, which discusses religion and, among other things, abortion. From one of these discussions, tensions rise between Mark Brittain, a devout Christian student, and his girlfriend, Jody, who is also Eric's secret crush. The reader discovers that Jody had been pregnant, but Mark encouraged her to abort the child. From the tensions surrounding these conversations, Jody breaks up with Mark, and Jody begins to date Eric. Mark is distraught and attempts suicide, but he does not die. After helping Sarah hide, Ms. Lemry decides that they need to find Sarah's mother, because she is the only person who has seen Sarah's father be abusive. In his search for Sarah, her father ends up attacking Eric, stabbing him, and Eric is only able to make his way to the house of former bully and friend Dale. Sarah discovers what has happened and wants to run away, hoping to save her friends from more attacks from her father. Also looking to help, Eric's mother's boyfriend lays a trap for Sarah's father. Although he successfully traps Sarah's father, after her father is injured in the trap, Eric's mother's boyfriend ends up in jail.

The book won a number of awards, including the *School Library Journal* "Best Book" award and the American Library Association's "Best Book for Young Adults" award. The book also got positive reviews from *Publishers Weekly* and *Children's Literature*. It also sold well, as have many of Crutcher's books.

Despite the accolades and awards, the book did receive some challenges. In Missouri, in the Smithville Public School District, a parent's challenge about the book's portrayal of sexual and disturbing material did result in removal of the book from the classroom. However, after the school board changed the policies for book approvals, not only was the book reinstated, but the high school's English honors society also changed its name to the Sarah Byrnes Society. The book was also challenged in New York, Ohio, and Wisconsin, among other places, complaining of its use of obscenity and its perceived negative portrayal of Christians. After the challenges, Crutcher posted on his website an open letter to the school districts claiming that the challenges were rooted in parental objections, making them not about students' rights but about parental preferences or curricular decisions made by teachers. He also published letters from readers praising the book. Crutcher's work to support his book and the teachers using it have helped it to maintain a strong and dedicated readership.

See Also: *The Sledding Hill*.

FURTHER READING

Daley, Patricia A. "Isler, Crutcher, and the Reader: Creating the World of Sarah Byrnes." *Journal of Children's Literature*, Spring 2002, Vol. 28, Issue 1, pp. 32–38.

Hofmann, Mary. *"Staying Fat for Sarah Byrnes." School Library Journal*, November 2005, Vol. 51, Issue 11, p. 59.

Lockwood, Lucinda. "Book Review: Junior High Up." *School Library Journal*, March 1993, Vol. 39, Issue 3, p. 218.

The Stupids Series, Harry Allard
(Houghton Mifflin, 1974–1989)

The Stupids is a fictional family that is the subject of a series of books by Harry Allard. The books always center around the family's absurd behaviors and the consequences of their idiotic behaviors. In the first book of the series, *The Stupids Step Out*, for instance, the family showers together, fully clothed before visiting their grandparents. They dress in bizarre ways, like wearing a cat for a hat. In other books, such as *The Stupids Have a Ball*, the family hosts a party to celebrate after the children come home with awful report cards.

The books sold relatively well, with both Allard and illustrator James Marshall having established reputations prior to the series that helped to bring attention to it. The book series was also adapted into a film, *The Stupids*, in 1996, though the film performed poorly.

Although many readers found the antics of the family to be more silly than troublesome, some readers did object to what they perceived as encouraging bad behavior. The rewarding of bad report cards in *The Stupids Have a Ball*, in particular, drew fire from some parents. While this book bore the brunt of criticism, after it caught attention, the series in general was challenged a number of times. Beyond the specific behaviors of the family, there was criticism of using the word "stupid" in the title and regularly throughout the book. While the book was challenged surprisingly often, making it up to the twenty-sixth spot on the American Library Association's list of "Most Challenged Books" from 1990 to 2000, the responses to the book have been more subdued than to other books with more charged material.

FURTHER READING

Holtze, Sally Holmes. "*The Stupids Die* (Book)." *School Library Journal*, February 1981, Vol. 27, Issue 6, p. 53.

Jeschelnig, Virginia E., Trevelyn E. Jones, Luann Toth, and Virginia M. J. Staff. "Starlight Goes to Town." *Publishers Weekly*, August 11, 2008, Vol. 255, Issue 32, pp. 46–47.

Suhr. "*The Stupids Go to Town* (Book)." *School Library Journal*, October 1989, Vol. 35, Issue 14, p. 72.

7

GRAPHIC NOVELS AND CENSORSHIP IN AMERICA

This chapter focuses on graphic novels. This genre is slightly different than comic books in a few ways. While comic books are serialized, usually put out on a monthly basis and focusing on small, self-contained stories, graphic novels, by contrast, have longer, coherent narratives like a novel. Because they are longer, the conflicts and plots within graphic novels are more complicated than in one-shot comic books, though some comic book titles have run longer story arcs that get collected into graphic novels. It could be argued that the readership of graphic novels has changed more than any other genre. This is largely because many parents and authority figures do not make a genuine distinction between comic books and graphic novels, and they view these genres as intended for children. Some of this assumption comes from the confusion of comic books with comic strips, the print cartoons that appeared in newspapers. This confusion led many parents to view both comic strips and comic books as either silly diversions to entertain their children or even as positive portrayals of American ideals. Figures like Captain America and GI Joe, in particular, were seen as wholesome heroes who children could look up to. During World War II and shortly thereafter, in particular, many American comic books portrayed Nazis or other perceived anti-American entities as the embodiment of evil.

However, in the late 1940s and early 1950s, publishers like EC Comics began putting out titles like *Tales from the Crypt* and *The Vault of Horror*, with stories of death, violence, and the occult. There were also titles focusing on war and detective stories, but it was the horror comics that would receive the harshest criticism and most attention. Although these were often written off dismissed by adults, some contemporary critics argue that there were redeeming values within the stories, with some being adaptations of Ray Bradbury stories and many confronting societal ills like corruption and racism, just with a gory twist to serve justice at the end.

Although these titles were commercially successful, they began to receive criticism. Psychiatrist and social critic Fredric Wertham began publishing articles claiming that these sorts of comics led to juvenile delinquency and that all comics diminished the reading skills of young people. In the mid-1950s, Wertham published the book *Seduction of the Innocent*, a sensationalist discussion of the influence that comic books had on young people. While Wertham's theories have since been largely debunked, at the time, there was enough of a controversy that Congress held hearings on the matter of comic books and young readers. The result of the trial was that the comic industry developed "the comics code" and the Comics Code Authority, a body within the industry to whom all publishers would have to submit material prior to publication to receive the seal of approval. While this body was rigorous and it was a significant shift from previous practice within the industry, it also meant that the comic book industry could avoid direct governmental censorship. While much of the code might seem innocuous (no glorification of drug use or violence, no overtly sexual material), enforcement of it was inconsistent. EC Comics ended up receiving undue scrutiny for their material. One of the most famous examples was when a judge told the publishers that the main character in a story on racism could not be black. Difficulties like this led the publishers of EC Comics to end up leaving behind many of their horror and science fiction titles altogether.

While the Comics Code Authority did restore trust in the industry for many parents, it also created pressures that led some writers and artists to begin publishing "underground" titles—titles that neither sought nor earned the seal of approval. Artists like R. Crumb published frank and explicit titles that quickly built cult followings for being outside of mainstream comics and touching on material that mainstream comics could not.

By the 1970s, things were changing for mainstream culture in general and for the comics industry in particular. The code relaxed on some components, like the portrayal of crime. In fact, some prominent comics writers were sought out to confront social issues that were coming to the surface in mainstream culture. In 1971, DC Comics published two issues of *Green Lantern/Green Arrow* (written by Dennis O'Neal) in which Green Arrow discovers that his sidekick, Speedy, is addicted to heroin. The book was part of an ongoing series in which the duo of Green Lantern and Green Arrow traveled the country, confronting societal ills like racism and class inequality. Marvel Comics also tackled issues like drugs and juvenile delinquency, adding a complexity to the stories and an urgency to the types of struggles that young readers saw heroes dealing with. Even major characters experienced problems, like Iron Man's alcoholism.

In the 1980s, a group of comics, including *The Dark Knight Returns* by Frank Miller and *Watchmen* by Alan Moore continued to change the nature of comic books. Both featured radically different portrayals of heroes, examining the kinds of inner tensions and drives that would be required for someone to carry out acts of vigilantism. After the breakthrough of writers like Frank Miller, Neil Gaiman, and Alan Moore, comics often became more daring as well as more focused on the inner struggles of characters, going beyond the physical confrontations between heroes and villains.

After the turn of the millennium, comic books experienced a resurgence, with many film franchises feeding out of established heroes. They were often inspired by the newer breed of comics that were less campy and more rooted in the psychologies of the characters, though there were some successful films, *Guardians of the Galaxy* and director Sam Raimi's take on *Spiderman*, which were more rooted in fun and entertainment than in complex portrayals of the characters. This focus was augmented by the entry of comic books into scholarly study. As cultural studies programs and conferences on pop culture sprang up, comic books gained a respectability that had been absent from previous eras, and this respectability and rigorous examination, in turn, led many comics to embrace more complicated and abstract examinations of people. While this led some comics to no longer be appropriate for younger readers, there still are many comics that are designed to bring younger readers in, grooming them for more complex works as their reading tastes mature.

Comics have also expanded their readership by taking on more diverse characters, having more female heroes as well as characters of color and of different sexual orientations. These sorts of changes and emerging characters have continued the work originally set out by writers like Dennis O'Neal in his work on *Green Lantern/Green Arrow*. With web publishing and other innovations, comics have continued to change, finding niche audiences and producing a wide and sometimes challenging variety of genres. Nevertheless, the medium has firmly established itself as a significant cultural force. Naturally, as this status has been achieved, challenges to comic books have come regularly. While they have not matched the kind of large-scale, though largely groundless, attack that Fredric Wertham brought, these challenges have been numerous and sometimes quite damaging for individual titles, authors, and artists.

TIMELINE

1905—*Little Nemo in Slumberland*, Winsor McCay, published, becoming the first comic strip to have an ongoing storyline

1917—Comic book writer and artist Jack Kirby born; also comic book writer and artist Will Eisner born

1922—Stan Lee, creator of the Hulk, Spider-Man, Iron Man, and more, born

1927—Comic book writer and artist Steve Ditko born

1934—DC Comics founded

1937—*Detective Comics* first published by DC Comics, setting the ground for Batman's eventual premiere

1938—*Action Comics* published by DC Comics, starting the run of Superman

1939—Batman makes his first appearance; also Marvel Comics founded

1941—Captain America first appears, becoming the first superhero in what will become the Marvel Universe; also Wonder Woman first appears

1943—Comic book writer and artist R. Crumb born

1944—EC Comics founded

1954—Comics Code established

1965—*Fritz the Cat*, R. Crumb, first published

1970—First Comic-Con held in San Diego

1982—*Love and Rockets*, Hernandez brothers, first published; also *Creepshow* released as a film

1986—Art Spiegelman's first work on what would become *Maus* published; also Dark Horse Comics founded

1987—*Watchmen*, Alan Moore and Dave Gibbons, published as a collected work

1988—First Eisner Awards presented

1989—*Sandman* by Neil Gaiman and Alan Moore's run on *The Swamp Thing* mark the beginning of DC's Vertigo imprint, establishing the practice of publishing adult-themed comic books pushing the boundaries of the Comics Code; also *Tales from the Crypt* premiered on HBO

1991—*Sin City*, Frank Miller, first published

1992—Superman dies, though he will later be revived

1999—*The Boondocks*, Aaron McGruder, first published

2005—*Sin City* adapted as a film by Frank Miller and Robert Rodriguez

2006—*Pride of Baghdad*, Brian K. Vaughan, published; also *9/11 Commission Report* adapted as a graphic novel by Stan Lee

2008—*Iron Man* and *The Dark Knight* both released as major motion pictures

2009—*The Color of Earth*, Dong Hwa Kim, published; also *Watchmen* adapted as a film by Zack Snyder

2012—*Saga*, Brian K. Vaughan, first published

Batman: The Killing Joke, Alan Moore
(DC Comics, 1988)

Batman: The Killing Joke is a stand-alone comic book that imagines a "final confrontation" between Batman and the Joker. The book opens with Batman visiting the Joker in Arkham Asylum, telling him that the pair of them need to come to some type of understanding, or one of them will kill the other. While giving his speech, Batman realizes that the Joker has escaped, and the man that he is talking to is actually an imposter. The book then pursues two storylines, one that looks at the Joker's probably origin story, where he was a chemist who left behind his work in order to pursue a career in stand-up comedy. After his pregnant wife dies and he is disfigured in an accident, his mind snaps. The book gives glimpses into this backstory while also telling a present story where the Joker and his henchmen break into Police Commissioner Jim Gordon's apartment, kidnapping Gordon and shooting his daughter, Barbara, in the spine before taking pictures of her being raped. The Joker takes Gordon to an abandoned amusement park, where he shows Gordon the pictures of Barbara and mocks and terrorizes him. Batman arrives at the park, and the pair fight, with Batman eventually defeating the Joker. Batman again makes the offer to the Joker to help him overcome his demons and become rehabilitated. The Joker says that it is simply not possible, that he has gone too far. The Joker then tells Batman a joke, and the book closes with police cars coming and both men laughing at the Joker's joke. The ending is ambiguous and is interpreted as some as a fulfillment of Batman's opening prediction that one would kill the other.

The book was part of a major revival of interest in American comics during the 1980s. Moore's contributions to this boom included his time as a writer for *Swamp Thing* and his graphic novel *Watchmen*. Like these other texts, *The Killing Joke* examined the complex and unusual psychology of both superheroes and villains. The Joker's goal, in this piece, is also unconventional for a comic book. Rather than trying to steal money or control or destroy a city, the Joker tries to use James Gordon, a supposedly sane and regular man who the Joker believes can be broken and driven mad, thereby proving to Batman that anyone can be broken with sufficient pressure. The book was met with very positive reviews from critics and fans alike, winning an Eisner Award in 1989 and making it onto the *New York Times* best-seller list, also being reprinted more than once. Many readers consider it to be the best Batman/Joker story ever written.

Although it was generally hailed as original, creative, and complex, *The Killing Joke* was also met with criticism over its content. In 2013, there was a request put to the board of the Columbus, Nebraska, public library to remove the book from the shelves. Although the book had not been shelved in the children's section, a minor had checked the book out, and the minor's parent objected to the material within, claiming that the book glorified rape. The library's board refused the request to remove the book, indicating that it was properly placed outside of the children's section and also that the rape was perpetrated by the book's villain. The book also received some notoriety in 2015, when DC Comics pulled copies of a *Batgirl* issue in which the cover had the Joker holding a gun in one hand and Barbara Gordon (as Batgirl) in the other. The cover was widely and heavily criticized by those who saw it as trivializing the rape and torture of Gordon. The company recalled the issue, and the artist responsible for it made multiple apologies to anyone who found it trivializing rape or sexual assault. Throughout the handling of the controversy, the artist and company both remained complimentary of *The Killing Joke*.

See Also: *Watchmen*.

Blankets, Craig Thompson
(Top Shelf Productions, 2003)

Blankets is a graphic novel examining the author and illustrator's experience with leaving the Evangelical Christianity of his parents. The book opens with Craig's adolescence, in particular looking at his relationship with his brother, Phil. Craig portrays his childhood as troubled, with both he and his brother being sexually abused by a babysitter and also with this being bullied at both school and church. Feeling like an outcast, Craig finds a small group of other misfit youths at a Bible camp, and he connects most deeply with Raina. Although the two are geographically separated (Craig lives in Wisconsin and Raina lives in Northern Michigan), they stay in touch, deciding to spend two weeks together at Raina's home. Craig finds that Raina's household is different from his own, with Raina having two adopted brothers that she helps care for. While Craig and Raina are very close during the visit, when Craig has to return to his home, the two drift apart. Although there is no major fallout, their dwindling relationship leads Raina to cut things off with Craig. The breakup is amicable, with the two agreeing to remain friends. After the breakup, though, Craig destroys most of what he has that might remind him of Raina, keeping only a quilt that she made for him. Craig keeps the blanket at his childhood home while he moves out to become more independent. He talks to his brother about their childhood and his feelings on Christianity, indicating that he has lost interest in identifying as a Christian, though he still values the teachings of Christ. When Craig returns to his childhood home, he finds the blanket, and he recognizes how much he has changed since first receiving it.

Upon its publication, *Blankets* was very well received within the comics community. Both commercially successful figures like Neil Gaiman and Alan Moore and more independent or alternative artists like Eddie Campbell and Art Spiegelman praised the book for its courage and emotional core. Even beyond the world of graphic novels, the book garnered significant attention, receiving glowing reviews from venues like *Time* and *Publishers Weekly*, who heralded Thompson as a significant new talent. In 2004, the book won a number of awards, further cementing Thompson's success as a writer and artist.

Despite these positive reviews, the book did meet with challenges. In 2006, there was a move in Missouri to have both *Blankets* and Alison Bechdel's graphic novel, *Fun Home*, removed, claiming that both works were "pornography." For a time, the works were both removed, with the library stating that a committee had been formed to examine the selection process for materials purchased and made public. Eventually, the library instituted a clear policy for the selection of materials, but they also stated that they would not set off or label any work included in the library's collection, citing concerns that this would be the first step toward out-and-out censorship. At this time, the library also returned both books into circulation.

Although the complaint indicated that the challenge was a result of the portrayal of sex and sexuality (and, indeed, there were frank portrayals of both sexual desire and sexual abuse), supporters of the book believed that the roots of this objection came from the book's portrayal of religion and the skepticism toward organized religion. While it is not possible to fully prove or disprove this theory, the subject matter of the book and the discussion of the objections do give it some credence.

The Color of Earth, Kim Dong Hwa
(First Second, 2003)

The Color of Earth is a graphic novel looking at gender and coming of age. The book follows a young girl, Ehwa, in a small village in Korea. After her father has died, Ehwa is raised alone by her mother, who owns a tavern. The book has a methodical narrative, not necessarily following a strong or fast storyline. Many chapters have examinations of animals and other natural symbols and their meaning in the culture in general as well as to the characters themselves. But this meditation on the natural scenery of the small village gets upset when Ehwa's love interest, Young Master Sunoo, leaves the village on a train, presumably heading for a more urban environment. The book also has Ehwa observe adults talking about issues like marriage and sex in coded ways, again turning to natural symbols like sparrows and gourds to suggest observations without having to make them directly. Against this narrative, the reader also sees Ehwa watch as her mother finds love again, leading Ehwa to ponder relationships and desire.

The book broke ground in a number of ways, with some critics suggesting that it was an early entry from Korean artists into a realm previously dominated by Japanese manga artists. It also was received very well by a number of critics and organizations. The Young Adult Library Services Association included it on their Great Graphic Novels for Teens list in 2010, and *Booklist* included it on their "Top Ten" list for graphic novels for young adults. Although the book did not necessarily gain a large mainstream readership, many readers of independent comic books and graphic novels responded favorably to the book.

Given the inclusion of direct discussions of sexuality and sexual desire, it is not surprising that the book has received challenges and, in some cases, has been banned in school libraries. It was, in fact, the second most challenged book in 2011, according to the American Library Association. Interestingly, while the reasons given were typically that the material was "inappropriate" for the age group, many of the conversations where Ehwa seeks out advice from her peers in regard to sex eventually end with her discussing these matters with her mother, getting parental advice rather than only learning about sex from other adolescents. Still, the book saw a wide variety of challenges, though, as with some other books, it is difficult to fully determine whether these challenges hurt or helped the book's image, sales, and prominence. In the end, the book has become an object of interest to scholars for a wide variety of reasons, from its portrayal of a particular culture and era to its consideration of gender and coming of age to its position as a frequently read and frequently challenged text.

The Dark Knight Returns, Frank Miller
(DC Comics, 1986)

The Dark Knight Returns is a four-issue miniseries that was collected into a graphic novel. It was one of the two or three core texts that helped to garner attention for graphic novels to scholarly and mainstream audiences. The story takes place in the near future, after Batman has aged and retired. Bruce Wayne comes out of retirement after seeing Gotham City become overrun by a brutal gang calling themselves the Mutants. In one of his adventures, Batman saves a teenaged girl, Carrie Kelley. Inspired by Batman's reappearance, Kelley buys a Robin costume and begins adventuring on her own, hoping to find Batman and become his new sidekick. Kelley's dream is realized after she saves Batman during a fight with the Mutants. After recovering from the fight, and after getting aid from James Gordon and Kelley (now officially referred to as Robin), Batman is able to defeat the Mutant's leader. After this victory, the Mutants change their name to the Sons of Batman, and, instead of committing crimes, they begin to fight crime, albeit in an extremely violent way. Meanwhile, Superman, now working for the American government, is told that he needs to stop Batman. Back in Gotham, the Joker comes back into power. Batman and the new Robin track down the Joker, but, before they can bring him to justice, the Joker kills himself, trying to set Batman up for a murder charge. Meanwhile, Russia attacks America, knocking out its power. Batman turns to the Sons of Batman, asking them to temper their methods but to continue fighting crime in the aftermath of Russia's attack. The success of Batman and his vigilante crew embarrasses the federal government, and the president asks Superman to take Batman down. The pair do face off, and Batman, with the help of Green Arrow, defeats Superman. After Superman is subdued, Batman tells him that he could have killed Superman, but he simply wanted to send him a warning so that Superman did not try to interfere again. After Batman gives Superman this warning, Batman falls over, apparently dying of a heart attack. At the funeral, Superman realizes that Batman faked his death, but he makes no move to alert anyone. Batman and Robin then meet up with the Sons of Batman, announcing that they will start policing Gotham City.

The Dark Knight Returns was a significant critical and commercial success. Many critics and publications (including prominent comics publication IGN) have declared it to be the greatest Batman storyline of all time. The combination of gritty but realistic crime and violence gives it a feel that many of the Batman comics of the 1950s and 1960s lack. It also had a number of technical innovations, like the slang that author Frank Miller developed and the use of person-on-the-street interviews to show what the citizens of Gotham might feel about Batman. It also sold extremely well, and it led to multiple continuations of the storyline along with the regular inclusion of Carry Kelley as one of the Robins, something that does not always happen for "noncanonical" comic storylines. Still, not every reader or critic was satisfied. The *New York Times*, for instance, cited that the story was sprawling and, at times, unfocused. Many readers also did not care for Miller's distinctive artwork, though a number of critics and readers felt that its uniqueness actually matched Miller's distinctive storytelling. Overall, the book met with more praise than criticism.

Beyond its critical reception, the book was a huge influence on generations of writers and critics. *The Dark Knight Returns* and *Watchmen*, the graphic novel by Alan Moore, are the two primary works (and, to a lesser extent, *Maus*) that are cited as helping to popularize the genre of graphic novel and give it the credibility to be a legitimate object of study by scholars. In addition, the book has been cited as an influence for a number of adaptations of films and television shows, including an episode of *Batman: The Animated Series*, an animated film version of *The Dark Knight Returns*, and, in some ways, the film franchise directed by Christopher Nolan and starring Christian Bale. The work has also been referenced in a variety of media, from other comics to video games.

The graphic novel along with its sequel, *The Dark Knight Strikes Again*, have both been challenged in a public library in Ohio. The principal objection was that the book was too intense and violent for young readers. Although the challenge did not succeed in removal of the book, the book was re-shelved to the "teen" area, presumably putting it out of the hands of most younger readers. Interestingly, this response was imitated on a television show, *Girl Meets World*, in which a new teacher assigns the book to his students, and the principal objects. This is one of the few cases of a portrayal in popular culture of a challenge to a real-world book that has been challenged itself. Despite the objections of both real and fictitious figures, *The Dark Knight Returns* remains one of the most widely discussed works in the graphic novel genre.

FURTHER READING

Bernardin, Marc. "Dark Inspirations." *Entertainment Weekly*, July 11, 2008, Issue 1001, p. 34.
Finigan, Theo. " 'To the Stables, Robin!' Regenerating the Frontier in Frank Miller's *The Dark Knight Returns*." *ImageTexT: Interdisciplinary Comics Studies*, Winter 2010, p. 5.

Fun Home, Alison Bechdel
(Houghton Mifflin, 2006)

Fun Home is an autobiographical graphic novel focusing on Alison Bechdel's formative years. The text is difficult to summarize because it narrates several events multiple times, giving the reader a different perspective with each retelling. One of the core conflicts of the book is Bechdel's relationship with her father, who is an English teacher and funeral director. Although the text is based in fact, some of the details, the funeral home that functioned as the family business, for instance, are surprisingly rich with figurative meaning. Another example comes from early on in the book, when the father is trying to restore his family's Victorian home. The need to maintain a sense of tradition and his focus on appearance more than connecting to his family are symbolic of many of the complaints and concerns lodged against the father throughout the book. This anxiety is tied to the self-hatred that Alison assumes that her father feels from his homosexual relationships. Some of these relationships include sexual interactions that the father had with his high school students. After Bechdel's mother asked for a divorce, her father died after being hit by a truck. In the text, Bechdel states that she believes that her father committed suicide. The narrative examining her father's sexual desire is paralleled by Bechdel's handling of her own sexuality. Bechdel discusses several significant pieces of her sexual development and identity, including masturbation, fantasies, and her first romantic and sexual experiences with women. Another overlap between the characters revolves around their common struggles with obsessive–compulsive disorder. The visual style of the book is relatively simplistic, not striving for the sort of stylistic realism that some superhero comics from the same era strove for. That said, the style was not overly simplistic or cartoonish. Bechdel took photos of herself posing as various characters, giving a general outline and sense of the characters before giving it her own particular style.

Fun Home was Bechdel's first stand-alone book, though she had regularly published *Dykes to Watch Out For*, a comic strip featuring exaggerated versions of many of Bechdel's real-life friends, for two decades before writing and illustrating *Fun Home*. The book achieved significant commercial success, staying on the *New York Times* best-seller list for two weeks. In addition to the commercial success, *Fun Home* was met with significant critical acclaim, receiving a number of awards and positive reviews and also being turned into a musical, which won a number of Tony Awards. It was seen as a significant work as a graphic novel, a memoir, and a piece of "queer literature."

Although much of the reaction to the book was positive, it did meet some significant challenges. Perhaps most notably, in Marshall, Missouri, in 2006, a resident tried to have the town's public library remove *Fun Home* and Craig Thompson's *Blankets*, claiming that there was too much sexual content, even trying to characterize the book as pornography. Although these charges were certainly serious, they resulted in only a temporary removal while the library's board reviewed both the material and their general policy for ordering and keeping books. Bechdel was not particularly bothered by the challenging, even referring to it as an honor rather than an upsetting event. This was not the only challenge to the book. In Utah, a college student objected to having had to read the book as part of a literature course, but little reaction came from this complaint. Most notably, in South Carolina, the book's inclusion in the curriculum at the College of Charleston was met with significant challenges. After a conservative group challenged the use of the book, Bechdel herself weighed in, stating that the group's label of "pornography" was not appropriate for her book, because pornography was designed to arouse the reader, but her work was not in any way arousing. After the college refused to pull the book from the classroom, the state legislature cut funding to the College of Charleston. This sparked a major backlash, with groups like the American Civil Liberties Union (ACLU), the Modern Language Association, and the Association of College and Research Libraries (among many others) siding with the College of Charleston and Bechdel. Eventually, the funding was restored, but with a number of stipulations that made sure that the funding would not go toward the purchase of books like Bechdel's. Despite these major challenges (and, in fact, because of them, according to some critics), the book has become and remained a significant piece of American literature.

See Also: *Blankets*.

FURTHER READING

Lydenberg, Robin. "Under Construction: Alison Bechdel's *Fun Home*." *European Journal of English Studies*, April 2012, Vol. 16, Issue 1, pp. 57–68.

McBean, Sam. "Seeing in Alison Bechdel's *Fun Home*." *Camera Obscura*, 2013, Vol. 28, Issue 84, pp. 102–123.

Warhol, Robyn. "The Space Between: A Narrative Approach to *Fun Home*." *College Literature*, Summer 2011, Vol. 38, Issue 3, pp. 1–20.

The Graveyard Book, Neil Gaiman
(Harper Collins, 2014)

The Graveyard Book has been published in both novel and graphic novel formats. Both editions were written by Neil Gaiman, and the graphic novel was illustrated by P. Craig Russell. The story opens with Jack Frost murdering his family. He thinks that he has killed all of them, but he is not aware that a toddler, later to be named "Nobody," has left his crib to explore the house. The toddler crawls to a nearby graveyard, where the ghosts debate what to do. Eventually, a ghostly couple, Mr. and Mrs. Owens, decide to take in the toddler, and the toddler gets protection from both the dead and the living, being granted ghostly powers like the ability to pass through solid objects. He is also protected when the caretaker, Silas, leads Jack Frost away from Nobody. Nobody grows up in the graveyard, interacting with both ghosts and, less often, the living. His principal living friend is Scarlett Perkins, a young girl who becomes convinced by her mother that Nobody is her imaginary friend rather than a living boy. Nobody has a number of interactions and adventures, with Scarlett's family moving to Scotland after she disappears with him for a short time on an adventure. Nobody also meets a variety of creatures and ghosts, including a werewolf, Miss Lupescu, who serves as his tutor, and Elizabeth Hempstock, the ghost of a woman who was murdered after being wrongly accused of being a witch. Nobody does try to attend school but quickly drops out after facing too much attention when he tries to stop two bullies from picking on other children in the school. As Nobody goes through his adventures, he begins to discover and master the abilities that are unique to him, like the ability to become invisible and to control people's dreams. As Nobody grows older, he finds out that Jack Frost is still hunting for him, because he believes that if Nobody is left alive, he will destroy a secret society (the Jack of All Trades) to which Jack Frost belongs. Scarlett Perkins and her mother move back to town, and she shares with Nobody that there is a local historian, Jay Frost, who is researching the house that Nobody grew up in and doing shadings of the grave markers in the graveyard. When Nobody goes to the house, hoping to find out more about his family, he discovers that the historian is actually Jack Frost. Jack and some other members of the Jack of All Trades follow Nobody, but Nobody escapes to the graveyard, where he is able to outwit and defeat everyone but Jack Frost, who has taken Scarlett as a captive. Nobody is eventually able to outwit Jack Frost, getting him to try to claim power that ultimately undoes him. Silas comes to Nobody's side, revealing the full rivalry between the Honour (a league that a number of Nobody's friends are part of) and the Jack of All Trades. Despite Jack Frost's having taken her hostage, Scarlett is disappointed in Nobody's role in his death. Silas and Nobody debate whether or not they should tamper with Scarlett's memory, with Nobody saying that it would be wrong to do so, but Silas saying that it is necessary. In the end, Scarlett does lose her memories of Nobody, and Nobody loses her. At the book's close, Nobody is beginning to lose not only his ghostly abilities but also his ability to even see the ghosts in the graveyard. Silas gives him some money and a passport, sending him off to have new adventures.

As stated above, the book was originally published in prose format 2008 and was later published as a graphic novel at 2010. Both versions were very well received, with the novel format winning a number of major awards, including the Newberry Medal and the Hugo Award for Best Novel of the year. The book was a commercial success as well. Gaiman had already established a very positive reputation in the worlds of both comics and young adult literature before *The Graveyard Book*, having received significant acclaim for his run on *The Sandman* and for more adult works like *American Gods*. Also, his book *Coraline* had been published as both a prose novel and a graphic novel, quickly inspiring an animated film that received an Academy Award nomination for Best Animated Picture. With this level of success, it is little surprise that *The Graveyard Book* attracted sufficient sales and attention to be adapted as a graphic novel and as a film.

It was, however, with the publication of the book as a graphic novel that the challenges to the book began. The book was challenged in 2015 by parents whose children found it in a middle school library. The book was, indeed, put under review, but, in the end, it was deemed to have sufficient literary merit to offset the violent imagery that parents had objected to, and the book remained on the shelves.

Oddly enough, there was another challenge to the book that came not from parents but from librarians. A group of librarians formed to request that the book be stripped of its Newberry Medal on the grounds that it should not have been found eligible. Their argument was that portions of the book had been previously published, and, therefore, it was not an original work published only in the year that the book should have been under consideration. These concerns were quickly dismissed, and some speculated that the true reason for this push was more related to concerns about the book's content than about the technicalities cited by the challenging group. In fact, one of the key members of the group had challenged other books in the past because of their content, lending credence to the theory that the true objection was not the one stated by the group. In the end, the challenge amounted to little more than another strange splash of publicity for the book and the author, and Gaiman himself was dismissive of the challenge, seeming to find it more humorous than genuinely threatening.

FURTHER READING

Barbieri, Richard. "After Potter, What?" *Independent School*, Summer 2009, Vol. 68, Issue 4, pp. 118–120.

Robertson, Christine. " 'I Want to Be Like You': Riffs on Kipling in Neil Gaiman's *The Graveyard Book." Children's Literature Association Quarterly*, Summer 2011, Vol. 36, Issue 2, pp. 164–189.

Schneider, Dean. "It Takes a Graveyard to Raise a Child." *Book Links*, March 2010, Vol. 19, Issue 3, pp. 6–8.

The League of Extraordinary Gentlemen: The Black Dossier, Alan Moore
(Wildstorm Comics, 2007)

The League of Extraordinary Gentlemen: The Black Dossier is a companion book to The League of Extraordinary Gentlemen series, containing excerpts of texts (both real and fictitious) referenced in the series. The central story of the book follows Allan Quartermain and Mina Harker (both members of the League in the first two books of the series) as they search for the black dossier, a book containing notes on the League members. A government agent, James Bond, tries to seduce Mina Harker. When she resists, he attempts to overpower and rape her, but she knocks him unconscious with a brick in her purse. Allan Quartermain then joins her, and the two find the black dossier. The British government's secret forces send agents to apprehend Quartermain and Harker. The agents catch up with the two as they are preparing to board a spaceship. The ship crash-lands, though Quartermain and Harker are able to escape before it does. They are met by the secret agents, but, when they reveal the full extent of their history to them, also explaining that their superior is a double agent working for the United States, they let the pair go. They then escape to the Blazing World, a sort of utopia where they can be safe. The narrative is interrupted at times by excerpts from the dossier, with references to the original two volumes of the series and other major pieces of British culture, including Shakespeare and a cutaway of Nemo's ship, the *Nautilus*. Like many of Moore's works, some of the interstitial pieces were straight prose works rather than comics.

The book was very well received, being praised by critics both inside and out of the comics world. It also won an Eagle Award for Favourite Original Graphic

Novel. Moore's reputation as a writer for comics had been fully established by the time that the book was published.

Still, the book was met with significant challenges. In 2009, Jessamine County Public Library in Kentucky saw a scandal that resulted in the termination of two employees. After discovering that the book had graphic content, one employee had tagged the book to be moved from the graphic novels section into the adult section, which was standard practice. When the board reviewing such requests determined that the book did belong in the graphic novels section, the employee then checked the book out and continued to renew it for a year, trying to keep it from being checked out by any young readers. When a patron requested that the book be returned, another employee cancelled the request after finding out the requester was a minor. In the end, the employees (neither of whom were in positions of significant authority in the library) received disciplinary action for their roles in the attempted censorship. While the book itself was not the most widely recognized of Moore's works, it was another example of a widely respected book written by Moore and unsuccessfully challenged by a small group of readers.

FURTHER READING

Cozine, Joshua. "Mina: The Magical Female. Inferential Sexism in *The League of Extraordinary Gentlemen*." *Film International*, 2007, Vol. 5, Issue 2, pp. 43–47.

Jones, Jason B. "Betrayed by Time: Steampunk & the Neo-Victorian in Alan Moore's *Lost Girls* and *The League of Extraordinary Gentlemen*." *Neo-Victorian Studies*, 2010, Vol. 3, Issue 1, pp. 99–126.

Shepard, Lucius. "Lucking Out." *Fantasy & Science Fiction*, February 2004, Vol. 106, Issue 2, pp. 82–87.

Maus, Art Spiegelman
(Pantheon Books, 1991)

Maus is one of the first independent graphic novels to gain significant cultural and critical prominence. The book is structured as a set of interviews between Art Spiegelman, the writer and artist of the book, and his father, a Jewish refugee who survived the Holocaust. In the book, Jews are portrayed as mice, a reference to Nazi propaganda film that equated Jews with mice, Germans are portrayed as cats, Poles are portrayed as pigs, and Americans are portrayed as dogs, though all of the animals are anthropomorphic. The book opens with a brief reflection on Spiegelman's childhood, where his father dismisses the younger Spiegelman's suffering and frustration, implying that he does not understand true suffering or friendship. The narrative then jumps to an adult Art visiting his father. It is established that Art's father, Vladek, has remarried after Art's mother committed suicide. Art asks his father to tell him about the Holocaust. Before discussing the Holocaust directly, Vladek gives Art some background on the family's origin, telling him about having to court Art's mother, who was wealthy and whose parents were not immediately fond of Vladek. Vladek tells of how his business acumen helped him to gain a positive reputation, eventually helping him to impress and win the hand of Art's mother. He also tells Art about his mother having a nervous breakdown after giving birth to Richieu, Art's older brother who did not survive the Holocaust. Vladek also pleads with Art not to include any of these sorts of details in the book that Art is working on, though the inclusion of these details in *Maus* demonstrates that Art did not, in the end, follow through on this promise. The family leaves their home, seeking a place for Art's mother to recover. When she does, they return to their home to hear that the Nazis are exerting more and more pressure upon Poland, and anti-Semitic feeling is rising as this pressure continues to increase. Vladek is drafted into the Polish army to fight the Nazis. He is soon captured as a prisoner of war, but he is able to escape and reunite with his family. As Vladek recounts these stories, there are moments of the present storyline, with Art and Vladek failing to understand each other on a personal level. Art also finds in his father's house an underground comic that he had published where he talks very frankly about his mother's suicide and the repercussions of it for his family. He is particularly struck by the fact that his father not only read it but held onto it. The narrative of the Holocaust begins again, now with Vladek describing how they were forced to leave their home as the Nazis took over. In an attempt to keep Richieu safe, Vladek and his wife send him to stay with a family member, but she ends up poisoning herself and the children that she is watching rather than let them be captured by the Nazis. Vladek and his wife continue to find hiding places, but, as they begin to run out of money, they seek a way out of the country. Unfortunately, they find that the people supposedly helping them to escape have betrayed them, and the couple is taken to the concentration camp in Auschwitz. In the present timeline, Art asks Vladek if he can have his mother's diaries, but Vladek admits that he burned them, not wanting to read them after her suicide. Once he is out of earshot, Art calls Vladek a murderer for this act. This marks the end of the first book of *Maus*. The second book opens up by examining the success of the first book. Although it was well received and became a source of pride for Vladek, Art finds himself feeling pressured and not able to continue producing when he is expected to be the voice of the Jewish experience. Art sees a psychiatrist, who also is a Holocaust survivor. The story returns to Vladek recounting his experiences to Art, discussing how he managed to survive, how he made efforts to stay in contact with Art's mother, and of the difficult decisions that he had to make, sometimes seeing other Jews died while he and his wife survived. In the present timeline, Vladek and his current wife argue, with Art offering sympathy to his stepmother but not able to help his father in any real way. Vladek tells Art about the end of World War II, his reunion with his wife, and how they came to America. As the story winds down, Vladek accidentally calls Art by the name of Richieu, but Art does not point out the error. The final image of the comic is of gravestones reading Vladek and Anja, Art's parents.

The book was generally well received, earning praise for both its stylistic innovations and its examination of weighty content. It was seen as a significant breakthrough for comics as well as a companion text for history courses. That said, the book struggled in some ways, because its distinctiveness made it very hard to classify. It had the distinction of being on both the fiction and nonfiction lists for the *New York Times* best-seller list, a move that led to some criticism of the *Times*, who eventually shifted the book back to the fiction list. The book also earned many awards, including a Pulitzer Prize. Many point to it as a source for the development of interest in comic books and graphic novels as legitimate texts for study. That said, not every reaction to the book was positive. Some Holocaust survivors felt like comic books were not the appropriate venue for this sort of story, and even some prominent comic book artists, Harvey Pekar, for instance, stated that they found the use of anthropomorphic animals to rely on stereotypes more than they interrogated those stereotypes. Some critics also objected to the characterization of Vladek, likewise finding it to be stereotypical (an observation that Art Spiegelman himself engages in the book) and not sympathetic enough. Still, the book has established and maintained its reputation as balancing a very personal story with a larger historical and social message.

The book has been met with challenges both in America and abroad. In California, a Polish American parent objected to the book for its characterization of Poles as pigs. Also, there were questions as to whether the discussion of the Holocaust, suicide, and sexual desire were appropriate for young readers. The challenge had little impact, and the book continued to be read and studied, with the objection dismissed as a simplistic attempt at censorship. The more serious challenge came in Russia in 2015, where officials had copies of the book pulled from stores. While the official reason given was that the cover features a swastika, going against the policy of not allowing any Nazi propaganda to be sold, most analysts suspect that the increasingly repressive Putin regime deemed the story too subversive. Despite these challenges, the book remains a favorite among independent comic enthusiasts, many scholars and a large group of readers.

FURTHER READING

Adams, Jill Petersen. "Acts of Irreconcilable Mourning: Post-Holocaust Witness and Testimony." *Culture, Theory, and Critique*, July 2015, Vol. 56, Issue 2, pp. 228–244.

Hutton, Rober. "A Mouse in the Bookstore: *Maus* and the Publishing Industry." *South Central Review: The Journal of the South Central Modern Language Association*, Fall 2015, Vol. 32, Issue 3, pp. 30–44.

Solomon, Alisa. "The House of *Maus*." *Nation*, September 15, 2014, Vol. 299, Issue 11, pp. 35–39.

Palomar (Series), Gilbert Hernandez
(Fantagraphics Books, 2003)

Palomar is a series of graphic novels originally published serially in the comic book series Love and Rockets. The series is set in the fictional Latin American town of Palomar. The Palomar subset of the Love and Rockets stories follows some of the inhabitants of Palomar as they travel to America, negotiating difficult and sometimes dangerous territories like the world of organized crime. It also takes on significant parts of American culture, and it looks at hot-button issues like sex and politics. The series has been long running and has received significant critical acclaim as well as a strong cult following. The collection titled Palomar is one of the many popular entries in this series, and it was met with positive reviews and sales for an independent comic.

Despite its popularity, the series received a significant challenge and serious accusations. At a high school in Rio Rancho, New Mexico, parents led a harsh challenge to the book, claiming that it was unfit for young readers and even going as far as calling it child pornography. One reason for the incendiary nature of this challenge is that the parent of a fourteen-year-old student who had checked out the book took her complaints straight to the local media, not giving the library, the school district, or the author a chance to respond to her allegations. The media only exacerbated the issue by airing a report but stating that the images in the book could not be aired on television, leading many viewers to immediately side with the parent, despite the fact that they had not seen the images themselves. Subsequently, the book was pulled from school shelves. Eventually, more people began to see that the book was well received by many readers and a number of critics, including prominent reviewers like *Publishers Weekly*. This came largely from when the Comic Book Legal Defense Fund, a group dedicated to defending challenged comic books and graphic novels, became involved, filing a case indicating that the school district had not followed its stated guidelines for reviewing books. The Defense Fund's argument was successful, and after this case, the school board voted to bring the book back to shelves, though it was also designated as needing parental permission for any student under the age of eighteen. Although the book did not necessarily become a major piece of social discussion nationwide, it did make for a meaningful example of how the media's discussion of challenged books can impact the overall treatment of the books.

FURTHER READING

Braybrook, Roy. "Love and Rockets." *Armada International*, August/September 2015, Issue 4, pp. 22–29.
Markee, Patrick. "American Passages." *Nation*, May 18, 1998, Vol. 266, Issue 18, pp. 25–27.
Saxey, Esther. "Desire without Closure in Jaime Hernandez's Love and Rockets." *ImageTexT: Interdisciplinary Comics Studies*, Summer 2006, Vol. 3, Issue 1, p. 3.

Pride of Baghdad, **Brian K. Vaughan**
(Vertigo Comics, 2006)

Pride of Baghdad is a graphic novel written by comics and television writer Brian K. Vaughan. The story follows a group (or pride) of lions who are freed from the Baghdad, Iraq, zoo as a consequence of American bombings during the second Iraq War. The story of lions being freed from a zoo because of the bombings does have grounding in real events, but the story itself is mainly extrapolation and projection. There are four lions, and, while three of them leave the zoo when the opportunity presents itself, the oldest lion, Safa, decides to stay at the zoo as a result of earlier trauma from her days in the wild. The group experiences various adventures and hardships, such as when one of them, Ali, is kidnapped by apes hoping to use Ali as a threat to other animals. When the remaining two lions fail to free Ali, Safa comes to the rescue, killing the apes and freeing Ali. The lions try to navigate the new world of animals, letting an antelope survive, for instance, to try to maintain an alliance that could later help them. After hearing a turtle describe to them a statue of a heroic lion, the group decides that they should enter the city proper, searching for the statue. The group continues on, trying to avoid being seen by soldiers and trying to decide how to properly exist outside of the confines of the zoo. Eventually, they find an emaciated lion being held captive by a bear. The lions fight the bear, hoping to free the captured lion. While they are able to defeat the bear, it comes at a significant loss, with Safa being blinded in the fight. The pride continues on, stopping to enjoy a sunset. As they are looking at the sky, they are shot to death by American soldiers. The story closes with a bird narrating the events of the story from an animal's perspective.

The book was very well received, being named the Best Original Graphic Novel of 2006 by comic publication IGN. It also sold relatively well for a series with no preexisting comic book characters. Readers and critics noted an appreciation of the complex work within the book, both empathizing with and critiquing a variety of perspectives on war, politics, and freedom.

Like a number of challenged books, it can be difficult to pinpoint what the true reason for the challenges to *Pride of Baghdad* are. The most frequently cited reason for the banning is sexual content (the genders of the various animals often come into play with the challenges and hierarchies of animals within the book). In 2007, in Millard, Nebraska, for instance, parents argued that the violence and sexual content made the book inappropriate. While the violence no doubt played a role, *Pride of Baghdad* is not significantly more violent than other comics that have not faced such challenges, leading some critics to suspect that the challenge came partially because of the backdrop of the Iraq War and the negative portrayal of American soldiers. Despite the challenges brought against the book, it has almost universally remained on shelves and been hailed as a major work of contemporary comics.

See Also: Saga.

FURTHER READING

Connors, Sean P. "Altering Perspectives: How the Implied Reader Invites Us to Rethink the Difficulty of Graphic Novels." *Clearing House*, January 2012, Vol. 85, Issue 1, pp. 33–37.

De Lint, Charles. *"Pride of Baghdad." Fantasy & Science Fiction*, March 2007, Vol. 112, Issue 3, pp. 40–41.

Mangum, Teresa, and Corey K. Creekmur. "A Graphic Novel Depicting War as an Interspecies Event: *Pride of Baghdad.*" *Society & Animals*, October 2007, Vol. 15, Issue 4, pp. 405–408.

Saga Series, Brian K. Vaughan
(Image Comics, 2012–)

Saga is a comic book series written by Brian K. Vaughan that has been collected into graphic novels as well. The series follows different alien races through their conflicts, focusing upon two aliens in particular, a couple who are from feuding species of aliens. The first storyline shows how the couple, Marko and Alana, meet. Alana is from a technologically advanced species, and Marko is from a species of alien who possesses magic. The conflict between their two races has spread throughout the galaxy, causing a large-scale war that has damaged a number of places and beings. Marko was a prisoner of war in a jail that Alana was guarding. Not long after meeting, Alana decided to help Marko escape, and they became a couple, eventually having a child, Hazel. Because of their association with each other, Alana and Marko are outcasts from both of their societies. Both societies hope to capture or kill the family before news gets out that peace between the races is possible. Alana's people send Prince Robot IV to bring them back, and Marko's people send The Will, a bounty hunter, to find and capture them. Alana, Marko, and Hazel (along with a ghostly figure, Izabel) successfully evade capture after Prince Robot IV and The Will interfere with each other's pursuits. The family is then joined by Marko's parents, who help them to continue staying safe. Subsequent storylines introduce more characters, including a writer, D. Oswald Heist, Upsher and Doff, two reporters who also pursue the family, and The Brand, The Will's sister, among many others. These characters and events introduce both more of the main characters' backgrounds and more of the universe that Vaughan has created.

Brian K Vaughan was already known for his work in both comics and television before he started writing Saga. His work on original comic book series Y: The Last Man and Ex Machina earned him a following of readers and many awards and critical acknowledgments. He also was a writer for the television show *Lost*, a major pop culture phenomenon. Image Comics, the publisher of Saga, also has a very positive reputation, being the publisher for major independent comic book titles like *Spawn* and *The Walking Dead* before the beginning of Saga. Next to Dark Horse Comics, Image might well be the most well-recognized publisher of independent comics. With the name recognition of both the press and the writer, it is not surprising that the series has garnered a good deal of attention despite occasional breaks in publishing as Vaughan has taken time off to pursue other projects.

Saga has been a significant commercial success in both its single issues and its collected novel forms. The first issues of the series sold out, with the first issue going into five printings, the first printing selling out before it had even reached bookstores. The first two collected editions also did very well, with the second edition reaching the number one position on the *New York Times* best-selling graphic novels list. Saga also garnered significantly positive critical reception, earning positive comparisons with other science fiction and fantasy touchstones like Star Wars and *Game of Thrones* while also being recognized for incorporating elements from mythology, Shakespeare's writing, and other "high culture" sources. It also has won a number of Eisner Awards, comics' highest honor.

Despite these accolades, the book has faced censorship and challenges from parent groups and even from comic book stores. One issue's cover featured Alana breastfeeding Hazel, and some comic shops refused to carry it. Another issue that featured two male characters engaging in oral sex (albeit on a screen within the panel rather than part of the core narrative) was not sold by Apple Inc., making it difficult for users of some of Apple's devices to obtain the issue, though whether this challenge came from Apple Inc. or ComiXology, the digital distributor used by Apple, is a matter of some dispute. In addition to these distribution issues, the series has been challenged for its depiction of sex and nudity, with some groups referring to the series as being "antifamily" and not appropriate for readers under the age of eighteen. This charge in particular makes it difficult to know if the principal objections are toward the portrayal of sex or the incorporation of homosexuality into the narratives. Still, the high praise that the book has received and the reputation of Vaughan and Image Comics have helped to establish the book as a major work within the world of independent comics.

See Also: *Pride of Baghdad*.

FURTHER READING

McArdle, Megan M. "Saga." *Library Journal*, March 1, 2015, Vol. 140, Issue 4, p. 56.
Thornell, Peter. "Saga." *Library Journal*, June 1, 2014, Vol. 139, Issue 10, p. 53.
Wolk, Douglas. "Masters of the Universe." *Time*, August 5, 2013, Vol. 182, Issue 6, p. 54.

SideScrollers, Matthew Loux
(Oni Press, 2006)

SideScrollers is a graphic novel exploring gender and power in young adults. The story follows three male friends, Brian, Brad, and Matt. The theme of gender and strength is set from the beginning, with the three principal characters arguing about various cartoon mascots and which of them would win a fight. While the trio heads out to find some snacks, they see Amber, a girl that Matt has a romantic interest in. She is walking with Richard, a quarterback that all the three boys dislike because he has bullied them. They try talking to Amber as they see her, but she turns away from them, showing her preference for Richard. As the three boys reach a parking lot, they see Richard's car, and they decide that they will vandalize it. Two other boys come along and join in. While the three principal boys run off, the other two are caught by Richard, and they implicate the principal three. The three then spend most of the day trying to avoid Richard, only to end up seeing him (along with his football teammates) at the mall. While there, they overhear Richard telling the other football players that he intends to sleep with Amber, diminishing her reputation in school. When Richard and the other players see the three boys, Richard threatens them, telling them that they will suffer if they tell Amber about Richard's plan. The three boys are able to escape with the help of the two boys who helped to vandalize Richard's car. Amber denies Richard his attempt for sex after he becomes too aggressive, and Brian eventually defeats Richard in a fight, and the boys enjoy their success.

The book was met with reasonable success for an independent comic. Although the book was not a major commercial success, it did get some very positive reviews. It was listed as one of the top ten graphic novels for 2008 by the Young Adult Library Services Association. It also earned favorable reviews from *Publisher's Weekly*.

While the book did receive these positive reviews, it also received a significant challenge. The challenge took place in Connecticut, and it was unusual in a number of ways. Most clearly, the challenge was difficult to situate, because it came against the book while it was on a list of choices for reading rather than on a required text list. The challenging parent claimed that the book had too many sexual references, and the parent also claimed that the request to have it removed from the list of options did not constitute censorship despite the fact that it effectively took the option of reading the book away. In the end, the book was indeed removed from the list of options, despite the stated policies of the Enfield, Connecticut, School District, which indicated that no parent or child could demand the removal of a text from such a list of options. Although this single challenge was successful, the book had an established and loyal following in many other places.

FURTHER READING

Chipman, Ian. "Truth or Dare about Dr. True." *Booklist*, January 1, 2010, Vol. 106, Issue 9/10, p. 72.

Staff. "*SideScrollers*." *Booklist*, March 1, 2008, Vol. 104, Issue 13, p. 15.

Staff. "*SideScrollers*." *Publishers Weekly*, November 20, 2006, Vol. 253, Issue 46, p. 46.

Watchmen, Alan Moore
(DC Comics, 1986)

Watchmen is a graphic novel that was originally published as a series of twelve individual issues. It is widely considered to be one of the greatest graphic novels ever written, and it also is seen as one of the texts that helped to bring new readers and interests in the graphic novel medium. The narrative is a complex one following several characters over many years with a variety of flashbacks and shifts in perspective. The story opens in New York City, where the police are investigating a murder. In addition to the police, Rorschach, a masked vigilante, is investigating, and he finds out that the murdered man was also a vigilante, and he operated under the name of The Comedian. Rorschach then warns other former heroes, including Dr. Manhattan, a superpowerful being, the Silk Spectre, Dr. Manhattan's love interest, Adrian Veidt, a brilliant and rich former vigilante, and the Nite Owl, Rorschach's former partner. The reader also finds out that the world is an alternate reality where President Nixon has usurped power and is effectively a dictator. There also is a clear threat of nuclear war between American and Russia. During his investigation, Rorschach gets taken in by the police, who are hostile to vigilantes. This helps to bring the Nite Owl and the Silk Spectre out of retirement. They break Rorschach out of jail and begin working together. Dr. Manhattan fleas the planet, and he takes the Silk Spectre with him to talk to her about the nature of life and the world. Rorschach and the Nite Owl discover that Adrian Veidt is orchestrating a major plot and that he was responsible for Rorschach's arrest. They all confront Veidt, only to find out that he's blown up much of New York, tricking the world into thinking that there's an alien invasion. This unites the world, eliminating nuclear war in favor of defending themselves against the aliens. In the end, the crew agree to not reveal Veidt's secret, except for Rorschach, who lets himself be killed rather than agreeing to go along with the plot. The book closes on an uncertain note as to whether or not Veidt's secret will be revealed through Rorschach's journal, which he had sent to a tabloid newspaper.

The book was a significant commercial and critical success. Along with *The Dark Knight Returns*, it was seen as one of the principal texts that brought credibility to the graphic novel genre. It was particularly noteworthy because it received critical claim both inside and outside of the comics world, gaining significant praise from a variety of well-known writers and artists in the field as well as major mainstream publications like *Time* magazine. In particular, fans and critics have shown appreciation for the careful portrayal of the characters' inner lives, adding a level of realism that had often been absent from mainstream comics. It also won a Hugo Award not long after its publication.

From the beginning, there were conflicts over the book's ownership and production. There were delays in some of the issues in the original run, and, after the publication of the issues as a graphic novel (a book that included additional, interstitial material like excerpts from books and interviews referred to in the comic), there was perhaps one of the most hostile conflicts over ownership of the intellectual property in the history of comics. Moore consistently accused DC Comics of cheating him and the artist, Dave Gibbons, out of their rightful ownership while DC has consistently claimed that Moore and Gibbons were fully aware of all of the ownership terms in the contract. This conflict and one stemming from Moore's work on *V for Vendetta* led Moore to sever all ties to DC and mainstream comics in general. In fact, he has consistently distanced himself from further work on the series, and he has not had a good relationship with Gibbons, either. Despite these disputes, there was eventually a live-action film and an animated version of the book. The film was a commercial success, with some critics appreciating the entertainment value of the film with others accusing the director of failing to adhere to the vision of the original text. There have also been "prequel" comics, following each of the major characters of the book prior to the central story of the original book.

Despite all of the positive attention that the book and its spin-offs have received, there have been challenges. On two separate occasions, the book has been challenged for appearing in high school libraries. This is not surprising, given the book's frequent use of profanity, violence, and references to sexuality. Less obvious but still present are references to homosexuality and questioning portrayals of religion. If anything, given this material, it is surprising that the book has not seen more challenges and that the challenges that it has faced have not been more successful. It is, perhaps, the position of the book as an early entry into the most well-known of graphic novels that have given it a protected place from challenges and outright bans.

See Also: *Batman, The Killing Joke.*

FURTHER READING

Keating, Erin M. "The Female Link: Citation and Continuity in *Watchmen.*" *Journal of Popular Culture*, December 2012, Vol. 45, Issue 6, pp. 1266–1288.

Kim, Ann. "The Watchmen Cometh." *Library Journal*, September 1, 2008, Vol. 133, Issue 14, pp. 32–33.

Prince, Michael J. "Alan Moore's America: The Liberal Individual and American Identities in *Watchmen.*" *Journal of Popular Culture*, August 2011, Vol. 44, Issue 4, pp. 815–830.

BIBLIOGRAPHY

Alderdice, Kit. "Brock Cole: Children Braving an Adult World." *Publishers Weekly*, February 17, 1997, Vol. 244, Issue 7, pp. 197–198, 2p.

Back, Harry. "Censorship of Library Books and Textbooks in American Schools." *Journal of Secondary Education*, 1965, Vol. 40, p. 14.

Bartlett, Myke. "Violence and Entertainment in *The Hunger Games*." *Screen Education*, Winter 2012, Issue 66, pp. 8–17, 10p.

Blume, Judy. "Is Harry Potter Evil?" *New York Times*, October 22, 1999, Vol. 149, Issue 51683, p. A27.

Burress, Lee. "Orwell and Censorship." *Social Education*, March 1984, Vol. 48, Issue 3, pp. 186–187.

Cannon, Bob. "No Way to Treat a 'Lady.' " *Entertainment Weekly*, June 11, 1993, Vol. 1993, Issue 174, p. 72, 1p.

Carpenter, Marilyn. "A Conversation with Chris Crutcher." *New Advocate*, Summer 2000, Vol. 13, Issue 3, pp. 201–212.

Charles, Ron. "Dystopia on Our Doorsteps." *Washington Post*, January 8, 2014, p. A6.

Chen, David W. "Horrors! *Carrie* Is Back at School." *New York Times*, April 5, 1998, Vol. 147, Issue 51118, Section 4A, p. 7.

Davis, Terry. *Presenting Chris Crutcher.* New York, NY: Twayne, 1997, pp. xxvi, 144.

Donaldson, Scott. "Censorship and *A Farewell to Arms*." *Studies in American Fiction*, Spring 1991, Vol. 19, Issue 1, pp. 85–93.

Editors. "Censorship Roundup." *School Library Journal*, March 2005, Vol. 51, Issue 3, p. 25.

Editors. "Censorship Update." *School Library Journal*, November 2001, Vol. 47, Issue 11, p. 22.

Editors. "Harry Potter Tops List of Challenged Books." *Curriculum Review*, March 2002, Vol. 41, Issue 7, p. 2.

Editors. "NC School Board Retains *Brave New World*." *School Library Journal*, February 1981, Vol. 27, Issue 6, p. 9, 1p.

Evertson, Matthew. "The Call of the Critics: Jack London, *The Call of the Wild*, and Its Early Reviews." *Call: The Magazine of the Jack London Society*, Spring–Winter 2007, Vol. 18, Issue 1–2, pp. 5–11. 7p.

Ferguson, Christopher J. "Is Reading Banned Books Associated with Behavior Problems in Young Readers? The Influence of Controversial Young Adult Books on the Psychological Well-Being of Adolescents." *Psychology of Aesthetics, Creativity, and the Arts*, August 2014, Vol. 8, Issue 3, pp. 354–362.

Fialkoff, Francine. "The New Censorship." *Library Journal*, January 1, 2002, Vol. 127, Issue 1, p. 76, 1p.

Ficociello, Tony. "Censorship, Book Selection, and the Marketplace of Ideas." *Top of the News*, Fall 1984, Vol. 41, Issue 1, pp. 33–38.

Foley, Louis. "The Badness of Bad Words." *Reading Horizons*, Spring 1973, Vol. 13, Issue 3, pp. 115–119.

Fox, Bette-Lee. "Naked Lunch." *Library Journal*, March 1, 2013, Vol. 138, Issue 4, p. 51, 1p.

Gewertz, Catherine. "*Captain Underpants, Bluest Eye*, Top Most-Challenged-Book List." *Education Week*, April 23, 2014, Vol. 33, Issue 29, p. 5.

Goldman, Albert. "The Trial of Lenny Bruce." *New Republic*, September 12, 1964, Vol. 151, Issue 11, pp. 13–14, 2p.

Goodman, Michael B. "The Customs' Censorship of William Burroughs' *Naked Lunch*." *Critique*, 1980, Vol. 22, Issue 1, pp. 92–104, 13p.

Grossman, Anna Jane. "Is Junie B. Jones Talking Trash?" *New York Times*, July 26, 2007, Vol. 156, Issue 54017, pp. G1–G6, 6p.

Heer, Jeet. "Pow! Wham! Permission Denied!" *Lingua Franca: The Review of Academic Life*, March 2001, Vol. 11, Issue 2, p. 21, 1p.

Jackson, Gardner. "My Brother's Peeper." *Nation*, January 15, 1930, Vol. 130, Issue 3367, pp. 64–65, 2p.

Jemtegaard, Kristi Elle. "James and the Giant Peach." *Horn Book Magazine*, March/April 2004, Vol. 80, Issue 2, pp. 198–199, 2p.

Jenkinson, David R. "The Censorship Iceberg: Results of a Survey of Challenges in School and Public Libraries." *School Libraries in Canada*, Fall 1986, Vol. 6, Issue 1, pp. 19–22, 24–30.

Kaplan, Fred. "The Day Obscenity Became Art." *New York Times*, July 21, 2009, Vol. 158, Issue 54743, p. 21.

Kneen, Bonnie. "Neither Very Bi nor Particularly Sexual: The Essence of the Bisexual in Young Adult Literature." *Children's Literature in Education: An International Quarterly*, December 2015, Vol. 46, Issue 4, pp. 359–377.

Lahr, John. "The Goat Boy Rises." *New Yorker*, November 1, 1993, Vol. 69, Issue 36, pp. 83–91, 9p.

Lazaro, Alberto. "James Joyce's Encounters with Spanish Censorship, 1939–1966." *Joyce Studies Annual*, Summer 2001, Vol. 12, pp. 38–54, 17p.

Marowitz, Charles. "Remembering Lenny Bruce." *New Theatre Quarterly*, August 2014, Vol. 30, Issue 3, pp. 214–217, 4p.

Martinson, David L. "School Censorship: It Comes in a Variety of Forms, Not All Overt." *Clearing House*, May/June 2008, Vol. 81, Issue 5, pp. 211–214, 4p.

Molson, Francis J. "Harriet the Spy, Another Look." *Elementary English*, October 1974, Vol. 51, Issue 7, pp. 963–970, 8p.

Monks, Merri M., and Donna Reidy Pistolis. *Hit List: Frequently Challenged Books for Young Adults*. New York, NY: ALA, 1996, p. 92.

Oliver, Kelly. *Hunting Girls: Sexual Violence from The Hunger Games to Campus Rape*. New York, NY: Columbia University Press, 2016, pp. ix, 203.

Parrish, Timothy. *Ralph Ellison and the Genius of America*. Amherst, MA: University of Massachusetts Press, 2011, pp. xiv, 253.

Pizzino, Christopher. "The Doctor versus the Dagger: Comics Reading and Cultural Memor." *PMLA: Publications of the Modern Language Association of America*, May 2015, Vol. 130, Issue 3, pp. 631–647, 18p.

Power, Brenda Miller, Jeffrey D. Wilhelm, and Kelly Chandler. *Reading Stephen King: Issues of Censorship, Student Choice and Popular Literature*. New York, NY: National Council of Teachers, 1997, p. 246.

Reichman, Henry. *Censorship and Selection: Issues and Answers for Schools*. New York, NY: ALA, 1993, p. 172.

Roach, Julie, Trevelyn E. Jones, Luann Toth, Marlene Charnizon, Daryl Grabarek, and Dale Raben. "And Tango Makes Three." *School Library Journal*, July 2005, Vol. 51, Issue 7, p. 81.

Rosen, Judith. "Extending the Reach of Banned Books Week." *Publishers Weekly*, September 21, 2015, Vol. 262, Issue 38, pp. 5–6, 2p.

Scales, Pat. "It Takes Three to Tango." *School Library Journal*, July 2007, Vol. 53, Issue 7, p. 24, 1p.

Soocher, S. "2 Live Crew: Taking the Rap." *Rolling Stone*, August 9, 1990, Vol. 21, Issue 584, pp. 19–21, 3p.

Stanek, Lou Willett. "*Huck Finn*: 100 Years of Durn Fool Problems." *School Library Journal*, February 1985, Vol. 31, Issue 6, pp. 19–22.

Sutherland, Janet R. "A Defense of Ken Kesey's *One Flew over the Cuckoo's Nest*." *English Journal*, January 1972, Vol. 61, Issue 1, pp. 28–31, 4p.

Symula, James Francis. *Censorship of High School Literature: A Study of the Incidents of Involving JD Salinger's* Catcher in the Rye. Buffalo, NY: State University of New York, 1969, p. 162.

Tally, Robert T., Jr. "Bleeping Mark Twain? Censorship, *Huckleberry Finn*, and the Functions of Literature." *Teaching American Literature: A Journal of Theory and Practice*, Spring 2013, Vol. 6, Issue 1, pp. 97–108, 12p.

Vanderham, Paul. *James Joyce and Censorship: The Trials of Ulysses*. New York, NY: New York University Press, 1998, pp. xii, 242.

Waldman, Amy. "Self-Censorship or Kid-Sensitivity?" *New York Times*, March 22, 1998, Vol. 147, Issue 51104, Section 14, p. 5.

Weber, Bruce. "Lenny Bruce, Pardoned and Laughing." *New York Times*, December 29, 2003, Vol. 153, Issue 52712, pp. E1–E3.

Will, Barbara. *"The Great Gatsby* and the Obscene World." *College Literature*, Fall 2005, Vol. 32, Issue 4, pp. 125–144, 20p.

Yagoda, Ben. "Trial and Eros: When *Lady Chatterley's Lover* Ran Afoul of Britain's 1959 Obscenity Law, the Resulting Case Had a Cast Worthy of PG Wodehouse." *American Scholar*, Autumn 2010, Vol. 79, Issue 4, pp. 93–101, 9p.

Young, Craig A. "Creating a Controversial Picturebook: Discussions with the Creators of 'And Tango Makes Three.'" *Journal of Children's Literature*, Fall 2011, Vol. 37, Issue 2, pp. 30–38.

Zeisler, Andi. "And Tango Makes Three." *Bitch Magazine: Feminist Response to Pop Culture*, Fall 2005, Vol. 10, Issue 30, p. 87.

INDEX

ABOUT THE AUTHOR

Zeke Jarvis is an associate professor of English at Eureka College in Eureka, Illinois. He is the author of *So Anyway...*, *In a Family Way: Stories* and *Lifelong Learning: Stories*, and he was the main author and editor of Greenwood's *Make 'em Laugh: American Humorists of the 20th and 21st Centuries*.